# THE GAME OF OUR LIVES

## ALSO BY DAVID GOLDBLATT

*The Ball Is Round: A Global History of Soccer*

*How to Watch the Olympics: The Essential Guide to the Rules,*
*Statistics, Heroes, and Zeroes of Every Sport*
(co-author with Johnny Acton)

*Futebol Nation: The Story of Brazil through Soccer*

# THE GAME
## OF OUR LIVES

The English Premier League
and the Making of
Modern Britain

## DAVID GOLDBLATT

NATION
BOOKS
New York

Copyright © 2014 by Tabacco Athletic Ltd.

First published in 2014 in the UK by the Penguin Group.

Published by Nation Books, A Member of the Perseus Books Group
116 East 16th Street, 8th Floor
New York, NY 10003

Nation Books is a co-publishing venture of the Nation Institute and the Perseus
Books Group.

Books published by Nation Books are available at special discounts for bulk
purchases in the United States by corporations, institutions, and other
organizations. For more information, please contact the Special Markets
Department at the Perseus Books Group, 2300 Chestnut Street, Suite 200,
Philadelphia, PA 19103, or call (800) 255-1514, or e-mail special.markets@
perseusbooks.com.

Library of Congress Cataloging-in-Publication Data
Goldblatt, David, 1965-
   The game of our lives : the English Premier League and the making of
modern Britain / David Goldblatt.
      pages   cm
   Includes bibliographical references and index.
   ISBN 978-1-56858-506-2 (hardback) — ISBN 978-1-56858-507-9
(electronic)
   1. F.A. Premier League—History.   2. Soccer—Great Britain—History.
3. Soccer—Social aspects—Great Britain.   4. Great Britain—Social
conditions—1945-   I. Title.
   GV943.55.F36G65 2014
   796.3340941—dc23
                                                            2014031665

First Edition
10 9 8 7 6 5 4 3 2 1

# CONTENTS

# PREFACE TO THE NORTH AMERICAN EDITION

Recently, while teaching at Pitzer College in Los Angeles, I noted almost immediately how little news there was in the *Los Angeles Times* and elsewhere about Britain. A shift of sentiment in the Beijing housing market or a speech by the Japanese Prime Minister was far more likely to feature than any news from back home. And why shouldn't it? Britain is a tiny island 6,000 miles from Southern California whose cultural, political, and economic reach, although out of proportion with its size, seems less significant with every passing decade.

My students, although familiar in passing with bits of British pop culture, comedy, and music, were neither Anglophobe nor Anglophile. Britain appeared too small a feature on their radar to evoke such extremes, but for one thing: football.

For what it is worth as sociological evidence, the course that I offered on British national identity since the Second World War attracted just nine students. My football course was four times the size and could have been double that again. Perhaps I just wasn't concentrating, but over a few days spent in Manhattan and Brooklyn I failed to see a single Mets or Yankees shirt but I saw a lot of Chelsea and Manchester City tops. But then the combined television audience in the US for the final day of the English Premier League (EPL) in 2014 was larger than the UK audience.

I'm not suggesting that football is the only way America engages with Britain—our mutual security services and military industrial complexes have a lot to talk about—but it is a rare popular bridgehead. The popularity of English football is, I think, a function of the much wider rise of football as a recreational sport, commercial spectacle and popular culture in the United States, yet the EPL is not the only game in town; there are, amongst America's many soccer cultures, devotees of La Liga and Serie A and diasporic support for teams in the Mexican Liga. However, measured by the value of TV rights if nothing else, the EPL reigns supreme among American cosmopolitan football fans.

Why? In part it must be a matter of language and a long established if little known presence of English football fans left over from the days of the North American Soccer League (NASL). In part it is because the spectacle is tremendously good. Now the richest league in the world and blessed with an extraordinary roster of global talent, the EPL also offers a style of play—a seemingly relentless end-to-end intensity—that the more measured Mediterranean leagues cannot match. In contrast to the almost invariably half empty stadiums of Spain and Italy, the EPL delivers loud full houses on almost every occasion. The UEFA Champions' League is perhaps the most favored foreign football of all, but you cannot lose your heart to a tournament or love a football confederation, for that you need a football club.

Every one of my students had their English football club and all the strange and serendipitous reasons that people acquire them; family connections, time spent in Britain, a club that felt in some way like the baseball or basketball franchise they supported in the States, because they were winners, because they weren't winners, liked the uniform, liked a player and got hooked on the club, etc. I imagine that most if not all American readers of this book will have a similar tale to tell. But by whatever route you have arrived in English football and whatever your intentions, you have stumbled across the most extraordinary prism for understanding England and Britain.

I apologize in advance for the use of the first person plural in this book. I wrote it in my head as a direct address to England and English football. It is not intended to be exclusionary and recognize that in our post-modern global world, the nature of "we" is always shifting, communities of fate cut across national boundaries. Perhaps then it is better to read "we" in this book as those who consider English football more than a mere commodity and spectacle for a disengaged global audience, but who think that its values and its pleasures grow out of an old, deeply rooted and richly textured sporting culture that is unmistakably, idiosyncratically English. The "we" are those who believe that a cosmopolitan outlook is predicated on respect for the local, and that is not a matter of citizenship or location. These are surely the dispositions and attitudes that a global cosmopolitan culture requires in profusion. Making these notions the common sense of the global order is an inconceivably hard task, but that we might achieve a fragment of this from our engagement with football is our good fortune.

# England Is Paradise

When you arrive in England for football it's a paradise.

ERIC CANTONA

I.

Sir Richard Turnbull, the penultimate governor of Aden, told Denis Healey, then Britain's defense secretary, that, "When the British Empire finally sank beneath the waves of history, it would leave behind only two monuments—one was the game of association football, the other was the expression 'Fuck off'."[1] Spoken in the mid-1960s as the last remnants of the British Empire were abandoned, Turnbull's predictions were perhaps overly pessimistic. A case can still be made for the lasting impact of English jurisprudence, engineering, and education. The canon of English Literature may not have the demotic presence of rough Anglo-Saxon cursing, but it continues to shape the linguistic imagination of much of the world. Yet Turnbull was right to believe that among the most important legacies of nearly two centuries of global influence was a product of working-class industrial Britain. Cricket, the game of gentlemen, would leave its mark in much of the Empire, but football, the game of the people, would be present everywhere.

Working-class industrial Britain, certainly one that Turnbull and Healey would have recognized, has gone the way of the Empire, sunk beneath the waves of history. Even as they spoke, the long process of deindustrialization was underway. Yet among the rubble of industrial Britain, football was still standing. In fact, football had reached its nadir in 1985, the year of the catastrophic events in Heysel and Bradford, and the game's lowest-ever attendance figures. Since then audiences had been growing, and the first serious television deal in the English game's history was signed with ITV. The Hillsborough disaster in 1989, a culmination of the dire state of British stadiums and policing, shook the game but did not destroy it. In fact the Taylor Report on the disaster would be the catalyst for profound reform. Despite the desperate tragedy of Hillsborough and the wide opprobrium in which it continued to be held, football endured. What could explain the game's seemingly ineradicable appeal? Writing in 1990, Roy Hattersley, then deputy leader of the Labour Party, thought that "Football does more than provide unrivalled pleasure on a Saturday afternoon. It keeps us in romantic association with our individual and collective past. It is a game of industrial England. It is no longer the exclusive preserve of men and women who work in the mines and factories. For the mines and factories are not the force they used to be . . . But in general it is a game of the sons and daughters of that old working-class."[2]

Although change was coming, football had not been entirely sanitized. Its rough edges remained on view and that, paradoxically, is what allowed its reincarnation. Its crowds still offered a raucous chorus. Its locations, its players, its character, and demeanor retained a distinctive urban working-class form. Its iconography, identities, and narratives were drawn from the fine grain of almost every corner of urban Britain. This made it rare. The already uneven distribution of wealth, power, and influence between north and south, and between London and the rest, was magnified greatly under the Thatcher governments. At the moment of its rebirth, football was drenched in nostalgic affection for the social formation that had just passed into history, for a world where large numbers of people would gather under one roof or in one industrial place; for a realm in which the old geography of Victorian industrial Britain still meant something.

Donald Trelford, an editor of the *London Observer*, argued that "Very often, as they move up the social ladder, these memories of queuing and jostling among football crowds are the only vivid recollection of the physical realities of working-class life," and recalled the metronomic solidarities of his own youth in Coventry: "All the men solemnly reversing their small cars out of their garages into the communal back entry at exactly the same time on a Saturday afternoon. It was a ritual, like the carriages going to church in Jane Austen's England, as they set off for the ground in time for the 3:00 p.m. kick off."[3]

Published in 1991 and 1992 respectively, on the eve of the Premier League, Pete Davies's *All Played Out*, a sharp yet delirious odyssey through Italia 90, and Nick Hornby's *Fever Pitch*, that brilliantly entwined the coming-of-age tale with the life of a football obsessive,[4] were hailed as the voice of the new football. Self-reflexive, confessional, and sociologically literate, they certainly heralded a new and diverse wave of football writing. They were, however, to a much greater extent, an elegy for the old football. While neither author was sentimental about the violence of the 1970s and 1980s, or the dilapidation and danger of its stadiums, both venerated the atmosphere and collective energies of the dwindling crowds, and sensed the arrival of the new commercialism which would sanitize them.

In the near-quarter of a century since the fall of Margaret Thatcher, under conditions of immense change, these sentiments have not disappeared; indeed, they remain integral to football's popular cultures: loyalty is prized but the dilettante, the arriviste, and the mercenary are damned; the active commitment of match attendance stands morally superior to the passivity of distant TV spectatorship; connoisseurship is preferred to consumption; there is space for individual brilliance but there is also a powerful sense of the value of collective action and a moral and sporting sense of the common good. It is this thick web of values, rituals, histories, and identities that, I imagine, Eric Cantona sensed when he came from French to English football in 1992 and found it a paradise. Philippe Auclair recounts Cantona's memory of his first goal in English football: "At the exact moment when the ball entered the net, the thousands of supporters who were behind the goal seemed to dive toward the pitch." Only in England, he said, could such "ecstasy be found." Only in Britain could the delirious celebrations of young men have become the central expressive ritual in an act of historical remembrance.[5]

## II.

Cantona scored that goal for Leeds United, the champions in the last season of the old First Division. He would win the championship again the following season but for Manchester United in the Premier League. A transitional figure, with a foot in both historical eras, (Cantona relished the delirium and theatricality of the old game, but became the first star of the new era—acquiring wealth, celebrity, and status far in excess of his predecessors. He was touched by the raw passion of the English crowd, but he heralded a league in which the English would provide less than a third of the players and managers and less than half of the owners. He saw his own performances as a gift to the fans, but the charismatic brilliance of his play was instrumental in popularizing a game that was consumed by money. It is at this intersection of Britain's deep-rooted cultural relationship with football with the arrival of new media and new money that the contemporary form of the game has emerged. The Premier League, in particular, likes to date the transformation of the game to its own inception in 1992 and explain its success in narrowly economic terms: the arrival of television money combined with investment in all-seater stadiums and the creation of the Premiership meant better players playing better football in a safer and more comfortable environment, and therefore attendances across the leagues have been rising ever since. All, in part, true, but without the inheritance of over a hundred years of football culture and the good luck to acquire it at a moment when its social and historical meanings were more powerful than ever, the stratospheric ascent of the new game would have been impossible.

Together these economic and cultural changes have produced a remarkable shift in the place of football in British society. Once merely popular, even widespread, now football is ubiquitous and its status in both popular and elite cultures greatly elevated. Four things illustrate this: first, the relative size and importance of football when measured against similar phenomena—from theater going to soap-opera audiences;

secondly, its presence in both popular and elite cultures—from television drama to poetry; thirdly, the degree to which a publicly advertised interest in football has become the norm among Britain's elites; and finally, the degree to which the nation's political commentators have taken on football as a metaphor for the nation's ills.

Football is a complex phenomenon with family resemblances to many other cultural forms but identical to none. In its capacity to gather significant numbers of people on a highly regularized calendar, in a highly ritualized fashion, and, on occasion, to create moments of community and collective ecstasy, it has something of the church about it. Shorn of any religious dimension, it is closer to the theater. Like the cultures of music it combines a professional commercialized circuit with a huge web of amateur organizations and a great hinterland of informal play and practice. And ultimately, when seen not just as a sequence of unrelated individual matches but as the multicharacter, multilayered narrative of a season, football's closest competitor is soap opera. On their own territory, football gives all of these activities a run for their money.

Both soap operas and professional football are significant components of Britain's popular culture, but they are sharply separated by gender. Soaps retain a predominantly female audience and offer an infinitely more gender-balanced array of characters. Football, despite marginal shifts in the composition of its crowds and the growth of grassroots women's football, remains an overwhelmingly masculine world. The leading British soap operas attract regular audiences that are easily in excess of most live football and collectively offer a weekly program at least as extensive as the football fixture list. *Coronation Street* and *EastEnders*, the old form of the genre, have the same kind of narrative and romantic connection to working-class urban Britain that football has acquired. The shows, like football, find themselves referenced and debated in a variety of other media, their stars endlessly featured in other contexts and their storylines taken as a sustained real-time commentary upon contemporary events. Football now manages all these and on a scale equivalent to the entire genre of soap opera. Moreover, beyond the emotionally disturbed, the soaps do not evoke collective ecstasy or carnival, nor do they provide the bedrock of collective identities. The Church, the theatre, festivals, and soap operas—football has acquired a place in British culture that exceeds them all, for it alone is the equal of each in their own domains of ritual, performance, ecstasy, and national narrative.

The sheer volume of newsprint and digital space occupied by football is the most obvious marker of the game's ubiquity. From just a few pages a day in the 1970s, even in the most football-heavy papers, Britain's tabloids and broadsheets started devoting many times that kind of space to football. Football's presence on the Internet has grown even faster as websites, podcasts, and blogs proliferated.[6] In a media culture in which professional journalists have always interceded between players and fans, Twitter has proved an immensely popular alternative circuit of communication. The marriage of digital technology and football has been particularly successful in the realm of gaming, which itself has become a huge consumer market and a virtually ubiquitous practice among young men. Between 1995 and 2012 the single most successful video games in the UK have been the FIFA football series. *Championship* and *Football Manager* and the other simulation games have sold fewer units, but in console form, as well as the online fantasy football leagues run by the Premiership and national newspapers, they have over four million players annually.[7]

Perhaps a better measure of football's new cultural weight than the sheer volume of news output or the uncountable hours devoted to video games in bedrooms across the nation, was the degree to which the game had become the subject of other cultural forms. Television, although it had covered football for over two decades from the mid 1960s to the late 1980s, had never really explored its possibilities beyond the sports slots. Outside of highlights shows and *Football Focus*, there were just a handful of documentaries and one-off dramas, like John Boorman's *Six Days to Saturday* or Jack Rosenthal's comedy *Another Sunday and Sweet FA*. In the 1990s this changed. *Fantasy Football League* brought together the worlds of stand-up comedy, the chat show and football fanzine trivia, the hosts both languorous and loquacious stitching it all together from the couch. Drama departments, which had steered clear of football, dipped their toes in the water: Cheri Lunghi took on the dressing room as *The Manager*, in which, quite unbelievably for the time, a woman was made the coach of a struggling professional men's team; Arthur Smith's bitter sweet comedy *A Night with Gary Lineker* was hugely popular on

TV and in the theater. ITV ran its sex, shopping, and shooting soap *Footballers' Wives*. Sky made ten series of *Dream Team*, *Roy of the Rovers* for the Premiership era, reduced eventually to *Dynasty* levels of implausible plot line, death, and betrayal.[8]

From almost a century of cinema up until 1990, British football had been featured in just a handful of films: the backdrop to a whodunnit in the 1939 *Arsenal Stadium Mystery*; the jaunty art-house documentary *Goal!*—the official film of the 1966 World Cup; in the early 1980s, there was the sweetly observed teen romance of *Gregory's Girl*; and the hapless hi-concept of Sly Stallone's *Victory*, Hollywood's take on "football meets the prisoner of war escape movie." They were all eclipsed by the short, but utterly heart-rending, football sequence in Ken Loach's *Kes*, in which Brian Glover's PE teacher treats a coaching session as a chance to regress to his inner playground bully. The last twenty years, by contrast, have seen dozens of football movies released. The Sisyphean task of bending the arc of a Hollywood script to English football culture was tried again, but both *Goal!* and *When Saturday Comes* looked clunky and clichéd. A slew of hooligan movies, drawing on the new genre of hooligan memoirs, were equally dismal. *Bend It Like Beckham* had the easy charm of *Gregory's Girl* transported from new-town Scotland to multi-ethnic London, but was slight. *Mike Bassett: England Manager*—a low-budget comedy about the trials of the England manager—had its moments, but it paled beside the real thing: Channel 4's documentary *Impossible Job*, which followed Graham Taylor's final days as England manager, was cruelly funny but bathed in the most acute pathos. As with so many attempts to dramatize football, fiction has found it hard to compete with football's own spontaneous capacity for narrative. The art-house montage *Zidane*, released in 2007 and produced by the Turner Prize–winning artist Douglas Gordon and French filmmaker Philippe Perreno, succeeded by abandoning narrative entirely. Only *The Damned United*, an adaptation of David Peace's coruscating novel about Brian Clough and his time at Leeds United, and Ken Loach's *Looking for Eric* have risen to the challenge. Loach's film manages this by combining Mancunian magic realism with *Ealing Comedy*, gently telling the tale of a struggling post-office worker and Manchester United fan who sorts out his life with the help of a magical Eric Cantona, played by himself.

Neither TV nor film was ever going to bestow serious cultural capital on football. Its elevation in British cultural life owed more to the sudden engagement of key members of its male literary elite with the sport. What sporting energies had existed among British writers had hitherto been directed elsewhere, towards cricket especially, but the haul of literary encounters with football was meager.[9] In the 1980s and early 1990s this changed. Martin Amis, Julian Barnes, Sebastian Faulks, Geoff Dyer, Blake Morrison, and Nick Hornby all published pieces on football. The leading literary journals, previously football-free zones, took note. Karl Miller, editor of the *London Review of Books*, started commenting on the 1990 World Cup in the magazine's Diary section, while the following year Granta published Ian Hamilton's *Gazza Agonistes*.[10] Literary England had deemed football a permissible topic of inquiry, but despite this rapprochement football acquired only a very marginal place in the fictional landscape, more often than not used as a jokey satirical stage, like its cameo in Marin Amis's *London Fields*.[11] Rare exceptions to this have been D. J. Taylor's *English Settlement,* in which money laundering at a south London club becomes entangled in a wider story about the rise of the city, David Peace's *The Damned United* and its follow-up *Red or Dead,* which fictionalizes the football life of Bill Shankly.[12]

Of all the arts, poetry's relationship to football has been the easiest and closest, an amity facilitated by the shared interest of poets and crowds in chants, rhythm and rhymes. Three of the most significant postwar poets—Philip Larkin, Seamus Heaney, and Ted Hughes—all found space for football as a potent childhood memory or a telling element of the urban landscape.[13] In the last twenty years poetry and football have moved closer together. Brighton and Hove Albion made Attila the Stockbroker, the postpunk poet and troubadour, club poet in residence; Ian McMillan was awarded a similar position at Barnsley. Andrew Motion, when Poet Laureate, backed the establishment of a nationwide football laureate.[14] More substantively, Tony Harrison's "V," still the most significant poetic reflection on the end of industrial Britain, drew widely on the oppositional and conflictual imagery of the game. Motion's successor, Carol Ann Duffy, wrote a poem for the nation on David Beckham's Achilles Heel, while Simon Armitage declared that "I'd always thought of poets as the goalkeepers of the literary world." Don Paterson, one of

Scotland's leading modern poets, framed his own poetic account of national postindustrial decline through the story of a failing football club in his long collection *Nil Nil*.[15]

The Royal Family had graced football with their official patronage, and their actual presence on the big occasions, since before the First World War, but they had hitherto been studiedly nonpartisan. In the last decade the royal house has let it be known that Her Majesty is a fan of Arsenal, a preference inherited from her mother. Prince Charles later revealed he was a longstanding supporter of Burnley; Prince William opted for Aston Villa, Prince Harry for Arsenal.[16] Postwar prime ministers had been equally reluctant to reveal any affiliation, if indeed they had one at all. Harold Wilson had made a few headlines with his support for Huddersfield Town but Clement Attlee, Harold Macmillan, and Alec Douglas-Home all preferred cricket; Ted Heath was a sailor and Margaret Thatcher simply loathed the game. John Major's arrival signaled a degree of change, for although predominantly a fan and a scholar of cricket, he liked to watch Chelsea. However, it was with Tony Blair's election as prime minister in 1997 that a deeper shift in attitudes to football at Westminster became obvious. Blair's media chief, Alastair Campbell, was a long-standing fan of Burnley (something he shares with the Prince of Wales), Blair was a less obsessive Newcastle supporter. In the run-up to the 1997 election, Campbell used football as stick to beat the Tories with, authoring articles by Blair in the tabloids. He also ensured there were plenty of photo opportunities of Blair playing keepy uppy or sitting with his family in the royal box at Wembley. Football became both a political tool and the currency of everyday networking in the upper echelons of New Labour.

The Conservative and Liberal Democrat parties have for the most part kept their distance from the sport, many preferring individual games and country pursuits. Tory William Hague's thing is judo while his colleague George Osborne plays computer games.[17] Nonetheless, Prime Minister David Cameron has considered it politic to make his love for Aston Villa well known (something he shares with the duke of Cambridge). Michael Howard, home secretary under Major and leader of the Tory Party between 2003 and 2005, was sufficiently engaged with the fate of Liverpool FC to publicly criticize manager Gerard Houllier and call for his resignation.[18] Vince Cable, the Liberal Democrat, has publicly declared his obsession with York City and has not been averse to the use of football metaphors in his speeches.[19] The City of London, Britain's financial district, has been much less reticent about wearing its football colors. Mervyn King, governor of the Bank of England for over a decade, claimed in a television interview that "Supporting Aston Villa is much more stressful than being governor of the Bank of England," and chose an obscure amateur celebration of the club's European Cup victory in 1982 as one of his desert island discs.[20] At one point both the archbishop of Canterbury, George Carey, and the chief rabbi, Jonathan Sacks, were very public Arsenal supporters.

The new football emerged in an era characterized by increasingly wide economic and social inequalities in Britain and the very high concentration of wealth among small elites. This shift was accompanied by the development of a new vocabulary of high-end consumption and social differentiation: luxury goods, premium services and business class. At the same time a key tool of public policy was the use of league tables in the measurement of services. Thus the language of football and the special aura of exclusivity and quality that surrounded the Premiership found their way into areas of cultural life previously off limits to the game. Reviewing the Booker shortlist in 1996 the *Independent* remarked that "Margaret Atwood is, by general consent, near the top of the world's Premier League of novelists."[21] Opening its survey of the state of British science the Royal Society claimed that "The UK has been in the top two of the scientific premier league for the last 350 years."[22] From primary and secondary schools to hospitals and Michelin-starred restaurants, all could be promoted to or relegated from the Premier League. Martin Sorrel, the most important figure in the British advertising industry, attempted to explain the new economic global order in similar terms.[23] The art world, not known for its close links to football, extended the metaphor. Damien Hirst's split from his long-standing gallery was seen in terms of the transfer market: "'It's not so much that these are defections, more that artists are more in control,' said Renton. 'It's like Premiership football. Why did Man City not get Robin Van Persie when they offered more than Man United? When you're already worth tens of millions, it's not just about money.'"[24] At the other end of the table, the *Mirror* argued that "a new

'Premier League' of art galleries and buyers fuelled by new wealth money was emerging, leaving smaller galleries and artists fighting for crumbs."[25]

For most of the postwar era politicians and commentators had been reluctant to use football as a guide to the state of the nation. In the twenty-first century they couldn't stop. For some, like Prime Minister David Cameron, the Premiership was an unproblematic export success, an exemplar of Britain's potential and a bridgehead to the rest of the world. Speaking in India he said, "We brought one of Britain's great exports to the world, Premier League Football, in which I think you take quite a close interest in India as well."[26] The left seized on the business practices of the game to denounce Britain's wider economic structures and the attendant problems of under regulation, vulnerability to globalization and soaring inequalities. Will Hutton went as far as to argue that "The beautiful game embodies everything that's bad about Britain," above all a political economy in which private ownership and profit always trumped public provision and social needs. In a similar vein, Jonathan Freedland, writing after the Glazer family's leveraged buyout of Manchester United, compared the deal to Kraft's buy-up of Cadbury: "Selling off the crown jewels of our collective culture in the name of a rampant capitalism that is both unsustainable and ultimately joyless. That doesn't just sound like the state of the national game, that sounds like the state of the nation."[27]

Predictably the right worried less about economic inequalities and injustices and more about football's meanings and moralities. Craig Brown fumed, "I hate its imbecilic chanting and its self-righteous saloon-bar expertise, its ersatz working classness."[28] Peter Hitchens, in the *Daily Mail*, asked, "Is football a pagan cult?" and concluded that it probably was. This, he wearily accepted, was the inevitable consequence of the failures of modern liberal Christianity, but football fans' shallow ninety-minute popular nationalism was another matter: "I am almost permanently furious that they can rush on to the streets to show 'patriotism' over a football game, but appear unmoved by the theft of our national independence, the rape of our countryside, the destruction of our culture and all the many real and lasting ways in which this country daily loses the Real World Cup of Nationhood."[29] The guileless masses soon transmute into the irrational mob. Michael Henderson, writing in the *Spectator*, thought that "If you were looking for the authentic voice of the football supporter, at the start of another season, Mr. Angry would make a fair representative." Incivility and crudity were bad enough from the working-class, but what really appalled him was that "These were not proletarians but well-paid professionals affecting to be working-class. They swore loudly and behaved in an obnoxious way because that is how they thought working-class folk behaved."[30] Henderson preferred an imagined golden age, when the salt of the earth would respond to a Johnny Haynes miss at Fulham with the words "Oh luckless Haynes." For a certain kind of conservative, football before the 1970s came to represent a much better Britain in which the working classes were deferential and the middle classes knew their place and voted Tory.

Now a metaphor of choice among elite commentators across the political spectrum, football's cultural ascent was unmistakable. Quite what it revealed remained to be seen.

## III.

What football reveals is the subject of this book. It is too soon to write a narrative history of British football since Hillsborough. We are only really beginning to get to grips with the 1980s. Yet when the histories of modern Britain begin to cover the 1990s and the early twenty-first century, we can be sure that football will play a bigger part in them than in any earlier era. While the dust is settling it seems wiser to review this era essayistically and thematically, and to ask how football both reflects the main trends of economic and social change in Britain, and where it runs counter to them. In chapter 1, "Aspiration and Illusion," I argue that the emergence of highly commercialized football in general, and the Premiership in particular, was only made possible by dismantling the defensive regulations of the old order in which competing economic, sporting, and social objectives were more finely balanced. Once these barriers had been swept aside the new forces of the postindustrial global economy could truly transform football. As with the wider economy, this has been a mixed experience: success and excellence at the top, uncertainty and hidden poverty at the bottom.

Potentially one of the most troubling aspects of football's commercialization has been its impact on the staging of the match itself. In chapter

2, "Keeping It Real?," I look at the changing composition and behavior of football crowds. I argue that for all the efforts of the media–football complex to control the event and shape it as a TV-mediated spectacular, the British crowd has resisted. The capacity to create collective identities, interests, and cultures around the watching of football has survived. This is why football remains entwined, in both real and metaphorical ways, with the creation of class and urban identities and the politics of ethnicity and nation.

In chapter 3, "English Journey," I take a tour of football in urban England from metropolis to small-town backwater. I contend that, in the absence of powerful local government or strong provincial civil societies, football clubs have become a vital component in sustaining distinct urban identities. The location and architecture of football stadiums have become important components of both economic regeneration programs and the definition of the wider cultural landscape. In the last couple of decades the already fraught relationship between club owners, their fans, and their cities has become more conflicted. The arrival of embezzlers and crooks has produced struggles for the very survival of clubs. Asset strippers and property developers have used clubs as speculative investment opportunities rather than sporting organizations. Commercially minded owners have sought to appeal to global audiences at the expense of local traditions. As with much of local politics in England, the balance of power continues to lie with owners and developers, but football has proved a surprising site of local resistance.

Football clubs may have been a fount of civic identity, but it was not one always accessible to all. The players and much of the crowd were working-class; part of the crowd and most of the shareholders were middle class; women were accommodated in small numbers; and until the 1960s they were almost all white. In chapter 4, "Playing the Race Game," I begin by retracing the emergence of Britain's pioneering generation of black players from the late 1970s to the mid-1990s, who publicly took the brunt of the game's and the nation's racism and made themselves an immovable part of English football. Alongside campaigners and supporters, they profoundly shifted the terms of the debate on ethnicity and made public racist abuse unacceptable in football and more widely. For once not merely a metaphor, football was at the leading edge of change.

Whether it can continue to be so in the face of institutional racism and the new global migrations to Britain remains to be seen.

In chapter 5, "Football at Twilight," I look at the way in which the United Kingdom's complex system of national identities has been reflected and even shaped by international football. Rarely among public or private institutions, the national football teams of the United Kingdom precisely correspond to the borders of the four constituent nations of England, Scotland, Wales, and Northern Ireland. Neither church, nor state, nor parliaments do this. In the international sporting realm tennis, rugby league, and most Olympic sports field British teams. In rugby union, Ireland is an all-island affair, so, too, in cricket where England and Wales are conjoined. In golf we are all part of Europe. In Northern Ireland football has been embroiled in the ethno-nationalist conflict since the creation of the province. In the years since the Good Friday Agreement it has come to reflect the ineradicable differences and uneasy compromises of Northern Irish society rather than a new-found unity. In Wales, where the international game lives in the shadow of rugby union, club football has been an arena in which the nation's complex relationship to its huge neighbor has been played out. In Scotland the game appeared to be an important component of the broad social alliance in favor of devolution and the reassertion of Scottish civic nationalism but in recent years the Tartan Army has fought shy of supporting the movement for independence, and the political edge of football has been softened by the success of devolution. At the same time the nationalists have found that the penurious state of the game, inevitable for a small fish in the very big football pond, and its enduring sectarian problems, make football a much less attractive vehicle for their political ambitions. In England, the nation most bereft of unique civic institutions around which to construct a contemporary sense of national identity, the story of the England football team has been an unruly exercise in nation-building.

Cutting across the first five chapters of the book is the issue of governance. Who, if anyone, has been in charge of this process? Who, if anyone, represents the public interest and the common good? Who allowed the old economic regulations to be abandoned? Who was on watch when the flood of dubious owners took over much of professional football and the match fixers and double-dealing agents rode into town? The answer is the FA, and its fate over the last twenty ears is an exemplar of a wider range of problems in British politics. In chapter 6, "You Don't Know What You're Doing," I maintain that the FA was utterly unprepared for the world of football after Hillsborough. It lacked the skills, the structure, the capacity or the intellectual energy to redefine its role in an era of highly commercialized football. Consequently it ceded enormous authority to the professional game in general and the Premier League in particular. The considerable efforts of the political classes and organized football supporters to force reform on the FA and the wider structures of power in football have been poorly rewarded. The governance of football represents the wider triumph in contemporary Britain of private interests and economic imperatives over the public good and social needs.

In all of these domains, from economics to politics, from race relations to civic nationalism, the last twenty-five years of British football have seen gains and losses, advances and reverses. The economic penury and dismal infrastructure of the past have gone, but the creeping anodyne uniformity of consumer capitalism has replaced it. Crowds are bigger, the football is better, but the atmosphere, more often than not, falls short of expectations. The culture of football has been opened up to women and minorities, but its ruling masculinities remain stuck in a narrow groove. Football fans are more organized and networked than ever, but the governance of the game feels less democratic. We have been mourning the passing of industrial Britain for over two decades. The further we are removed from that era, and what we remember as its values, the more football has kept those notions imaginatively alive. Yet at the same time its ruling institutions have created an economic model and a system of governance that nurture their opposites. If England is, as Cantona thought, a paradise where the ecstasy of the crowd puts us in touch with a lost and venerated world, then we should leave the final word to Milton and *Paradise Regained*:

> The happy place imparts to thee no happiness, no joy –
> Rather inflames thy torment, representing
> Lost bliss, to thee no more communicable;
> So never more in Hell than when in Heaven.

# CHAPTER 1

# Aspiration and Illusion

## The Economics of the New Football

Football is an optimistic, upwardly mobile, aspirational business

RICHARD SCUDAMORE,
Premier League Chief Executive, 2011

Where's the money gone?

FOOTBALL CROWDS, ANON

I.

A quarter of a century ago, the *Sunday Times* of London saw football through the lens of urban decline and described it as if it were the game of the feckless and undeserving poor: "A slum game played by slum people in slum stadiums."[1] Now it is being spoken of in the same terms as the private housing market and speculative property development, alongside banking the quintessential industries of the long boom and asset-price bubble that ran from the early 1990s to 2007. The new football economy is certainly a child of that boom and like the property market has lived in a dream world where investors believe that the miraculous is possible, that growth never stops, and that the future will always be benign. Football, though, has outstripped the real estate market and continues to grow at a rapid rate through the recessions of the last five or six years.

Like the bankers, perhaps, the game has continued to prosper and pay a small number of remarkably high salaries whatever the economic outlook, and we, the public, have continued to pay the clubs to do so. The idea that football is a business, that money shapes the game is not new, but over the last twenty years these notions have become almost the defining feature of the game in Britain. Clubs refer to themselves as brands, and accountancy firms publish earnest reports on the business of football. The financial pages have acquired sports sections, the sports pages dwell on financial matters and publish rich lists. The conversations that roll around the grounds, Internet fan forums, and talk radio turn on greed and excess, implausible salaries, record transfer fees, and the corrosive impact of cash. All dwell on the notion that the Premiership is the richest football league in the world. The play-off game that decides who gets the final promotion spot to the Premier League is ritually discussed as a multimillion pound match—the figure rising with every passing season. Football, it is claimed, is not just business but "big business."

Like a lot of the claims made for the new football economy, this is an illusion. As Simon Kuper and Stefan Szymanski pithily put it, "Football is neither big business nor good business. It arguably isn't even a business at all."[2] Despite the rhetorical hype of the new football industry, in absolute terms, it remains a pygmy. The average Premier League club has a turnover only slightly larger than the average Tesco supermarket. At the lower end of the leagues, clubs look more like small packaging firms stuck in the corner of a grim industrial estate turning over a couple of million quid a year while they rack up another expensive overdraft. Collectively the entire turnover of the professional football industry is smaller than the consumer markets for pet food or prepared sandwiches. If it were a single company its turnover would only put it in the lower reaches of the top 500 companies listed on the London Stock Exchange; not that one could now float the football industry anywhere and expect many takers.

Over the last twenty years all of Britain's professional football leagues have run at a net loss. Cumulative losses, one way or another, end up as debts and debts lead to bankruptcy. During the game's most lucrative years insolvencies have become commonplace. Coming up to half of the current members of the English Football League have spent a period in administration since 1992. The situation in Scotland is similar. This is not an economic sector that, on the face of it, rational investors looking at rates of return on capital would be investing in; better to put the whole lot in treasury bonds. The stock market has delivered a withering assessment of the football business. Between 1983 and 2001, twenty-five clubs listed on one of the UK's stock exchanges. Today only seven remain there. All of them, after an initial burst of baseless optimism, collapsed in price. Arsenal's shares are almost entirely held by two investors and none are openly traded; the rest of the clubs are still trading but at a tiny fraction of their original flotation price.

The reason that the new football economy football has proved to be such a bad business is that, despite discovering commercialism and having been flooded with new revenue, its key decision-makers have, so far, retained the preferences and outlook of the old order, choosing competitive football and access to social networks and status over bottom-line profits. If football is a business it is a very unusual one. For almost a century, British professional football was a network of social enterprises rather than a cutthroat economic sector of competing profit-driven firms. While clubs attempted to stay afloat, the basic orientation of directors and fans was to see as much good football as the budget would allow rather than spending money on investments or distributing profits. The wider culture in which football was embedded—above all, of urban collective identities—provided status and networks that proved much more powerful incentives for club directors and shareholders than acquiring dividends or salaries. Today's directors and owners, although they are partial to a dividend and a salary, are not dissimilar. The kinds of network and the reach and forms of status that the Premier League can deliver are richer, more complex, and influential than the old football, but in the end it is the same stuff that the chairmen crave.

Yet despite all of these caveats, the football industry tells a very celebratory story about itself. In this version of economic history British football is cast in the role of the ailing heavy industrial giants of the late 1970s: relics of the nineteenth century, beset by conflict, prone to outbreaks of unruly behavior, burdened by a century of under investment and amateurish management practices, churning out an unattractive product for a declining market and steadily being driven out of business by its new competitors. Breaking from the past, the Premier League and British Sky Broadcasting Company (BskyB), the Rupert Murdoch-owned satellite TV company, unleashed a commercial dynamism in English football that brought in new investments in stadiums, new professional practices of crowd control and management, created a huge rise in attendance, put on a world-class spectacle and created a massive export success. All of which, up to a point, is true—but it leaves a number of matters unexamined.

Turning the old theater of English league football into a globally attractive televised spectacle did not happen by the application of commercial acumen alone. Rather, it required three other changes: first, a kind of modern institutional enclosure, in which the common property of football clubs' identities and histories were, by stealth and legal maneuver, taken into private hands in the form of holding companies; secondly, a rewriting of the old rules established by the FA and the Football League to regulate commercial activity and mitigate the worst forms of financial inequality between leagues and within leagues; and thirdly, the force of the state to insist that the clubs do what they should have done a long time beforehand—invest in and transform their stadiums, a demand sweetened by very considerable public subsidy. Having done this the leading clubs were in a position to make the most of the arrival of the new digital technologies, above all pay TV via satellite and cable, which transformed the market for football. Without the new communications technologies football would no doubt have still changed, but the arc of its financial and cultural ascent would have been much more modest. It would probably feel different, too, for television has not only transformed the revenue stream of the industry but steadily helped reshape and reinvent the game; both play and coverage have been raised to new levels of technical excellence while mutating into an increasingly managed and commercialized experience.

English football is an industry with a globally renowned capacity for increasing turnover. However, it distributes that income very unequally and combines this with a pitifully limited capacity to control costs. There are two problematic consequences of this business model. First, the game is awash with debt and, not surprisingly, plagued by insolvencies and administrations; these particularly affect the divisions below the Premiership, which carry the costs of turbulence and disruption. Secondly, the widening structural inequalities in income distribution have not only encouraged reckless financial gambling by clubs but have made individual games and the championship as a whole less competitive. However, football clubs are not businesses like any other. They can attract massive capital injections as a down payment on glamour and status rather than future profit and they can go bankrupt and discharge their debts without actually disappearing. A glance at the attendance data and viewing figures for football suggests that whatever the theory may predict, there is no lack of appetite for an increasingly predictable competition—quite the contrary. Like much of British life, the new football economy is unfair but functional, wincingly unequal but never boring.

## II.

Like the railways, the sewers and the red-brick terraces of urban Britain, the basic grid of the nation's football was the product of a Victorian boom and an Edwardian consolidation. By 1914 the pitch had acquired its familiar markings, participants their familiar equipment and the broad style of play had been settled. Fields would remain unchanged until the introduction of coaches' technical areas in the 1990s. Uniforms would add squad numbers, boots would get screw-in studs and the ball would eventually acquire a modicum of waterproofing, but they remained essentially unaltered until the 1980s. The rewriting of the offside rule in 1923, requiring just two rather than three defenders to play an attacker onside, was the last significant rule change before the back-pass rule was introduced in 1992. Even then it only marginally altered the balance of attack and defense rather than fundamentally changing the geometry of the game. The shift from individualistic dribbling to collective passing, from all-out attack to a balance of offense and defense, had long been settled as the game's norms.[3] Similarly, the club as the basic social and sporting unit of the sport had been set and in turn the basic geography of British football was established: over 85 percent of the current members of the Football League were members in the early 1920s, the vast majority of them on the same plot of land that they acquired in the first quarter of the twentieth century.[4]

As football completed its mutation from an idiosyncratic aristocratic pastime to the most significant popular cultural practice of working-class life, it came to embody, in its sporting, cultural, and commercial norms, the changing class balance and political compromises of the age. It was a complex mix. On the one hand, the game retained traces of the rough and the rowdy, the spontaneous and the carnivalesque that characterized popular forms of folk football, both urban and rural. These games had been tied to saints' days, local festivities and rituals, and proved too boisterous and too threatening for the more rigid order of the Victorian city. Judicious use of the Riot Act, as well as rural depopulation, meant that these games were all but extinguished by the 1850s, but they lived on in the ludic zoos of England's elite private schools. Here, football first served as a form of pedagogic social control and was then shaped into the proving ground of a new Christian masculinity; the game, half-civilized and half-regulated, became an exemplar of the pluck and courage, the healthy mind and body, the steel-edged fair play that would characterize a race fit to run a global empire. For much of the 1860s and 1870s, the Football Association (founded in 1863) and its newly published rules presided over a small, almost cultic practice, made up of clubs that had their roots in the nation's leading public schools and military regiments. Yet the aristocracy never quite had the field to itself. In the public schools, universities, and professions they were joined by the football-playing sons of the haute bourgeoisie. The middle classes followed suit as the game was spread to the grammar schools, teaching colleges and urban parishes of Britain, driven with almost evangelical fervor by university-trained teachers and priests.

By 1875 the game had reached working-class Britain where its instant popularity made it something of a craze. In the cotton towns of the Lancashire valleys, in the steel towns of south Yorkshire, in the factories of the Midlands, and the working-class slums of Glasgow football mania took hold. By the mid-1880s working-class clubs and the increasingly large working-class crowds that came to see them had engulfed the hitherto exclusive world of amateur aristocratic football; and the challenge was not just on the pitch, where northern working-class teams were now regularly thrashing their southern amateur counterparts, but in ethos, too. With the crowds came money and with money came payments to players. Football was increasingly about winning not merely playing.

Something would have to give, and it was the FA that shifted position. In 1885 professionalism was legalized.[5] Within the FA there was a fundamentalist wing that would not accept professionalism at any price. They went on to create a doomed amateur-only breakaway in the south of England and staffed the ranks of the Corinthians—a strictly amateur touring club that, for a short period, combined brilliant football with an exaggerated gentlemanly sense of fair play.[6] However, it was the pragmatists among football's elites that won the day. Like their political equivalents they recognized that they had to accommodate some of the demands of the industrial bourgeoisie and the newly organizing Victorian working class, the former due to its financial wealth, the latter due to sheer weight of its numbers. The gradual widening of the male suffrage and the introduction of a regulated professionalism were, in the worlds of politics and football, prices worth paying for staying in overall control. Moreover, in both politics and football, accommodation created enough room for maneuver for the old elites that the new settlement could be made on their terms. Universal male suffrage would sit alongside a constitutional monarchy and an unelected hereditary house of parliament; professional football as a mass cultural phenomenon would be permitted, but the social and moral consequences of unregulated commercialism would be checked, and the still-aristocratic FA would remain the sovereign body of the football nation.

Once professionalism was permitted, the largest and most popular clubs established themselves as limited companies. This legal move protected shareholders and directors from the large financial liabilities clubs were taking on as they began to enlarge their facilities and build the first wave of industrial stadiums. It also opened up the possibility of clubs being run primarily as a source of income rather than as a sporting organization. To counter this possibility the FA made a series of rulings in the 1890s that were condensed in its eponymous rule book as Rule 34. This stated, first, that the dividend payments that clubs could pay to their shareholders were to be restricted to just 7.5 percent of profits; secondly, that no director could be paid by the club or work directly for them. Finally, to prevent asset-stripping scams in which clubs' stadiums and land were sold off and the limited company liquidated, any surplus from winding-up sales could not be taken by shareholders but had to be donated to a sporting charity.[7]

If this system of football governance was a trade-off between the aristocratic FA and the urban middle-class professionals and businessmen who formed the majority of the football directorate, two further deals were required to make the model work.[8] First, among the directors of clubs, and especially among the founder members of the Football League, there was a recognition that a good show required a degree of competitive balance, one jeopardized by the significantly different size of clubs' crowds that provided the overwhelming source of their income. Thus, from its inception, the Football League insisted on clubs sharing a slice of the gate receipts with the away team. Initially this was set at a flat rate of fifteen pounds and then in 1919 changed to 20 percent of the gate—an arrangement that endured for over seventy years. Secondly, the inevitable competition among clubs for players gave labor a significant bargaining advantage, which would, other things being equal, push up wages and consistently favor the bigger clubs who could pay the higher salaries that a competitive market would create. Labor was kept in check by two mechanisms: hire-and-retain and the maximum wage. The creation of the draconian hire-and-retain system left clubs holding players' licences. Without the licence they could not move to another club, whether they were under contract or not and whether their current contract was improved upon or not. In effect, once you were signed to a club you would play there and only there unless they decided otherwise. Having limited labor mobility and players' exit options, the authorities then ensured they would not be able to exercise significant power within the clubs. In 1901 the Football League introduced a maximum wage of £10 a week.[9]

Thus the Edwardian football club was neither a business nor a charity but a form of social enterprise-cum-civic association, collaborating, and competing with other clubs in a complex set of sporting and business networks. Institutionally and economically they were controlled by the urban middles classes, but the cultural compass of the game was set by the tastes and dispositions of the working class. What, ultimately, made professional football such an important cultural phenomenon was the enormous appetite of the British working man for playing it, watching, it, reading about it, and gambling on it. The crowds, although hardly angelic and occasionally drunk and spiteful, were large, loyal, and boisterous, often well informed and opinionated, and predominantly self-regulating with a repertoire of applause, banter, and the occasional music-hall singalong. The players were a skilled working-class aristocracy, depicted by the press as natural gentlemen, boys next door, and the salt of the earth. Fans did not pick and choose among competing clubs or switch their allegiance in line with fashion, but for the most part, stoically supported their local team. In turn, clubs did not look to make profits or to expand their fan base by buying out other clubs or attracting the opposition's supporters; rather they sought to maximize what the economics profession refers to as utility—which in this case constitutes competitive football in a given league on a break-even budget. Directors and club boards were pilloried, not for their profligacy or extravagance, but were cast as tight-fisted, mean-hearted skinflints: making an annual contribution to their club's never-ending overspend and debt became the price of admission to many football clubs' boards.[10] Once there you could indulge your love of football, make all sorts of useful connections and deals, maybe even have some business put your way if catering or brewing was your game, elevate your status in the local civic pecking order—but you weren't going to make a fortune. When the Premier League and the new football economics emerged they did not do so out of nowhere; this old order and its interlocking forms of economic and cultural organization had to be unpicked.

For nearly seventy years almost nothing changed. Match day remained the overwhelming source of clubs' income. Sponsorship was absent; advertising was rare, cheap, and confined to ad hoc boards and posters. The arrival of the pools industry—based on a new form of gambling in which participants tried to predict the scores of each weekend's games and shared a pool of prize money—in the 1930s was met with disdain even though it eventually yielded an important additional source of income. Radio arrived in the 1930s, television was pushing to cover league football from the 1950s, but even the arrival of regular TV highlights in the 1960s brought only a trickle of money into the game. Not surprisingly, hardly any extensive stadium development occurred. Some war damage was repaired in the late 1940s and early 1950s, and some of the bigger clubs invested in a single new stand, but the basic infrastructure of the game remained its architecturally precious but now ageing Edwardian inheritance. The one thing that did decisively change was the end of the maximum wage, finally abandoned in 1963 after a sustained campaign by the newly militant

Professional Footballers' Association led by Jimmy Hill, a Fulham player who went on to become a famous sports broadcaster. Wages for players rose and the finances of the clubs became more precarious.

In its twilight years, the old order of British club football enjoyed a remarkable late sporting renaissance. Between 1974 and 1985 British teams contested sixteen European finals and won seven European Cups, two Cup-Winners' Cups, and three UEFA Cups. Liverpool may have been the hegemonic team of the era, but there was enough room for smaller teams to win the league—Derby County and Nottingham Forest for example, while Aberdeen and Dundee broke the stranglehold of Celtic and Rangers on the Scottish title. Still the attendance figures continued to fall. Except for a couple of seasons in the 1960s, they had been falling every season since their all-time peak in 1951. Football's core working-class urban constituency began to shrink demographically, and competition in the Saturday afternoon leisure market appeared in the guise of DIY, gardening, and shopping. The fighting and disorder of the early 1970s became a permanent feature of the game, spreading to smaller clubs and European fixtures. The Edwardian infrastructure of the game was in visible decline, from turnstiles to toilets, from leaking roofs to rusting terrace barriers. Like the creaking remnants of the British manufacturing industry, undercapitalized and beset by conflict, something needed to change if it was to survive.

In 1983, the year of the Conservatives' second consecutive election victory, the Thatcherite project was consolidated, sealing the fate of Britain's old manufacturing sector. It was also a decisive moment in determining the direction of the football economy. Early in the year a report on football's league structure written by Sir Norman Chester was published. The Chester Report opted for a form of rationally managed decline, a defeatist but humane social democratic restructuring. On the one hand Chester called for a greater professionalism in the running of the clubs and a more commercially minded outlook, especially with regard to supporters' comfort.[11] Chester couldn't have been entirely convinced that this could be willed into being, as he also advocated retrenchment: reducing the size of the top division, cutting the size of the league as a whole and regionalizing the lower tiers to save money. Above all, he recognized that if a more socially and equitably minded settlement could not be negotiated now, a completely different settlement would be imposed by the bigger clubs "who know from conversations in the advertising and entertainment world that if they were free agents they would be likely to secure for themselves a much higher revenue than if they are treated as but part of ninety-two clubs. This is the issue which, if not settled amicably in the near future, could split the League."[12]

No sooner had the report been published than it was ignored. As with the wider economy, in the absence of a collective plan the running was made by piecemeal deregulation and exotic legal and financial practices. In 1981 the FA had begun the process by relaxing the rules on dividend payments and directors' pay, in the hope that full-time directors would bring more rigor to the game's economic governance. In 1983 the agreement to give the away team a share of the home gate, a practice beneficial to the smaller clubs, was revoked. Later in the year, as the Chester Report was buried, the real forces of change began to emerge: Tottenham Hotspur were floated on the Stock Exchange. The club had been bought by the property developer and tax exile Irving Scholar, who brought a new commercial sensibility to club management. He introduced pitch-side advertising to White Hart Lane, and negotiated lucrative sponsorship deals with kit manufacturers, but as with so much of the era his real innovation was a form of financial and legal engineering. Scholar and his team came up with the idea of creating a holding company, which would wholly own a football club as a legal subsidiary. The FA's remaining financial restrictions would still apply to the subsidiary club, but the actual ownership of the club, the power to run it and move its money around, lay with the new holding company to which no such restrictions applied. Spurs wrote to the FA to let them know what they were doing, but they never received a reply. In a single legal maneuver, Irving Scholar had found a way to circumvent the Victorian system of restricted civic commercialism, and nobody at the governing body noticed.[13]

This kind of legal chicanery opened up the possibility of shareholders making a quick buck by selling up their shares, but the basic problem of getting more money into the game and thus increasing the value of those shareholdings remained. As match-day attendances continued to decline and the income available from other sources remained minuscule, the biggest and most powerful clubs took a different route: keeping more of what money there was in football for themselves. In both 1983 and 1986 the clubs that made up the Scottish Premier League threatened to break away entirely from the Scottish Football League with its long tail of small-town clubs and sporting minnows. Significant concessions were extracted. More pools money was routed to the leading clubs, a new voting structure allowed them total administrative control and relegation from the top division was reduced to just one club a season. In 1986 the richer English clubs, especially the group known as the big five—Liverpool, Everton, Arsenal, Spurs, and Manchester United—began to organize and act. The Football League was reorganized to give Division One four of the nine places on the League's management committee. Simultaneously the majority required for rule changes was reduced from three-quarters of the members to two-thirds. Television money was reallocated upwards, with Division One clubs now receiving half of all the income, while the League's own levy on gate receipts was cut from 4 to 3 percent. Two years later the process went a step further—for many years Britain's only commercial TV broadcaster' broke off its relationship with the state-funded BBC and sought to outbid and exclude its erstwhile ally, negotiating directly with the biggest clubs and promising them guaranteed shares of the TV money in a breakaway league. A compromise was negotiated and the Football League remained intact, but Division One now received 75 percent of the £44 million ITV paid over four years for live football.

The final years of the old order were curious. On the one hand, football seemed more mired than ever in the complex of economic and social problems that had brought about its decline. In 1985 thirty-five people died beneath a crumbling wall at Heysel Stadium in Belgium as they fled from a terrace charge just minutes before Liverpool were due to play Juventus in the European Cup final; a few weeks earlier fifty-six people died in an inferno at Bradford City after a lit cigarette ignited half a century's worth of accumulated rubbish lurking beneath an old wooden stand. The live television pictures of a full-scale and violent pitch invasion by Millwall fans at Luton Town were extreme, but this was just one of hundreds of incidents of disorder in British football. English clubs were banned by UEFA from European competition; Lord Popplewell's report on the Bradford fire castigated the industry for its pathetic levels of investment and inattention to the safety of fans. The reaction of the government was to publish the draconian Football Supporters ID scheme. It looked as if foot-

ball would be caught in a downward spiral of declining income, investment, and attendances driven faster and further by policing levels and
techniques that were closer to those used against political demonstrations
than something appropriate to the entertainment industry.

Yet, at the same time, there were indicators of change. The first signs of
a new fan subculture began to emerge. In 1985 the Football Supporters'
Association was founded, offering a more politicized organizational voice
than the old federation of supporters' clubs. The following year, *When Saturday Comes* made its debut as a bi-monthly independent magazine and by
1990 was available in mainstream newsagents with a considerable circulation.[14] The climax of the 1989 league season saw a final day deciding match
between the top two—Liverpool and Arsenal—played on a Friday night,
shown live on TV and delivering a last-minute winner for the underdogs
Arsenal. Greg Dyke, head of ITV and the key figure in the station's pursuit
and use of live football, couldn't have concocted a better script.[15] The following year, England's performance at the 1990 World Cup had a similar
energizing effect on the standing of the game, made all the more powerful
by its intersection in the media with pop culture (through New Order's
England song "World in Motion") and high culture (the use of Pavarotti
wailing "Nessun Dorma" as the BBC's World Cup theme tune).[16] Perhaps
most significantly of all, football attendances had actually begun to rise
from the low point reached in 1985 and were gathering pace.

In this context the Hillsborough disaster and Lord Justice Taylor's report on the events appear as both the almost inevitable outcome of thirty
years of accumulated problems in British football and the decisive moment at which new forces of change could emerge.[17] The most important
impact of the Taylor Report was that the long-running attempt to deal
with football predominantly as a public-order issue requiring more draconian forms of surveillance and control was abandoned and reconceptu-
alized as a problem of public safety and economic management. Taylor's
forensic dissection of the institutional failures of the police and other
emergency services, and the football clubs and football authorities that
shaped the disaster, were given additional legitimacy as they came in the
wake of a whole series of non-football disasters attributable to underin-
vestment and regulatory laxness: the King's Cross underground fire, the
Piper Alpha Oil rig disaster, and the sinking of the ferry *Herald of Free*

*Enterprise.* The depth of institutional failure in the legal system, in the coroners' court, and above all in the police force would have to wait another twenty years to emerge, but even so the report's recommendations acquired such unassailable authority that they would reshape British football. A proposed ID card scheme was abandoned and a long series of changes in policing and stewarding at football was initiated.

The second key feature of the Taylor Report was to address the problem of the game's Edwardian infrastructure head-on. Taylor not only called for a fundamental refit of the basic structures of the nation's stadiums, but argued that perimeter fences should be removed, that the clubs be required to have a designated safety officer, and that venues for the top divisions in England and Scotland, at the very least, should have all-seater stadiums. This turned out to be the single most significant change in British football's infrastructure, culture, and economic model since the coming of professionalism.

In the strictly economic realm, the Taylor Report's main impact was to help force a shift in football's business model by making clubs invest in infrastructure, provide a higher level of "service" and ask more money for it in return. Taylor's initial estimate of around £150 million to carry out these changes was a considerable underestimate, but even on the basis of these figures it was clear that the football industry was in no state to fund the change itself. The Major government relinquished over £100 million in levies on the pools and other forms of betting, and passed it on to the Football Trust. The Trust, in turn, and for no stake or equity, passed the money to the clubs, in chunks ranging from the £2.5 million for Leeds United to the nearly £4.5 million given to Chelsea and Sheffield Wednesday. Compared to the public money lavished on Wembley (over £100 million) or the City of Manchester and London Olympic stadiums (around £200 million each), which were effectively gifted to Manchester City and West Ham United, this may seem small fries. However, this injection of public money, probably around a quarter of the first wave of stadium redevelopment costs, was the essential financial catalyst for change. Alongside the subsidized reconstruction of their grounds, clubs took the opportunity to start raising ticket prices at considerably above the rate of inflation, not as a one-off price hike to fund the rest of the cost of stadium reconstruction but as a central component of their business model.[18]

Thus the new football economy did not begin with a burst of revolutionary entrepreneurial energy or the invigorating arrival of private capital, rather it was triggered by an entirely avoidable tragedy and disaster; it was steered down a particular path of development by the hand of the British state; and a good chunk of the investment costs was paid by the taxpayer. Moreover, it inherited a vast body of cultural capital, of accumulated meanings, stories, collective memories and symbols whose value had not been tarnished by the problems of the 1970s and 1980s. Indeed, as the real industrial Britain from which they emerged, receded, they were burnished. The final act in the process was to monetize this new potential. As ITV's four-year deal, due to end in 1992, ran down, English football made its final fateful decisions on how the game would be run for the next two decades. The Football League had attempted to set the terms for this debate by publishing *One Game, One Team, One Voice* in 1990. It offered a new model of governance in which the League, the FA and an independent arbiter would resolve their collective problems and maintain a degree of financial solidarity across the divisions. It would also bypass the FA Council (the body's large, cumbersome ruling committee) and give the League a bigger say in a whole series of areas that the FA had traditionally considered its own, from youth development to the England team.[19] From the moment of its publication there was considerable resistance to the proposals from the FA, for obvious reasons, but from the biggest clubs as well. Their chairmen opposed the plan, arguing that they would not be able to control the newly empowered Football League or their proposed joint board. Above all, they would have to share much more of the money that appeared to be on offer with the lower leagues and they had no intention of doing that again. In an alliance of convenience the FA and the big clubs delivered their riposte: *The Blueprint for the Future of Football.*[20] It was a vacuous and disingenuous reworking of the League's proposals but shorn of the proposed FA–League committees. Instead, it provided a threadbare form of ideological legitimacy for the formation of, in effect, a breakaway league of the largest clubs, approved and anointed by the FA Chairman Bert Millichip. Twenty-two clubs resigned from the Football League in the summer of 1991, formed the Premier League, and invited the TV companies and sponsors to bid and the subscribers and season-ticket holders to pay up. They all came, and in greater numbers than anyone could have imagined.

## III.

The new football economy has been characterized by two key features: its extraordinary capacity to collectively generate income and to distribute it among the clubs in an unequal fashion; and, simultaneously, its complete inability to control the costs of doing business. As fast as the money comes in, it has been going out the other end. The Premier League's total annual turnover, currently standing at over £2.3 billion, is the biggest of any football league in the world: 66 percent bigger than Spain's La Liga, nearly half a billion a year more than its nearest competitor, Germany's Bundesliga. The Championship is by some way the wealthiest second-tier league and in the overall financial standings it is the ninth largest of any football league in the world. In the Premier League's first season, the twenty-two clubs raked in £170 million, which was a quantum leap from the final year of the old Division One. Just seven years later, at the turn of the century, twenty clubs were bringing in over half a billion pounds; by 2005 the figure had reached £1.3 billion. In 2013, the first year of the League's most lucrative TV deal yet, the Premiership as a whole turned over £2.3 billion, a figure almost fifteen times the League's turnover in its inaugural season. That computes as an annual rate of growth that exceeds even the asset-price bubble of the raging London property market.[21]

Football makes money in three ways: across the Premier League as a whole, half of that £2.3 billion is money from television and other media rights, a quarter comes from match-day income (tickets, pies, and banquets) and a quarter from other commercial activities including sponsorship, naming rights, property deals, and selling souvenirs. Twenty years earlier only 10 percent of a club's income came from TV. Now, in the case of smaller clubs in the Premier League, up to 80 percent of their income arrives this way. What accounts for such an extraordinary leap in the value of TV rights? In part, of course, it is about the quality of the new product, yet for all the hype of the Premiership's opening season the product was really not very different from the final year of Division One. Clubs, squads, style of play, and the state of the stadiums had yet to undergo really significant change. Change would come in all of these features of English football but the initial leap into the new economy was a matter of good fortune: to have the right product at the right time in the right place. Although the value of television rights had been creeping up through the 1980s they remained, historically speaking, very inexpensive. The existence of only two bidders, BBC and ITV, and their tendency to collude, kept the cost of football rights down. Moreover, although both channels considered the acquisition of football rights to be important—increasingly so at ITV—it was not the epicenter of their business models, a matter of make or break. Neither was going to go to the wall to get football on TV: indeed, they were prepared to call the Football League's bluff and show no football at all if necessary.

For BSkyB it was another matter. Satellite pay TV began in the UK with the launch of two competing systems—Sky and BSB—in 1989. Burdened by the high start-up costs of satellite TV, and selling to a public accustomed to free-to-view television, both companies hemorrhaged money. If the business had a future, it was for just one channel and one system. Sky bought out its competitor in 1991, but the basic problem of attracting subscribers remained. Heavy investment in Hollywood movies had failed to lure them. It became clear to Sky's management that football might be a better draw, or, as Rupert Murdoch came to refer to it, "a battering ram" to get his boxes inside people's living rooms. Consequently when the Premier League was formed it had a bigger range of bidders than the Football League had ever encountered, and in BSkyB it had one bidder that had put football at the heart of its whole business strategy. It was ready to bid what seemed at the time an astronomical amount of money to get live football.[22]

Sky's judgement was correct. In the twenty years since it signed the Premier League TV deal, BSkyB has acquired over ten million subscribers, turnover has grown from just over £200 million to nearly £7 billion and for a decade it has, unlike its sporting partner, posted pretax profits, currently running at over a £1 billion a year. Indeed, the BSkyB brand has become virtually synonymous with the Premier League, placing an even greater premium on the company's valuation of football. BBC and ITV effectively withdrew from the field though their appetite for highlights packages has sharply driven up the value of the weekend review slot. In the last decade other buyers have appeared. After a series of court rulings that forced the league to sell its rights in smaller packages to more bidders, Setanta, ESPN, and most recently BT have bought a share of the action. The arrival of a truly huge corporation like BT, searching for content, has pushed the price of TV rights up to another level: from around a million pounds a match in the 1990s, BT and Sky are now paying over £6 million a match and showing almost three times as many games.[23]

The capacity of the Premiership to attract subscribers rather than just one-off viewers, and the clear preference of many international audiences for English football over other European leagues, has made Premiership rights the jewel in the crown in dozens of sports television markets. From almost nothing, global sales of the League's TV rights now exceed domestic income. In the most recent round of bidding, Abu Dhabi Sports paid $200 million more than the previous winning bid from Showtime Arabia. In Singapore, with a population of less than five million, Singapore Telecom spent $200 million to acquire the rights from its main rival. NBC, in what was once considered the very marginal US market, was ready to pay a quarter of a billion dollars to win the rights and will be showing every single game with commentary in two languages.[24] Over the last decade the largest clubs have assiduously cultivated these markets, through social media and by staging longer and larger preseason tours to Europe, Asia, and North America. The Premier League itself has held a short knock-out competition in Asia every other year since 2003. In an attempt in 2008 to capitalize upon these markets even further the Premier League proposed a thirty-ninth game each season to be played in foreign cities which would bid for the rights to stage the game—a business model that promised each club around £5 million a year.[25] In a rare misjudgement of official and public reactions, the proposal was actively opposed by FIFA, UEFA, and fans and eventually buried. Instead, the biggest clubs with a known global profile have created their own alternatives. In the summer of 2013 Manchester United toured Australia, Japan, Hong Kong, and Thailand; Chelsea played Thailand, Malaysia, Indonesia, and the United States; Manchester City were in Hong Kong and South Africa; Arsenal found time for Japan, Indonesia, Malaysia, and Vietnam; and all were getting paid around $2.5 million per game.[26]

Match-day income, primarily from tickets, makes up just a quarter of the League's income but has nonetheless swelled in absolute terms to over half a billion pounds per year. This has been achieved, with considerably smaller ground capacities in all-seater stadiums, by the simple expedient of making tickets a lot more expensive. Broadly speaking, season tickets at the cheaper end of the market have increased in cost by 500 percent in the last twenty years, even allowing for inflation. Stadium renovation has made sure there are many more expensive seats, seats with cushions, seats with drink holders, seats in boxes, and seats outside boxes, and they have all increased in price even faster. In the case of TV rights the Premier League was both prescient and lucky. The growth of global digital communications arrived at just the right moment, widening the number of TV companies bidding for content, opening up new markets and with consumers ready to pay higher prices. None of these conditions was created by the Premier League, but it can claim to have cultivated them assiduously. In the case of ticket prices, clubs have just pushed their luck. The demand for football tickets proved to be remarkably price inelastic. Clubs raised prices in every market segment and have found, overall, that demand increased rather than decreased. This happened because the new football has been able to replace older less affluent fans that wouldn't pay the new prices with new more affluent punters that would. In part it happens because many fans are, for a complex mix of personal pleasures, obsessions and notions of loyalty, ready to pay more whether they can afford it or not. They are not exactly a hard market to work with.

The final quarter of the clubs' income—what gets lumped together as commercial, as if the TV and ticket sales were an act of charity—is where the real innovation in income generation has come. It has been effective but vulgar. Again, some of the groundwork had been laid in the 1980s with the arrival of pitch-side advertising, kit deals and shirt sponsorship, but there has been a step change in the scale of these activities. The cost of putting your brand on a Premier League shirt has risen considerably, with the leading clubs getting around £20 million a year; the smallest clubs get perhaps a tenth of that. Stadium-naming rights have also been up for sale. Football has baulked at renaming old stadiums, though one suspects more because of the considerable brand value of their current names than out of respect for history and tradition. When it comes to new stadiums, the names have been sold off. The new geography of football includes the Reebok, Emirates, Britannia, and Etihad.

However, sponsorship possibilities do not end there. Taking their cues from the model developed by FIFA, the IOC, and other global sporting mega events, football clubs have acquired a long list of official suppliers, friends and partners, carefully calibrated to ensure a single brand in each sponsorship slot. The language of this world hovers between the bureaucratic, the euphemistic, and the absurd. Clubs don't merely have sponsors, they have partners, and not merely partners but official partners, helping out with responsible drinking and gaming (boozing and betting) and providing financial services (payday loans and legal loan sharkery). Manchester United now has twenty-nine different corporates paying up: a roster that includes official paint, integrated telecommunications, and medical systems partners, an East Asian official noodles sponsor, and wine and beer specialists to support poor old Smirnoff with the task of responsible drinking at Old Trafford.

Professional football was always an unequal competition, with inequalities of income between the leagues and within the leagues. In the Premier League the richest clubs now have incomes more than four or five times that of the clubs at the bottom of the league. In 2012 Manchester United, Chelsea, and Arsenal all had revenues over £220 million, while Blackpool, Birmingham, and Blackburn had a quarter of that. Those clubs in turn have an annual turnover more than three times the average budgets of the clubs in the Championship. In Leagues One and Two the average club had a turnover of £5 million and £3.5 million respectively, making the bottom two divisions into smaller businesses than Manchester United or Arsenal alone. The inequality between the leagues, previously a function of the size of a club's fan base, is now overwhelmingly determined by the value of the TV rights they can command. In a winner-takes-all market, where for the general viewer there is only room for one major football league product, the better league will get all the income, not just a share of it. That's the point of the Premiership. On top of this, of course, the same league can command higher ticket prices and will attract the vast majority of the corporate and high-end customers. Finally, in an economic competition in which the glamour, status, and meaning of your club identity/brand is the key to unlocking sponsorship money, the lower leagues simply can't compete.

This degree of inequality within the Premier League is, perhaps, surprising given that three-quarters of the TV money (half of the domestic income and all of the overseas income) is divided equally among the twenty clubs. The other half of the domestic money is distributed on the basis of how often you are on TV and how high you finish in the league—factors which give the top clubs perhaps 50 percent more of this tranche of money than those at the bottom. But what really drives the income difference among the clubs is the same logic of status and sponsorship that divides the Premiership from the leagues below it: the size and income of club's crowds and the impact of elite European competition. The range of sponsorship and commercial income in the Premier League is huge. In 2012 Wolverhampton Wanderers, Stoke City, and Norwich City raised less than £20 million, while Bolton Wanderers managed less than £10 million; twenty miles down the road the two Manchester clubs raised over £100 million apiece. Match-day incomes show a similar spread. Manchester United and Arsenal have by some way the largest stadiums combined with the most extensive hospitality packages and high-end corporate seating and in Arsenal's case the most expensive ticketing across the board. In 2012 they brought in from match-day sales £99 million and £95 million, respectively: almost twenty times what Blackburn Rovers could muster, ten times what Stoke City could manage. A few clubs are able to stay in touch: Chelsea and Spurs have smaller stadiums but a fan base with incomes sufficient to pay very high prices, while Liverpool and Newcastle charge less in poorer cities but have bigger crowds. Manchester City and Chelsea have also received some of the biggest, softest loans on record but the rest of the Premier League has no prospect of catching up.

Finally, there is income from competitions other than the Premier League. Revenue from the FA Cup and the League Cup, while welcome to smaller clubs, is too little to account for the growth of income inequalities. European football is another matter. The UEFA Champions League, reformatted and launched in 1992, has been phenomenally successful, bringing in enough money to make it the sixth, possibly even the fifth biggest league in Europe and with very high revenues directed to the leading clubs in the largest TV markets. In 2011, for example, Manchester United made £50 million from the TV income from the Champions League alone. This was more than Barcelona received after beating them soundly in the final and more than the total broadcast income of nearly half the clubs in the Premier League.[27] In the same year, Arsenal, who only made the round of sixteen in the Champions League, received £30 million. With the same remorseless logic of winner takes all, the second-tier European competition, previously the UEFA Cup but now hopefully rebranded as the Europa League, brought in only around £6–7 million for the English clubs that took part in it. This massive annual injection of cash, and the huge increase in global coverage that Champions League participants receive, has been one of the key reasons that the top of the Premier League looked so similar for so long—dominated by Manchester United, Arsenal, Chelsea and Liverpool who were in the competition every season.

Unequal or not, one might expect that this deluge of income, steered by the great entrepreneurial wisdom of club boards and owners, would have produced some extraordinary profits. But perhaps the most amazing thing about the new football economy is that it has barely produced profits at all. On the most generous measure possible, the Premier League has collectively managed to generate a small operating profit most seasons, though even this has collapsed from around 16 percent of turnover to less than 4 percent. However, when we add in the capital account—the cost of paying debts, the decline in the capital value of assets like players and losses on trading in the player market, as well as tax—then, in the Premiership and every other league in the country, there have been no overall profits at all. In 2010, for example, the Premier League clubs made pretax losses of £445 million.[28] In the same year, the Championship clubs made a collective loss of £133 million, and Leagues One and Two made operating losses of £52 million and £8 million, respectively.[29] Of course, there have been some very large variations among clubs in each of the leagues. A handful of clubs break even or even make a small profit. Manchester United have regularly made money, as have Arsenal since they moved to the Emirates. Occasionally an exceptionally well-managed smaller club will make a profit for a season or two in the Premiership—Swansea City and West Bromwich Albion, for example—or a lower league side will make some money on an exceptional cup run or a carefully husbanded transfer policy, but they are few and far between. More emblematic of the game as a whole are the record losses clocked up in 2011 by Manchester City (£197 million) and Chelsea (£68 million). In this at least, the new economy is a democracy of profligates, as operating losses, though smaller, are found right across the leagues. In the same year League One clubs were losing an average of £2.4 million a year on an average £5 million turnover; in League Two they did a little better, losing an average of just £300,000 a year on an average turnover of £2.4 million.

How has British football managed to create a business model in which as turnover rises, so do losses? The problem is not really on the capital account side, though interest payments on accumulated debt and losses on player transfers don't help. The problem is the current account. Alan Sugar nailed it: "The money coming into the game is incredible. But it is just the prune-juice effect—it comes in and goes out straight away. Agents run the world."[30] In Division One's final season, wages consumed 44 percent of the league's income. Ten years later players had secured 60 percent of the Premier League's far larger turnover and by 2010 they had taken their share of club expenditure to 70 percent. In the Championship the average share is even higher—around 90 percent of clubs' income in 2011—with at least six clubs spending more on wages alone than their entire revenue.[31] Given the huge leaps of income between the leagues, players' wages have moved in the same way. In 1992 the average wage of players in the Premiership was £75,000 a year; by 2010–11 it was £1.4 million a year, which is around £26,000 a week.[32] In the Championship the average player's wage in the early 1990s was £50,000 a year, two-thirds of the wages in the division above. By 2011 they were earning less than a seventh of players in the Premiership, at just over £200,000 a year. In League Two, the old Division Four, players were earning an average of £15,000 a year in 1992. Now they are bringing in £40,000 a year. The ratio of wages in the bottom division to Premiership wages has shifted from 1 to 5, to 1 to 35. There are of course considerable differences within leagues and within individual clubs. At the highest end of the Premiership the structure of inequality is repeated again, with an elite handful of players being paid £5 to £10 million a year.

Why is it that players have managed to capture such a huge slice of football's new money? Why are clubs prepared to pay wages so high that they are running at a permanent loss? The core reason is that the relationship between wages and winning in English football is pretty straightforward. The higher your wage bill, the more points you will win, the higher up the league you will finish. The transfer market in players, and the wages they can command, while not perfect indicators of ability and performance, are sufficiently good for this relationship to hold. Clubs can do better or worse than their wage bill would predict. A mixture of luck, smart dealing in the transfer market and good managerial decisions will shift you a few places up or down the league. But not more than that.

This in itself is not enough to ensure that the entire industry will operate on a permanent loss-making basis. It needs to be combined with a set of employers whose decisions on expenditure, wages and transfer policy are primarily concerned with winning football games and not with making a profit. There are exceptions. The Oyston family, owners of Blackpool, took the opportunity of a season in the Premier League to recoup their investments rather than funding a realistic stab at staying up. The wage bill was frozen at Championship levels, Blackpool were duly relegated, and the Oystons scooped up around £40 million from a year of broadcast fees and four years of parachute payments (i.e. payments to relegated clubs to cushion the reduced TV and gate income). At the other end of the scale the Glazers, having obtained the single most powerful brand in English football, have been busy making it sweat through a combination of huge directors' fees, soft loans to the family and a small stock market flotation. Yet even they recognize that all of this booty is dependent on putting out a highly competitive team that keeps Old Trafford full. Thus the labor market in football is full of hyper-competitive, over-optimistic buyers motivated by winning rather than profit: a guarantee of massive wage inflation. This dynamic was given a further boost by the impact of the new inequalities within and between the leagues. The massive increases in income and status derived from playing in European competitions, or from promotion to the Premiership, have encouraged more risk-tasking. More clubs have been prepared to spend more money and go into more debt to make the jump across one of these key thresholds, thereby helping to push wages up even further.

It is precisely these kinds of problems that have led some professional team sports to collectively impose salary caps or limit the degree on clubs. This is the norm in North America where all the major leagues—the NFL, MLB, NBA, and the NHL—attempt to restrict player share of turnover to a specific maximum and limit the degree of income inequality between the largest and smallest clubs. However, there has been little taste in the Premier League for similar institutional machinery. The Football League has recently imposed a salary cap on League Two, but the turbulent free-for-all in the labor market has continued unabated above it. The absence of any kind of attempt to control wages collectively is curious. In part it is a consequence of the very limited administrative machinery of the Premier League—which is essentially a branding machine and TV-rights-selling business. The FA effectively retreated from any engagement with the economic regulation of the leagues in the early 1990s. Above all, it has been impossible to get any kind of consensus among the twenty club chairmen who at any one time are the actual decision makers. The biggest clubs have feared that they would no longer be able to compete in unregulated European labor markets, smaller clubs have wanted to hang on to the opportunity of gambling and going for the top, and clubs funded by soft loans and their owners' capital have wanted to keep that as an option. Competition for players has been so fierce that not only have wages risen but clubs have been unable for the most part to impose contracts that reduce players' wages in the event of relegation and a catastrophic decline in income.[33] A modicum of sanity and restraint has been applied to this downward spiral of market fundamentalism by a dose of European corporatism: UEFA's Financial Fair Play regulations, fiercely opposed in some quarters in England, which have begun to limit clubs' accumulation of debt. Manchester City were fined £50 million at the end of the 2014 season and the size of their Champions League squad reduced. Whether this kind of penalty will be sufficient to cool the football bubble at the very top end of the market remains to be seen.

Unable to protect themselves from themselves, the clubs have been further weakened in the labor market by a series of legal changes that have shifted the balance of power towards the players. In 1995 the European Court of Justice ruled, in the case of the little-known Belgian player Marc Bosman, that a club's ability to hold on to a player who was out of contract as long as they offered him a new one on at least equal terms was an illegal restraint of trade. Players that were out of contract could now move to a new club with no transfer fee being paid. As a consequence, transfer fees have disappeared altogether and a club that does buy a player still under contract to another club effectively buys him out of that contract rather than paying a fee. While this ruling gave players more freedom it also helped open up a much bigger pool of labor for the competing clubs. All restrictions on the numbers of EU players in a squad or a league had to be abandoned. Players from the European Union are not considered in labor law to be foreigners at all and the EU has expanded from twelve members in 1992 to twenty-eight members in 2012. The global pool of talent available widened even further as clubs' scouting networks began to look at Africa, Latin America and Asia as well. This should have shifted some power back towards the clubs, but demand was so high and with quality the key threshold, the main effect of opening up the global talent pool was not to reduce wages but to displace British players from the top end of the market. From just eleven foreign players in the squads of the clubs that played the opening season of the Premiership in 1992, less than 3 percent of the work force, by 2012 it was touching 60 percent. On the opening weekend of the 2013–14 season English players made up just 37 percent of the first XIs that played.[34]

The impact of these changes is usually considered in relation to the fate of the England national team, the global appeal of the league and the relationship between fans and players. I return to all of these later, but in more narrowly economic terms this form of globalization did not benefit the clubs for they did not have the institutional machinery or personnel to capture and use their new-found power in the market place. In fact, the new football labor market cruelly exposed the weaknesses in British football clubs' scouting networks, transfer policies and negotiating skills. Until very recently enormous power was vested in just the manager or a very small number of key individuals in clubs. The virtues of collective discussion and critical examination were considered less important than the gut instincts of old-school gaffers. The innumerable mistakes, systematic biases, and expensive miscalculations that this style of personnel policy produced have finally seen English football clubs make transfer policy the responsibility of directors of football rather than first team coaches, and brought a modicum of reasoned discussion to clubs' transfer spending.

Even so they have some way to go to catch up with the other side, where football agents have made themselves vital figures in the football economy. Unregistered before 1995, the agency business has grown as fast as its clients' wages. Agencies have proved adept at playing clubs off against one another, keeping abreast of the ever rising industry wage standards and using the story-hungry media to manipulate bargaining positions. Some have branched out into the role of middlemen, not merely representing a client to a club but acting as a personal gatekeeper, earning a range of introduction fees for connecting buyers and sellers, before going on to represent the player in the deal as well. In both roles they have been amply rewarded.[35] Though it is impossible to calculate the sums involved with any real accuracy, it is clear that the football agencies have been earning their share of their players' astronomical wages and up to another £100 million a season lubricating other transactions.[36] This might seem odious and unfair. It probably is, but agents are just a symptom of the absurd business model that the commercialization of football has produced, in which record growth produces record inequality, in which the ever larger and faster turnover of clubs is converted more efficiently into uncontrollable wage bills and overall losses.

## IV.

The new football economy might by conventional reasoning be considered absurd, a madly spinning wheel of ever larger cash flows that enriches a very small and highly specialized labor force, but produces no profit. On the other hand, as the viewing and attendance figures attest, it is putting on a very popular show and that, in the end, is what it is there for. Critics argue that issues of social justice or economic efficiency aside, there are two trends created by the new model that are truly problematic: the rise of football debt and insolvencies, and the decline in the competitive balance of the game. When companies make persistent losses, for whatever reason, they inevitably accumulate debt. English football is awash with it. UEFA reported that in 2008 the English Premier League alone accounted for 56 percent of all the debt held by European football clubs. In 2010 net debt held by Premier League clubs stood at £2.6 billion, and had been as high as £3.3 billion in 2008.[37] At the same time Championship clubs had racked up £0.9 billion of debt. Scottish football has been a much smaller economic operation, with just twelve teams in the SPL, but the League barely breaks even most years and by 2009 the clubs had accumulated debt of over £100 million.[38]

Debt, in and of itself, is not a bad thing. It all depends on what kind of debt and how much. In Arsenal's case, debt borrowed at a sensible rate of interest to pay for a new stadium with a much higher earning capacity would appear entirely reasonable. Debts incurred in the form of soft loans (at low or zero interest rates with no threat of foreclosure) from rich owners might be considered a form of unfair competition by less fortunate clubs and they create a financial situation where a club's fate hangs on the whim of one person, but in pure accounting terms they are tolerable. Fulham, Chelsea, Newcastle, and Manchester City have all been substantial beneficiaries of this form of support. Manchester United are a special case: their debt arose from a leveraged buyout, after which the new owners put their borrowing onto the club balance sheet; this is risky to say the least, but it remains a one-off, albeit a very large one-off debt.

These cases aside, the vast majority of indebted clubs have got there because they persistently spent more than they were bringing in. Accumulated losses turn into debts and in most fields of business accumulated debt usually leads to one of three outcomes: takeover by a competitor, radical internal restructuring, or insolvency. Takeovers never happen in football. It makes no sense for one club to buy another—what would one be buying? Players, but they can be bought anyway by the buying club. Why double your wage bill but still play the same number of paying gigs? A club might acquire a stadium, which is a capital asset but one that the buyer almost certainly already possesses. Even if didn't, a rival's stadium is going to be in the wrong place and with a customer base that is unlikely to keep coming.

The internal restructuring option is possible. This usually combines massive cuts in expenditure, essentially players' wages, with a sale of assets including players and grounds. Then an attempt can be made to stabilize the club, albeit at a lower level in the league or indeed in a lower league entirely. However, it is rarely popular and sometimes unsuccessful. A sharp reduction in expenditure can lead a club into a downward spiral of declining income without any reduction of debt. Alan Sugar's reign at Spurs was a rare example of a truly cost-conscious management trying to deal with a big debt problem and refusing to overspend. The consequences of this regime were financial stability and small profits but at the cost of a decade of mid-table finishes that remained profoundly out of kilter with the club's self-image and its fans' expectations. Successful or not, it was a strategy that ran right against the grain of unvarnished optimism that permeates football.

Insolvency, by contrast, has proved a remarkably good business strategy. Unlike other kinds of company, the clubs do not disappear. Despite more than a hundred cases of administration since 1923, 97 percent of the Football League's clubs are still in existence and 85 percent of them are still in the League itself.[39] Total liquidation is very rare indeed. Clubs cut a deal with their creditors, shed the majority of their debt, and immediately go back into business as a new entity under the same old name and usually with their stadium as well; for what in the end is a football club but a name and a complex set of stories, memories, traditions, and histories that this embodies? No amount of red ink can eradicate them or diminish their value for those who consider them important—important enough to go and pay to watch a team with that name. The arrangement has generally worked well for other clubs, too. Under the Football Creditors rule they alone are the preferred creditors of the clubs and must receive their money in full before any is apportioned to Her Majesty's Revenues and Customs—Britain's tax collectors—club suppliers or even voluntary organizations like the St. John's Ambulance.[40] Indeed, these arrangements worked so well for heavily indebted clubs that the Football League has had to impose penalties and loss of league points on clubs that go into administration, to discourage the practice from being used even more regularly than hitherto.

Insolvency in English football is nothing new. Either side of the First World War clubs went bankrupt in most years and in the 1930s, as the depression lengthened, more went under. In the postwar era, bankruptcy was rare, with just two clubs getting into serious trouble in the 1960s.[41] In the mid-1980s winding-up orders were on the rise again; a dozen between 1984 and 1994. Since then the numbers have grown: another twenty-seven clubs went bust between 1995 and 2002, when eleven clubs in a single year went into administration. In the next decade over thirty more clubs, some admittedly coming back for a second bout of administration, went down the tubes. Around 10 to 20 percent of football insolvencies have an element of criminal or fraudulent behavior as one of their causes. Given the exceptionally weak financial and legal regulation of football clubs, they have proved very attractive to a variety of hucksters, fraudsters, and villains bent on insurance fraud, money laundering, dodgy land deals, and straightforward embezzlement. The collapse of Exeter City, Barrow, Wrexham, York City, and Doncaster Rovers, for example, could be traced to precisely these kinds of management techniques. The other 80 percent of insolvencies stem from the same basic problem of too little income and too much expenditure, often exacerbated by a protracted run of poor performance on the pitch, which turns into a downward spiral of income and attendance. Already fragile clubs are then particularly susceptible to shocks and sharp changes in circumstances that tip them over the edge; the run of insolvencies in 2002 and 2003 fall into this category. Clubs that had already stretched themselves were maintained as growing concerns by the promise of continuing to receive money from ITV Digital—a short-lived pay TV venture that had offered to pay the Football League £315 million over three years. When the station collapsed in 2002 the successor TV deal was worth less than a third of the previous arrangement, leaving a gigantic hole in clubs' budgets.

However, neither criminality nor external shocks helps us understand why there have been so many more financially vulnerable clubs who eventually get tipped over the edge. At least part of the explanation lies with the much higher levels of inequality that now exist in British football. As the financial gap between the leagues has grown sharply, the benefits of promotion and the costs of relegation are greatly magnified. Football clubs, hitherto, have focused on the former rather than the latter. Given the already strong, virtually compulsory, preference for optimism over pessimism in the business, more clubs have placed themselves at risk by borrowing and spending—in effect gambling on promotion or another season in the Premier League, and with it another huge financial windfall. Since 2002 the most high profile insolvencies have been the slew of medium-sized clubs who had been relegated from the Premier League and then went into free fall.[42] Bradford City are considered the archetypal case, when after a successful season in the Premiership surviving on the last day, the club chairman inaugurated what became known as "six weeks of madness" in which the bounty was spent, the wage bill went through the roof, and the club acquired a squad of mismatched players on immense salaries who had neither the cohesion nor the grit to keep the team up for a further season. Multiple relegations and administration followed soon afterwards.[43] Yet Bradford City did not disappear. Indeed, the club has bounced back, free of debt, and made it to the final of the 2013 League Cup. Administration and insolvency are certainly forces for destabilization. They can, in extremis, threaten a club's very existence but it rarely comes to that. They waste a lot of people's time and energy, and they are mean and unfair to the small commercial and voluntary-sector creditors of the football clubs. However, in the absence of a very different regulatory framework this is an inevitable consequence of the new football's insatiable, aspirational appetites.

Perhaps the most vexed question surrounding the sporting impact of the new economic order is the question of competitive balance. Given that wages are the central determinant of club performance and given that the economic structure of British football produces very sharp inequalities both between leagues and within leagues, does this mean that the game—at the level of individual matches as well as the contest for the League itself—has become more predictable and therefore less interesting? At one level this is a technical and statistical question. A variety of econometric studies have examined the problem. Some, looking at individual match data, have found that home advantage has been steadily declining, making more games more uncertain.[44] On the other hand, studies at the level of the season examine what share of points in the League are taken by the top five clubs, and what share has been taken by newly promoted clubs.[45] In both cases, relatively steady levels of inequality and imbalance from the 1940s to the early 1990s show a sharp increase over the last twenty years.

Translated into the narrative experience of seasons and championships, the Premier League certainly appears to be a highly limited competition. Between 1992 and 2004 only three clubs won the title: Blackburn Rovers once, Manchester United eight times and Arsenal three times. From 2004 to 2014 Manchester United have again been the leading side, winning five titles, and they have been joined by Chelsea with three and Manchester City with two. Five different champions in twenty-one seasons, with one dominant club, is actually not hugely different from Liverpool's era of hegemony (1970–90) when they won the League eleven times leaving space for only six other clubs (Arsenal, Everton, Leeds, Nottingham Forest, Derby County, and Aston Villa). The common assumption is that fans and viewers will tire of these predictable outcomes and desert the sport. However, all the evidence so far is to the contrary.

The data on match attendance, television-viewing figures, radio-listening data, and the consumption of news all suggest that this highly unequal, stratified League is incredibly popular, and the more uncompetitive it has become, in strictly econometric terms, the more the world seems to want it. Clearly the palate of the football public is much more complex and diverse than the economists have so far allowed for.

In fact fans like balanced and unbalanced games. The former offers the prospect of a closely fought battle decided by minute but brilliant margins; the latter offers David and Goliath, the possibility of the humiliation of the favorite and the triumph of the underdog. The point is that fans like games that mean something, and winning the title, while a key narrative, is not the only story on the boil. In its second decade the Premiership has settled down into three or four simultaneously occurring contests: the race for the title itself; the contest for the top four places and thus entry to the Champions League; the miserable struggle of the middle-range clubs for the minor European slots, which are so much less remunerative or glamorous; and then a long tail of teams struggling to stay up in a contest that is often considerably closer and more dramatic than the title race itself.

The fact that such a narrow range of clubs has actually won the title, infuriating as it is to the nearest but titleless challengers, has not been bad business for the League as a whole. The Premier League, indeed the whole of professional football, is not consumed in individual morsels or conducted like an exercise in the ethics of distributive justice—it is experienced as drama and story. Manchester United function as the villain of the piece and this is a part of the reason that their away games are so popular with other fans and can command such a premium. Manchester City and Chelsea both have provided sporting competition and extended the rogue's gallery that any long-running melodrama requires by turning themselves into vulgar nouveau riche arrivistes. In fact, the multilayered contests of the new football offer more than just soap opera but something closer to a state-of-the-nation novel: the debt-fuelled antics and bitter conflict of the rich and famous; the long-suffering mediocrities and disappointments of middle England; the high hopes and harshly dashed aspirations of the hardworking poor; and in the lower leagues the great provincial small-town masses, permanently excluded from the center, charting their own small courses. This is a world that is highly stratified and becoming more so, where mobility between those strata becomes rarer and harder, yet which believes itself to be a meritocracy. While the preference of the public is for social realism, the rising competitive imbalance of British football will be an economic strength, not a weakness.

This is the strange world that the entrepreneurs and commercially minded managers of the new football created: a boom that produces inequality, growth without profits, insolvencies without liquidation and an ever-narrowing competition that becomes more compelling as it becomes more unjust. Now they have moved on. The key figures at the head of the football clubs that made this economic revolution have cashed in and sold up. Irving Scholar got himself and Spurs into financial trouble in the early 1990s and was forced to sell up to Alan Sugar: he missed the gold rush. Martin Edwards at Manchester United spent nearly twenty years looking for a way to cash in the chips his father Louis Edwards had so painstakingly amassed. Edwards sold a tranche of the club's newly floated shares in 1991 and would love to have sold the rest to BSkyB in 1999, but was thwarted by the Monopolies and Mergers Commission. In the end they did him a favor, as he did even better selling his shares in tranches to other investors over the next four years. He left the club with a profit of something in the region of £100 million. However, when it came to screwing every last penny available out of their football club, Sir John Hall and the Shepherd family at Newcastle United were the real professionals. Dividends between 1997 and 2005 amounted to nearly £20 million despite the club's minuscule operating profits and overall losses. Salaries were generous—Hall's son Douglas and Freddy Shepherd were on director's salaries of £5.3 and £4.7 million respectively while numerous members of both families acquired well-paid non-executive directorships. Hall also sold shares from as early as 1998 and made over £50 million this way. The Shepherds ended up with another £30 million when forced to sell their stake to new owner Mike Ashley. Between them they managed to extract just over £145 million from the club that they had bought for just a few million.

Given the Stock Exchange's accurate and damning assessment of football's long-term profitability, Manchester United aside, most of Edwards' generation of big club shareholders were unable to turn their paper into a small fortune by selling off their stake on the open market. The only way to make the game pay was to find someone or something that was ready to buy your shares as an investment in a unique and globally visible form of status and power rather than on the basis of rates of return. Once again the Premiership chairmen have been lucky, for that is precisely what a selection of the world's super rich—American billionaires, postcommunist oligarchs, Middle Eastern royal families, and industrial tycoons from Asia—have been looking for. David Dein bought his first shares in Arsenal in 1983, 16.6 percent for just £292,000. He sold the bulk of them to the Uzbek-Russian oligarch Alisher Usmanov in 2007 for £75 million. Ken Bates exceeded even this kind of rate of return, having bought his share in Chelsea for £1 in 1982 and recouped around £17 million when the club and its gigantic debts were sold to Roman Abramovich in 2003. This wave of foreign billionaire owners in the Premier League has made rich men even richer. In 2006 Terence Brown sold his share in West Ham, where he was pulling in a million pounds a year in salary, pension, and expenses anyway, to Icelandic investors for £35 million. Doug Ellis had made a killing first time around at Aston Villa. When the club was floated on the stock market, at a preposterously high price, Ellis cashed in £4 million in shares. As the share price tanked, he switched methods and drew himself a fabulous salary as chairman and director, directed very large dividends to himself, and then sold up the club entirely to American billionaire Randy Lerner in a deal worth over £60 million.

At least Lerner was relatively benign; some of the old school shareholders have made more money selling their clubs to even more inappropriate new owners. Manchester City's owners took £80 million off ex-Thai Premier and fugitive from national and international justice, Thaksin Shinawatra, in 2007. John Moores, the long-term owner of 50 percent of Liverpool, got £89 million when the club was sold to the American robber barons Hicks and Gillett. Of all the strange and ugly elements of the new football economy, this process was the strangest of all, that these clubs, essentially Victorian working-class institutions, and their complex sporting culture should prove to be unique objects of desire for the new global elite, and that the biggest money of all would be made by those who appropriated them and then so carelessly sold them on.

# CHAPTER 2

# Keeping It Real?

## Match Day in the Society of the Spectacle

Longing on a large scale is what makes history. This is just a kid with a local yearning but he is part of an assembling crowd, anonymous thousands off buses and trains . . . and even if they are not a migration or a revolution, some vast shaking of the soul, they bring with them the body heat of a great city and their own small reveries and desperations, the unseen something that haunts the day.

**DON DELILLO,** *UNDERWORLD*

I.

Guy Debord, consumed by his alcoholic melancholy, foresaw a world in *The Society of the Spectacle* in which cultural life was increasingly colonized by commercially manufactured imagery.[1] It was a future in which distant, mediated, artificial events were the central nodes of an atomized culture held together by a shared addiction to stupefaction and the spectacle. The intimate, the immediate, the unscripted, and the authentic would eventually be driven out, leaving just the simulacrum of the world—a copy of a copy. Precisely this outcome has arrived in the shape of reality television, "structured" documentaries, celebrity diaries, and talent shows. Sport can be cast in this mold, too, as media companies, dissatisfied with the games on offer, have invented their own, creating in WWE, for example, an entire parallel universe of wrestling. What saves football from this fate is the fact that the raw material out of which the media–football complex constructs the spectacle remains intensely local. If you have ever watched a game played in an empty stadium after some punishment has been issued for fan misbehavior, you will know that there is nothing quite as lonely and maudlin. Until the broadcasters can perfect a digitally enhanced crowd, there is no spectacle without them.[2] In the last twenty years, the crowd and its behavior, and the look and choreography of the experience of going to the game, have been profoundly shaped by the demands of television and the other commercial and cultural forces at play in the world of football. However, the experience has also remained stubbornly the same, resisting the encroachment of commercialism. In the heart of the media spectacular remains the grit of the real match. Here, the spectacle, notionally pure imagery, must wrestle with both the material reality of a stadium full of people and the tangible social relationships that exist between them.

The single biggest difference between a game today and one played in the mid-1980s is that the crowd is bigger, much bigger. In 2012 the total attendance at English football topped 30 million people in a season, a level only previously reached in 1968 and that was a one-off, tapping into the short-lived, post-1966 World Cup football frenzy. Prior to that, one has to go back over half a century to see such big crowds.[3] The economists and the club marketing departments have argued that this growth can be explained in terms of the product on offer: safer, more comfortable all-seater stadiums plus better football means bigger crowds. The broadcasters congratulate themselves that football's exposure on live television has helped make attendance all the more attractive. There is, of course, some truth in these arguments. But they are not the whole story. The last time there was such a surge in numbers attending football was the late 1940s. The end of the Second World War was followed by the restart of the Football League, and the crowds surged: from 27 million in

1938–39, the last full season before the war, to 35 million in 1947–48, peaking the following season at over 40 million.[4] After six years of rations and bombing it is hard to argue that the product on offer was any better than before the war: many stadiums were unusable due to bomb damage; players, even those who had turned out for the armed forces, were hardly at the peak of fitness; teams long broken apart had to be hurriedly reassembled. Even so, as demobilization began, millions of young men returned to civilian life after their wartime adventures, and among them there was simultaneously a desire for both a return to normality and for some flash of color in the unbearable drabness of postwar Britain.

What is it then that our own generation has hungered for and found at the football game? Sky and their advertising copywriters think they know the answer. Looking at the adverts the company ran in 1992 announcing the first season of the Premiership, it appeared it was just good wholesome fun that we were after.[5] Mum, dad, and the kids are opening up their Christmas presents and guess what Santa has brought them? A phalanx of players from all twenty-two teams in the new league running out of the tunnel together in their shiny new shirts. Just five years later this kind of family-friendly jollity seemed embarrassingly naive, psychologically too shallow to explain the miracle that football on Sky had become. The Premiership was no longer just Christmas and your birthday in one, it was the Second Coming. For this one needed the actor Sean Bean, ransacking the clichés of obsessive football fandom but giving them a sham aura of profundity by his terse diction and intense unblinking stare. All of this was delivered close-up in Spartan monochrome and intercut with highlight-reel football and fan reaction. "We all need someone to rely on, someone who's gonna make you feel like you belong, someone constant. It's ecstasy, anguish, joy and despair. It's part of our history, part of our country. It's theater, art, war and love. It should be predictable but it never is, a feeling that we can't explain but we spend our lives explaining it. It's our religion. Football."[6]

It is hard not to be cynical about Sky as anthropologists. As the brilliantly graffitied billboard read, "We know how you feel about football because we feel the same way . . . about money." The company's central thesis that the structural parallels of ritual and meaning between religion and football make them equivalents is an old trope. The language of faith and salvation, miracles and curses is long established in the game, but in the absence of any real belief in the supernatural or the divine, let alone an established theology and morality, the comparison simply will not hold. What remains of religion in a secular world—and Britain has become among the most secular of societies—is the abiding need for collective energies, identities, and shared meanings. As Durkheim put it over a century ago, "The only way of renewing the collective representations which related to sacred things is to retemper them at the very source of religious life, that is to say in assembled groups . . . men are more confident because they felt themselves stronger; and they really are stronger because forces which are languishing are now reawakened into consciousness."[7] In recent years the British public has assembled in increasing numbers, not only at football, but other sporting occasions, evangelical gatherings, carnivals, street parades, music festivals, royal celebrations, and urban riots.

Why? Secularization is not the only social change at work here. The passing of industrial Britain has thinned the great crowds that once assembled in huge workplaces and fragmented the communities of the old urban working class. There have been immense individual gains from breaking with the narrow life courses and suffocating conservatism of these communities, but as the growth of these new postindustrial crowds suggests, there is also now a longing for the communal and the public in an individualized and privatized world. Perhaps the most salient social change of all in modern Britain is the fact that we increasingly live alone. In 1971 just three million people in England lived by themselves. By 2005 nearly seven million lived alone and the number of single-person households is projected to rise to around nine million; a shift from 6.5 percent of the population to around 17 percent and constituting more than one-third of all households. If we add the households where there is one parent and kids, then over 40 percent of households have a single adult.[8] Eating together, our most basic common activity, has become less prevalent in households of all kinds. By contrast, we go to the football match together and not just as a single unstructured mob, but as couples, families of all kinds in various cross-generational combinations, as well as in loose skeins of acquaintance and tight networks of friends: less than 10 percent of football crowds go to the game alone. We also, increasingly, live apart. The long-term polarization in the distribution of wealth, in England, combined with the geography of the housing market and schools, has produced a society in which rich and poor, indeed every gradation of the class culture, are less likely to live and learn in a broad social mix.[9] Football, by contrast, remains a place of social mixing, where crowds gather and make space, if only for a short moment, truly public.

One of the main ways in which the pleasures of football were expressed in the past was as escapism. Escape from the drudgery of work, from the rigidity of social norms, from externally imposed restrictions and deprivations of all kinds. This remains important. The misery of the mass production line may have gone, but work remains no less fragmented and boring for the new white-collar proletariat of the call centers, the imposed emotional labor of the retail and personal services industries no less alienating. However, in the last twenty years there appears, in the written record at least, another kind of escapism, from a damaged self rather than an authoritarian society; a phenomenon that tracks both more open attitudes to discussing mental illness and a real rise in their incidence. John Crace described the close connection between his mental well-being and going to the football.

> At the best of times the idea of milling with crowds of shoppers on the high street makes me anxious and homicidal. Yet even when I'm nuts, I feel safe in a football crowd: over and beyond a sense of common purpose. I feel as if I am in a bubble, where there's nothing getting between me and the moment . . . there is no me: only football. It is the most perfect time off, time out from myself.[10]

Or Nick Hornby, depressed, on the way to the game after visiting his shrink: "I felt better, less isolated, more purposeful . . . I no longer had to try to explain to myself where I was going or where I had been."[11] In this guise football appears as a salve for the fragmentation of society and the psyche, for the diseases of affluence rather than the cruelties of poverty.

Finally, there is the longing for narrative, for stories that make sense. This includes the match itself, but more than that, in an era of incredible social and technological change, football offers a sense of how each match and each season fits into a wider and meaningful narrative of personal, sporting, and social history. Certainly the football memoirs and oral histories of the last two decades have often been set over the course of a whole life of watching football and structured around the transition from childhood to adolescence, from adulthood to middle age. They invariably track the shifts from the postwar consensus (the golden age of the terraces) to the death of social-democratic industrial Britain (the rise of hooliganism, Thatcherism, Hillsborough, and its aftermath) to the emergence of the deregulated, globalized and deeply polarized postindustrial economy of the twenty-first century (the era of the Premier League).[12] Nearly all are afflicted by a real melancholy that entwines the coming of age with the loss of a gilded if problematic past. From the very earliest days of its new commercialism football was simultaneously serving as a giant obituary notice for the death of industrial Britain, the passing of a masculine working-class world, rough but impassioned and alive, and its replacement with the comfortable but effete bourgeois world of the high arts. As David Thomas predicts, in the *Daily Telegraph*:

A decade or two from now, the roar of the crowd may well have dwindled to an appreciative murmur as upscale audiences applaud the subtle interplay of footballers moving with balletic grace…. But as dusk approaches, the ghosts of footballing legends, will look down from on high. They'll remember the passion. They'll think of the steam as it rose from a pulsating, shouting, singing crowd, who watched hard men play a hard man's sport.[13]

Nostalgia now moves at the speed of light. Once the whirlwind of economic restructuring and commercialization unleashed on football and society alike in the 1980s and 1990s had struck, the past looked different. Just five years on from Hillsborough, the old forms of football culture were being turned from a deadly pathology, a cancer in the body politic, into a golden age of benign communality. The 1970s, previously cast as uncivilized and dangerously ungovernable, now appeared as a lost world of authentic solidarities. The gains of the new order were already being measured against the long-term losses and, try as they might, the masters of the spectacular have not been able to eradicate these stories and these longings. They are the "unseen something that hangs in the day." History is still being made at the match.

## II.

Since the advent of half-day working on a Saturday, a concession won by the new trade-union movement of the late nineteenth century, British football operated on industrial time: the structured regularity of the new factory, clocking on and clocking off, a five-and-a-half then a five-day week, with summer shutdowns in the factories, mines, and shipyards. Football started in September and finished in April, matches kicked off at three o'clock on a Saturday, the FA Cup final marked the end of the season. The arrival of floodlights, still rare in the 1940s, brought the bonus of midweek night games and, for the few, excursions to exotic European destinations.

Today's game could be taking place on any day of the week, and if it is being played at the weekend, in any one of eight different time slots. Post-modern times? Certainly our use and perception of time has become more complex and fragmented. The steady mechanical beat of an economy built around mass production has given way to the endlessly flexible rhythms of the postindustrial economy: deregulated opening and closing times, 24/7 services, the multiple time zones of globalized markets. Football schedules, shaped by the needs of broadcasters and the expansion of European competition, mirror this. In 2002 when Middlesbrough were playing in the UEFA Cup they had just one 3:00 p.m. Saturday kick-off at home between August and January. Late and early starts make for a day's blockbuster viewing and lucrative advertising but they also make life for the traveling away fan more expensive, sometimes simply impossible. But it is not just a question of efficiency and practicality, it is a question of meaning and values; fan surveys continue to highlight a hunger, nostalgic or not, for the 3:00 p.m. kick off, for a sense of temporal order, an acknowledgement of the ritual status of going to the game.[14]

Whatever day it is, whatever time it is, we probably drove here.[15] Almost half of the crowd will have arrived in their own car and another 10 percent will have hitched a ride. Historical data is hard to come by but the film and photographic evidence of crowds just thirty years ago suggests that the car, although present, was not ubiquitous. The steady shift away from walking and public transport is hardly surprising in a society where the car has remained the priority of all transport policy and planning for half a century. It is also reflective of an ageing crowd where the numbers of youth coming unaccompanied (and therefore without a car) have plummeted. The relocation of some stadiums to out-of-town retail parks and trunk road junctions—Reading, Derby, Bolton, Chester, and Coventry, for example—has made the car almost compulsory; the numbers who walk or cycle to football remain stubbornly at around just 5 percent.[16] There are exceptions. In London especially, where public transport works and grounds are situated close to stations and busy bus routes, car journeys are actually in the minority. Newcastle's Metro and the new tram routes in Manchester which run direct to the stadiums are pushing up the numbers who arrive at Premiership games by public transport to almost 30 percent. However, for the most part, home fans arrive by car, park where they can (an entire pop-up economy and geography all by itself), and then walk the final stretch. Large stadium car parks on the American model that allow one to drive straight in, circumventing any public gathering, are still few and far between.

On the approach to the ground you might have felt for the money in your pocket. You still might at lower league grounds where you can just roll up, pay cash, and walk in, but more likely you're feeling for the plastic swipe card that is now your season ticket or the glossy embossed tickets you bought on line. The gnomic characters that used to stand outside games—an open satchel or sack strung across their chest and a homemade sign in the hand saying, "used tickets stubs please"—already rare, are now a threatened species. If it's a big game the scalpers will be here, too, striding through the crowd, eyes on a pivot, buy tickets, sell tickets, but they, too, have moved online; a ticket that fell off the back of the sponsor's allocation will more often than not have been bought on the Internet and delivered to your hotel.

However you bought the ticket, it cost more than last time. If the game is in the Premiership then it cost a lot more. Football players and managers are fond of the notion of giving 101, 110, 150, or even 200 percent of their effort to a game. Extraordinarily, the real rate of price inflation in football actually exceeds this kind of hyperbole. In 1989 the cheapest season ticket at Liverpool was £60, and £96 at Manchester United. If prices had risen in line with inflation they would have cost £106 and £170 in 2011. In actual fact they cost £725 and £532, respectively, real rates of inflation of over 500 and 300 percent respectively. If today's game is against a big club, then we will be in an even higher price bracket. Entrance to the North Bank at Arsenal's ground at the time Highbury to see Chelsea in 1989–90 was five pounds. Twenty years later the cheapest seat at the Emirates for the same game was £51; taking account of inflation that's a price rise of 920 percent.[17] The biggest clubs aside, the cheapest season tickets hover around three to four hundred pounds a season, and a one-off ticket is around £20, though these may be hard to pick up. Sheffield United and Huddersfield Town were still charging just £10 to stand in 2012, and in the real bargain basement, Montrose in the Scottish Third Division, they'll let you in for just six quid.[18] But the trend has been unmistakable: football at every level has got much more expensive. For the very poor and the very young, even an occasional visit is going to take a serious slice of disposable income. For those on a low to median wage it's still doable, but a season ticket at a leading club will bite deep into your leisure budget. As Rogan Taylor, one time chair of the Football Supporters Association and long standing season ticket holder, put it, "When I go to Liverpool now I don't mostly see a bourgeois, middle-class crowd, but ordinary people who must be stretching to afford it."[19]

In the hour to hour-and-a-half before the game begins, crowds still mill around in whatever public space or concourse is available to them. They gather in complex and shifting ways, spilling out of the pubs en route and onto the roads normally busy with cars, they knot on noted corners, pause in parks, move in a steadily thickening stream towards the entrances. As late as the mid-1990s, the landscape would have probably still included the high crane-like struts of floodlight towers and the humped backs of cinder-banked terracing, both now a rarity. In this blur of movement and color we might be struck by something that is motionless and unchanging. Cast in bronze, raised up on marble, occasionally painted like the saints of a medieval cathedral, there are statues. Once unknown at British football stadiums, they have multiplied rapidly. As late as the 1980s football was not a patron of the visual arts or a place where one publicly remembered the dead. It rarely thought of itself as the custodian of a history worth publicly commemorating. Arsenal had long had a bust of Herbert Chapman but kept it away from public view in the marble halls of Highbury's East Stand. When a sculpture of Stanley Matthews was first made in the 1980s, it was placed in his hometown Hanley, not at Stoke City's ground. The public attendance at funerals and the minute's silence held at Old Trafford for the victims of the 1958 Munich disaster were the exception not the norm. Art was for museums and collective acts of mourning were confined to the war dead, the monarch, and Churchill.

The first hint of change came in 1981. Liverpool responded to the death of Bill Shankly both officially and spontaneously. Flags were flown at half-mast on civic buildings, a minute's silence was held at Liverpool games. Handmade banners announcing "the King is dead" were hung from a block of flats near Anfield, along the funeral route and on the terraces at home games. The crowd began to sing, "We all agree, name the stand after Shankly."[20] He didn't get a stand but he did get some ironwork; the creation of the Shankly gates at Anfield in 1982 being an early instance of what has become a flood of commemorative architecture and installations at football grounds. When Jackie Milburn died in 1988 there were 20,000 people lining the route to his funeral through Newcastle; homemade banners said "Wor Jackie" and "Thank you for the golden goals, Thank you for the golden memories." By 1990 Milburn had a stand named after him, and statues in his hometown of Ashington as well as Newcastle city center.

Hillsborough was mourning in a different key, the mourning for those who were like you, not the demi-gods of the football pantheon. This raw public grief could not be dissociated from the wider social conditions that brought about the tragedy. It was apparent to all that Hillsborough was, in some way, a summation of many of the changes that football and the nation had undergone. Thus remembrance of the dead and remembrance of time past became indissolubly linked in the collective football imagination. This connection was made again when, in 1993, Bobby Moore died at the age of just fifty-one. Remembered, above all, as the captain of the victorious 1966 World Cup team, his death was marked in rituals of public mourning at West Ham and across the football world. The *Guardian* described the feel of the moment: it was "another kind of mourning; for a world, as it seems looking back, when things sometimes used to go right."[21] It was a time when England won the World Cup and heroes were kept unblemished; when a working-class boy could metaphorically become a gentleman, when the captain wiped the mud from his hands before shaking the Queen's. It was of course a restrained, predominantly masculine kind of mourning, stifled tears and bluff determination. To make this deeper trend in the emotional life of the nation apparent it would need a feminine touch. That arrived when Princess Diana died in 1997. The same elision of a private individual tragedy with the emotional hurts of many other lives, the same need for collective commemoration that had emerged in football culture, became tangible to all.

Since the mid-1990s, football clubs have made up for lost time. There has been a frenzy of commemorating. Players and managers, founders, benefactors, and directors have been immortalized in official addresses, stands and restaurants. They have been given memorial plaques, gates and street names, and, in the case of Tom Finney at Preston, a mosaic composed of bucket seats in the stand. A dozen clubs, including Arsenal, Chelsea, Liverpool, Newcastle, and Wolves, have actually opened museums at their grounds. However, to truly stake a claim in the wider historical memory one must be cast in bronze. The pantheon falls into four categories. First, the inter-war and immediate postwar greats including a second Stanley Matthews, this time at Stoke's Britannia Stadium, Billy Wright and Stan Cullis at Wolves, Tom Finney at Preston, Dixie Dean at Everton, and Wilf Mannion at Middlesbrough. Secondly, the managers who, in keeping with their ascent in the game's division of labor and power, are for the most part of a more recent vintage. Statues include Bill Shankly, Matt Busby, Don Revie rehabilitated in bronze at Leeds, Alf Ramsey and Bobby Robson. For Brian Clough, the biggest ego of them all, there have been three statues, in Middlesbrough, Derby and Nottingham. Among the living only Sir Alex Ferguson has been immortalized before his time. Administrators, patrons and directors are the third group to be honored in this way, with Brother Walfrid at Celtic, Jack Walker at Blackburn Rovers, Jimmy Hill (astonishingly supported by public subscription) at Coventry City and William McGregor, the founder of the

Football League, at Aston Villa. Finally, there are the players of the first televised era—as yet overwhelmingly drawn from between the early 1960s and the late 1970s. In 2011 the figure of Thierry Henry, kneeling in post-goal celebration outside the Emirates, was a rare example of a Premiership era player and the first black and the first foreign player to be welcomed into this haphazard canon.

The best of this oeuvre have been those pieces that retain something of the motion and movement of football: the Stoke triptych of Stanley Mathews at three stages of his career captures the bend of his body as he shapes to cross; Billy Wright, upright, forthright, and ever ready, almost bounds off his plinth and onto the field at Wolverhampton Wanderers; Preston North End's Tom Finney, skidding through a huge muddy puddle, virtually horizontal to the ground, remains poised and balanced, carving a deliberate arc through the spray. Less successful perhaps is the cast of Bob Stokoe, manager at Sunderland when they won the FA Cup in 1973, depicted skipping across the pitch at Wembley. He looks spritely but somehow sinister, too; a bad leprechaun or the child catcher of children's nightmares. By contrast the majority of statues of more recent players, particularly those that made their name in the 1960s and 1970s, are more static. Billy Bremner at Leeds and Jimmy Johnston at Celtic seem poised between a jig and a jump for joy, but for the most part they are a stoical bunch, all standing, eyes focused on the horizon, ball in hand or lightly held beneath a boot: John Greig at Rangers, Johnny Haynes at Fulham, and Peter Osgood at Chelsea have mass but not gravitas. The rather frail physiques and almost spindly limbs of Best, Charlton and Law looking onto Old Trafford feel less staged but they also seem a little sad, dwarfed by the towering bulk of the rebuilt stadium. Some pieces are just bad. The statue of Ted Bates, player, coach, and director for over six decades at Southampton, erected in 2007, was simply awful; the likeness was compared to both the disturbingly strange British comic Jimmy Krankie or, worse, the Serbian chairman of rivals Portsmouth, Milan Mandarić. It was removed and a new piece commissioned. The second statue is bland but at least it looks like dear old Ted.

Encoded in all of the pieces there is still a gentlemanly vision of the game and its players. Football's past remains the heartland of an aristocratic manliness and Corinthian honor, long after the landed elite and the global empire that created them have been swept away. As the inscription beneath Bobby Moore's statue at Wembley Stadium reads:

> Immaculate footballer. Imperial defender.
> Immortal hero of 1966.
> First Englishman to raise the World Cup aloft.
> Favourite son of London's East End.
> Finest legend of West Ham United.
> National Treasure. Master of Wembley.
> Lord of the game. Captain extraordinary.
> Gentleman of all time.

There is in Britain no equivalent to the French bronze of Zinedine Zidane outside the Pompidou Centre in Paris that captures the moment toward the end of the 2006 World Cup final when he head-butted Marco Materazzi. We prefer our heroes steadfast, imperturbable, tough but never wantonly aggressive; players are always cast alone or with their teammates, the game's gladiatorial dimensions sidelined. The past is golden.

Match day always had its many pleasures. Drinking, smoking, eating, and betting have been part of the day out for most of the twentieth century, collectively remembered as a pie and a pint, a fag and flutter. All of these remain, but in each case they are utterly different, too. Eating at football, like the wider food culture of the nation, has fragmented and now encompasses grim burger trucks outside the stadium, unadventurous mass catering inside, and high-end client account restaurants in the boxes. Given the size of football crowds and their apparent appetite, it is amazing how little street food is available for sale in the vicinity of the stadium. Grounds still located in older working-class neighborhoods have their share of local chippies, kebab houses, fried chicken joints, and full English breakfast cafes, and in the north of England reasonable to excellent pie shops can be found nearby, but it is the mobile burger van that is the most ubiquitous presence. Scanning the away fan guides and their comments, it is hard to find anywhere that can boast a food truck rising above burnt onions and soft rolls. Honorable exceptions are Mick's Monster Burger Van in Portsmouth, Mr. Tikka at Wolverhampton, the organic burger truck that parks up near Fulham and Piebury Corner on the way to the Emirates. At least the vans keep the crowds in the streets and bring life to the space around the stadium. At some grounds, and not just those that have been located in out-of-town retail or industrial parks, the main options are warehouse-scale branches of the big chains, the same depressing litany of KFC, Burger King, McDonald's, Harvester, Subway; though in a rare concession to locality the McDonald's near the Reebok Stadium is a Bolton Wanderers–themed experience and at Blackburn Rovers they do a match-day walk-through service.

Inside the stadium, for most of the crowd, the eating options are little different from the 1980s: long queues; fizzy drinks, tea, and a variety of bad instant coffees; chocolate bars, crisps and bags of sweets; worryingly pale hot dogs. Resistant to innovation, impervious to the arguments of the healthy eating lobby, stadium food is perhaps the one element of match day that has stubbornly resisted the tide of change. The emblematic football snack remains the meat pie, not merely the biggest selling item on match day but a baked good of unique cultural connotations: the sturdy yeoman's lunch, the honest working man's pleasure. The pie, as Harry Pearson reported, seems to transport us to the lost world of the music hall and the banter of the works' canteen:

> A crop-haired youth of . . . vast proportions . . . came into the Gallowgate eating a pie. It was one of those special football pies with asbestos-grey pastry that cracks to release the odor of a thousand year old tomb . . . "Who ate all the pies?" the crowd howled . . . "you fat bastard, you ate all the pies."
>
> The blubbery boy responded to this by shoving half the pie in his gob and then laughing . . . "He's fat. He's round. He sprays his pie around . . . fat bastard" . . . the crowd celebrated.[22]

Our young friend is not alone. A lot of people eat pies at football. According to Pukka, one of the leading manufacturers in the £3 million-plus pie economy of British football, "Among the 35–40 clubs we supply, you usually get 15–20 percent of supporters at the ground buying a pie . . . at Rotherham that jumps to 40–50 percent." The south favors steak and kidney, the north opts for meat and potato, and everyone's second choice is the Chicken Balti pie that emerged in the late 1990s in homage to the nation's postcolonial devotion to anglicized curry. As mass manufactured food goes, the football pie has proved reasonably savory, even if the texture of its pastry is prey to the vagaries of microwave ovens. Ingredients wise, it may not be organic or locally sourced but the only football club forced to withdraw pies during the 2013 horsemeat scandal was Aberdeen.[23] Intriguingly, over the last five years a better class of pie had got a look in. Of course, some redoubts of the craft in the north have been producing excellent products for a long time, Poole's Pies in Wigan being a notable example. They are now being joined by others. Morecambe FC's Chicken, Ham, and Leek Pie, competing well beyond the comfort zone of football-only goods, won the title of Supreme Champion at the British Pie Awards 2012. The Scottish Football Pie of the year was won by old school Highland butchers, showcasing the distinctive mince and pepper Scotch football pie.[24]

Vegetarianism and the green commitments to local and organic sourcing have made little headway in football food culture, but in 2010 it finally acquired a champion: Forest Green Rovers. The club, which plays in the upper reaches of the Conference, is based in Nailsworth, South Gloucestershire. Effectively they are the team of the greater Stroud area, noted for its recent concentration of bohemians and environmentalists. Forest Green was bought by Dale Vince, the founder of the green energy company Ecotricity. As part of a wider commitment to create the first sustainable football club in the country, Forest Green's stands now boast hundreds of solar panels, horse manure is spread on the pitch as part of an effort to get it certified organic by the Soil Association, and the squad has been encouraged to adopt a vegetarian diet. For the crowd it is compulsory as meat has come off the menu, replaced by the Rainbow Koblenz Wrap with pumpkin humus, grated beets, and carrots, the Green Man Pie filled with leeks and zucchini, and the Portobello Mushroom Burger.[25]

The real business of food is elsewhere. Three million pies with around a pound mark-up on each is a nice little earner, but an *amuse bouche* by comparison to what is going on in the boxes and the lounges high above the stadium's main concourses. Match-day catering and entertaining accounts for around 8 to 10 percent of the annual turnover of the biggest clubs. Chelsea boast on their website about the CV of their executive chef and installing an upscale American restaurant chain into their stands, while at Manchester City, where as late as the early 1990s the club directors dined on homemade cakes brought by their wives, they now tempt you with the promise of a fusion menu. At the high end of the trough people are eating top-class client account food; maybe not a Michelin star but smart, corporate, and unadventurous, spiked with reassuringly expensive ingredients. The Connell Club, Manchester City's most expensive offering, kicked off its 2012 menu with *Velouté of New Season Asparagus with Lemon Butter Sauce* or *Goose Liver Parfait, Foie Gras, Blackstone Cherry Glaze and Truffle Toast*. You can imagine the rest of the script. Even here, where clubs have tried to evoke the cultural capital and status of a metropolitan restaurant, the urge to theme everything in sight is irresistible. At the Connell Club, you'll be finishing up with petit fours and coffee in a pod named after one of City's new corporate virtues—generosity, glory, loyalty, honor, and bravery.

Lunch is for wimps though; a whole hospitality package is available for the masters of the football universe. It seems there is no limit to how much fun, food, drink, relaxation, and excitement can be built into the match-day experience for those willing to pay. The 1882 package at Tottenham, coming in at around £500 a person, gets you a parade of legends, silver salvers, framed photos, another legend at your table, souvenir gifts, and the judging of the man of the match competition from the "high backed Olympian style chair with heating."[26] The presence of a club legend, as they are generally referred to, is the linchpin of the next level of hospitality down from the boxes. From Liverpool's Boot Room to City's Legends Bar to West Ham's 1966 Club, bigger stadiums now have lounges, bars and diners where celebrity contact and reminiscence are the key items on the menu. As the pitch from Fulham puts it, "When you choose the George Cohen Restaurant, you'll receive a personal welcome from George himself, who will stay to share his nostalgia."[27] Of course, if you prefer your nostalgia on the cheap there are still those who bring their own Thermos flask and sandwiches, ritually eat a Wagon Wheel or some other ailing brand of snack at half-time and share their bag of pick'n'mix sweets with you.

After food and drink the traditional match-day purchase has been the official program. It, too, is a lot more expensive than the one you bought in the late 1980s; three or four pounds today against change out of a pound then. It's worth buying though if you have patience, for football programs are among the most prized of football memorabilia; the rate of inflation for rare, collectable programs far exceeds the already dizzy rise of match-day prices, driven on a complex wave of nostalgia, compulsive completism, and affluence among football fans. By the late 1980s programs were already assuming something of their current form, as glossy paper and wall-to-wall color photography became the norm and the first steps towards conscious commercial branding were made. What had once been produced in-house or by dedicated teams of semi-official fans and helpers was steadily being outsourced to marketing companies. Two decades later that process is complete, with the result that almost every trace of eclecticism, variety, and originality has been drained from the form. Where once there was a dizzying array of design styles, experimental fonts, thoughtful use of color and beautiful hand-drawn artwork, today's charmless and increasingly expensive documents are visually soulless and a poorer read than the average airline magazine.

This is not to suggest that the programs of the postwar era were uniformly interesting. There was a lot of dross. In the style of the kids' magazines like *Shoot!*, programs specialized in excruciatingly cheesy player profiles. They took a leaf out of the tabloids' book with photos of all those City girls and United lasses, "kitted out and ready for action," and the whole era was garlanded with the lamentable punning of local firms' advertising copy, as in this example from Norwich City in 1972: "Make your goal the Mustard Pot, within shooting distance of this ground." Yet for all the kitsch there was something warm and human about them. As late as 1998, the novelist and critic D. J. Taylor still found the Norwich program an "oasis of decency, humility, and good humor" and full of "politenesses and courtesies."[28] It was a publication that referred to Ghanaian girls seeking Norwich pen friends as "those young ladies," the referee as the "man in the middle" and even hoped he enjoyed his night at Carrow Road. Another decade of commercialization later and this voice is very rare. Where would it belong in a text that apes the layout and feel of aspirational men's health magazines? Programs were turned into magazines as the crowd increasingly turned to the Internet and smartphones; the arrival of the digital program for tablets and e-readers seems unlikely to halt the format's stylistic decline. The same problem has confronted the fanzines. While at most grounds one still finds two or three characters with a small cardboard box (always the small cardboard box from the printers) hawking their wares, online fanzines, popular blogs, home-grown podcasts and social media have squeezed the market for alternative commentary and helped shape a new generation of fans who find it hard to comprehend why anyone would ever pay for something that you read.

While alcohol in general and beer in particular remains the drug of choice at English football, it is more closely policed than in the past. It remains the drug of choice in Scotland, too, but overwhelmingly at the pub. The draconian Criminal Justice Act of 1980 remains in force in Scotland where it is a crime to be in possession of alcohol or drunk on the way to a football match and alcohol is banned within the stadium. A similar law was passed in 1985 for England and Wales but it allows drinking in the stadium, though not in sight of the pitch. Despite pressure from the clubs and the alcohol industry, who are of course huge sponsors of the game, there has been no change.[29] How much this has contributed to changing behavior inside and outside the stadium is not clear—at best alcohol was only one factor in explaining elements of the disorder of the 1970s and 1980s. It certainly doesn't mean that people won't be drunk. Many continue to drink heavily before the game and outside the stadium rather than endlessly queue for a pint that you then have to drink in a cold breeze-block corridor.

One unambiguous change is football's relationship to tobacco. Football players on collectable cigarette cards made their first appearance in the 1890s; in the 1920s Dixie Dean was endorsing Carreras Clubs and as late as the 1950s Stanley Matthews lent his name to Craven A. The mutually reinforcing and compulsive nature of both nicotine addiction and football spectatorship meant that the stands were full of smoke, and from the 1980s not just tobacco smoke. Nick Hornby recalled a night at Aston Villa for a League Cup quarter-final in 1986: "there was . . . an interesting historical element to the evening; the freezing January air . . . was thick with marijuana smoke, the first time I noticed that some sort of terrace culture was emerging."[30] Today all you're likely to smell is stale beer and cooking oils. Tobacco advertising and sponsorship were banned in 1998, and in 2007 smoking was banned in all stadiums. For a taste of the past one must head for the corners of car parks and the small outdoor spaces some clubs make available for a half-time cigarette break.

Football's relationship with gambling was once uneasy. In the late nineteenth century FA Cup games in particular attracted wild and self-destructive betting by fans with illegal bookmakers. In the 1920s the football pools arrived and by the 1950s this complex communal sweep-stake had almost half the adult population returning a coupon. The Foot-ball League had at first fought the pools companies, lost, then came to an uneasy accommodation with them that endured through to the 1980s; but there remained an air of moral disapproval, of patrician concern for the dangers of gambling and a practical worry about its impact on players who might be tempted to throw a game. Since then the pools have shrunk and the National Lottery has taken a huge share of the casual small-stake gambling market, while the new types of football betting, with online bookmakers and in the betting shops, have taken the more "sporting" component off the market.

During the 2011–12 season over £1 billion was staked on football in betting shops, and perhaps another couple of hundred million online.[31] Moral and practical concerns have been thrown to the wind. The lifting of the advertising ban on online gambling sites in 2005 blew hard. By 2012, in the Premier League alone, online betting sites sponsored the shirts of five clubs (188bet at Bolton and Wigan, SBOBET at West Ham, Sporting Bet at Wolves and Tombola at Sunderland); and nineteen out of twenty clubs had an official "gaming partner," as the bookmakers are eu-phemistically described. Only Manchester City, under their new owners from Abu Dhabi, declined their money. Consequently many clubs now have betting shops within the stadium, and prominent links to online bookies on their own websites. Football has good cause to pursue this new relationship more cautiously than hitherto: first, because there are so many footballers who have, in their long off hours, fallen prey to gam-bling addictions made all the worse by the ease and solitary nature of betting online or by mobile. Not merely role models, footballers are the vanguard of a steady rise in serious problems of gambling addiction, un-sustainable debt, family breakdown, and mental illness.[32] And secondly, because the global wave of match fixing for betting syndicates in football may yet destroy the credibility of the game—and if the audience think the show is no longer ad libbed but scripted in advance, they may well just stop coming.

Gambling and corruption are old sins. What of the addiction of our own times? Shopping. Thirty years ago clubs had souvenir shops not super stores, and a rag tag of hawkers outside the ground did most of the trade in memorabilia and clothing. Now they have been driven to the margins, fought in the courts over trademark infringement and beaten. If you want to shop, the club's shop is the only game in town. At Celtic the corrugated warehouse that serves as the club shop looks like it's been taken straight out of a small industrial estate and set down in the car park. It looks at home. Inside the shop has all the fixtures and trappings of the mainstream mall: beige fascias, chrome rails, flat screen TVs selling you leisure clothing, branded frippery, and coffee-table books all under bright lights, heavy security, and plenty of CCTV. It is a formula repeated across all the bigger clubs, though Manchester United's pitch-black interior décor and tasteful, sparse display of merchandise is more Urban Outfitters or Hollister than Celtic's BHS. Lower down the leagues, Bristol City's offering is closer to the kind of eccentric high street sports shop destroyed by the big chains like Sports Direct: a brick and glass extension, a kind of prepacked conservatory on the back of an old stand, it is cramped and chaotic. Bristol Rovers' shop, hidden away under the stand, is more like a failing sub-post office that has desperately tried to stay afloat by becoming a club-color-themed pound shop: fake tattoos, garden gnomes, shot glasses, fluffy dice, and beach towels. Enough. The lure of the stands, the site of the pitch, the sound of a crowd gathering are still electric, still enough to pull us away. It's time to join them.

## III.

Stadiums fill in complex but predictable ways. The earliest arrivals are in the executive boxes where, depending on how grand your entertainment package is, there will be signings, photo opportunities, guided tours, and complimentary refreshments for up to four hours before the game. Away fans will tend to arrive early as police and club officials try and get them into their zone and away from everybody else as soon as possible. The clubs would like more of the home crowd to arrive early, too, and, of course, spend money, but only around a fifth of the crowd will have actually entered the ground more than half an hour before kick-off; maybe another two-fifths are milling around outside or just arriving and the rest are still on their way. Then the rush begins, peaking fifteen minutes before kick-off. The bulk—maybe two-thirds of the people—make their way from the turnstiles to their seats in this short slot.[33] The mass of colored bucket seats becomes fragmented, broken by islands then archipelagos, then craggy-coasted continents of people. Then, in the final five minutes, the late hurry in, the languid saunter to their spot and the last out of the pub stumble to theirs.

Imagine, as the first tranche of the fans drift into the stand opposite us, that we can arrange them demographically. There are twenty-five rows, from A to Y, each a thousand seats long: a 25,000-seat stand with every row standing for 4 percent of the crowd. What do we see now? If we line them up by gender it will confirm what has been obvious from the day so far. Everybody in rows A to V is a bloke. Surveys from 1997 found that only 12 percent of football crowds were female. Despite the claims of a notable upturn in women at football, Premiership surveys show that the female share of the crowd had crept up to just 15 percent—just the back four rows. Some clubs, especially newly promoted sides like Leicester City and Ipswich Town, have seen female attendance climb as high as a quarter, but these changes were balanced out by the seemingly impregnable male bastions of more established crowds; as late as 2007 women made up only 5 percent of the crowd at Aston Villa and just over 10 percent at Spurs and Chelsea.[34]

If the changes in gender balance have been marginal, there is no doubt that the crowd is getting older. Although there is some tendency, particularly from the photographic evidence, to overemphasize the number of youths at football in the 1970s and 1980s, the data that is available is unambiguous.[35] At Coventry City in 1983, 16–20-year-olds alone made up 22 percent of the crowd. A decade later this cohort made up a quarter of the crowd at Aston Villa and 17 percent at Arsenal. By the mid-2000s the numbers of 16–24 year olds, double the cohort size of the earlier research, had fallen to around 10 percent of the crowd, occupying just rows W–Y in the nosebleed seats. Thirty years ago they were more like rows A–G, a quarter of the crowd, out in front and often setting its tone. The percentage of season ticket holders over forty has risen from 41 percent in 2001 to 54 percent in 2011, while the average age of the crowd inched up from the late 1930s to the mid-1940s. Greyer and balder, the crowd's everyman was forty-four years old in 2007.

Although there has been considerable turnover in season-ticket holding, with fans dropping in and out of the game at different times in their lives, this predominantly older male core of the crowd retains a deep attachment to club and locality. On average the crowd comes from a thirty- to thirty-five-mile radius around the stadium, and around 85 percent live less than fifty miles away, though there are significant variations. At the smaller northern clubs locals rise to 90 percent or more of the crowd, while in London those who live within ten miles of the stadium make up less than a quarter. The biggest clubs in the regions, especially Leeds, Liverpool, and Manchester United, do have large contingents of long-distance travelers. Some are tourists but above all they are English economic émigrés.

The only reliable data of any kind on the ethnic makeup of football crowds comes from surveys of the Premiership between 1997 and 2007.[36] Over that decade the percentage of the crowd describing itself as white British dropped from 98.8 percent to 95 percent, leaving the other 5 percent split between British ethnic minority groups and foreign fans. At Chelsea, the number of foreigners in the crowd was over 3 percent in 2007, almost a whole row in the stand by themselves, while Middlesbrough had just 0.1 percent of the crowd from overseas. Foreign residents with the cash for Premier League football and regular football tourists (like the Scandinavian contingents at Newcastle, Liverpool, and Manchester United) are only found at a handful of clubs.[37] The 3 to 4 percent of the crowd from a minority ethnic background masks very wide discrepancies among the clubs; some have crowds who are less than 1 percent non-white, while others have a significantly more diverse audience. In 2007 Arsenal, Spurs, and Fulham had a minority presence of around 7 to 11 percent in the stands, while both Coventry and Leicester have managed to attract a British Asian following of around 10 percent of the crowd.

The most common assumptions about the contemporary football crowd compared to the 1980s is that it is now richer and significantly more middle-class. The best available data on the crowd before 1990 shows that, in fact, a stable class structure of around two-thirds middle class and one-third working class long predates the Premiership. A cluster of surveys of both the Premier League and the Football League taken around 2000 showed little change.[38] Of course, both these class categories are complex, the former stretching from senior professionals to low-skill white-collar workers, the latter conjoining the skilled working class with those on the fringes of the labor market and those outside of it altogether. However, the figures do suggest that the basic shift away from football crowds as overwhelmingly working-class in composition occurred long before the economic and cultural transformations of the 1990s. What the new football order has done is to accentuate and polarize those shifts. Thus, in 2007 the Premiership crowd had shifted a little further up the class ladder. The upper-middle classes took up nearly half the seats from rows A–L. The lower-middles classes are in rows L–S; together they make up over 70 percent of the crowd. The skilled working class are in rows T–W and the semi-skilled and those outside the labor market get just the two back rows X and Y.

Not surprisingly the massive structural differences in wealth and labor markets across England show up in the crowd. At the big London clubs, the working class are restricted to the back six rows, of which the part time and unemployed are confined to row Y. At Spurs, Arsenal, and Chelsea, the broadly defined middle class has crept up to three-quarters of the crowd. By contrast the comfortable middle classes make up just a third of the crowd in Sunderland and Middlesbrough. Income figures for season-ticket holders confirm this kind of polarization; in 2007 30 percent of Chelsea and Tottenham fans were earning more than £50,000, the figure in Sunderland and Bradford was 7 percent and in Middlesbrough just 6 percent.[39]

Does this crowd feel like the country? Can it stand proxy for anything other than its own peculiar rituals and behaviors? Football is certainly not the only realm in which older white middle-class men predominate and set the codes of behavior and outlook, and the class composition of the crowd is not hugely different from the wider social structure. Premiership crowds in particular are more polarized. The unemployed, students and those in unskilled work, make up around 9–10 percent of the labor force, but 2 percent of the crowd. Professionals are slightly over-represented, but the basic shift from an industrial society to a postindus-trial society, in which both an enlarged middle and shrunken working class are deeply stratified by skill, income and status, is clearly on show. Geographically the crowd certainly follows the demographic contours of the nation, accurately registering the differences between north and south, London and the rest.

Class, in the end, will only take us so far in understanding the make-up of the nation and the crowd. It is equally instructive to look at the crowd by mode of consumption rather than by mode of production, and to recognize that cutting across the divisions of class, gender and age are differences in styles of support and emotional relationships to football.[40] Richard Giulianotti has divided the crowd along two axis: first, the old school of support, local, committed and long-term, against the delocal-ized, contemporary and consumer-driven fan; second, those whose emo-tional relationship is intense and whose self-identities are closely bound up with the game, against those whose relationship is more distant, tran-sient and reflexive. Our four types of fan produced by these scales are thus the old school, divided between intense supporters and more dis-tanced followers; and the new school of maniacal fans and wandering flaneurs, dropping in for their little dose of football. Other writers have suggested that the taxonomy of the crowd should also include a new gen-eration of traditional lads, the old boys, who are the retired and semire-tired crews of the hooligan era, as well as the new consumers divided between the stands and business and executive box elites.[41]

All of these models point to important elements of the crowd but what in the end is so remarkable is that whatever the internal complexity of the crowd or its relationship with the real social structure of the na-tion, both sociologists' models and the everyday conversations of British football culture pivot on a series of interconnected binary oppositions: the authentic and inauthentic, the real and the fake, the sincere and the insincere, those who really love the game and those who are merely buying into it. The postwar economic and technological revolutions that turned the labor force and the football crowd from predominantly working-class to predominantly middle-class happened a long time ago. Under the heightened conditions of polarization in the new era of commercialized football, this socio-economic shift has been given cultural and moral weight. Those that preserve and honor the imagined past of authentic football support, whatever their actual class origins, are real. Long after its death, football fandom has become a significant place in which to misremember and mourn the strange disappearance of industrial Britain.

## IV.

Around twenty-five minutes before kick off the squads dribble out on to the pitch in their tracksuits. A man with a huge sack of footballs walks towards the goals where the goalkeepers begin to limber up. The fanatical are watching but it is rare for the crowd in Britain to engage with the players' warm-ups much beyond a few desultory claps and the odd boo. Even in front of the most enthusiastic fans, it is hardly Istanbul, where every member of the squad must go through a complex choreography of cheers with the crowd before the game starts. In any case, the stadium is only half-full at this point. If mercifully the PA system has been turned down, it's a moment of rare quiet when the eye and mind can wander.

Take a look at the pitch itself. On balance it's going to be in a better state than when we were last here. Clubs have invested in complex systems of irrigation, drainage, and under-soil heating so cancellations due to frost, mudbaths, and puddles are things of the past, great bare patches of soil are rare, and the use of intense grow lamps keeps the grass growing whatever the vagaries of the British weather; though, as with almost everything in football, levels of investment steadily decline lower down the league ladder. Standing terraces are only seen in the lower leagues, replaced elsewhere by the plastic bucket seat. The stands themselves are transformed out of all recognition: all the fencing and wire have gone, exits and entrances are wider, clearly marked and more numerous. Most of the old roofs that required poles to support them have been replaced by cantilevers—though endearingly, if infuriatingly, they remain in place at a number of grounds. Executive boxes, present in the 1980s, have proliferated. Inserted into the long sides of every stadium, sometimes stacked two or three high, their blank glass exteriors visually break the crowd in half. The bench, as it is still quaintly referred to, is no longer just a humble bench. The concrete boxes, the tin sheds, and the semi subterranean bomb shelters have been swept aside. The contemporary bench is now set into the terrace, lavishly equipped with padded and branded chairs, packed with substitutes, coaches, and medical assistants. They are almost all the same, only the peculiar red-brick construction at Old Trafford, described as a "monstrosity normally seen in a suburban housing estate," stands out.[42] And everywhere there are stewards in what appear to be ever brighter shades of electric lemon yellow and nuclear tangerine high-vis vests and jackets. Where once they were invisible, they now appear like an army of cones and traffic lights marking out a complex set of road works.

While the gains accrued from these changes have been considerable in terms of comfort and safety, order and civility, there is an increasing uniformity of aesthetics, architecture, and choreography within the stadium, and that is a loss. Look now, while you can, at the last idiosyncratic gems in the grounds that have yet to be entirely redeveloped. In one corner of Bristol City's Ashton Gate there is a long-disused kiosk molded in the shape of a pot of branded instant coffee; at Anfield the salvaged mast of the SS *England* still serves as a flag pole; a single plane tree as high as the stands is visible inside Craven Cottage, the last tree within a ground in Britain; the sci-fi brutalism of Tottenham's polyhedric crowd-control center still hovers improbably above the crowd.

The alphanumeric system of touchline boards changed by hand that used to indicate scores at other games has gone. In photographs of the era their arcane codes appear indecipherable—forgotten runes. Scores are now announced with clarity at halftime and the final whistle, and shown on the stadiums' screens, and for those that cannot wait there is now the mobile phone. Absent from any football stadium in the 1980s but for the most expensive executive boxes, it is now ubiquitous. Crowds have acquired a stage set of collective ticks, individual movements and glances as they continue to check and use their phones throughout the game, texting, surfing, calling, tweeting, and increasingly taking pictures and filming video. It is hard to know quite what the overall impact of this has been on the crowd's demeanor, but it is hard to imagine that it can be anything other than a force for fragmentation and distraction, another barrier to achieving the unbroken engagement and shared experience that make crowds live.

The mental fragmentation and neuronal frenzy that has been created by the mobile phone is replicated visually. Of course advertising has been part of the visual landscape at football for over a hundred years, but it was once more restrained and less intrusive. The Second World War cleared most stadiums of their inter-war advertising and as late as the 1970s clubs like Spurs, Arsenal, and Wolves resisted the introduction of perimeter boards. Some advertising became in effect absorbed, collage-like, into the fabric of grounds, long after its initial pitch had dimmed: the M&B logo was synonymous with Birmingham City's Railway End, the West Reading Laundry hoarding erected behind a stand at Elm Park, John Smiths Bitter on the pitched roofs of old-style stands at Barnsley, Ismail and Co. Cafe at Blackpool, and Captain Morgan's Rum ("for the taste of today") at Cardiff. Relocation and redevelopment have seen nearly all of these depart, to be replaced with a micro-managed environment of coordinated branding, global rather than local advertisers and LED boards with moving imagery. If this is not enough to distract us from the game there are also the big screens. These began to appear in the mid-1980s, the first one installed at Highbury in 1984, and have now become widespread at the bigger clubs—only St. James' Park, home of Newcastle United, is among the biggest stadiums without a screen or a clock.

Grit your teeth, for the prematch entertainment is about to begin. Even among the more ambitious and showbiz-minded clubs of the pre-Premiership era, the build up to the kickoff and the halftime entertainment were more county show than Super Bowl with a motley cast of military brass bands, pipe bands in Scotland, police dog displays that combined Crufts with a canine assault course and amateur majorettes, their white rah-rah skirts splattered with cold mud.[43] A table and chair might have been brought onto the edge of the pitch for the ceremonial signing of a contract, but often there was just nothing but the noise of the crowd and your own thoughts.[44] Perhaps there were announcements and music, too, but it barely mattered for the sound systems of the time had the same kind of acoustic clarity as a crackling pub PA. As Harry Pearson remembered, "Someone played the Power Game theme to me . . . the music Middlesbrough used to run out to . . . I realized, despite the fact that I had been present at the playing of this tune hundreds of times, I had only ever heard the first few bars of it, the rest had been drowned out by the noise of the crowd."[45] Not any more. The PA systems of the modern stadium are big and loud and terrifyingly clear. They have been handed over to egomaniacal deejays and overenthusiastic amateur callers who, given the chance to fill the stadium with their voice, do so. The feel of the entire performance is that of the most anodyne local radio: a musical mix of golden oldies and contemporary pap, melded together by birthday greetings, shout outs, raffles, and competitions. In a few stadiums there will be some minor interplay, a tiny hint of call and response, that enlivens the preprogramed sterility of the performance. At both Wolves and Bristol Rovers, "Hi Ho Silver Lining" is punctuated with a big shout of the club's name. At West Bromwich Albion the crowd memorably responded to an on-pitch marriage proposal with the chant "You don't know what you're doing." More commonly the crowd is battered into submission by the sheer volume of the music. The DJ's relentless upbeat jollity stands in sharpest contrast to the crowd in the lower leagues: Exeter's use of James Brown's "I Feel Good" suggests football, like so much of the consumer culture, is paranoid that the audience might, just might, feel like this is not the greatest day of their life.

When it comes to cheerleaders, British football has trod carefully. West Ham for a short period in the 1990s experimented with the Hammerettes and Crystal Palace continue to have their troupe. While both of these efforts approximated to the high-kicking perma-tan-and-glitter model of the Americas, Bristol Rovers did it on the cheap. The Blue Flames were perhaps the saddest example of prematch and halftime entertainment in the Football League: essentially a schoolgirl outfit from Filton, they were simply awful, out of time, overawed and under-rehearsed.

Among the supporting cast is a man or woman in a hot synthetic foam animal suit forlornly working the crowd up and down the touchline: the club mascot. He wasn't here last time either. At the end of the nineteenth century football clubs and military regiments often adopted real animals as their ceremonial totem.[46] Manchester United were among the earliest, employing Major the St. Bernard dog and Billy the Goat, while Preston North End took on a stray black cat that had walked across the pitch. After the First World War animal familiars gave way to human mascots but they were invariably self-appointed, only acquiring a modicum of official standing after many years' presence. Darkie at Aston Villa was an odd take on minstrelsy: a blacked-up white man in top hat and tails. At the Den you could find the Millwall Lion, who bore an uncanny resemblance to the weedy and forlorn specimen in the Wizard of Oz. Hoppy Thorne, the one-legged wonder, had served during the First World War, lost a limb and ended up as a cleaner at Old Trafford. He made himself mascot at Manchester United by taking off his prosthetic leg and hopping around the pitch in the build-up to the game. He fell out with the club in the 1940s and was replaced by Jack Irons, who spent the 1950s parading in a red and white dinner suit, holding a red and white umbrella and sporting a red and white bowler hat. None of them seemed to do much cheerleading, in fact Jack Irons seemed to spend a fair amount of time signing autographs.

The contemporary British football mascot takes its cue from the American theme park. Plundering the aesthetic codes of mid-century American animation, football is awash with lions and elephants, robins, cats, and dogs, all anthropomorphized with a rictus smile, a dumb gaping mouth, and huge immobile eyes. Given how few children are present these days, and given how old the crowd is, their sub-standard cheerleading and excruciatingly inept clowning just feel infantilizing. The mascots only get a big response when they transgress the anodyne rules of playacting. The celebrated roll of dishonor includes Wolves' mascot Wolfie, who slugged it out at Ashton Gate with one of Bristol City's three little pigs, and Bury's Robbie the Bobby, named after the founder of the modern police force Sir Robert Peel, who was sent off for "mooning" at fans at Stoke, then ripped the ears off Peterborough's Peter-Burrow rabbit, a trick he soon repeated with the head of Cardiff City's Bartley the Bluebird before finally being fired. Swansea's Cyril the Swan went through a difficult period at the turn of the century. He was fined £1,000 for a one-bird pitch invasion after the team scored in an FA Cup tie against Millwall, received a two-match ban after clashing physically with Norwich manager Bryan Hamilton, threw a pork pie on the pitch against West

Ham and tore off the head of Millwall's Zampa the Lion before drop-kicking it into the crowd.[47]

It's just a few minutes before kickoff. Although in the past there were variations in etiquette, and the biggest matches would be choreographed, often teams used to turn out alone rather than side by side, and there were latecomers and stragglers. Today it will be different; sponsors' boards brought onto the pitch, sometimes a little garden archway of advertising, perhaps a group of kids waving sponsors' flags in a complex but utterly unfocused manner. The officials line up in the center of the ensemble, the teams, often accompanied by kids in replica kit, take their places and all face the cameras. In 2004 handshakes along the line were added to the tableaux; like the bad mascots, a performance that only has any traction when there are unpleasant words, withdrawn hands and deliberate blanking going on.[48]

And then silence. No, not at every match, but the commemorative imperative in football has reached here, too, as minutes of silence and acts of remembrance have become more common. Nationally held and officially endorsed minutes of silence outside of football were, for most of the twentieth century, reserved for Armistice Day. This began to change in the 1990s as nationwide silences were held for the victims of the Dunblane shootings in 1996 and Diana's death in 1997. The new century saw the rate of commemoration accelerate with silences held for the victims of 9/11 in 2001, the Asian tsunami in 2004, and the 7/7 London bombings in 2005. Silences became longer, shifting to two minutes on Armistice Day and then three minutes for the Asian tsunami, and more institutions adapted their timetables to encompass them (public transport and supermarkets, for example), provoking in some quarters an accusation of a silence inflation that diminished the ritual's value.[49] Given this wider shift in the observance of public acts of mourning, the football authorities embraced the change with greater fervor than most institutions, acknowledging a sense of the game as a site of national solidarities while also being acutely conscious of the potentially negative impact of not observing these rituals on live television.[50] In 2001 all matches marked 9/11, followed in 2004 by a minute's silence for Ken Bigley, the British hostage executed by jihadists in Afghanistan, victims of the Asian tsunami, and the deaths of John Peel, the radio DJ, and Pope John Paul II.

Unlike supermarkets and train companies, football also added silences for its own pantheon. In 1989 a chain of scarves created by Liverpool and Everton fans marked the victims of the Hillsborough disaster,
but it was a rare, even a unique act of spontaneity from below. For the
most part, in the early 1990s football's acts of remembrance were organized from above, confined to the deaths of players, and then held only
at their own clubs; Bobby Moore's death in 1993 was marked at West
Ham but not across the League. In 2013 the anniversary of his death was
marked by acts of remembrance across the country. By then it was just
one of many, with almost every club holding a minute's silence for someone during their season. The first public opposition to the silence inflation in football came in 2007 when the early death of Phil O'Donnell, a
little-known player for Celtic and Sheffield Wednesday, was marked
across British football. Colin Calderwood, manager of Nottingham Forest, went on the record as saying, "I don't think it's appropriate to have
them for every tragedy that happens. Sometimes it needs to be a bit closer
to home." Four years later little had changed, as the *Economist* caustically
remarked: "It felt as if every fixture was preceded by players standing
around the center circle, head bowed, remembering the death of ever
more obscure players."[51]

Silence is golden but easily broken, and segments of the crowd have
on occasion taken the opportunity to break it. Fighting broke out between Stoke and Wigan supporters in 2001 after a minute's silence for
Stanley Matthews. The silence for George Best's death held all over the
country had to be cut short when broken by chanting Liverpool fans.
Even the national football silence held for the Hillsborough victims was
broken in some grounds.[52] The fiftieth anniversary of the Munich disaster fell on the day of the Manchester derby in 2008, prompting an emotional debate over whether the minute's silence could be maintained. It
was, but the perennial anxiety that these occasions induce has seen a shift
to applause as an act of remembrance.[53] In part it is a practical measure,
but there is also a reaction to the dominant Victorian model of solemnity
as the only acceptable demeanor for these occasions. The silences held on
the death of Alan Ball—one of the members of England's 1966 World
Cup winning side— in 2007 were broken by spontaneous celebratory
applause, and this has become the sanctioned norm for marking the

death of national treasures like Bobby Robson and Nat Lofthouse. Football, like the rest of the culture, is stumbling towards a new concord with death and mortality. The silence ends. The players take up position. The whistle blows. The game begins.

## V.

English football retains enough diversity and unpredictability to ensure that we could see *any* kind of game on any given day, from a League Two contest in a mudbath to a pulsating Premiership contest, but at the highest level there is a wide consensus: the football played is better, faster, more skillful and engaging. Comparisons of the style and patterns of play from different eras are complicated by a number of factors. First, the unreliability of human memory and the many ways in which the reading of an individual game is shaped by interests and biases. Few observers watch one side as keenly as another, few fans perceive their own side's fouls and misdemeanors with the same rigor as their opponents'. Secondly, for longer than most sports, football resisted the use of statistics for analyzing the game. There has been a persistent preference for artisanal knowledge, accumulated over a lifetime of observation and inclusion within the clannish inner structures of football clubs. And the complexity of a game constantly in three-dimensional flow made coding and recording the action impossibly hard. By comparison, the sequential and slower pace of baseball and cricket made the systematic scoring and recording of play a much simpler operation.

Over the last two decades these barriers have been swept aside. The arrival of digital technologies has made possible the collection of gigantic amounts of data about professional football and its players. OPTA, Prozone, and a dozen other companies are measuring a thousand variables and micro-incidents in every game played. Two examples illustrate the way in which the collection and analysis of this data makes the game look different, challenges football's folklore and is beginning to change the way the game is actually played.[54] A standard trope of commentators, after a team has scored an opening goal, is to remind the audience that they are now "at their most vulnerable." However, a pretty basic look at the data suggests precisely the opposite. Opponents are most likely to get a goal back in the last quarter of the time remaining to them. Similarly, crowds value corners, in England especially where they respond with great vigor and anticipation, expecting their tall central defenders to come forward into the opposition's penalty area. However, the numbers say otherwise. Only one in five corners turns into a shot on goal and only one in nine of those scores a goal. In actual fact Premier League clubs score a goal from a corner once every ten games and there is a considerable price to be paid for attempting it since defenders are out of position and vulnerable to a counter-attack. Barcelona have abandoned the ball-into-the-box tactic altogether, preferring to treat the corner as an opportunity to regain controlled possession.

Thus football in the twenty-first century has become a highly self-reflexive game, in which participants are analyzing their own and their opponent's actions with greater detail and intensity than ever before. They are also modifying their own play and behaviors accordingly. Consequently, styles of play are in a constant state of flux, with new playing positions and movements being created, only to be rendered redundant by a newly coined counter-tactic. For a period in the early 2000s, playmaking central midfielders seemed on the decline as holding and defensive midfielders took their place. Less than ten years later, Barcelona's relentless possession game gave pride of place to the distributors and attacking midfielders.

One of the reasons that so much of this data-driven change can take place is that the basic framework of format and rules has remained doggedly the same; a long-term stability that encourages micro-innovations within it. The back pass to the goalkeeper was outlawed in 1992, tackling from behind has been both banned and more rigorously refereed, and tweaks to the offside rule have been made, but otherwise the game is formally identical.

There have been some small alterations to the cast, the stage and the costume. The referee is now accompanied by two assistant referees (the term "linesman" was officially abandoned in 1996) and the enigmatically titled fourth official, who was added in 1991. As with the players, their kits are now sponsored; the "Man in Black" is now occasionally not a man, and often he is not in black.

The only change to the pitch markings is actually off the pitch—the coach's technical area, introduced in 1993, which is defined by a broken white line in front of the bench. Managers trying to direct the game, and substitutes waiting to come on, are confined to these zones. They have become a stage all of their own—a grassy podium where the coach's own performance can be highlighted, an invisible cage in which the coach's tics and neuroses are given center stage. The zone is closely patrolled by the fourth official whose conflicts with managers who persistently escape the narrow compound are now a pleasing cameo for viewers.

The players, visibly taller, heavier and better conditioned, are kitted out much as they were, in club and sponsors' liveries, but have added gloves, snoods, and colored boots to their wardrobes. The use of gloves, in particular, is an invariable cue for commentators to remark on foreign players' difficulties in adapting to the bitterness of the English winter.

The game still lasts ninety minutes, though on average the ball is now actually in play for more of the game. Injury time, now called additional time, and added at the discretion of the referee, is now announced on the PA and gives the fourth official their best lines—holding up an illuminated board to show the same.

Formations, the most basic way of organizing the division of the labor in a team and allocating players to different tasks and parts of the field, have diversified. While there has always been variation in English football, the early 1990s were dominated by one simple model. As Arsène Wenger put it, "When I arrived in England I would say there was one rigid formation, 4-4-2. Today teams are more versatile, they can go to three defenders, five defenders, they can go to 4-4-1-1, 4-3-3 . . . all kinds of variants."[55] If there is a pattern to all of this, it is that the weight of play has moved towards the midfield. Many coaches set out their team on four bands, with in effect two bands of midfield players. Players, notionally designated as forwards, are expected to be part of their midfield for much of a game. Even so, across a season and even within a single game teams can modify or even completely transform their shape according to circumstances—a degree of flexibility that was, previously, very rare.

The game itself, as before, is dominated by passing and possession, but the data from the last two decades is unequivocal on this: there is more passing and more successful passing. The average number of passes in a Premier League game is now around 1,000. Compared to even a decade ago more of those passes require only one or two touches from the players, and the vast majority of them are short passes, nearly four-fifths less than 25 yards. Teams still play long balls, a few specializing in them, but sides that do so, to the complete abandonment of controlled possession, are, as Wenger noted, extinct. "Remember you had Wimbledon before—that was a shock for any foreign player who came here, but doesn't exist anymore."[56]

Teams that pass the ball more need players who make space to receive it comfortably. Teams that prize possession are making greater efforts to press the opposition and get the ball back. Players, now obviously fitter and better conditioned, are running further than they did twenty years ago. In 2006, the average Premier League midfielder ran 11.5 kilometers per game, while the average center-back covered 10 kilometers per game. At the same time the ground covered by players while sprinting increased by 40 percent between 2000 and 2006 alone: a sprint is classed as a run made at quicker than 7 meters per second, equivalent to running 100 metres in 14 seconds flat.[57]

There is also more variety in passing, more examples of demanding ball control, more use of what in Britain are, almost derisively, referred to as tricks and flicks. As Philippe Auclair realized on his arrival in England, "The French had at their disposal an arsenal of descriptive words or phrases which English press box colleagues had yet to coin." For example, he found no English equivalent to "Pigeon wing . . . a marvellously evocative semantic shortcut . . . running forward the player receives the ball slightly behind him, and by shaping his leg as a trussed bird's wing flicks it in front of him with the outside of his boot."[58] While not absent from the English game, the presence of this kind of technical language and skill has been massively expanded by the arrival of foreign coaches and players in such large numbers.

Goalkeepers, their options transformed by the back-pass rule, now touch the ball with their feet seven times more often than they do with their hands. Their closer integration into the flow of play has not as yet altered their status as the odd man out, or diminished interest in the peculiar psychological and emotional position they occupy in the game. Defenders spend less of their time man-marking, organized instead to defend space. They now pass more often, and in the case of attacking fullbacks, they are often the players that cover the most ground in the match, providing attacking options down the wing but also required to sprint back to return to their defensive duties. The rule changes on the tackle from behind and the close policing of violent fouls have required defenders to move more and kick less, though all seem to agree that shirt pulling and grabbing in the penalty box at set pieces has increased. Midfielders, as we noted, have become ever more important to the game, running further and faster, and making and receiving more passes than the rest of the side; equally important, they are increasingly multifunctional, capable of switching positions, and adapting to a variety of tactical circumstances.

Finally, there is the dwindling band of out and out strikers. Here again there has been a change, with many sides abandoning the use of a conventional center-forward. Yet in transfer-market terms at any rate, forwards are still the most prized members of the team, for overwhelmingly they are the goalscorers and goals remain rare and difficult to come by. The long decline in average numbers of goals in professional football matches appears to have bottomed out, with just over two goals a game now the average and the vast majority of matches clustering around the scores 1–0/1–1/2–1. Those goals, as before, come overwhelmingly from open play, then from penalties and last and rarely from set pieces. Where there has been change is that more of these goals result from long and complex sequences of passes.

There remain sides that have tried to run against the grain of the rest of the Premier League. Stoke City under Tony Pulis actually preferred to play with as little possession and actual playing time as possible, and scored a considerable number of goals from the long throws of Rory Delap and the ensuing penalty box melee. Wigan under Roberto Martínez consistently outperformed more accomplished opponents by eschewing the long passing move and specializing in shooting from distance, goals from free kicks, and long-ball counter-attacks. Mainstream or marginal, the speed at which contemporary football is played, the level of technical skill and athleticism of the players is clearly superior to that of the past. It's the kind football that should have us getting to our feet.

## VI.

The single most important change in the football crowd is that during the game it now spends most of its time sitting, when it used to spend most of its time standing. You can still stand at some grounds in League One and League Two, but these stands are small and often half-full. Even when the stands are full the predominance of season ticket holders and the strict controls on moving around the stadium, have meant that the old self-selecting clusters of standing and singing fans have been bureaucratically fragmented. We won't be seeing again the great swaying waves of humanity that washed across the old terraces or the ragged lines of kids squeezed up against the perimeter board. Where once the crowd's density and shape would shift with their mood and movement, there is now a grid-like visual rigidity in the all-seater stadium, only broken by the vertical rise and fall of standing and sitting, standing and sitting, as the ball moves and the drama shifts. Even this has been a subject of regulation by overzealous clubs who have threatened to remove supporters who stand too long and too often.[59] Thus the bucket seat not only transformed the economics and demographics of the British football crowd, it was also the key technology of surveillance and control.

The worst excesses of the past—dangerous crushes, stampedes, pitch invasions, arson, attacks on visiting fans inside the stadium—have almost entirely disappeared. Indeed, misbehavior of all kinds is at a record low. During the 2010–11 season there were just over 3,000 arrests for football-related disorders of some kind—the smallest number of arrests since comparable records began in 1985. At a considerable number of games, over a quarter, there were no arrests at all, and the average number of arrests at a professional game was just one.[60] Aggressive stand-offs, let alone actual fights inside the stadium, are very rare indeed. Seating is not the only reason why. Policing, banning orders, stewarding, and CCTV surveillance have all played their part, but the seats do more than just physically regulate, they dampen the emotional tenor of the crowd. The kinds of collective delirium, aggression and abandonment required for mass disobedience are very much harder to evoke when you are putting your feet up.

Despite this it might appear that little has changed. The non-verbal repertoire of the crowd has shifted remarkably little in the last twenty years. The generous use of insulting hand signals are still the norm. The crowd, despite the seats, still jumps for joy, and the walls of scarves still appear alongside key songs and at key moments in a match. There have been minor innovations in goal celebrations with Celtic fans adopting "the Huddle" and Rangers fans "the Bouncy." Manchester City fans copied the Polish fans of Lech Poznan who celebrate a goal by turning their backs to the pitch, linking shoulders and bouncing up and down. Known as "Le Greque" in Poland it became "The Poznan" in Manchester.[61] Yet there is a pervasive sense that something is not right. Despite the obvious gains in safety and comfort that the new stadiums have brought, there remains a strand of discontent among many supporters. On a thousand message boards and fan blogs one reads that same story. Yes, the stadiums are better now in innumerable ways, but we just don't sing like we used to. Indeed, the sound of the crowd in the 1970s and 1980s has come to be seen as the gold standard of authentic support, and first among equals was Liverpool's Kop. Yet in 2012 Gareth Roberts, more in sorrow than in anger, wrote:

> For the second time in as many weeks the home "support" was outsung and out-shouted by a group of away fans following a club promoted from the Championship . . . On both occasions not only were the visiting contingent louder, more visibly passionate and more obvious in their backing for their players, they also took the piss out of us: "Where's your famous atmosphere?" "Your support is fucking shit" . . . "This is a library," etc., etc . . .[62]

The Kop is not always like this today, but that it could be like this at all is a measure of the massive changes in the behavior of football crowds. The recent attempts to establish singing and standing sections at many leading football clubs are testament to the deep vein of concern that runs through football administrators and crowds—that something important and valuable is going to be lost if the best of the old era's atmosphere, camaraderie and noise cannot be passed on.[63]

Singing and chanting are in fact just one element of a bigger culture of performance that is passing. For example, photos of the crowd from the seventies and eighties, particularly at the biggest games, include an eclectic assortment of homemade costumes and banners. These date back to the early twentieth century and were certainly a feature of FA Cup finals, and included remodeled or homemade top hats in team colors, teddy bears in handmade club strips, gigantic rosettes and above all flags and banners with the words spelt out in the characteristically blocky, angular shapes of cut tape: "Jesus Saves, but Pearson nets the rebound," "Red Hot Irons burn Arsenal's Willy," "Joe Jordan Strikes faster than British Leyland." There are remnants of this craft culture in today's crowd, particularly when protesting the ownership or the direction of the club—especially at Liverpool. Sometimes they are surreal: "Martin Škrtel is so hard he asked for a Big Mac in Burger King and got one"; sometimes angry: "Built by Shanks, Broke by Yanks." Leeds fans acidly responded to Galatasaray's "Welcome to Hell" slogan with a handmade sign of their own: "Welcome to Civilization." There may be some of those banners today, but more likely we will be faced with a wall of replica shirts: almost entirely absent from football grounds in the 1970s, they are now the single most worn item in the stands. While at the level of consumption the crowd appears increasingly homogenous, the British continue to resist the repertoire of the continental European ultras. The British crowd has proved largely indifferent to chanting orchestrated by megaphones and drumbeats, the widespread use of naval flares, smoke bombs, and fireworks and the intimidation of players and coaches outside the stadium.[64]

One of the most eccentric elements of crowd behavior still present in the 1980s, but sadly absent today, are the streakers and the mooners. Their contemporary equivalents are the beer bellies, particularly at Newcastle, who parade without shirts in the freezing cold. Perhaps a more fitting style of football exhibitionism in an era of obsessive celebrity culture was Karl Power's Zelig-like pranks. In 2001 he managed to insert himself into the Manchester United team line-up before a Champions League match against Bayern Munich. In 2003 before a United game with Liverpool he orchestrated the re-enactment of a goal scored in a previous encounter during which Liverpool's goalkeeper Jerzy Dudek had let a ball through his legs giving an easy tap-in to Diego Forlán. Power's eleven man troupe then ran to the corner flag to taunt the Liverpool fans before being banned from the stadium for life.[65]

The crowds of the 1980s may have been unruly enough to invade the pitch themselves, but they were relatively circumspect when it came to throwing objects on the pitch. The grenade chucked into Brentford's goalmouth in the 1960s was a rarity. In a more light-hearted vein Newcastle fans threw Mars bars at the stocky Paul Gascoigne when he returned to the club playing for Spurs. Gazza, to his eternal credit, picked one up and ate it. From the mid-1980s on, Chelsea fans celebrated victories by throwing bunches of celery on the pitch, until the club clamped down on the practice in 2007.[66] In the early 1990s there was a short season of inflatables, most memorably the massed ranks of blow-up fish at Grimsby Town, but the most common projectile was the banana—the choice of demeaning insult for the most actively racist component of the crowd, but a phenomenon now virtually unknown. We are now more likely to see objects thrown in protest over the running of the club. In 1997 Hull City fans, appalled by the management of the ex-tennis player turned health club entrepreneur David Lloyd, threw hundreds of tennis balls onto the pitch. More recently, Blackburn fans, protesting against the willful stupidity of the club's owners Venky's—a poultry processing Leviathan from India—released chickens onto Ewood Park.[67] There is also a high-tech option for the malicious. Look for the dots of sickly green light that appear in the eyes of a player about to take a penalty or dance across the faces of goalkeepers awaiting a set piece. These are produced by laser pens or pointers. They were first noted in the late 2000s in European games and then began to appear at home as well; the most widely reported incident involved Chelsea fans during a game against Manchester City in 2011.[68] There is still, however, a taste for more primitive technologies. Crowds will, if sufficiently roused, pelt players and officials with coins and lighters.[69]

Thus, despite all the changes to the emotional architecture of the stadium, despite the stewarding and the surveillance, British football crowds have both embraced the carnivalesque and retained the unpredictable edge of the mob. Today's crowd, at its loudest and most engaged, can still generate an extraordinary atmosphere. In the dying days of the 2009 season, Newcastle United played a must-win-or-be-relegated night game against Middlesbrough at St. James' Park. For most of the ninety minutes, it was simply impossible to hear oneself talk or think. A wall of human energy, part communal roar, part thunder, a force field of white noise and whistling, the soundscape enveloped and then consumed the senses. What happens the rest of the season though? What is the average experience and how does it really compare to the past? Here, more than anywhere perhaps, the pathologies of golden age thinking are at their strongest. However, there is barely any reliable sound archive against which to test the nostalgia-infused collective memory. One of the very few systematic attempts to listen to the football crowd in the 1970s and 1980s was conducted by Desmond Morris for his book *The Soccer Tribe*.[70] Morris had a number of Division One games recorded and transcribed as well as half a season's worth of games at Oxford United in the Third Division, and his summary of the findings is a good place to try and begin that task of comparison.

The basic classifications of noise and song that Morris used in 1981 remain in place today. First, crowds continue to alternate between periods of general noise, whose emotional tone and hue can vary greatly, and periods of silence. Secondly, some noise is directed at specific events on and off the pitch, other sounds are more general mood music, and some are unexpected spontaneous eruptions. Thirdly, whatever the noise, most of it tends to start in the home end behind the goal and spread to other stands more sporadically. Away fans are vital in creating atmosphere and a kind of collective ill-tempered dialogue of claim and counter-claim, insult and injury across the pitch. However, while today's soundscape is structurally similar to the world Morris depicts, there is a quantitative difference. Morris noted that in most games there are around 130–160 distinctive crowd chants, songs or collective noise in a game, around one every thirty seconds. Hardly scientific, but this seems significantly higher than most Premiership games today. Moreover, casual observation suggests that many of the chants that we hear today are sung by a very small section of the crowd, and that genuinely stand-wide or stadium-wide singing is rare.

As with the 1980s the main components of the collective score are songs and chants of support, encouragement and praise. Variants on "Que Sera, Sera," "You Are My Sunshine," and "When the Saints Go Marching In" remain standard fare. Abuse of the referee and the away fans are in the same groove—"You don't know what you're doing," "The referee's a bastard," "Are you Scotland in disguise?" Individual songs for players are still common, both short chants and extended paeans, and here at least the inventiveness of the modern crowd remain intact: Habib Beye celebrated to the *Happy Days* theme tune at QPR, or Liverpool's affectionate tribute to their hapless defender to the tune of Michael Jackon's "Blame It on the Boogie": "Don't blame it on the Finnan, blame it on Traore. He just can't, he just can't, he just can't control his feet." Fans commented on Alan Shearer's disastrous switch from *Match of the Day* pundit to Newcastle United manager, to the tune of "Guantanamera," "You should have stayed on the telly." The same refrain was used by Bristol Rovers fans who sang to their opponents from blighted seaside town Torquay, "You only work in the summer." Chants that are no longer heard or only surface as a kind of historical re-enactment are abuse of the police and threats of violence: "If you all hate coppers clap your hands," "We all hate pigs and we all hate pigs" are now hardly ever heard. Similarly, "You're gonna get your fucking head kicked in," "See you all outside," "You're going home in a London ambulance" and "You'll never make the coaches' have gone but for the occasional piece of pantomime. Much more likely from the new terraces is self-deprecation. Fans of Manchester City, 7–0 down to Middlesbrough, sang "Can we play you every week," and at 8–1 down broke into "Easy! Easy! Easy!" The crowd may not be singing like it used to, but that it is still singing and performing as it does after all the changes in the staging of football is a remarkable act of resilience.

Seven minutes to go. If you look up from the game a strange choreography will have already begun. The tangerine and lemon stewards will begin, in lumbering unison, to take up new positions, descending from on high in the stands to the entrances and exits, or heading off to the touchline where they will create a new defensive line between the crowd and the pitch. At the same time individuals and small groups will be getting up out of their seats and heading for the exits. Some will linger at the tunnel, look over their shoulder and check their watch or phone. Most will try and look invisible as they press their way through the tightly packed rows of seats. These people are leaving early, and not because they are disgusted and simply can't take any more—those guys will have left with a more theatrical flourish at 5–0 with twenty minutes to go. No, these folks are leaving to make a quick getaway and to beat the traffic. Again, this is not a new phenomenon and the nature of the all seater-stadium exposes the early leavers in a way that the old grounds did not, but it appears to be a more widespread practice. It is a small but significant phenomenon, especially given how much the seat will have cost and how often crucial decisions and goals come in the final minutes as players tire and mistakes multiply.

The whistle blows. Game over. The crowd roars, boos, grunts, and instantly begins to fragment as people hurry for the exits. Some linger, particularly those that still like to clap the home side off, but the backdrop of the spectacle has already began to shift to the sponsors' boards. Cameramen, sound recordists, and besuited presenters swarm across the pitch and accost the unlucky players. The PA is cranked back up to full volume, now booming inside a space whose acoustics are getting shriller by the moment as people and life drain from the stands. The away fans will, most probably, be kept behind for another twenty minutes. The army of low-paid labor that collects the rubbish and cleans the seats begins to drift in.[71] The game is giving way to the spectacle, the day appears to be disappearing entirely into media land, postmatch interviews and press conferences. Unhinged now from the real, the play is being edited, cut, replayed and analyzed in a hundred blue and chrome studios, in subterranean edit suites, migrating and mutating on Facebook and YouTube. Then it will be reinvented in the studios of the radio phone-ins, on the pundits' sofas and in the match reports already being posted on the sports and news websites. A million words and images, but they will capture so little of the day. Shankly's scarf softening his sharpened bronze features. The sound of a thousand hands pummelling the corrugated iron shed you stood in. The strangers that hugged you and made you dance a turn in the aisle when we scored. The away fans, faces pressed to the glass of their coach windows, bawling you out. These thoughts and sensations are the fine ash of a distant volcanic eruption thrown high into the atmosphere now come back to earth, settling deep in the sedimentary layers of individual and collective memory. To paraphrase Don DeLillo:

> All the fragments of the afternoon collect . . . Shouts, step-overs, cruel chants and stray shots, the sand-grain manyness of things that can't be counted. It is all falling indelibly into the past.[72]

# CHAPTER 3

# English Journey

## Football and Urban England

Hillsborough Stadium—North Stand. Constructed: 1961. Capacity: 9,255 (seated). The North Stand runs along the long north edge of the pitch, and is one of the earliest examples of football stands having a cantilever roof, and the first in England to run the entire length of the pitch.

---

**NIKOLAUS PEVSNER**

## I.

It is a terrible irony that Hillsborough is the only football stadium to receive an entry in *The Buildings of England,* Nikolaus Pevsner's otherwise encyclopaedic survey of England's urban landscape. The stadium, picked out in characteristically terse tones for its structural and technological innovations, was of course the site of English football's worst disaster. Among the many factors that explained the awful chain of events on the day was the antiquated character of the stadium and its infrastructure.[1] Pevsner's successors as itinerant architectural critics have proved to be a little more sensitive to the place of the football stadium in the mosaic of

English cities. In the mid-1970s Ian Nairn made two short films called *Football Towns*; one pitted Halifax against Huddersfield, the other featured Bolton and Preston. They were, he argued, exemplars of "industrial places—where the real hard stuff of Britain is going on . . . and mostly unvisited, unless you go there on business . . . or to the match."[2] However he only used the game as a structuring device, in which he refereed a contest between the townscapes rather than reflected on the actual place of the sport in English urban life. More recently Owen Hatherley's splenetic, architectural autopsies of New Labour's "urban renaissance," *A Guide to the New Ruins of Great Britain* and *A New Kind of Bleak*, crisscross every conceivable urban environment, and remark upon every kind of building, but there is only a handful of references to football stadiums. In Manchester he manages a quick peek at Old Trafford, but more characteristic is Hatherley's glance back over his shoulder at the Millennium Stadium as he hurries on to the waterside redevelopments and *grands projets* of Cardiff Bay.[3]

In their defense Pevsner might have amended his own dictum: "A football stadium is a building; Lincoln Cathedral is a piece of architecture. Nearly everything that encloses space on a scale sufficient for a human being to move in is a building; the term architecture applies only to buildings designed with a view to aesthetic appeal."[4] While it would be unfair to say that the huge wave of stadium redevelopment in English football has been conducted without any regard to aesthetic appeal, it would be hard to argue that it has been much of a priority. In her survey of the iconic buildings of the North of England, Laurie Peake noted that "The multitude of stadia springing up . . . are rarely given prime spots in the topography nor the kind of design treatment that allow them to show off their monumental potential . . . Given that the football industry bestrides the region like a colossus, not one stadium imposes itself."[5] Nonetheless, amid out-of-town retail parks masquerading as grounds, the chaotic, ugly signage and grimly lit refreshment zones, there are a handful of more confident architectural statements: the New Wembley, St. James' Park, and the Emirates, for example. Moreover, it is not necessarily the showcase pieces and the prizewinners that most closely reflect the physical grain of England's towns and cities; their real vernacular vocabulary might be better explored through the crass, the mediocre and the unimaginative.[6]

If English football has offered thin pickings for the architectural traveler, its detailed patchwork of peculiar localism is surely richer fare for popular scrutineers of national identity. England's football stadiums are the places where the team and the crowd are *at home*. J. B. Priestley was sufficiently alert to the emotional and cultural significance of the game to open his 1929 novel *The Good Companions* with a long description of a match, alert above all to the fantastical realm of popular theater and collective identity, "an altogether more splendid life" that football had become: "To say that these men paid their shillings to watch twenty-two hirelings kick a ball is merely to say that a violin is wood and catgut, that Hamlet is so much paper and ink. For a shilling the Bruddersford United AFC offered you Conflict and Art."[7] In *English Journey*, published in 1934 and now the template for many similar travelogues, Priestley described the Nottingham derby between Forest and County. Here, he cut his own and the crowd's sentimentality with a shot of cynicism but without relinquishing a sense of the game's pervasive cultural importance: "Nearly everything possible has been done to spoil this game: the heavy financial interests . . . the absurd publicity given to every feature of it by the Press; . . . but the fact remains that it is not yet spoilt, and it has gone out and conquered the world."[8] His successors did not take note. Orwell's journey to Wigan Pier through the working-class cultures of the North did not include a match, while Bill Bryson stopped only to note Liverpool's "pathetic reliance" on their football team to furnish an identity; a comment he might like to discuss further with all the Everton fans in the city, as well as the Hillsborough support groups. Jeremy Paxman's *The English* only finds room for football in the guise of the hooligan abroad as a crude cipher for the nation's martial and xenophobic qualities. Sir Roy Strong's *The Story of England*, unsurprisingly a football-free zone, clings to the shibboleth that the England of the imagination remains overwhelmingly rural.[9]

Encoded in this combination of lack of interest in and hostility to football is the longstanding anti-urbanism of much of the English intelligentsia and its strange cultural snobbery towards sport.[10] It makes them look a little ridiculous. The idea that contemporary England, where over 90 percent of the population lives in urban areas, could be properly imagined through its rural landscapes, bucolic art or its ecclesiastical architecture is absurd. The idea that one could write football out of the narrative of English identities, or reduce its contribution merely to hooliganism, is equally foolish. D. J. Taylor's description of the relationship between Norwich and football, though locally specific, can also stand proxy for almost every town and city in England:

> Norwich is a small city, a couple of MPs , nothing between it and the sea . . . Supporting the local football team consequently is an essential part of local patriotism, of identity, definitive proof of Norfolk's superiority to Suffolk, of Norwich's superiority to Ipswich . . . even today, walking back through the Norwich suburbs on a Saturday afternoon in October wearing your yellow and green scarf you can count on being stopped by the old woman emerging from the shadows with her dog to enquire "How'd City git on?"[11]

In some countries the meanings of football's geography and its place in the urban landscape are obvious. In Italy the towering economic predominance of the north is reflected in the total football hegemony of Turin's Juventus and the two Milanese teams. The overwhelming centralization of Argentina and Uruguay can be read from their top divisions, which, until recently, were almost exclusively composed of teams from the capital city. England's footballing landscape is more complex, but equally illuminating. Look at a map of the country, with the motorway network included. In the bottom right-hand corner the orbital ring of the M25 sends spokes in all directions, its key branches being the westerly M4 and the north–south double spine of the M1 and the M5/M6. The vast majority of professional football clubs—more than 90 percent— lie either inside of the M25 or very close to this narrow, shrunken urban core. Beyond this are the national parks and their inhabited fringes, the faceless edgelands and exurbs, and the wealthy gulags of executive mansions and gated villages; the badlands and the deserts, bereft of professional football teams. It is interesting to note than only three clubs with a good motorway connection—Luton Town, Stockport County, and Cambridge United—have disappeared off the football map and slipped into the Conference in the last twenty years: indeed, in 2014 Luton and Cambridge managed to clamber back into the Football League. By contrast, the teams east of the A1 and M1, like Scarborough, Rushden and Diamonds, Boston United, Lincoln City, Mansfield Town, Grimsby Town, and Darlington, have all but been wiped out. With the demise of Wrexham and Chester, the only professional football between the West Midlands west of the M6 and the Irish Sea is in the micro-enclaves of Hereford, Shrewsbury, and Cheltenham.

English football is not only quintessentially urban, but, the architectural travelogue aside, an unusual context in which the great diversity of English urbanism is simultaneously on show. In the football fixtures and league tables we find metaphorically, but literally, too, new metropolitan elites and old inner-city proletarians (Chelsea and West Ham United), cathedral and university cities (Norwich City and Oxford United), garrisons and ports (Colchester United and Southampton), new towns and market towns (Milton Keynes Dons and Chesterfield), suburbs and seaside resorts (Crystal Palace and Southend United), retirement bunkers and commuter dormitories (Bournemouth and Wycombe Wanderers). Football's relations with urban England and the nation's civic identities are more than just metaphorical though. In the last twenty-five years football clubs' new stadiums have altered the urban fabric, old stadiums becoming the object of desire for unscrupulous developers. In some cases the clubs have become direct players in large-scale urban-regeneration projects and local strategies for economic development; in others they served as a key trope in city-branding exercises.

Our *English Journey* begins in the core of football: the axis of enmity that runs between Merseyside and Manchester and on the pitch between Liverpool and Manchester United, which is by far the most bitter and emotionally wrought derby in English football. In Liverpool in the 1980s football success peaked alongside the last wave of radical municipal socialism before both team and city were broken. In Manchester, by contrast, local government pursued the new entrepreneurial urbanism of culture-led regeneration, and Manchester United pursued the most aggressive commercial strategies of any English football club. In both cases Manchester outstripped its near neighbor. In the 1990s these cities were joined at the core of English football by London. As in the wider economy, the city benefited disproportionately from the import of foreign talent and capital that was the basis for the Premiership titles achieved by Arsène Wenger's Arsenal and Roman Abramovich's Chelsea.

It also received the lion's share of public money and media institutions in the form of the New Wembley national stadium and the headquarters of Sky and the Premier League. Nonetheless, the influx of money into these cities has not been equally distributed. Indeed, the more money and status that flow to the core, the more its own football barrios struggle. There is precious little trickle-down economics in football as the fates of Tranmere Rovers, Oldham Athletic, Leyton Orient, and Barnet make clear.

English football's semiperiphery comprises six regions, all of which possess clubs who have been regular if not permanent members of the Premiership and sides with the occasional title of some sort to their name. The North East has, by virtue of distance alone, always stood at one remove from the core, but in terms of crowds, fervor, and the production of players it considers itself second to none. Despite this its leading sides have not permanently established themselves in the Premiership, nor won a league title for a very long time. In Newcastle, in particular, this enduring gap between potential and actual results has been the fuel for a hugely ambitious football project that has entwined sporting success, the postindustrial regeneration of Tyneside and a vision of regional political autonomy. The North West and the Midlands were both once part of the nation's football and economic core, the inaugural Football League being made up of twelve clubs from just Lancashire and the Midlands. Despite this heritage both regions have fallen on harder times and, with the exception of Blackburn Rovers' league title in 1995, there have been precious few triumphs. Indeed, there is a gathering sense that now, expelled from the core, they may never get back. This kind of realism has not afflicted Yorkshire, where despite all evidence and advice to the contrary, Leeds, Bradford, Barnsley, and the Sheffield clubs have flown too close to the sun, trying to buy their way to the top, before ignominiously crashing. In contrast to the northern narratives of decline the small cities of the South East have been on the way up: Southampton and Reading have made regular Premiership appearances; Portsmouth, albeit fuelled by a torrent of foreign debt and fictive money, won the FA Cup in 2008 and were runners-up in 2010 before spectacularly imploding, while Brighton has finally roused itself and joined the ranks of Premiership contenders.

England's football periphery, as one would expect, lies in the zones at the very edge of or beyond the motorway skeleton, where clubs are few and far between and those that do manage to carry on are rarely seen outside the lower divisions. In the great stretch of Eastern England that runs through Humberside and Lincolnshire professional football has been banished to the urban redoubt of Hull. In East Anglia it can be found only in the isolated outposts of Norwich and Ipswich. Northumberland beyond Tyneside and the whole of Cumbria appear football-free zones but for embattled Carlisle on the Scottish border. In the South West football begins petering out after Bristol and disappears altogether beyond Plymouth. Finally, beyond the periphery, in the fourth world, are the ghost towns, populated by the small semi-professionalism of the Conference.

Perhaps, most interestingly of all, a new wave of clubs has begun to emerge: the DIY self-build solutions, the fan-created clubs that have risen up the football ladder like AFC Wimbledon and FC United of Manchester. In an era that liked to think of itself as an urban renaissance, a time of regeneration when the dilapidated social and physical capital of the nation would be rebuilt, these experiments are the smallest but greatest successes.

## II.

A measure of just how long ago England's industrial revolution began is just how early its great manufacturing cities began to shrink. Both Liverpool and Manchester peaked in size around 1930 before losing almost half their populations by 2001. Both cities were devastated by containerization and the shrinkage of their docks, and both hemorrhaged manufacturing jobs. Manchester's industries employed 225,000 people in 1961; by the turn of the century it was down to 35,000. In the 1980s alone Liverpool lost one-third of all its employment. By the early 1990s, deindustrialization had left a pockmarked urban landscape in which vacant land, empty factories and derelict buildings accounted for around 15 percent of both cities.[12] Liverpool responded to the decimation with defiance. Militant, the Trotskyist group, had infiltrated the husk of the old Labour Party and then led the Liverpool Council and the rest of the city into an unwinnable battle with the Thatcher government. As the city decayed Liverpool Football Club blossomed, winning ten League titles between 1977 and 1990 and four European cups. Everton, although always in their shadow, won two League titles themselves and the European Cup-Winners' Cup in the mid-1980s. Football offered a parallel universe of success alongside the otherwise vertiginous urban decline of the city. Hillsborough seemed to put an end to all of this. Liverpool won the League in 1990, but that was the last time they have done so. Everton have won an FA Cup since then, but nothing else. Of course, Liverpool continued to win cups, three alone in 2001 and their fifth European Cup in 2005, but the title has eluded them.

The deep antipathy between the two cities stretches back at least as far as the construction of the Manchester Ship Canal in 1887—the purpose of which was to allow Manchester merchants a way of avoiding Liverpool's docks—but over the last couple of decades their footballing encounters have had a peculiarly barbed edge as the struggle to be the cultural capital of the North and the footballing capital of England has swung decisively towards Manchester and Manchester United. Each Manchester United title over the last twenty years brought them closer to Liverpool's record of seventeen, until finally they surpassed them, or as Alex Ferguson succinctly put it, "knock[ed] them off their fucking perch." It has made for a cruel and volatile atmosphere. Liverpool fans have been known to sing of the Munich air disaster to the tune of "Always Look on the Bright Side of Life," "Always look on the runway for ice."[13] United fans have responded with a similarly heartless range of chants. Straight Scouse caricature ("they're hard, they're scouse, they'll rob your fucking house") is the staple but there have also been songs about Heysel.[14] The Hillsborough tragedy has also been directly referenced: "You used to sing Munich but not any more, since ninety-six Scousers lay dead on the floor."[15]

Hillsborough's impact on Liverpool's football culture has been multi-faceted. The sheer emotional blow of the moment shaped and then broke the relationship of many people with football. Others clung harder and faster than ever. The waves of shock then mutated into the long terrible era of black propaganda, Murdoch scuttlebutt and the painful lying and denial by the authorities. Because so much of the story woven by the Murdoch press, the South Yorkshire police and their many allies turned on the disreputable character of Scousers and their city, the emotional and symbolic relationship between the game and Liverpool was perhaps wound even tighter.

More prosaically, the necessity of building all-seater stadiums that Hillsborough initiated has become the central financial problem for both Liverpool sides. In contemporary football terms, Anfield and Goodison Park do not make enough money. They are not large enough to meet current or potential demand, nor are they kitted out in a way that would allow the clubs to extract sufficient money out of the crowd. Arsenal, once established at the Emirates Stadium, could rake in over four times the takings that Everton could manage even when Goodison Park was full. However, the stadiums of both Liverpool clubs have become so super-saturated in local meanings and histories, so emblematic of the relationship between fans, city and club that their redevelopment, let alone their relocation, has become highly contentious.

The stadium debate also points to some of the problems with the city's wider regeneration strategy. Liverpool's big problem was getting access to capital to rebuild the city. As far back as 1997 Everton's board considered moving out to Kirby, only four miles away but outside the city precincts. Knowsley City Council was desperate enough to offer them free land and a partnership with the supermarket chain Tesco, who would make a contribution to the stadium costs. Fans bitterly opposed this option, and the group Keep Everton in Our City has been an important force in monitoring and challenging the club. When this option was blocked the club explored both a new city-center stadium—at the King's Dock on the old waterfront—as well as a ground share with Liverpool in the New Anfield that they have been trying to build for fifteen years. The ground-share scheme, despite interventions from the then Minister of Sport and regional development agencies, was simply not acceptable to anyone. How could it be acceptable for Everton fans to watch their team from a consciously remodeled version of the Kop? The King's Dock project, which would have placed football at the geographical and architectural heart of the city's waterfront, was widely supported by fans, but faltered because Everton couldn't find the £155 million it needed.[16] Bill Kenwright, the beleaguered owner and chairman of Everton, has made it clear that he is simply not rich enough to overcome the multiple obstacles in the path of Everton's development.

Liverpool had plans to build a new stadium in Stanley Park as early as 1999, but failed to consult the area's residents before they sprung on them their intention to demolish 1,800 houses. A fierce political back-lash followed that forced the club to retreat, and then opt for yet another design in Stanley Park. By the time the costs of building this ground had been calculated the price had soared. Liverpool's owners, the Moores family, were reluctant to spend more of their own fortune and were un-able to raise the capital necessary to start work. Thus planning blight and uncertainty were added to the woes of one of the poorest and most run-down parts of Liverpool.[17] Money was spent on foreign players and for-eign managers, and this kept Liverpool at the top of English football without ever quite threatening to dominate it. Under Frenchman Gerard Houllier and then Spaniard Rafa Benitez, Liverpool found some of their old swagger and fielded a blend of Scouse icons (Steven Gerrard and Ja-mie Carragher) and adopted sons (Sami Hyypia); the side's miraculous recovery and penalty shoot-out victory in the 2005 Champion's League final suggested that a return to the summit of English football was possi-ble too. However by 2007 it was clear that this was not enough either to build a New Anfield or win a title; the Moores family were prepared to sell. They rejected offers from Thailand and Dubai and consciously sought out a set of owners who would in some sense understand and honor the Liverpool way—of discreet patrician conservatism. It was their misjudgement and Liverpool's misfortune that they should sell to two Americans who were richer but unashamedly more venal than them.

Tom Hicks and George Gillett were a shotgun marriage. Both had prospered through a mixture of risky leveraged financing, property spec-ulation and development and professional sports franchise (ice hockey and baseball).[18] The two never got on, but they did agree that Liverpool in a new stadium was a cash cow. This was not however their pitch to Merseyside. They persuaded the Moores family to sell and much of Liv-erpool's fan base to accept their arrival by making all the usual financial promises but in the guise of a conservative patrician ethos that chimed with Liverpool's own traditions; portraying themselves, in contrast to the Glazers at Manchester United, as custodians not owners. Given the city's long connections with the United States and recognition among the fans that the club had always, in part, been a commercial entity and needed now to be a better one, the prospect of American tycoons owning the club was less unpalatable than one might imagine. Moreover, Liverpool fans did not have a history of radicalism or protest, rather loyalty and an apolitical focus on the football was their default mode. There were signs of change in the early twenty-first century as first the Keep Flags Scouse and then the Reclaim the Kop campaigns sought to police the behavioral codes of the stands—no crass goading of opponents, no singing about clubs that weren't present, no excessive display of recent purchases in the club store—but questions of high politics and ownership did not concern them.[19] It is testament to the cultural insensitivity and level of self-interest displayed by Hicks and Gillett that they were able to rouse a more militant fan culture.

The Americans' core problem was financial. They had bought the club and its debts on the basis of gigantic short-term loans from the Royal Bank of Scotland and Wachovia, who were two of the many banks whose liquidity froze during the financial turbulence of the following three years. For the next two years, as the global credit-crisis unfolded, they failed to find a long-term solution to their own and the club's spiralling debts, and made no progress on building a stadium that might have saved them. After a short honeymoon period protest erupted. In 2008 over a thousand fans broke from the club to create their own side, AFC Liverpool.[20] Among those who stayed the most militant gathered as the Spirit of Shankly group. Over the next eighteen months they publicly confronted the owners, orchestrated email blitzes of their business and led the anti-songs inside Anfield.[21] Hicks and Gillett hung on for as long as they could for as high price as they could; a stance that forced RBS to install its own chairman and make the sale. In 2010 the club was sold against the wishes of Hicks and Gillett for £300 million to Fenway Sports and John Henry, the banker-patrician who owned the Boston Red Sox.

While the switch from malign hucksters to a relatively benign tycoon has calmed the fury—and in 2014 brought a league title tantalizingly close—it has not brought peace or success. The former for sure, but perhaps the latter too, await the conclusion of the long political and legal struggle over Hillsborough. Here, at last, there has been real progress. Twenty-three years after the disaster the Hillsborough Independent Panel, chaired by the Bishop of Liverpool, and given access to 450,000 documents previously unavailable, delivered their report.[22] It was unequivocal. Liverpool fans were not in any way responsible for the tragedy. The blame squarely lay where it always had, with an antediluvian infrastructure and appalling, incompetent policing. More importantly, the report made clear that there had been a systematic effort by the South Yorkshire police to protect themselves and blame the fans; that the decision to restrict the original coroner's inquests to events before 3:15 p.m. on the day was unsustainable and required a re-examination of the actions of police and emergency services after this; that the West Midlands police force inquiry into South Yorkshire was the threadbare apology of an investigation everyone always knew it had been. Liverpool has its truth now. Justice awaits.

If football and politics in Liverpool in the 1980s had an air of magic realism, even of full-blown fantasy, Manchester was rather more social realist. Both City and United went through the 1970s and 1980s in a state of advanced mediocrity. Manchester City Council and the ruling Labour Party had followed a similar if less aggressive agenda of municipal socialism and resistance to Westminster, to the one pursued in Merseyside. However, after the Tories had won their third successive general election victory in 1987, the city and its elites shifted direction.[23] Manchester City Council now embraced—indeed, they effectively invented—a new entrepreneurial urbanism in England: local government's main task was to rebrand the city, attract investment in the new service and knowledge economies and catalyse multiple development projects through alliances with the private sector and regional quangos.

Simultaneously, change came to Manchester United. First, in the guise of Alex Ferguson, whose appointment in 1986 signalled the beginning of a long era of success. Secondly, the flotation of the club on the stock market in 1991 was the first step in a two-decade campaign of relentless commercialization. The two processes of urban and sporting regeneration were not just comparable, shaped by adaptation to the same neo-liberal environment, but intimately linked. United's global reach, which long preceded the coming of the Premiership or satellite television, made sport in general and football in particular an obvious resource for the rebranding and renovation of Manchester. The council and local business elites launched two bids to host the Olympic Games; neither was successful but both created an enhanced global profile for the city and a swathe of new sports and transport infrastructure projects. The

1996 IRA bombing of the brutalist Arndale center gave an unexpected boost to the process, clearing away acres of ageing property and opening the way to another round of high-end retail development and inner-city lofts and apartments.

Central Manchester is now transformed. From a population that had dwindled to less than four hundred there are now over 20,000 people living there. It is home to four universities, major arts venues, and has the biggest gay quarter in the North. Unfinished and still pock-marked by spaces of decline, it has nevertheless acquired a more varied and vibrant urbanism, culturally and architecturally, than anywhere in England outside of London. What gives the city this sense of scale is that Manchester's transformation is not dependent on this core of activity alone. In actual fact the city's two biggest poles of development lie on either side of the center, to the south-west where the massively rebuilt Old Trafford sits at one corner of a zone of development across Salford Quays and Trafford Park; and to the east, where you will find the City of Manchester Stadium, now home to Manchester City and the anchor of the New East Manchester project. Salford Quays were once the epicenter of the world's leading industrial city; the terminus of the Manchester Ship Canal. Trafford Park, just across the water, was home to the world's first purpose-built industrial estate. Today they are conjoined in a sculpted postindustrial landscape that houses Daniel Libeskind's Imperial War Museum North, the Lowry gallery and factory outlet mall and the complex of offices and squares branded Media City. Where once manufacturing was the source of wealth, value is now conjured from the archaeological remains of the industrial. It is an architectural testament to a new economy built on sport and art, the monetary valorization of history and memory, and, of course, the ubiquitous presence of the mainstream media, chain restaurants and indoor shopping. Yet bigger and more eye-catching than all of them is the garish scarlet neon of Manchester United's signage and the sparkling white crown of tubular steel cantilevers that ring the top of the stadium.

Close up, Old Trafford is a paradoxical building to read. Located on a small plot of land, it is sharply bounded by an eighteenth-century canal, a working Victorian railway line, a messy goods yard and a few streets of tightly bound red-brick terraces. It is rooted in a place that is unmistakably industrial, a location mirrored by the stadium itself, much of which is undistinguished and functional; all high blank brick walls and metal fascias that appear to have been cannibalized from shipping containers, punctuated by the occasional porthole window. The high walls of the east stand have been wrapped with a tinted glass fascia that would just pass muster in the large office blocks of a high-end science park. Below and immediately around this facade, the red-brick walls have been clad in what looks like green faux-marble tiles from a bathroom superstore, serving as the splash plate for the club megastore on the ground. A temple of football mammon perhaps, but in actual fact the shop is barely the size of a large Gap and certainly smaller than a high street Marks and Spencer's. Yet the stadium as a whole has a huge unabashed rectangular presence, its height and mass emphasized by the narrowness of the concourse around it; on the slip roads to its east the signs announce "Welcome to Salford," but they are visually and symbolically rendered irrelevant by Old Trafford. Belying the usual stereotype of the club as a commercial rather than a footballing operation, Old Trafford's architectural strength is ultimately where it should be, within. The self-appellation "theater of dreams" is perhaps a little too cloying for all but the faithful, but one cannot help but be awed by the scale, drama and sightlines of the largest club stadium in the country. It remains, despite the commercial clutter and confetti of brands strewn across its fixtures and fittings, a breathtaking place in which to watch football. It is from this strand of the club's culture that a contrary identity was nurtured, where the popular conception of United fans as mere glory hunters, exiles, and tourists was challenged by a renewed emphasis on the Mancunian quality of the club and where something of the old Mancunian radicalism—that gave birth to both the trade union and cooperative movements—could find a place in the new football and the new Manchester.

Martin Edwards' years as owner and chairman had spawned three independent fanzines—*Red News*, *Red Issue* and *United We Stand*—with plenty to gripe about and an audience hungry to hear it. In 1995 they helped create the Independent Manchester United Supporters Association (IMUSA), which campaigned against high ticket prices, for standing areas at Old Trafford, and attempted to build a base of small shareholders. It was this coalition that helped defeat the proposed BSkyB takeover in 1999, their politically connected lobbying helping influence the decision of the Monopolies and Mergers Commission to reject the bid.[24] A less cerebral expression of United fans' new localism was the plan hatched in 2001 to celebrate the twenty-fifth anniversary of Manchester City winning nothing by holding a party in an executive suite at Maine Road. City got wind of the jape and cancelled it, but the party went ahead outside the gates of Maine Road. Across the Stretford End, banners expressing the new localism made regular appearances—the sentimental "Flowers of Manchester," the utopian "Manchester is my Heaven" and the more autarchic "Republik of Mankunia."[25]

Murdoch may have been seen off, but after the 2002 stock market crash, United were profitable, debt free and selling at a relatively low price. Someone was going to buy them up and Martin Edwards had been steadily selling off his shares to a variety of investors who might have a go. The first skirmish was really a phony war. It appeared that the Coolmore faction, the Irish gamblers, racehorse owners and thoroughbred breeders, J. P. McManus and John Magnier, who held almost 30 percent of the shares, might make a bid for the club. Alongside the usual forms of protest a new style of direct-action militancy made an appearance: United fans deliberately disrupted racing at Hereford to get at Coolmore on their own territory.[26] But the real danger lay elsewhere. The Glazer family had built a precarious fortune on debt, malls and the Tampa Bay Bucks of the NFL. By 2005 they had built up a shareholding of almost 30 percent in Manchester United, though they did not have the money to buy the rest. The Glazers then managed to secure a series of loans, many of them at exorbitant interest rates, and used this money to buy out the small shareholders. Once they had sold up, everyone else with more substantial holdings fell in. Now in complete control of the club, the Glazers delisted United from the Stock Exchange, made it a private company and most importantly of all, loaded all the loans that they had taken out to buy the club straight onto Manchester United's balance sheet. In a reversal of roles that only the voodoo of contemporary finance makes possible, the club would henceforth pay for the Glazers to own it.[27]

The protests engendered by BSkyB and Coolmore paled into insignificance. Joel Glazer's first trip to Old Trafford required the deployment of dozens of riot police and dogs, who eventually baton-charged protesting fans. Among mainstream fans the principal vehicle for protest has been the slogan (and group of the same name) "Love United Hate Glazer." Their most public weapon was the display of green and gold—the colors of Newton Heath, the nineteenth-century railwaymen's team from which Manchester United emerged. Flags, scarves and other insignia began to appear in the crowd at Old Trafford in 2009, and in 2010 at a televised cup game 30,000 supporters donned green and gold, and let off tens of thousands of balloons. On the fringe, the more radical model of fan protest acquired organizational form. The Manchester Education Committee, which communicated by press releases, appears to have been a cross between an old-school firm and an underground political cell.[28] This anonymous group of fans organized flash mobs in the city center in the shops of United's sponsors—the Nike Store ground to a complete halt. Endless bogus takeaways were delivered to the offices of PR companies working for the Glazers, great waves of faxes, calls and emails jammed their corporate communication systems. The Glazers' financial advisers Deutsche Bank were treated to the arrival of call girls at their Christmas party.[29] Less attractively, the group have mirrored the language of Belfast paramilitaries with their oblique warnings of "consequences" and in the case of Wayne Rooney's rumored move to Manchester City, a taste for intimidation.[30] However, neither peaceful nor violent strategies have come to anything. The Glazers are still in charge and United are still paying their wages, their bills and their debts.[31] For a significant group of active fans, as we shall see, the only option was to leave altogether. For those that stayed, the end of the Ferguson era and the appointment of his anointed successor David Moyes in 2013 exposed the depth of the problem. In their worst season for decades United finished eighth in the Premier League and failed to qualify for Europe. Moyes, unable to conjure miracles from an ageing squad whose quality could not match the hunger and vigor of its leading opponents, was sacked.[32]

Manchester's other pole of development lies to the east of the city center. Here the neon signage is blue. Manchester City's Etihad Stadium sits at the center of a gigantic zone of redevelopment projects. Indeed, in the last twenty years East Manchester has been subject to the attentions of more overlapping agencies and initiatives than any other space in the country.[33] When the new era of football began, City were still in their old home Maine Road, so decrepit that meeting the minimum standards of an all-seater stadium, let alone a more modern building, was financially ruinous. But Maine Road had soul, and through the 1990s that was the point. In the internal football culture of Manchester, United's global, commercial and deracinated growth was contrasted to the earthy, authentic Mancunian qualities of City. The club's self-identity as the perennial underdog, as the home of unbreakable support come what may, of the love of place over victory, was nourished by the team's erratic form, their sojourn in the lower divisions and disastrous management.[34] First under Peter Swales, then under Francis Lee and his consortium of Manchester businessmen, City went down to the third level and looked for a moment in 1999 like they might take another drop right to the bottom.

A decade or so later, City are probably the richest club in the world, owned by the royal family of Abu Dhabi. They may not have the revenue stream of either United or the Spanish giants, but they have a lake of oil behind them that no one can compete with. The sequence of events that brought about this extraordinary shift begins with the fall of Francis Lee and the takeover of the club by a group of Manchester businessmen headed by David Bernstein. Their key move was to cut an extraordinarily good deal with the Manchester City Council who, together with the National Lottery and Sport England, would not only build the new stadium for the 2002 Commonwealth Games but cover the costs of its conversion from athletics to football. City would only pay rent on ticket sales above the 32,000 seats they already had at Maine Road. In total this amounted to a public subsidy to Manchester City plc of around £125 million.[35]

Yet, even with this kind of largesse, full houses and a return to the Premiership, City were still losing money and its owners were ready to sell; ready enough to sell the club to the ex-prime minister of Thailand, Thaksin Shinawatra, no questions asked. Shinawatra had spent the previous five years between 2001 and 2006 as the Thai premier, a position built on a super-populist platform that appealed, in particular, to Thailand's rural poor. His party name translates as Thais Love Thais, and Thaksin was his own number one Thai. Although there was some small trickle-down of resources to the poor in rural Thailand, much of his rule was actually spent bullying the press and the opposition, cracking down on dissent and changing the law in ways that would benefit his and his family's fortunes. By 2006 he was reputed to be worth more than £2 billion.[36] Later that year while abroad, Shinawatra and his government were removed by military coup and some of his assets frozen. Consequently his year at City was just one long act of grandstanding from exile. City fans were appeased the same way he courted rural Thailand, with huge noodle kitchens dispensing free chow in public squares. Thai politicians and businessmen were wined and dined in the executive boxes, and Thaksin's face was beamed back to Thailand where Premiership football was hugely popular. It certainly endeared Thaksin to his core constituencies, who have continued to support him and the various political movements he has backed since his own party was dissolved. But it did not endear him to Thailand's judicial and military elites, who tried him in absentia for corruption, took away his passport and grabbed what they could of his fortune. City had been useful but it was time to go, and in late 2008 Sheikh Mansour and the ruling house of Abu Dhabi made their move.

A billion pounds and counting later, in 2012 City won their first League title for thirty-four years, a victory made all the sweeter by defeating United on the final day in the final minutes of the final game. Unlike at Liverpool or Manchester United, the arrival of the global super-rich has not produced a reaction, a breakaway club or a protest movement. In part, this is because there has been so little to protest about. The Al Nayan dynasty have proved to be highly competent, organized, well-mannered owners albeit with a streak of ruthlessness. Or perhaps it is because City fans, after enduring a culture of perpetual disappointment, believe that, whoever legally owns the club, nothing can erode their monopoly on the meaning of the club. While the gullible Scousers were sold a complete turkey, City's sharper scallies tell themselves they are laughing all the way to the trophy cabinet.

It will be interesting to see how long this deep emotional inoculation will sustain them. There are already signs that City and its New East Manchester home are semidetached from the rest of the metropolis. The club is now building a gigantic training and academy complex around the stadium, with seven full-size pitches and accommodation for a dozen teams, not to mention hotels and medical facilities. The sports city that Manchester's elites long imagined appears finally to be taking shape, but this will be a highly privatized city in which the club's contribution to the public realm is almost nugatory, amounting to a few acres in one corner of the complex with promises of a school to be built upon it.[37] On match days, despite the bustle around the Etihad, the vast majority of the pre-match ritual, the drinking and the smoking, the meeting up and the pleasures of collective anticipation, are experienced outside of New East Manchester in the old pubs round the back of Piccadilly and across the city center. Post-match bacchanalia spreads out across East and South Manchester to the curry houses of Rusholme and the pubs of Fallowfield and Gorton. And what of Maine Road? City gave it to the council, and though some of the land has been redeveloped into small housing units, much of it remains empty. There is a palpable sense of the old rectangle among the dead-end roads of red-brick terrace; and in the streets beyond, the boarded-up shops, the pubs for lease, the long-closed chippy, the last husks of the micro economy of football that was once here.

"Where's the money gone?" City's crowds have been known to sing. To answer that, you need a new map, one that charts the cartography of fantastical wealth and bizarre ambition; a map that features American robber barons in their new lair in Salford, an Arabian dynasty who have established an outpost in the ruins of Ancoats and an X to mark the spot of the hidden treasure. Far to the southwest are the golden fields of Carrington. Once merely a wealthy commuter village in the Cheshire countryside, both clubs have built opulent training facilities here, both hidden at the end of long uninviting lanes. Many players are known to make their home around Carrington, living behind the controlled gates and hidden CCTV of their neo-Georgian mansions.

Prior to the 1990s football was one of the very few institutions in England that reversed the usual North–South polarities of power, wealth and influence. Between Tottenham's League title in 1961 and the beginning of the Premiership in 1992, only Arsenal of the London clubs managed any others (1971, 1989, and 1991) and none of them had won a European Cup. The relative sporting underperformance of the capital city is not uncommon in European football. Madrid and Spain aside, the most successful clubs are often from large provincial industrial cities: Milan not Rome, Amsterdam not the Hague, Munich and Marseilles rather than Berlin and Paris, Porto over Lisbon, and Glasgow over Edinburgh. Though sometimes smaller and often poorer, these cities were much more completely and rapidly industrialized than their older capitals; this provided them with a larger working-class constituency from which to draw players and crowds and local elites with fewer opportunities for acquiring cultural capital, public profile and political influence.[38] The extraordinary concentration of power in London where the worlds of finance, law, politics, art, broadcasting, newspapers, theater and publishing all coalesce, makes the competition for cultural capital even fiercer.

The sheer size of London, perhaps four times the population of metropolitan Manchester or Liverpool, made it virtually impossible for any one side to capture the identity of the city as a whole, diminishing the wider cultural weight of any particular club's history. Of course, all clubs in the capital claimed the mantle of a more restricted area. However, the tumultuous waves of migration in and out of London over the last few decades have rendered the geographical relationship between club, neighborhood, and fans more elastic. The suburbanization of London, which had been gathering pace since before the First World War, was further accelerated by the huge slum-clearance programs of the immediate postwar era. This decanting sent hundreds of thousands of North and East Londoners to the garden cities and new towns of Essex and the home counties, and has produced a map of fandom that tracks these migrations. West Ham draws part of its crowd from Basildon and Gravesend. Tottenham and Arsenal pull significant numbers from Ilford and Enfield, from Hemel Hempstead and Welwyn Garden City. Simultaneously, what was left of the low-cost and public housing of inner London has taken in successive generations of new migrants who, while not entirely absent from these teams' crowds, are woefully unrepresented.

In the last twenty years London has begun to make up these historic deficits and challenge the Liverpool–Manchester axis. The single most important factor was the arrival in the capital of the global super-rich: they have arrived in the North, too, but really only for the football. In London the super-rich came to escape domestic political pressures, to keep an eye on their money, to pay remarkably little tax and to enjoy a very comfortable life. In fact, life is so comfortable in London that the super-rich have come in numbers sufficient to distort the city's property market and building plans and add significantly to its ever sharper social polarities and economic inequalities.[39] Their impact on football has not been dissimilar. Of the six biggest clubs in the city, five have been at one point or another owned by very rich foreigners (Arsenal, Chelsea, Fulham, QPR, and West Ham) while Tottenham are now owned by Joe Lewis, our very own home-grown billionaire-in-tax-exile, who made a big chunk of his money speculating against the pound during the Exchange Rate Mechanism crisis of the early 1990s.

Inner West London, which, over the last twenty years has became one of the most ethnically diverse zones in the whole country, has over the same period had football-club owners from four different continents. Mohamed Al Fayed, the Egyptian businessman, was, as he will loudly tell anyone within earshot, the trailblazer, buying Fulham in 1996 when they languished in the Fourth Division. Al Fayed, who was then also the owner of the Paris Ritz Hotel, the House of Fraser department stores and the ultimate retail trophy Harrods, picked up the club for just £6 million. Never one for half measures, he announced that Fulham would become the "Manchester United of the South." Nearly £200 million in interest-free loans and ten managers later, Fulham have established themselves in the mid-reaches of the Premiership and made the final of the UEFA Europa League in 2007, but Manchester United they are not. For traditionalists, the trade-off for this level of success has been relatively slight. Craven Cottage, despite Al Fayed's grandiose streak, remains a small picturesque ground that retains its mock Tudor gables and the lone plane tree in one corner; the only concession to bad taste and kitsch has been the statue of Michael Jackson erected outside in 2011. Jeff Koons lite, it commemorated Al Fayed's friendship with a man who had no interest in Fulham or football and visited the club just once. Harrods had long gone to Qatar for over £2 billion when, at the age of eighty-four, Al Fayed bowed out of football. His final act in 2013 was to sell the club to Shahid Khan, an exuberantly moustachioed Pakistani-American billionaire, who added the club to a portfolio that already contained a car-parts empire and the NFL's Jacksonville Jaguars. Al Fayed stipulated that the Jackson statue would be staying. It was, of course, removed, but perhaps the old boy knew something. Fulham's form disintegrated and in 2014 they were relegated from the top division for the first time in thirteen years.

QPR, Fulham's near neighbors, have gone through a similar process albeit later and at a more maniacal and accelerated pace. Marooned in the lower divisions for much of the 1990s and 2000s, the club was constrained by the small size of Loftus Road and the limited wealth of its owners. To make the jump into the Premiership in the contemporary era, billionaires were required and they arrived in the eclectic shape of the owner of Formula 1, Bernie Ecclestone, the infamous Italian impresario, ghastly self-publicist and unabashed bully Flavio Briatore, and Lakshmi Mittal, the Indian steel tycoon whose wealth put him in the top ten of the global rich lists. Four years of swearing and shouting, ten managers and a lot of money later the project peaked with a single disastrous year in the Premiership.[40] Bernie Ecclestone, with remarkable commercial acumen, passed on the circus, sold his share and took his profits before the team had kicked a ball in the Premier League. The new owner was Malaysian businessman Tony Fernandes, founder and owner of Air Asia, South East Asia's leading budget airline. A self-confessed West Ham fan, he tried and failed to buy that club, but the itch for Premiership football was too strong, so he settled for QPR. It has been, for such a remarkably accomplished businessman, a chastening experience. Fernandes blew another £50 million of his fortune in a doomed attempt to stay up. "I've seen all the parts that make football quite—maybe immoral is a strong word, but they would sell their grandmother to do something."[41]

West Ham's dalliance with the super-rich was even less successful. For over fifteen years the club was owned and run by Terence Brown, a Barking-born accountant with interests in holiday villages on the south coast. In 2006 he sold the club to two Icelandic entrepreneurs, pocketing around £34 million in the process. Not a bad payday on a £2 million investment. The front man of the new operation was Eggert Magnusson, head of the Icelandic FA and a biscuit manufacturer; but the real power was Björgólfur Gudmundsson. Gudmundsson had made and lost his first fortune in connection with a fraud and embezzlement scandal in Icelandic shipping for which he was convicted in 1991. Undaunted he made another fortune in the post-Soviet brewing industry—not a sector known for its probity or gentility—before coming home and scooping up the former Bank of Iceland in 2006. A year later Iceland went into financial meltdown and the banks that Gudmundsson owed huge debts to called them in and found that West Ham was about his only tangible asset. The club has been bailed out of this disastrous situation by a combination of Birmingham City's ex-owners David Sullivan and David Gold and the public purse; they will soon be playing, at very reasonable rates, in the 2012 Olympic Park.[42] Whether subsidizing West Ham United will prove to be a sensible public investment remains to be seen. At a symbolic level it is certainly intriguing to see a bastion of the industrial East End, long and deeply embedded in the old cityscape of the docks and the slums, relocate to the well-appointed but aseptic island of redevelopment that is the new Stratford. The exchange of soul for space, of community for convenience, is one that many of West Ham's older fans, traveling from the new towns and overspill of Essex and Kent to their childhood team, will be familiar with.

At the beginning of the 1990s Tottenham had looked like the commercial pacemakers: the first to float on the Stock Exchange, a cheerleader for a breakaway league, innovators in banqueting, branding and merchandising, and owned by the self-consciously street-smart multimillionaire Alan Sugar. Yet somehow Spurs missed the boat and spent almost two decades out of both the top and bottom six, a position only partially remedied by the arrival of the infinitely richer Joe Lewis as owner. Whatever the ownership or management structure of the club, Spurs, like Everton and Liverpool, remained uncompetitive at the highest level primarily because it couldn't move and build a big enough new stadium in its tightly packed urban neighborhood. In the absence of success, Spurs has taken refuge in its multifaceted identities—authentic Londoners in one of the poorest areas of the inner city; the team of Jewish London; the last sanctuary of good taste in football, connoisseurs of style and swagger.

While these strategies provided some balm for their fans, their potency was diminished by the fact that nearly all these things could be said of the New Arsenal. As the main challenger to the dominance of Manchester United for the first decade of the Premiership, Arsenal hardly looked like inauthentic Londoners. Indeed, at a moment when London was undergoing its biggest architectural, demographic and political changes since the 1930s, Arsenal looked much more like the public face of the capital city: ambitious, successful, comfortably multicultural, consciously Europhile and above all winning things—the title in 1998 and 2003. The club was taken in this direction by an alliance of the old guard patricians—the Hill-Woods and Bracewell-Smiths—and the new boys and their money, David Dein and Danny Fiszman. Dein's presence was just one indicator of many that Arsenal had acquired as large a following among London's Jews as Tottenham. The appointment of Arsène Wenger as manager and his introduction of a cosmopolitan and stylish array of players, most notably Thierry Henry and Dennis Bergkamp, meant Arsenal were playing the kind of football that Spurs just talked about. Moreover, while Spurs remained penned into White Hart Lane, Arsenal took the plunge and built a new 60,000-seat stadium on an old gas works just a stone's throw from Highbury.

Rather than fleeing the urban, the Emirates embraces it. It is placed right in the heart of an incredibly dense inner-city area and, rather than turning its back on the city, it is open to it—easily accessible by public transport, it also offers pleasing walking routes from a whole series of economically, ethnically and architecturally diverse neighborhoods. The stadium itself is an unbroken ellipse, set in generous and well-appointed public space. Although transparently a commercial operation the Emirates has a restrained good taste about its signage, its sponsors and its advertising hoardings. Inside it offers a superb stage for the spectacular. It is light, airy, uncluttered, everywhere seems close to the action and through the undulating panels of glass in the top tier there are hints of London's skyline. Yet, though it has been entirely full for most of its games, the atmosphere, a few derby games aside, is a shadow of Highbury's, and nothing seems able to change that.[43] Nor has there been much success to match these aspirations. Arsenal went almost a decade without a trophy until their FA Cup win in 2014. Arsenal are well appointed, solvent, with a manageable mortgage and now a seemingly benign American billionaire owner—Stan Kroenke. Is this what it is to be one kind of Londoner now? Good job but a narrowing of prospects and ambition; a nice house despite the crippling property market, tasteful decor; just about afloat and keeping up appearances; holidays and flights of fancy in France and a nice quiet afternoon out at the stadium?

Perhaps the greatest lesson from Arsenal is that rational business practices, even when conducted with care and caution, simply do not work in the Premiership any more and the reason why they don't work any more is Chelsea. Sited on one of the most expensive pieces of real estate in English football, since the 1960s Chelsea has been the place where the glamour and the gutter meet: a showcase for those tiny zones of transgression in the English class system where the wealthy and the famous rub shoulders with the roughs, the toughs and the undesirables. By the late 1990s, under the splenetic and byzantine leadership of Ken Bates, Chelsea had made the basic moves that would allow them to survive in the Premiership—an enlarged all-seater stadium, architecturally undistinguished leisure and retail facilities, a foreign coach, a lot of foreign players, some nasty looking debts and a very big wage bill; but they were never going to be champions of England or Europe. Now they have been both; all fuelled by the money and ambitions of one man, Roman Abramovich. Chelsea, it seems, were a central element of his long-drawn-out exit strategy from Russia where he had made his money in the oil and aluminium industries during the chaotic Yeltsin era (though this is stretching the meaning of made).[44] Immediately catapulted to a global level of coverage, Chelsea have provided vital protection and visibility in Abramovich's struggle to extricate himself from the altogether less oligarch-friendly regime of Vladimir Putin. While other tycoons have lost their fortunes and their freedoms, Abramovich has quietly and carefully got away with it, though he continues to pay up when required for Russian national football-team coaches, Siberian provinces' social-service bills and expensive bids for the World Cup. This has still left plenty to spare for Chelsea whose level of spending in the transfer and wages market has given an already overheated football economy a blast of nitro-glycerine.

Chelsea's crowd is probably the richest in the country. The average income of season-ticket holders is almost double the national norm, though one suspects this is a statistical artefact of the astronomical wealth of one part of the crowd balanced by the still working-class and lower-middle-class wages at the other end of the scale; but neither their own nor their club's economic good fortune seems to make them any more comfortable. There is something peculiarly mean about Chelsea. They possess a spiteful arrogant metropolitan superiority that, though present at other London clubs, receives its fullest expression here. No crowd spends quite so much time and deploys such verbal dexterity in demeaning their opponents. Songs, usually reserved for just Liverpool fans, are sung against northern teams of all kinds; the smallness, drabness, and grimness of opponent's grounds and hometowns is always remarked upon. Personalized abuse of individual players is a speciality. Few crowds mine their own violent pasts so effectively or continue to celebrate their reputation for disorder so loudly. While the worst racist excesses that lasted well into the 1990s have been quieted, the torrent of anti-Semitic abuse levelled by email at then manager Avram Grant and the blind doting of many on captain and, according to the FA, racist John Terry suggest that that voice has not gone away.[45]

At the other end of the scale are the small clubs of London's suburban peripheries who have been in a permanent state of financial crisis and scuttle along in the bottom two divisions or worse. Yet still they have been able to attract reasonable crowds and investors looking for somewhere to play. In the east Leyton Orient were taken over by Barry Hearn, the supremo of world snooker and professional darts, who has for purely sentimental reasons kept the club afloat. In the far west of the city Brentford chairman Dan Tana was well connected enough in Hollywood to enlist Cameron Diaz as a fan; he was followed by Ron Noades who sold out to the Bees United, the fan trust, and Greg Dyke, the former BBC Director General and now FA Chairman, who kept the club just solvent enough before selling it to online betting millionaire Matthew Benham. There are well-developed plans for a new stadium near Kew Bridge. In the north, Barnet was owned by the celebrity ticket tout Stan Flashman and then by Tony Kleanthous, who made a fortune in the early days of the mobile-phone boom. Despite spending their time in and out of the Conference, unable to find a new stadium in a long bitter battle with their local authority and often known as Arsenal reserves (who shared their ground), there was still enough status and money in Barnet for Edgar Davids, the Dutch midfield star, to come and play half a season before taking on an equally short stint as manager.

Life on the fringe is at least free from the disappointment that follows unrealistic expectations, the bitterness of getting close enough to the Premiership to dream but remaining outside, or worse even, getting in only to be found out and immediately ejected. This is life for the medium-sized clubs of South London who in both economic and football terms have long been the poor relations to the north and west. Separated by the Thames from the main centers of wealth and power, and poorly served by the capital's main transport arteries, South London's clubs are now the squeezed middle of a polarizing society: too big to be content with the footballing anonymity of the suburbs, but too small to get a foothold at the top. They have struggled to keep up with their neighbors and in the process they have managed to send themselves into administration, confound, impoverish, or bankrupt a whole series of multimillionaires, and in the case of Wimbledon extinguish themselves altogether.

Charlton Athletic appeared to have learned the hard way after they went into administration in the 1980s and were forced to play away from their home ground, the Valley. Under chairman and owner Richard Murray they proved themselves the very model of a modern club in the ensuing years: prudent, family-friendly, and community oriented, getting back to financial health and the Valley before getting themselves up into the Premiership. Once there, the club's organization and hard work on and off the pitch looked like it might make them permanent fixtures. Then, in 2007, seduced like the rest of the country by the seemingly endless growth of the long boom, aspirations and expectations got completely out of hand. The club swirled with rumors that Alan Curbishley, whose fifteen years as manager had proved so spectacularly successful, had "taken them as far as he could." Curbishley was sacked and replaced by a string of disastrous appointments that saw Charlton drop two divisions in three years and head back into administration: so much for aspiration.[46]

Crystal Palace had a brief period of success under chairman Ron Noades in the late 1980s and early 1990s. However, Noades was never prepared to risk his Surrey-based golf-course empire on improving the team. By 1998, with the club hemorrhaging money, he was looking for a way out and when Mark Goldberg came along, he simply couldn't have asked for more. A young multimillionaire who had made a fortune in executive search and recruitment, Goldberg abandoned whatever financial astuteness he had accumulated when it came to his childhood love—Crystal Place. He bought the club from Noades at the gargantuan, inflated price of £30 million (£5 million of which Noades loaned him), only he didn't get the whole club, just the team and the debts. Noades had managed to keep Selhurst Park for himself and proceeded to charge his old club a hefty rent. Over the next eighteen months Goldberg's financial backers evaporated, his own fortune went the same way and in a tragic act of self-destruction, he installed Ron Noades as the team coach. Palace imploded and went into administration again. The club was rescued by another lifelong fan, Simon Jordan, a youthful mobile-phone shop tycoon who had sold his business for around £35 million. However, Jordan's combination of financial generosity, business acumen and chutzpah was not up to the task. Over a decade later his fortune has dwindled and Palace went back into administration in 2010.[47] One multimillionaire owner is simply not enough to compete. Palace were back in the Premiership three years later but only just, and it has required a consortium of four very wealthy fans who made hundreds of millions in banking, property and insurance to get them there.

At least Crystal Palace is still in existence. Their near neighbors and rivals Wimbledon flew higher, fell further and then disappeared altogether. In the late 1980s, under the ownership of Sam Hammam, Wimbledon crafted a place in English football history as the Crazy Gang: rough, tough, unpredictable and horrible to play against, the South Londoners barged their way into the top flight and to an FA Cup final victory over Liverpool in 1988. In 1991 the club was forced to abandon its Plough Lane home, which was some way from meeting the new stricter standards for all-seater grounds. While Wimbledon were playing at Palace's Selhurst Park and ostensibly looking for a new ground in South London, Hammam took control of the old ground, bought out a council lease that restricted its use to sporting events, and, thus unencumbered, sold it off to Safeway. He made a killing for himself and nothing for Wimbledon FC. Now truly groundless, Hammam tried to take the club to Dublin, Belfast, Cardiff, and Milton Keynes, but faced huge resistance from both fans and the football authorities. Crowds that had once been numbered in the tens of thousands dwindled to less than four figures by the time Wimbledon played their last games in south London. On the pitch Wimbledon were on a downward slope, too, and as the debts mounted Hammam sold out to two of Norway's richest industrialists for the astronomically foolish price of £30 million, handing over a club in decline and without a stadium. The final act of destruction came when the Football League decided that Wimbledon's official metropolitan area was actually in south Buckinghamshire; a geographical recalculation that allowed Wimbledon to up sticks and relocate to Milton Keynes where they promptly went bankrupt and were bought up by pop producer Pete Winkelman.

Football in London appears a complex but appropriate mixture for a city that has grown divided in an era of unregulated globalization; there are flights of fancy and priceless glamour for the central and increasingly global elites; in the far suburbs there are hobbies and charities for mere millionaires; and, between them, in a cycle of boom and bust, the irreconcilable aspirations and economic realities of the middling sides. London derbies are certainly bad tempered and foul mouthed, but there is barely a trace of the old firms and crews, with the fights and stand-offs that used to close down the main stations in the capital late on a Saturday afternoon. For some trace of that London one has to go to Millwall, always the poorest relation of South London football, and the most badly behaved. In 2002, after losing a promotion play-off to Birmingham City at home, over 600 fans engaged the police for an hour with a fusillade of bricks, paving stones, flares and fireworks.[48] In 2009 a Carling Cup game saw over 2,000 Millwall fans at West Ham, where the vicious and violent rivalries of the 1970s were rekindled. Sporadic trouble before the game created a charged atmosphere redoubled by the wild taunting of the Millwall fans when they went a goal up. West Ham's three goals were all accompanied by celebratory pitch invasions creating a state of hysterical mutual hostility and collective indifference to the police and stewards. After the match both sets of fans gathered outside and for over three hours fought each other and the police who stood between them.[49] Yet such is the draw of English football that Millwall have found their very own American billionaire. John G. Berylson, a Boston-based banker decked out in his regulation cream trench coat and pinstripes, bought the club in 2010. This banker had done a tour in Nam. "I wasn't scared. Members of my family from the War of Redcoats have found themselves in harm's way. An astounding number in my family have been killed doing the right things."[50] In the early twenty-first century very rich Americans no longer hanker for the conventional trophies of success—art, yachts and iconic architecture—or seek to buy their way into the genteel antiquity of the aristocracy through the purchase of titles and stately homes. Doing the right thing has changed. Instead, they long for the best seat in the directors' box of a rough old working-class football club, easily accessible to the City of London and which might have a shot at the Premiership. Berylson's closest brush with success was Millwall's appearance in the semifinals of the 2013 FA Cup. Jostling and pushing turned into a full-scale fist fight among a section of the Millwall crowd at Wembley. Remarkably, the fighting was left unattended for twenty minutes, before the police eventually waded in with batons, arresting over a dozen people for affray and possession of cocaine.[51] The team lost.

## III.

Since the formation of the Premiership only one club from outside the Manchester–London axis has won the title—Blackburn Rovers in 1995. Newcastle United and Everton are the only other sides beyond the core to have ever finished high enough in the Premiership to play in the Champions League. Yet in all the regions that make up English football's semiperiphery there remains an enduring intensity about football culture; these are places where a significant part of the population invests in the meanings and fates of their football clubs: "Approach Sunderland north along the A19 and you come to the offices of the *Sunderland Echo*. Mounted prominently near the roof is an image of a football with arms, legs, a face and cap . . . if Sunderland have won he smiles; if they have lost, he frowns; and if they have drawn his mouth remains a flat line."[52] As the wins, draws and losses turn into seasons and decades, the narratives that have emerged from this encounter between contemporary football's economics and these deep-rooted cultures have an uncanny knack of revealing wider economic and urban trends.

St. James' Park sits on a high moor in the center of Newcastle. It is the only major football stadium in the country that by aspect and architectural ambition truly commands the city it surveys. On match days, patterns of movement that start on the banks of the Tyne seem drawn upwards through the city's labyrinthine levels towards it. From the main approaches through the small Victorian streets, St. James' suddenly rears up to show its newest silver stands, capped by a huge curving glass roof and supported by the longest cantilevered structure in all Europe. This combination of bold civic urbanism and leading-edge architectural technology reaches back to Tyneside's short liaison with the idea that iconic modernist architecture was the route to regional growth and status. In the early 1960s T. Dan Smith and the Newcastle Labour Party had envisaged "A Brasilia in the North." With the city already in decline and its Victorian slums untouched, Smith planned to reimagine the region and rehouse his electoral constituency in a huge program of municipal towers and concrete complexes. Smith's own ambitions outgrew Tyneside before much of the architectural vision was realized as he moved on to jobs in Whitehall, PR and property development before his conviction and imprisonment for corruption in 1974.[53]

Smith's Thatcherite successor as "Mr. Newcastle," as both have been known, was Sir John Hall. Plain John Hall grew up in a mining family in the pit village of Easington. Grammar school allowed him to escape the mines and take a job as a surveyor for the National Coal Board—an interesting place from which to observe the immense tracts of land that the collapse of the coal industry was making available in the North East. Starting with private housing developments and new-style warehouse industrial estates on precisely this kind of brownfield site, Hall went on to make the bulk of his fortune developing the Metrocenter shopping complex in Gateshead. T. Dan Smith had imagined the future to be in high-rise public housing and municipal arts complexes; Hall knew it was in housing bubbles and shopping as entertainment. In 1992 he bought Newcastle United for £3 million from the patrician solicitor Gordon McKeag after a bruising public battle in which Hall played the regional politics card. Hall wasn't merely seeking to buy a football club, it was "The Geordie nation, that's what we are fighting for."[54] Hall liked football, but as that pitch made clear his ambition was always much greater. Newcastle United was going to be the emblem of not just the city, but the entire region. It wasn't going to be just a football club but, like the Spanish giants Barcelona and Real Madrid, a multisport club. Together, the progress of its sports teams was going to lead the North East out of its beleaguered economic situation and into an era of prosperity founded on property development, retail, culture, sport, and entertainment; perhaps even lead the region into an era of political autonomy. Hall, in a truly odd parallel, suggested that Geordies were "the last of the Mohicans," but more often than not it was the regional renaissance of Catalonia that was his favorite comparison. Above all, they weren't going to languish at the bottom of the Third Division when the glamour and the money were to be found at the top. Hall appointed Kevin Keegan as manager, spent some money on the squad, lit the fuse, and watched.

It was quite a show. Keegan's messianic fervor and irrepressible optimism, combined with an almost suicidal insistence on attacking play, made Newcastle roar: successive promotions, third in the Premiership on their first season back, and then in spring 1996 they looked like they had the better of Manchester United and the title in their grasp. But the pressure got to everyone and the team buckled. The crowd, now known in the media as the Toon Army, swelled and sang in numbers last seen at Newcastle when they still built ships on the Tyne. That was the point: with no ships to build or metal to work, the collective celebration of Newcastle United had become the single remaining coordinate of an older masculine working-class culture that had otherwise disappeared.[55] When Alan Shearer was signed for a record fee in 1996, it was a homecoming for the prodigal son. Asked at the press conference whether the money would spoil him, he replied on cue, "No, I'm a sheet metal worker's son." The crowd that had assembled at St. James,' in considerable numbers on a working day, went wild. On match day, in the Sky directors' box, they were spoilt for choice: zooming in on the bare wobbling bellies of the Gallowgate End, or framing a picture of a distraught, tearful young woman, the Geordie nation was caricatured as hopeless overwrought romantics and drunken buffoons.

Newcastle had Shearer but they appeared to have peaked; for another decade they failed to improve on the best of the Keegan years and were often much worse. The ice hockey, basketball, and rugby teams that Sir John had assembled at St. James' Park did not ignite much interest. Hall decided to relinquish the chairmanship of the club in 1997 after a successful stock-market flotation of Newcastle United plc made him millions of pounds on what, it transpired, was almost no real investment or financial largesse. The books revealed that the new stadium developments were overwhelmingly paid for by bond issues, hugely increased ticket prices and loans from Hall to the club at wincingly high interest rates.[56] His worst legacy though was his replacements, his son Douglas Hall and the other major shareholder Freddy Shepherd. Venality and incompetence aside, their specialism was contempt for the Newcastle fans who were making them rich. Secretly taped in conversation with a reporter from the *News of the World* in a Spanish lap-dancing bar, Hall and Shepherd laughed at the gullibility of the Toon Army whose appetite for replica shirts made them "mugs" and the women of Tyneside who were all "dogs."[57]

The final payday came in 2007 when both families sold Newcastle United to Mike Ashley—the billionaire sports-goods retailer from Buckinghamshire. All told they made £145 million out of their stewardship of the Geordie nation. It has been a curious encounter. Ashley really does appear to be an uncomplicated if publicity-shy tycoon. He had worked in retail since the age of sixteen, built up his company Sports Direct, never gave an interview to anyone about anything and then floated the company on the Stock Exchange, which brought him his billion. He liked football, a beer, and hanging out with his London mates, and now he wanted some fun. Newcastle United fitted the bill; after all, his key retail strategy had been the purchasing of ailing but valuable brands. Ashley not only bought out the Halls and Shepherds but he covered the club's now considerable debts and overdrafts (which he had failed to notice when buying the club in the first place), put up £100 million of interest-free loans for players and expected, one suspects, love and success. When he first appeared among the Newcastle fans at a game at Arsenal, and went out for a pint in the Bigg Market, he got a taste of the love, but there has been precious little love or success since. And for a man who is so publicity shy, there has been an awful lot of bad coverage. Much of this was of his own making. Ashley's senior management team was an overwhelmingly London-based operation, nicknamed the "Cockney mafia" by fans and the local press, and including such luminaries as Mayfair casino manager Derek Llambias and the archetypal London cheeky-chappy Dennis Wise. Their touch when dealing with the regional sensibilities of the club was ham-fisted, rehiring and then quickly sacking Kevin Keegan again as manager and threatening to sell the club to Dubai, while Ashley's proposal to sell the naming rights to St. James' Park raised the opprobrium in which he was held to new levels. The second coming of Alan Shearer, this time as manager in 2009, may have bought Ashley a little respite but it didn't save Newcastle from the drop and an embarrassing year in the Championship.

If both the Hall–Shepherd and the Ashley regimes at Newcastle exposed the limits of the club's footballing pretensions, the 2004 referendum on the creation of a North East assembly terminated the last lingering elements of the regional political project. The successful *No* campaign mobilized a whole series of practical arguments and tapped into a wider disenchantment with the idea of more politicians, but ultimately the distinct identities of the region's other cities, Sunderland, Hartlepool, Middlesbrough and Darlington, and their shared distaste for the presumptions of the "Geordie Nation," were more significant than either of those factors. The enduring bitterness of the games between Sunderland and Newcastle is testament to the street-level antipathy between the regional metropolis and the others. Middlesbrough and Hartlepool have opted for sporting and political independence, rejecting the charms of Tyneside and voting for independent mayors. In the case of Hartlepool they elected the football-club mascot—a monkey called H'Angus—as mayor of the city in 2002. In his human form, Stuart Drummond went on to be reelected twice with increased majorities and dignified his office by abandoning the monkey suit and writing a column in the club program. It is hard to know whether his victory was a function of how little Hartlepool had come to trust its sclerotic ruling Labour Party, or how much it loved its football team, but as protest votes go it sure beats backing the neofascist British National Party.

A measure of the relative decline of football in the Midlands is that the League Cup and short-term Premiership survival represented the summit of regional achievement over the last twenty years. There were two titles for Aston Villa in the 1990s and one for Leicester City at their turn-of-the-century peak, but Birmingham City's win over Arsenal in the 2011 League Cup final seems emblematic of these pyrrhic victories—signalling a run of form that would see them relegated—and in possession of a majority shareholder in Carson Yeung who has been jailed for six years by a Hong Kong court for money laundering. Cities that retained a foothold in the top flight—Nottingham, Derby, Coventry, and Leicester—have seen their clubs burn out, go bust and/or be bought up by foreign conglomerates. This fate has proved painful in the East Midlands where the magical era of Brian Clough—which saw Derby County win the League in 1973 and Nottingham Forest win the European Cup twice in 1979 and 1980—appears unrepeatable under the current regime of football economics. But the malaise is at its grimmest in Birmingham, which as

Britain's second city, with a greater metropolitan area that is home to almost three million people, should on all normal demographic and economic indicators have produced more successful football teams. It is a narrative that could speak to any number of aspects of the region's economic and cultural fortunes.

In part it is a problem of urban geography, as the West Midlands conurbation is actually deeply fragmented. West Bromwich, Wolverhampton, and Walsall all prefer their own teams and grim town centers to Birmingham.[58] More than this, in a recent report from Birmingham City Council, it was made clear that many of the city's nearly two hundred ethnic groups find themselves completely detached from any sense of civic belonging, while the white working class that once typified Brummies have been scattered to the peripheries and in some cases sit and sulk on the sidelines of a city they feel they no longer know.[59] It is an emotional cartography of anonymity, dislocation and the anodyne. Owen Hatherley, viewing the city in terms of its architecture and urbanity, argues that Birmingham is the "accidental quintessence of urban and suburban Englishness, encapsulated in its utter lack of typological regionality, originality or eccentricity."[60] This texture of feeling, an absence of local idiosyncrasy, encapsulates the city's two football clubs.

Aston Villa and Birmingham both lie close to the city's small commercial center—itself separated from the Victorian suburbs by ring roads and wastelands. Aston is to the north, but the most telling fact about the place is that Aston University is located nowhere nearby, but is actually based in the city center. Perhaps the most significant structure in the neighborhood is the intersection of the M6 and the A38, better known as Spaghetti Junction. Aston feels like a place you go through rather than stop off at. After the motorway Villa Park is easily the most notable civic building. It at least could claim some architectural merit. The stadium was built when the club were truly among the footballing elite and was an extravagant but brilliant creation of architect Archibald Leitch and club chairman Fred Ridner. The Trinity Road stand was the pair's masterpiece, built without any aesthetic concessions to the modernism that was creeping into many stadiums. Its entrance was a magnificent red-brick concoction, in the style of many late-Victorian grand civic buildings. It was embellished with balustrades, beautiful wrought iron lamps and

Dutch gables. Its flanking walls boasted superb tile mosaics made by Italian immigrants to Birmingham. In keeping with the architectural sensibilities of the city as a whole, the stand was demolished in 1994 and replaced by more executive boxes and a modern building of remarkable mediocrity. Birmingham City's St. Andrews, perhaps fortunately, never had this kind of architectural or decorative heritage to vandalize. Its comprehensive rebuilding in the early 1990s made it functional but truly unremarkable.

If Birmingham's football grounds offer little to differentiate the city or expose something of its soul, the structure of its fan culture is equally blank. There has never been any obvious religious or sociological cleavage separating Villa and Birmingham fans. Villa's heartland support was drawn from the industrial north-east of the city—Perry Barr, Witton, Erdington, Aston—and the huge northern public housing estates of the 1940s and 1950s like Kingstanding. Birmingham City drew fans from Sparkhill and Sparkbrook to the south-east of the city, and the 1960s estates on the south side like Chelmsley Wood. Overwhelmingly white working class in their makeup, both clubs' support was leavened by a sprinkling of newcomers and suburban middle-class fans. Among the richer suburbs Edgbaston and Solihull have been Blues territory, Sutton was Villa's, though again their support seems a matter of proximity rather than anything else. The Irish in Handsworth, Perry Barr, and Erdington supported Villa, but the Sparkhill Irish were Blues, as were much of Birmingham's small Jewish community concentrated in Moseley. Black and South Asian fans, despite their communities' increasing presence in all these neighborhoods, were thin on the ground anywhere until the last fifteen years, and most Asians have chosen Villa.

Villa have certainly been the more successful of the two clubs over the years and have been able to attract a following from outside of the city. As early as the late 1890s special fan trains were being run to the ground, and today Villa have support in small towns like Stourbridge and Kidderminster. It can even attract fans from as far away as Oxfordshire and Gloucester, as the preferences of David Cameron and Prince William attest. Even so the usual binary contrast of the glamour hunters versus the heart and soul, the commercialized versus the authentic, or the long shadow of older sectarian divisions between Catholics and Protestants that have animated the football rivalries of Glasgow, Liverpool, and Manchester, have no purchase in Birmingham. Owen Hatherley draws a further interesting contrast:

> Manchester, Liverpool, Glasgow . . . each of these cities, notwithstanding recent decline, exhibits the overwhelming pride and scale of a metropolis. Birmingham doesn't, and it doesn't ever seem to have given much of a toss. It keeps itself to itself. It is fundamentally modest . . . unlike its competitors it does not export disgruntled expats to London en masse. Yet it never quite manages to elevate this modesty into a virtue, so that numerous successive plans to beef it up since the 1950s managed to make it seem more provincial not less.[61]

It is not an architectural or cultural tableau against which epic football rivalries are likely to be unveiled. Thus the city's football culture swings between two internal poles. One, at which the rivalries are so unremarkable that they allow for a considerable body of fans who will go and see more than one team. The other, where the narcissism of small differences predominates and gives the relationship between the Villans and the Blues an occasionally unpleasant, violent dimension.[62]

The medium-sized cities of the East Midlands have fared just as badly. In 1991 Derby County were saved from the clutches of newspaper tycoon Robert Maxwell by Lionel Pickering, who had made tens of millions from a chain of free local newspapers in the era before the Internet killed them. Pickering spent a part of his fortune wisely and steered Derby to the Premiership in 1995. He and his fellow directors also funded the move to a new stadium in 1997. Pride Park was basically an amended version of Middlesbrough's Riverside Stadium, plonked in a distant and uninviting business park on the periphery of Derby. What appeared an act of enlightened patronage was not always well received. As one Derby County fan wrote of his early experience in the stadium, "I feel like a nice elderly relative has given me an expensive high tech Xmas present which is just not quite what I'd asked for."[63] Although attendances held up, the move coincided with a decline in form that saw the team relegated in 2002 and sent into administration. Two consortia of local business and football henchmen later, the club was still deep in debt and taken over by GSE, the investment vehicle of Andrew Appleby, the American owner of the Detroit Pistons NBA basketball franchise. They inherited a club mired in scandal. In 2009 Derby's chief executive and its finance director, as well as Murdo Mackay, previously director of football, and a Monaco-based lawyer David Lowe, were imprisoned for defrauding the club of nearly half a million pounds. The four had taken illegal payments from the club while it was drowning in oceanic levels of debt.[64]

Further south Coventry City's course has been catastrophic. In the early 1990s they were founding members of the Premiership. Chairman Bryan Richardson was proposing the club build a new multipurpose arena as early as 1997 as a way of keeping it financially stable, but the club couldn't raise the money. After Richardson's resignation, the new board, including local Labour MP Geoffrey Robinson, came up with a plan. As befits a close acolyte of former British prime minister Gordon Brown, Robinson's wheeze had all the characteristic peonage of a debt leveraged buyout. The local authority was going to build and own the new stadium, the Japanese electronics firm Ricoh were going to sponsor and name it, and by the time it came to move, Coventry City were going to leave Highfield Road for a stadium they didn't own, couldn't fill and frankly couldn't afford the rent on. It has proved a disaster. Significantly, on its own website the Ricoh Company hardly mentioned the football team and at one point made no mention of Coventry at all. The stadium's distance from the city center, the lack of public transport and its lamentable atmosphere combined to reduce attendance by over a third. There has yet to be a full house for football since Coventry left Highfield Road. In fact, under the ownership of an anonymous venture capitalist firm called SISU, the club and the city have ended up with no house at all. In 2008 SISU bought the struggling club and proceeded to overspend wildly, which resulted in Coventry being relegated to League One.[65] In early 2013 the club was put into administration by its owners. They stopped paying rent to Ricoh with whom they had been in bitter conflict for a number of years, and began to plan to play elsewhere. The administrators then sold the club effectively back to SISU through a different corporate entity, though one without all the debt they had incurred first time around. The "new owners" refused to negotiate with Ricoh and arranged for the club to groundshare with Northampton

Town, necessitating a seventy-mile round trip for Coventry's angry and disappointed fans.[66]

Leicester City appeared the epitome of the sensible mid-sized city team in the 1990s, with the epitome of sensible phlegmatic management, Martin O'Neill, in charge. Seven seasons in the Premiership, two League Cups and two European adventures gave Leicester the confidence and wherewithal to build a new stadium, sponsored by one of the city's growth industries—the Walkers potato chips empire. But as with Derby County, financial miscalculation, followed by the collapse of ITV Digital in 2002, exposed the club and sent it into administration. Marooned for over a decade in the Championship the club passed from its local owners to the Serbian-American, serial football-club chairman Milan Mandarić and from him to a consortium of Thai businesses headed by Vichai Raksriaksorn, owner of King Power, a duty-free shop company. They returned to the Premier League in 2014.

Nottingham Forest were an enclave of the old school and seemed equally cautious in their business dealings, but it did them little good either. They only became a limited company in 1982 and retained a highly regulated multiple-shareholder model of ownership that kept outsiders and takeovers at bay. However, relegation from the Premiership and the financial decline of the late 1990s saw them sell out to a consortium of businessmen whose only contribution was to sell on almost immediately to Nigel Doughty. The private equity merchant and Labour Party supporter held the fort and paid out millions of his own money, but could not get the club beyond the play-offs for the Premiership. His planned resignation in 2011 was cruelly preceded by his death at the age of fifty-four; his estate sold the club on to the Kuwaiti Al Hasawi family, who have promised much but so far mainly spent their time sacking managers.

Events on the other side of the River Trent at Notts County were a mixture of charity and farce.[67] First, the charity. The club had spent the 1990s in debt in the lower divisions going nowhere before going into administration in 2002. The club was saved, primarily, by Hayden Green, an unassuming season-ticket holder who happened to be a millionaire. He bought 49 percent of the club and the council's leasehold on the ground, which he then rented back to the club on very modest terms. He went on to sell his shares, mainly to the supporters' trust who became majority owners, but generously deferred his payment. Now for the farce. In 2009 an unknown company, Qadbank Investments and its subsidiary Munto Finance, both registered in the British Virgin Islands, appeared on the scene. All that was known of them was that the latter was based in Switzerland, managing money for the former's anonymous Middle Eastern clients. This mysterious corporation tried and failed to buy BMW, a Formula One team, and then, in a dizzying switch of focus, settled for Notts County. The supporters' trust, faced with the possibility of money and ambition that could take Notts County to the top, sold up. For a few short months of madness Meadow Lane was going to be the start of a new Gulf dynasty in English football. Sven-Göran Eriksson was recruited as director of football, Sol Campbell and other ex-Premiership players were signed. Five months later a winding-up order against the club's parent company had arrived from Britain's tax authorities, Sol Campbell had left the club after one sorry appearance, and Qadbank departed as they had arrived, swiftly and enigmatically.

Like the Midlands, the North West was home to half the founding members of the Football League, which made Preston its headquarters and where the League remains.[68] The leading clubs—Blackburn Rovers, Preston North End, Burnley, and Bolton Wanderers—hail from the mill towns of the Lancashire valleys, which boomed in the late nineteenth century and then watched the textile industry and most of the light engineering of the region vanish by the end of the twentieth. Blackpool, on the coast, served as the Sin City of Victorian Lancashire, but its tourist industries and dance halls declined, its core working-class constituency preferring package tours to the sun and low-cost flights to the European capitals of stag and hen-night parties. Despite the region's problems football has been relatively successful, with only Preston unable to spend a season or two (if usually on the never-never) in the Premiership. What has sustained these clubs is a combination of the enduring civic identities they embody and a generation of local boys made good, whose life in tax exile saw them struck down by the kind of sentimental melancholy that makes you want to spend a large slice of your pile on your football club. Jack Walker led the way at Blackburn Rovers, buying his home-town club in 1991 as the fortune he had amassed from a steel-stockholding business reached half a billion pounds. He rebuilt the hapless if lovable Ewood Park, bought a competitive team and they won the Premiership in 1995. Wigan Athletic, who were only formed in the late 1970s, joined the town's two rugby clubs as part of the Dave Whelan sports-goods and sports-teams empire at the JJB stadium. Preston North End and Bolton Wanderers have both been kept afloat by businessmen born locally but now living in tax exile in the Isle of Man: Trevor Hemmings at Preston and Eddie Davies at Bolton. Burnley's benefactor was Barry Kidder, who made a fortune on scratch-card and bingo inserts in newspapers and magazines. This was a business premised on the idea that even when you have thought you have won, you have actually lost; a pretty reasonable approximation to Burnley's experience of getting into the Premiership and then being swiftly and ignominiously booted out. Promotion in 2014 may let them do it all again.

The fans have been equally passionate if rather less sentimental. The 2009 game between Blackburn and Burnley was preceded by Burnley fans dressing Jack Walker's statue in a Burnley kit and comedy wig which was posted all over the Internet. This brought a graffiti reprisal as BRFC was sprayed all over Burnley's club shop. It was, to be fair, the first Cotton Mill derby for over thirty years. The reward for the wait was a gigantic police presence, an atmosphere close to martial law and a major turnout by police helicopters and dog units. This was enough to control the crowd at the game, but not enough to prevent massive fights (probably prearranged) breaking out between fans at two city-center locations in Blackburn. The rematch in 2010 was almost as bad, with widespread fighting inside and outside the stadium.[69]

Sentimentality has not been the only emotional driving force in football in Lancashire—ambition, ego and access to global branding have all been part of the motivational mix for these owners—but sentiment has been the most important. At Blackpool under the ownership of the Oyston family and at Blackburn, sold by the Jack Walker Trust to Indian poultry magnates, this became no longer the case. Blackburn's story is a familiar one. An older generation of provincial philanthropic and/or egomaniac multimillionaires find that the club, even in the Premiership, is an unending drain on their wealth. They then sell to a foreign dynasty or oligarch who think that the global coverage and cultural capital of being in the competition is worth blowing a hundred million pounds on. Blackburn got the Venkys, together with the now familiar mixture of over enthusiasm, naivety and chaotic authoritarianism that saw the club relegated in their first season as owners.[70]

Blackpool's tale is different. Once home to Stanley Matthews, there are few more sepia-tinted images of the old football culture than Matthews winning the FA Cup for Blackpool in 1953. Owen Oyston grew up in Blackpool, imbibed the club, and dabbled in acting before getting into real estate. In 1987 he sold his estate-agency business, just before the stock market crash. He then set about acquiring a distinctly northern media empire of papers, radio stations, early cable TV franchises, the Miss World contest and down-at-heel Blackpool FC just before the ground was turned into a supermarket. Oyston's ambitions in business, politics, and football were effectively terminated by his conviction and imprisonment for rape in 1996; although still a shareholder in the club, he has been reclusive since his release from prison. In his absence the club has been run by his son Karl, who seems to have none of the sentimental attachments or regional ambitions of his father. It's all been business, in particular selling half of the club to Latvia's richest man, Valeri Belokon, whose money paid for a successful charge at the Premiership. Like a wild weekend in Blackpool, a fabulous long bender, a spree you can't afford on the slots and the roulette tables of the seafront, the club spent a year in the Premiership playing outrageous attacking football and almost getting away with it. But the real magic act was elsewhere. In an act of unique Gradgrindian financial control, the Oystons managed to pay their team the same in the Premiership that they had in the Championship while revenues increased by over £40 million. The club made an unheard-of £32 million profit.[71] They were, of course, relegated.

Although often described as a region, the greater South East is a complex and varied landscape, composed of beleaguered zones of open country-side, peri-urban ribbons and suburbs, studded with urban settlements as varied as ancient Winchester and new-town Hemel Hempstead, proletarian Portsmouth and the gilded estates of Guildford. If anything gives the region shape it is, first, the shared reality of being the great dormitory hinterland of London, and secondly, that despite its many small zones of decline, the South East has been the main beneficiary of each recent wave of national economic growth and property-price bubbles. For cities that are large enough and distant enough from the magnetic pull of London this has opened the way to a measure of footballing success; for those too close or too poor to even get on the football ladder, there has been decline and bankruptcy.

On the M1 corridor, just thirty miles north of London, Watford have been the winners and Luton have been the losers. Both towns were transformed in the nineteenth century by the arrival of the railways, connecting them to London and the North, and both were home to a wide range of manufacturing industries. In the last twenty years Watford has held on to some of this and made itself home to a cluster of multinational headquarters. Luton, which was a center of hatmaking and car manufacture, has lost both and a lot more besides. Watford have never matched their second place in the old First Division achieved in the early 1980s under owner Elton John and manager Graham Taylor, but in the modern era there was at least one brief stay in the Premiership. Luton, by contrast, have plummeted. As recently as 1992 they were in the top flight. By 2009 they were bankrupt and in the Conference where they endured five purgatorial seasons before winning promotion back to the league in 2014. For the most part, Luton fans have not been a happy tribe. At a League Cup game with Watford in 2002 they started fights in the local pubs and continued the brawl on the pitch, which meant that the game was the only one not to observe a minute's silence for the victims of 9/11.[72]

Gillingham sits in the middle of the urban patchwork that is Kent's Medway Towns—a catchment area of at least a quarter of a million people that runs along the River Medway. However, despite a decade-long resurgence the club simply cannot fill its ground, much to the endless dismay of chairman Paul Scally, who saved the club from administration in 1995. Scally made his money in photocopiers and used some of it to keep Gillingham solvent. He even got them promoted to the Championship, but the draw of London football keeps the crowds down; a hidden migration made transparent when Charlton Athletic proposed a Valley express bus route to pick up their fans from Kent and whisk them through Gillingham to South East London.[73] Under such inopportune geographical and economic circumstances, nurturing local support would appear essential. Unfortunately, Scally, who has been through four wives and considerable personal tragedy, has been ruled by a quick-fire temper that saw him sack his best manager Tony Pulis in a fit of pique, publicly rage at the failure of supporters to turn up, and then cut the crowd even further by banning reporters from the local newspaper and the ex-chair of the supporters' trust from the ground for life. He is currently a resident of Dubai, which doesn't suggest that he is getting any nearer to the people of Gillingham.

Directly west of London, football can be found in three small cities. Oxford have fared the worst of the three, dropping out of the Football League in 2006 for four years, but they retain a fearsome following and a special place in the city's life. The Kassam Stadium is one of the few architectural and social poles that leans closer to the *banlieue* of the massive Blackbird Leys public housing estate than the spires of the University.[74] Swindon Town got a single season in the Premiership, but without an external injection of cash have recently been stuck in the lower divisions. By contrast Reading have made major gains. The town itself, rather than being drained by its nearness to London, is the endless beneficiary of jobs and investment spilling out from its already overdeveloped western peripheries. The club was bought up by local patrician John Madjeski, whose enormous business empire was founded on the *Thames Valley Trader* magazine. His ego and largesse were sufficient to build a new stadium—the Madjeski, obviously—and a team that could get to the Premiership. Reading, which had a considerable light industrial base before the contemporary avalanche of back offices and finance companies, also possessed a hard core of support who thankfully rechristened the stadium the Mad House. They stuck with the team during some very dicey periods in the lower divisions, and at the nadir of the club's fortunes protested over the team's dire performance. On appointed PANTS (Players Are Not Trying Sufficiently) days, they took to waving their underwear in the stands and throwing used underwear on the pitch.[75] It is precisely these kinds of eccentric acts that make provincial football clubs such important vectors of surreal provincial pride; yet the economics of football mean that the old alliance of these fan cultures with locally rooted philanthropists is no route to success. Madjeski may not be a billionaire but his wealth runs into hundreds of millions yet still this was not deemed sufficient. In 2012, he sold a majority stake in the club to Anton Zingarevich, the son of a Russian billionaire.

The two rising stars of the south coast present an interesting contrast. Brighton and Hove Albion lost their old Goldstone Stadium to the original "separate and sell to the supermarkets" merchant, the absentee club chairman Bill Archer. Over a decade of massive community and municipal mobilization, they managed to keep themselves solvent and eventually paved the way for a move into a beautifully appointed new stadium in Falmer, from which they are mounting a serious bid to make the Premiership.[76] Further along the coast Bournemouth are looking to short-cut the long, slow processes of community involvement and catapult themselves out of obscurity. This plan combined the dubious talents of the property developer and serial bankrupt Eddie Mitchell and the money of his new partner, a mysterious Russian petrochemical trader called Maxim Demin. Demin has kept a low profile, and underwritten the biggest wage bill in their league, but Mitchell, whose demeanor is as large and flashy as the grotesque millionaire mansions he builds on the Dorset Riviera, has not. After a home defeat to Chesterfield he walked onto the pitch shouting into a radio microphone and offering to take on the crowd. "The lad in the leather jacket whose eyes seem to be popping out of his head . . . why don't you jump over the fence and come and have a chat with me? Come on then, one to one?"[77] Such is the marriage of money, ambition, and authority in contemporary England.

While all the small cities in the South East have had a sufficiently industrial past to create a small football culture, they were either too small or too near to the gravitational pull of London to take off. The only urban areas sufficiently working-class and distinct from London to establish a regular presence in the Premiership were the neighboring port cities of Southampton and Portsmouth. Both have undergone almost forty years of slow decline as defense cuts and containerization drained their docks of employment. Both have considerably higher rates of violent crime than their already poor economic fortunes would suggest. Their dreary car- and retail-driven urbanism has left them bereft of civic space and identity and in this context the football clubs appear to have acquired greater significance in marking out the cities' differences.

Encounters in the first half of the twentieth century were rare, with Southampton invariably in a higher division, and the atmosphere was competitive but entirely friendly. The first recorded instance of trouble at games between the two dates from 1966, when Southampton beat Portsmouth at Fratton Park on their way to promotion to Division One. There was a pitch invasion by both sets of fans. Since then there has been a steady series of incidents at and around games, most notably the 1984 FA Cup tie that saw Southampton's black players vociferously abused. In the ensuing fighting, fifty-nine people were arrested amid widespread damage to the neighborhood.[78] In the last decade and a half their encounters have been sour, and there exists, online and in the stands, an elaborate vocabulary of mutual abuse and an atmosphere of bitter rivalry.

Quite where this mutual loathing has sprung from is unclear. The two have never been direct economic competitors as Portsmouth was always primarily a military port, Southampton a civilian one. It is widely claimed that Portsmouth's use of the term "Scum" to describe Southampton supporters derives from a strikebreaking incident in the 1930s by the Southampton Corporation Union Men—a claim that is entirely unverified. It is strange that contemporary civic tribalism should be justified through an invented working-class history of loyalty and betrayal. Owen Hatherley on his journey through the architectural wastelands of Southampton wondered if this desperately felt but invented opposition arose from the failure to properly regenerate the area back in the 1960s when the Wilson Labour government toyed with joining the two together as Solent City. "The Southampton–Portsmouth football rivalry began in the late 1960s at the exact point that Colin Buchanan was . . . developing a plan for the 'Southampton-Portsmouth Super City.' It could be argued that the Saints/Pompey hatred is what happened instead of this south coast megalopolis. Rather than a real modernity, we got dimwitted atavism."[79]

Southampton has, but for a few short if disastrous years in administration and the lower divisions, maintained its place in the Premiership. The club has never threatened to win anything or go anywhere—at least since 1976 and the miraculous FA Cup victory for the then second division side over Manchester United. But it has held on tenaciously and nurtured some remarkable home-grown talents—Theo Walcott, Gareth Bale, Alex Oxlade-Chamberlain and Luke Shaw—who have inevitably been sold on to the richer metropolitan clubs. Portsmouth went for broke, and under chairman Milan Mandarić won the FA Cup in 2008, the club's first title in almost six decades. The city council honored the players, the town turned out for the open-top bus tour, and manager Harry Redknapp was offered the freedom of the city. Mandarić took the opportunity to sell the club for a handsome profit. The buyer, who didn't pay much attention to the books, was Alexandre Gaydamak, son of the Russian-Israeli businessman Arcadi Gaydamak who had dabbled in arms dealing, football and Israeli politics. Although Gaydamak junior claimed it was all his own money, it was interesting to note that his father's own financial and legal difficulties were shortly followed by the son's funding for Portsmouth drying up. The club, whose finances were totally unsustainable, went into administration in 2009. At one point it looked like the club would be bought by a Dubai-based property entrepreneur, Sulaiman al-Fahimon, then it appeared to be in the hands of the mysterious Ali al-Faraj, a Saudi Arabian who never made a public appearance. In the meantime, in order to stay afloat, the club took out a loan with Portpin, a Hong Kong company owned by Balram Chainrai, who eventually took the club out of administration as a way of protecting his own investment. He then sold Portsmouth on to a Russian, Vladimir Antanov, and retained a secured debenture for a debt of £17 million on the club itself—guaranteeing Chainrai that money if it should be sold on. When Antonov's other businesses went into administration, so did Portsmouth—for a second time. In the final stretch it came down to a struggle between the Portsmouth Supporters' Trust and Chainrai and his allies, who were determined to extract every last penny out of the club before letting it and his debenture go. With the club now in the bottom tier of English professional football, just five years after winning the FA Cup, the matter was finally settled in the High Court in a way which allowed Portsmouth Supporters' Trust to take the club over.

Football in Yorkshire has taken on something of the air of film noir. The landscape of corrupt property developers, crooked police, and clannish elites painted in David Peace's *Red Riding Quartet* thrillers was not far off the mark as the results of the Hillsborough independent inquiry make quite clear.[80] More theatrically, there has been plenty of surface swagger and secret deals that have seen football clubs exchanged in the night. For a region that had previously traded on its miserliness, Yorkshire football has proved particularly prey to the temptations of overspending and over-indulging. Leeds United and Bradford City "lived the dream" and, in a pyrotechnic display of hubris, exploded. Geoffrey Richmond, flush from his sale of a cigarette-lighter company, took Bradford from the bottom of the League to the Premiership and right the way back down again, bank-rupting the club and himself. After miraculously surviving their first year in the Premiership on the final day of the season, what followed was in Richmond's own words "six weeks of madness": extravagant spending, increased borrowing, appallingly bad transfers, and the firing of manager Paul Jewell, who had been the real architect of the club's success. The team headed to the bottom of the table and stayed there until mercifully put out of their misery by relegation. Leeds under Peter Ridsdale did the same, only bigger and better and louder, spending their way frenetically as far as the semifinals of the Champions League in 2001, before it was time to pay up. There followed two relegations, administration and a decade outside the Premiership.

In the former Socialist Republic of Sheffield, it has been two decades of almost unbroken underachievement. It is, after all, a city that can claim the oldest football club in the country (Sheffield FC, formed in 1858) and if not among the founders of the Football League, two profes-sional clubs that have had a major presence in every era of the English game. Sheffield Wednesday and Sheffield United were both founder members of the Premier League. United were relegated in 1994 and have since spent only a single season back at the top while Wednesday have slid as far as the third tier, perpetually hamstrung by momentous and it seems irresolvable debts. In Yorkshire, the plot lines are all dark, the end-ings have all been messy as God's own county swings between two unpal-atable but seemingly inevitable conclusions: slow, grinding decline or self-destructive bids for the top.

## IV.

Sporting life, for most clubs on the football periphery, has always been grim. In the last twenty years the concentration of wealth and status at the sport's core has made small-town provincial football look, to some, even more hopeless and distant from the action than ever. For the most part the game has been played in undistinguished, patched-up or decaying stadiums, in front of small crowds drawn from tiny catchment areas and all on precarious finances. In an era of saturation TV and media coverage for the Premier League, many fans' affections and wallets have migrated to the metropolis. For three dozen teams at least there is nothing but relegation battles and lower-league obscurity to look forward to, seemingly forever.

And yet still the crowds come: over 20,000 a week to see Wolverhampton Wanderers labor in League 1, more than 15,000 at Portsmouth at the foot of the fourth tier, 6,000 at Bristol Rovers, where a full house of almost 11,000 watched them descend to the Conference. If you have ever spent a Saturday afternoon at Bristol Rovers, you will know that football must offer a lot more than a love of the art or the taste of victory. Stripped of the possibility of anything but scratching around at the bottom of the football world, the fan cultures and the collective pleasures and purposes of football in the periphery are even more clearly exposed as an exercise in an imagined community. This role has been magnified over the last twenty years as other facets of a distinct local identity have disappeared. Regional economic specialisms and rooted local firms have been lost to global competition or foreign mergers and acquisitions while distinctive local high streets have been homogenized by the bland facades of chain stores and franchises.

It is particularly unfortunate then that the football peripheries serve as hunting grounds for the most venal, deluded and dubious club owners and directors. While the small number of bigger cities attract local multimillionaires, even the odd billionaire now, the tiny financial worth and often large debts of lower league clubs make them easy pickings for the determined. In an era of booming property prices, these clubs' only real asset became their stadiums, or rather the land that their stadiums were inconveniently parked on. Using the model pioneered by Bill Archer at Brighton and Sam Hammam at Wimbledon, stadiums have been detached from their clubs by shifting the ownership of the ground to shell companies. Unscrupulous owners have then sought all manner of ways of moving, evicting and liquidating their own clubs in pursuit of a land deal with a mega-supermarket or a battery-farm house builder. Where that has failed they have chosen to charge extortionate rents. Alongside the asset strippers there have been starry-eyed romantics, louche chancers, money launderers and wide boys on the final explosive arc of a lifetime of egomania. The fate of fan campaigns to challenge and oust this rogues' gallery is testament to both the tenacity of provincial civil society and the weakness of its position.

The only clubs to have made it out of the football barrios and into the Premiership in the last two decades are from the medium-sized but isolated cities of the East of England: Hull City, Norwich City, and Ipswich Town. All three failed to maintain their Premiership status and then underwent huge financial crises when they were relegated; Hull and Ipswich were forced into financial administration and Norwich was only rescued at the last minute from a similar fate. For much of the twentieth century the East Anglian clubs quietly prospered through an alliance of patrician local businessmen with their small working-class populations drawn from the region's light industries, agricultural machinery and food-processing sectors. In the early 1990s Norwich City and Ipswich Town were in the Premiership, with City good enough to take third place in 1993. Both, however, crashed out of the League in 1995 before a sustained stay could be consolidated.

Norwich's short period of success was conducted under the regime of Robert Chase, a successful local builder who rescued the club in the mid-1980s and wisely, but rarely for a Chairman, focused on bricks and mortar rather than picking the team. Indeed, he was known to refer to the squad merely as "the football department." The declining performance of the football department eventually jeopardized the rest of Chase's ambitions as relegation was followed by a fire sale of players, combined with increasingly bizarre spending decisions including notoriously thick carpets for the executive zone, a huge fleet of club cars and a match-day radio station. A year-long campaign by fans to displace Chase culminated in a small-scale riot at Carrow Road in which windows were broken and police dogs used on the crowd.[81] Chase sold out and his shares eventually wound up in the hands of TV chef Delia Smith and her husband Michael Wynn Jones. The pair have capitalized on Norwich's rare mix of cathedral-city gentility and small-town proletarian roughness. On the one hand, Norwich houses Delia Smith's commercial operations and provide, without question, the best catering at any English football stadium, whether it be the match-day burgers or the Michelin-starred dinners available to platinum season-ticket holders. On the other hand, the snake pit at Carrow Road, where Norwich's loudest fans gather, is known to sing in praise of Tony Martin, the Norfolk farmer who shot a teenaged burglar in his house, with "There's only one Tony Martin"; more pointedly, to the tune of "London Bridge is Falling Down," "Tony Martin is our friend, he shoots gypos."[82] These two sides to the club were brilliantly consummated when an emotional, even overwrought Delia Smith took to the pitch at Carrow Road at halftime. Norwich had thrown away a two–nil lead against Manchester City during the depths of the club's relegation battle. In an attempt to rouse the somnolent crowd she shouted into the mic: "A message for the best football supporters in the world: we need a twelfth man here. Where are you? Where are you? Let's be 'avin' you! Come on!" It's not a tone that works in popular cookery and it didn't seem to work on the pitch either. Norwich went on to lose 3–2 in added time. It did however gain Smith a kudos with the stands that had previously eluded her.[83] Her regime has been tough enough to survive relegation and come back to the Premiership without going bust. It has also acquired an odd, ironic cachet for its gentility; a shift underwritten by the appointment of Stephen Fry as a director and football ambassador and broadcast by the club's association with Steve Coogan's provincial radio DJ alter ego—Alan Partridge.[84]

Ipswich, in their 1970s heyday, possessed an even more convivial chairman in the shape of John Cobbold, who remarked of his management style at the club, "The only crisis here is when we run out of white wine in the boardroom."[85] His successor was another old Etonian, the mayonnaise magnate David Sheepshanks, who offered himself as a model of patrician obligation and financial prudence, steering the club back to the Premiership in 2000 without breaking the bank: "So much of football is about short term glory which leads so often to boom and bust. We're not about that."[86] And then they were. Ipswich got into European competition, spent a lot of money on new signings and were promptly relegated with a ballooning debt and an unsustainable wage bill that ended in a period of financial administration. Financial salvation came in the form of Marcus Evans, a little known but fantastically wealthy businessman, whose hospitality and conference group made a fortune from putting on global networking events for military and professional elites. He has, however, been reluctant to part with the kind of money that could get Ipswich back in the top flight and has in recent years displayed an increasingly paranoid attitude to criticism; paranoid enough for the club to deploy plain clothes police officers to intimidate and move on a fanzine seller (with his kids) from outside Portman Road.[87]

Until Hull were promoted in 2008, the city would self-deprecatingly boast that it was the largest in England to have never experienced top-flight football, a fate often attributed to the city's devotion to rugby league, for which it could sustain two teams, but in reality not unconnected to the caliber of the club's owners over the years. In the mid-1990s it was in the hands of Christopher Needler who had inherited the shares from his father. He pursued a strategy of destructive stasis: unwilling to invest in the side but at the same time emotionally unable to let the club pass out of family hands. In the meantime, his right-hand man, the chairman Martin Fish, managed to alienate a large section of support. The charge sheet included housing a huge contingent of Bradford away fans in the home stand and displacing local supporters; selling off a cherished club name plate without telling anyone; and taking the club to the edge of bankruptcy.[88]

Needler finally gave in, selling up to the unlikely figure of David Lloyd, a minor tennis professional turned aspirational health-club magnate. He at least had a plan, which was to combine the football and rugby league club, create what he called "an American leisure city" and, of course, to sell off Boothberry Park to a supermarket. Hull did not so much respond badly to Lloyd's charms as to barely respond at all. So it was with considerable relief that he found someone with an even wilder vision for the unlucky fans of Hull City. Enter Steven Hinchcliffe, a man described as "a living, breathing Mercedes-driving advert for a fit and proper person test."[89] Beggars can't be choosers and Hull's fans embraced the flamboyant Hinchcliffe. The city council, which uniquely in England had built and run its own telecoms company, sold up for a couple of hundred million and decided to invest in a new stadium for the local sports teams. With a significant population, and a new stadium on the way, Hinchcliffe was dreaming of the Premiership. In the end he went to prison and Hull went nowhere. His crazily irrational retail conglomerate FACIA went under in 1997. In 2001 he was sentenced to five years for corruption and bribery, and the football club went into administration. Initially rescued by ex-Leeds directors who had fled the wreckage at Elland Road, the club finally acquired owners with deep enough pockets and reckless enough instincts to get them into the Premiership and stay there for another season before the inevitable relegation and disintegration in 2010. A second period of administration followed, with the club now possessing outstanding debts twenty times larger than those accumulated just nine years beforehand. The promise of Premiership football though remains alluring, able to scratch the itch of even the most sober entrepreneur. Hull and its debts passed into the hands of the Egyptian-born industrialist Assem Allam, who over thirty years had quietly amassed a fortune in Hull with his diesel-engine company. Having accumulated something in the region of £150 million, he and his family put fifty million into the club and were rewarded with promotion back to the Premier League in 2013. Hull City may have been good enough for the Premiership, but for Allam not good enough for the global market. He changed the team's name to Hull City Tigers, and would have preferred to drop the City entirely. "Hull City is irrelevant," he said. "My dislike for the word 'City' is because it is common . . . It is about identity. City is a lousy identity."[90] For now at least this ambition was frustrated: a widely supported fans' campaign against the name change fought Allam all the way to the FA Council and won.

The smaller towns of the region did not fare as well, as one by one they were expelled from the Football League and cast out into the Conference: Boston in 2007, Mansfield on the outer edge of eastern Nottinghamshire in 2008, Grimsby in 2010, and Lincoln in 2011. While all these demotions were accompanied by a degree of turmoil, incompetence and bad luck none of them took on the pantomime quality of Mansfield Town's collapse. It is hard to know whether owner and chairman Keith Haslam should be cast as one of the Ugly Sisters, the Wicked Sorcerer, or Ali Baba and his Forty Thieves. Perhaps it is best to imagine him playing all three, especially the latter. In his twelve years in charge of Mansfield, Haslam received over half a million pounds in interest-free loans from the club, got another half a million from land he sold to the club for a youth academy that was never built and topped it all off with a generous salary of £66,000 a year. What is all the more remarkable, magical even, is that he managed to extract such considerable booty at a time when the club was consistently losing money and running on a pitifully small budget.

Haslam's level of contempt for Mansfield appeared to peak when, in 2008, it was announced that he was selling out to John Batchelor, a name guaranteed to put the fear of God into any football club. Batchelor had made a name for himself as an unsuccessful motor-racing entrepreneur and even more unsuccessful director of York City Football Club. His short but turbulent rule at York was eccentric. In an effort to crack the American market, he changed the team's name to York City Soccer Club. He signed a contract, though it was never fulfilled, to develop the club's stadium with Persimmon Homes, and then helped himself to some very large loans and dividends from the club coffers before bailing out, leaving them to descend into the Conference under the ownership of the supporters' trust. Batchelor's master stroke at Mansfield was to announce his bid and suggest that the club change its name to Harchester United, the fictional star of Sky's long-running soap opera *Dream Team*: "Harchester is more promotable than Mansfield. That's not any form of insult to Mansfield at all because it's a club with a long tradition, but it's just a fact. One club has been on the television for ten years and the other one hasn't."[91] He really wasn't kidding. Not only had Batchelor already changed York City's name, but in pursuit of sponsorship for his defunct motor-racing team he had changed his own name to John BandQ. Even Haslam didn't quite have the front to sell up to Batchelor, whose access to finance was in any case pretty unclear. Instead, Haslam awarded himself a £2.36 million dividend in 2008, and immediately used a chunk of the money to buy Mansfield's ground.[92] A few months later, Mansfield were being relegated from the Football League on the last day of the season. Home fans decided to storm the directors' box and a local businessman, who was in talks to buy the club from Haslam, took the opportunity to punch him in the face. Mansfield were homeless, relegated, broke, and paying Haslam £120,000 a year to play in their old stadium.

What makes the Mansfield story so grim is that Haslam never seems to have demonstrated a scintilla of love or romance, no flights of fantasy to blur the harsh edges of his greed. For this one must go west to Carlisle United and Michael Knighton. Knighton got a schoolboy trial at Everton and trained at Coventry City before an injury terminated his short career. Dreams curtailed, he went on to make enough money from property development and running a private preparatory school in Huddersfield to allow himself the luxury of tax exile in the Isle of Man. During the summer of 1989, while most of the country was absorbing the dreadful impact of Hillsborough and the seemingly unstoppable decline of English football, Knighton could see an upside: a world in which commercial chutzpah, intelligent marketing and the new television technologies would allow football clubs to exploit their readymade and well-known brands and turn them into multimillion-dollar businesses. Mobilizing some of his business contacts and a whacking great overdraft from the Bank of Scotland, Knighton charmed his way into the offices of Manchester United chairman Martin Edwards. Once there he painted a bold picture of the football world that was coming—above all the financial potential of the new television transmission systems that were just emerging—and offered Edwards £20 million for his controlling share in Manchester United. Edwards was keen to sell and the move was announced at a United home game. Knighton, beside himself with excitement, got hold of a training kit and went out onto the field to meet the crowd. They watched him do a little impromptu keepy-uppy before he gently volleyed three balls into the net. Edwards and the rest of the board suddenly got very queasy about who they were about to hand the club over to. Knighton was persuaded to drop the bid, and allowed to play director for three years.[93] Knighton was never going to be the boss at United and that is what he needed to be. He left the club to be the boss at Carlisle United at precisely the moment that Manchester United began its ascent to dominance over the English game with a strategy remarkably similar to the one he had first envisaged in 1989.

For a few glorious years Carlisle United provided the perfect vehicle for Knighton's brilliant capacity for self-promotion, raging ambition and unquenchable bonhomie. The club came cheap, just £75,000, it had no local competition and it owned plenty of empty land with all sorts of development potential. Knighton promised that they would be in the

Premiership within a decade. Promotion to the third tier duly followed in 1995, and in 1997 the Auto Windscreens Shield came to Cumbria. Then the momentum faltered and relegation followed, with Knighton himself now acting as coach. Still, if there wasn't success, there was melodrama. A year later the club was saved from a second successive relegation and the drop from the Football League in the final seconds of the final game by the last touch of the match—an equalizer from the foot of the goalkeeper Jimmy Glass. Backstage, and for some time now, the Knighton project had been crumbling. His prep school went bust in 1997, but not before the school had paid what was left in the bank to the Knighton family companies before the tax authorities or anyone else could claim their due. Later, in mitigation, Knighton admitted that the money was primarily used for Carlisle United. No longer an invulnerable entrepreneur, his other public persona as a romantic visionary took a knock when a local newspaper reporter revealed that Knighton had said that his inner drive came from following the advice of aliens who had come to see him in a UFO during his childhood. The money had gone; in 2002 Carlisle went into administration and Michael Knighton went out the door. The enduring symbol of Knighton's reign was the New East Stand; the only significant piece of rebuilding he managed. A reasonable if unexceptional structure, the stand is also considerably longer than the pitch that it faces. Consequently, much of its seating is marooned in one corner, waiting for the pitch move that never happened.

Carlisle United were destroyed by incompetence combined with vaulting ambition, whereas Chester City and Wrexham were plain robbed. In 1996 Mark Guterman took control at Chester City, his demeanor best characterized by a long-suffering Chester fan who wrote that Guterman was "generally described as a Manchester-based property dealer, though that could mean anything. Mark, a portly, bespectacled chap in his late thirties, drives an Aston Martin and likes to be seen at away games with glamorous female company."[94] At home games he was besieged by angry creditors as the kit washer withheld shirts that had not been paid for, players went without wages and the club was put into administration. A measure of how low Guterman's standing had fallen was that fans welcomed a bid from Terry Smith, an entirely unknown and relatively unsuccessful American football player and coach. Guterman could not believe his luck and scuttled off, leaving Smith in charge. Almost his first act was to fire the manager, take over himself and try out a few tricks from the NFL: captains for defense, midfield, and offense, and the Lord's Prayer in the dressing room.[95] It was new, it was different, but it didn't work. Smith took Chester to the bottom of the League, a position that, despite his resignation as coach, they never escaped from. In his first season in charge Smith had managed to take Chester out of the League for the first time in sixty-three years. The following season in the Conference ended with a widespread protest against Smith as fans paraded a Chester City coffin around the town center; at the final whistle of the last game club stewards threw their high-vis jackets on the pitch and unfurled a "Smith Out" banner. Chester's death knell was the arrival of Steven Vaughan, known as a Liverpool boxing promoter and then chairman of non-League Barrow FC.

In an illuminating turn of events, Barrow were drawn against Chester in the fourth qualifying round of the FA Cup just a month after Vaughan had taken over the Cheshire club. To avoid any conflict of interest, Vaughan sold his Barrow shares for a song to a painter and decorator from the town called Bobby Brown who sold them back to Vaughan after the game. Vaughan then sold his shares on, but tried to hold onto Barrow's ground until forced to return it by court order. If that style of operation wasn't enough to worry Chester City there was plenty of other information coming out on the Barrow Internet sites. Vaughan had certainly put money into the club and built a new stand, but he was never entirely candid about where the money had come from. The details are still unclear but in his autobiography the leading member of a Liverpool cocaine-smuggling syndicate, Curtis Warren, reports flying over Barrow's Holker Street ground and remarking, "I own that."[96]

For a couple of years Vaughan appeared to be bankrolling the side and Chester were promoted back up into the League in 2007. Despite this kind of success many remained suspicious of the chairman, an attitude confirmed by the club's decision to hold a minute's silence in remembrance of a significant benefactor who had recently passed away. Colin Smith, it turned out, was the number two in Curtis Warren's cocaine operation and had been gunned down by his erstwhile Colombian trading partners. Chester went straight back down the following year, and then into administration as its gigantic debts became palpable. By this time Vaughan himself had been found guilty of conducting a half-million-pound sales tax fraud at his Widnes rugby operation, a carousel scam in which sales tax is reclaimed on non-existent goods and false purchases.[97] With this Steven Vaughan had the honor of being the first person to fail the FA's new fit and proper person test for football club directors. Vaughan resigned from the board but the club remained in the hands of family and cronies. Chester fans responded by organizing a boycott of their own club, and attendance collapsed from a dismal 2,000 to a pitiful five hundred. Then a home game against Eastbourne was abandoned after an on-pitch protest by fans. In early 2010 the players, who hadn't been paid for months, snapped and refused to board the team bus heading for Forest Green; the following week the police refused to work the home game against Wrexham as they hadn't been paid either. The tax authorities delivered the *coup de grâce* and wound up Chester City, who were expelled from the Conference just before they were legally dissolved altogether. Steven Vaughan was last heard of punching a police officer in Liverpool and moving his passion for boxing and football to Malta.[98]

In 2002 Wrexham were bought by our old friend from Chester, Mark Guterman, now working with property developer Alex Hamilton. Guterman's arrival, given his disastrous tenure with the club's arch rivals, was treated with considerable suspicion. He told the fans to "judge him on the signings," and so they should have; particularly the agreement signed by the two owners where their plan for the club was spelled out with quite remarkable and refreshing candor: "The management of Wrexham Football Club is to be on an equal control basis with the main and sole objective to realize the maximum gain from the property assets of the Football Club for the benefit of Alex Hamilton and Mark Guterman."[99] True to their word, the pair purchased the freehold of the Racecourse Ground and passed it immediately to Crucialmove, a company owned by Hamilton. Another £300,000 was paid, in effect to themselves, to cancel the football club's 125-year lease on the ground and a new clause was inserted into the deal which allowed Wrexham's owners to expel their own club from their own ground on twelve months' notice. You can see where this is heading. Hamilton duly gave his own football team the order to quit in autumn 2004. However, the plan to get B&Q on the site faltered and the disastrous finances of the club saw it put into the hands of administrators who had one look at the paperwork and took Guterman and Hamilton to court on the not unreasonable grounds that they had not acted in the best interests of the company but engaged in the naked misuse of their positions. The ground was returned, but the damage was done and under new ownership Wrexham acquired another great pile of debt. Almost a decade later, the club has been through a raft of local businessmen as owners, a period of administration and in 2008 relegation to the Conference after eighty-seven years in the League. As with so many institutions that went to pieces that year, they have been saved by public effort and the public sector as the supporters' trust is now in charge and the Racecourse Ground was secured when the benign local university bought the freehold.

If the Welsh borders have proved to be harsh football badlands, a cursed earth that attracts the malevolent, then the South West is more a misty and perplexing bog, where progress easily falters, ambition sinks into the quicksand and normal logic breaks down. Bristol, depending on how you measure its population, is around the sixth or seventh largest city in England. It is well connected to the rest of the country and historically possessed a substantial industrial economy and a significant working-class population. Yet, despite all these basic preconditions of football success of a moderate kind, there has been none.[100] Bristol City, located in the south of the city, managed a run of five seasons in the top division in the Edwardian era but have only returned for a single spell between 1976 and 1980. Bristol Rovers, who have made their homes in the east and north of the city, have spent nearly their entire existence bouncing between the second and third levels of the League, but for their sojourns at the bottom.

The notion that the city is too small for two clubs and might benefit from a fusion has never gained any support from anyone—a fact underlined by the sour antipathy and occasional violence that the clubs' rare derby games have elicited. Indeed, as Bristol's distance from the new football heartlands appeared ever greater, the significance and volatility of the derby increased: in 1997 a last-minute Rovers equalizer at Ashton Gate triggered a pitch invasion by 400 City fans and widespread fighting; in 2004 the postmatch scuffling that followed an entirely unimportant Johnstone's Paint Trophy tie at Rovers' Memorial Ground required the deployment of helicopters, riot police and dogs in the genteel streets of Horfield and Bishopston.[101]

The competing attractions of rugby and cricket in the city are often offered as an alternative explanation for the lack of footballing success, but while both have drawn significant support from Bristol's more well-heeled citizens, neither Bristol Rugby Club nor Gloucestershire County Cricket Club is a force to be reckoned with in their own sport, and neither draws the kinds of crowd or fervor that could seriously undermine the football teams. Rather the clue to Bristol's footballing underperformance is in its urban landscape and geography. The center of Bristol, once home to the biggest port outside London, has lost almost every last trace of its functioning maritime and industrial base. The entire operation was moved to the coastal container port of Avonmouth, six miles down river. Similarly, the tobacco factories and warehouses in the working-class neighborhoods of South Bristol have closed, and many of the people who lived there and in older housing across the center of the city were long shipped out to the peripheral estates of Hengrove and Withywood in the south. The aerospace and engineering industries on the north side of the city and the old mining zones to the east are administratively not even part of the city but lie in South Gloucestershire and North Somerset respectively. Bristol, whether by intention or not, has perhaps more thoroughly than any other city cleared its inner urban neighborhoods of football's traditional working-class social base.[102] The fate of Bristol Rovers typifies this.

In the postwar era, the grubby but much loved Eastville Stadium, close to the city center, was home, though Rovers only rented the ground and had to share it with greyhound racing, speedway and a Sunday market. In 1986 the place caught fire and Rovers had to move out. A temporary departure became permanent when Eastville was pulled down and replaced by a gargantuan Tesco and an even larger IKEA. Nearly two decades in the wilderness followed. Rovers played their home games at Twerton Park in Bath while the city council repulsed all attempts to find a site for a new ground close to their old home. The normally apolitical Rovers supporters actually contested the 1994 local elections as the Bristol Party in an effort to highlight the club's problems. Rovers found temporary accommodation at the rugby club's Memorial Ground, and had the good fortune to be flush when their landlords went broke, enabling them to buy the ground. Unable to get planning permission for a stadium plus student housing development, they now propose to move out to the northern ring road, which is outside of Bristol proper but closer to the working-class fringes of Filton and Kingswood. This time their exit to the peripheries was meant to be on their own terms and they are going to leave a poison pill for the comfortable and mildly bohemian neighborhoods of North Bristol. Rovers are selling out to Sainsbury's, who plan to build a vampiric supermarket at the head of what has hitherto been Bristol's largest and most successful independent shopping street.[103] A series of legal challenges failed to stop them but the incompetence of the Rovers board and management just might. After two brushes with relegation, Rovers finally went all the way and on the final day of the 2014 season dropped out of the Football League for the first time. Whether a team mired in the Conference will be able to sustain the grandiose economic projections for the new Filton stadium remains to be seen.

Bristol City, always the larger of the two clubs, has remained at Ashton Gate for the whole of its existence and like Rovers has suffered from the exodus of the working class from the old terraces of Ashton, Bedminster, and Southville. However, since the early 1990s it has had a seriously rich owner: Steve Lansdown, who co-founded the investment brokerage Hargreaves Lansdown in 1980. By 2012, as he took up tax exile in Guernsey, Landsdown was reported to be worth around half a billion pounds. The problem then has not been lack of funds, the problem has been one that has afflicted the whole of Bristol—the seeming impossibility of getting major infrastructural development built. Football is just one planning bottleneck. Bristol, despite its reputation for musical innovation, cannot organize itself to build a reasonably sized arena for popular acts and is often missed off national tours. Its public-transport networks are laughable and in an era of iconic buildings it has managed to build none. Indeed, the entire cityscape suggests a place that has been bypassed by much of the best (and worst) of modern architecture. It lends the city an undeniable charm but it comes at a price, and not merely for its football clubs.

Beyond Bristol the star performer of the region is Somerset's only club, Yeovil Town, who, unusually for a region rich with New Age unreason and mystic pretensions, traded quirky romance for utilitarian reality. They left old Huish Park—the ground with the largest pitch incline of any in lower league football—and opted for something flatter: a proper pitch, stable management and careful finances. This has yielded results and since the move the club has risen into the Football League and in 2013 was promoted to the Championship, if only for a season.

Exeter City, by contrast, embraced the supernatural, with disastrous results. In 2002 John Russell and Mike Lewis bought the club on money secured against their apparently considerable business assets. In actual fact they had no money and no assets, and a track record of disastrous involvements with football clubs, Russell for three months at Swansea and Lewis at Scarborough where he had overseen their relegation to the Conference. Their secret weapon was to enlist an illusionist of even greater capacities than they. Uri Geller, the Israeli-born celebrity magician—though he was a self-proclaimed possessor of paranormal powers—had made his big break in the 1970s with a global tour of spoon-bending on the chat shows of the western world. Settled in the West Country, he claimed that his son's love for Exeter City had brought the club to his attention and he to the attention of Russell and Lewis. Appointed co-chairman, Uri gave the headline writers everything they wanted: "At no point will I use any paranormal powers to influence performances or results on the pitch." This was actually just as well. His only previous attempt to influence an Exeter City performance, back in 1997, saw him put crystals around the goalposts and the team go down to a 5–1 defeat.[104]

Geller's real worth was his remarkable capacity for diverting everyone's attention away from exactly where it should have been. For the next two years Russell and Lewis ransacked Exeter, paying themselves gigantic consultancy fees, diverting money for an academy to themselves, keeping gate money in the boots of their cars, bouncing cheques, and juggling debts. Meanwhile Geller had arranged for the magician David Blaine, singer Patti Boulaye, and the extraterrestrial Michael Jackson to come down to Exeter City for a fundraising gig that would split the proceeds between the club and local children's hospitals. Jackson entered the stadium twirling his umbrella from the back of an open-top vintage car, looking alarmingly like Willie Wonka with a perm. Blaine entertained the stands with a few card tricks, and Boulaye belted out some gospel.

Then Jackson took the stand and was soon freestyling: "We come here to support children with AIDS . . . and help the people of Africa find a solution against the spread of AIDS . . . Everyone hold hands . . . Tell them you love them . . . I see Israel, I see Spain . . ." The crowd cheered, the buckets were filled with change, and no one had the faintest idea what he was on. No matter, Jackson and Blaine were made honorary directors of the club and they were soon joined by David Prowse, the weightlifter-turned-actor who had played, if not voiced, Darth Vader in *Star Wars*. Geller, ever mysterious, explained Prowse's new-found love for the team, "There's something about Exeter City that's inexplicable . . . it has a positive power."[105] And he thought the influence might be reciprocated, "There is a psychological value . . . you can imagine when the players of an opposition team go out knowing that Darth Vader is watching them." Unfortunately the impact was minimal and the club was relegated to the Conference in 2003 before being sent swiftly into administration with outstanding debts of over £4 million. Russell and Lewis were arrested and convicted on a variety of embezzlement and fraud charges. Uri Geller moved on to the reality show *I'm a Celebrity . . . Get Me Out of Here!*

Another fifty miles past Exeter, the most westerly club in the Football League, Plymouth Argyle had been going through a good period, playing for five successive seasons (2003–8) in the Championship. What was needed, of course, was a dose of investment and entrepreneurial vim, and the usual plan to get into the Premiership. In 2008 this good news arrived in the shape of Sir Roy Gardner and Keith Todd, property developers who took a joint 13 percent stake. Together with the low-profile Yasuaki Kagami, a Japanese investor with a Tokyo office, interests in toy manufacturing and 38 percent of the club, they formed a majority.[106] It looked like another shady little property scam was in the making as the three formed a new company—Mastpoint—which took over ownership of Home Park and put most of their energy into lobbying for Plymouth to be an aspirant host city in England's doomed 2018 World Cup bid. Great vision but disastrous execution: the team were relegated and the club threatened with bankruptcy when the tax authorities issued a winding-up order for the three-quarters of a million pounds it was owed. At this point the wage bill was an astronomical 87 percent of the club's turnover—the kind of budgeting that makes the Premiership look parsimonious; total debt had risen to £13 million. Administration mercifully came in 2011, forcing Gardner out, but the ten-point deduction issued by the Football League guaranteed a second relegation, to the fourth level.

How many examples does one need to demonstrate that the combination of lower-league football clubs with the egomania and self-regard of property developers is a recipe for financial disaster and collective impoverishment? The pull of the Football League, and the distant city on the hill that is the Premiership, continues to fire the imagination of rich men with property interests, however little they know about football and however far away they sit. Kevin Heaney had worked his way into the lower reaches of the national rich list with his building company, Cornish Homes. Uninterested in football until then, he was persuaded to take a look at Truro City, a team that had played at least seven levels below the Football League for its whole existence. He concluded that three million should get them there, bought the club and paid up.[107] Truro achieved five promotions in six seasons, won the FA Vase at Wembley in 2007, and in 2011 began the season in the Blue Square South, just two levels below the Football League. In keeping with the regional-nationalist strategies of Cornwall's rugby clubs, Heaney had abandoned Truro's red and black strip, opting for the Cornish nationalist palette of black, white and gold. By late 2011 it was clear the bubble had burst: the players were not getting paid, the tax authorities were limbering up for yet another winding-up order, Heaney's own company was bust, and no one would buy the ground from him. Like so many of the incompetents and thieves who thought that they had the right to treat the common property, the accumulated cultural capital that truly constitutes English football clubs, as their own, Heaney's instinct was to look after number one. He sold the club's ground to his wife's company and walked away.

## V.

What happens when the rich man walks away or gets sent to prison? Given the reason that owners abandon the situation is that there's nothing left to take from a club but debts, the price of patronage and elite philanthropy is the perpetual threat of sudden extinction. For organized fans, driving out these rogues and rentiers is only the beginning of their troubles. In dozens of cases over the last twenty years, supporters' trusts have stepped in to try and salvage something from the wreckage of their club: York, Wrexham, Chester, Carlisle, Swansea, Wycombe and Darlington are just some of the examples.[108] Some supporters' trusts are like the armies of broom-wielding cleaners volunteering to sweep up all the shattered glass and burnt dustbins after the 2011 London riots: well-meaning, good-hearted, community-spirited and prepared to get stuck in, but bereft of ideas to prevent the situation happening again. While some of the trusts and their members have an ideological commitment to notions of mutualism, democracy and collective ownership, most have just focused on survival. That in itself is no mean feat. The levels of dedication, skills and organization required to keep a lower-league club afloat are highly demanding. It is little surprise that after a period of firefighting, fending off the tax authorities and doing a deal with creditors, most trusts have looked for new investors and perhaps board representation rather than consolidate their permanent ownership of the club. Notts County and Brentford, for example, both sold on their shares to businessmen they thought would truly transform the clubs' prospects.

Like many of the community-level organizations in England's cities, the supporters' trusts find themselves in a world where all the best properties have long been taken and which, at current valuations, will be impossible to purchase. While they have access to the ruins, they rarely have access to much capital and are condemned to doing repair work under constant financial pressure. In the current Football League only three clubs are entirely supporter-owned—Exeter City, AFC Wimbledon and Wycombe Wanderers. Exeter's trust managed not only to save the club but get them out of the Conference and back into the League. More fantastically, AFC Wimbledon, who were founded in 2002 after their old club was given permission to move to Milton Keynes, have managed to get from the ninth level of English football to fourth-level League Two in just nine seasons; they have also proved themselves among the most socially minded and active clubs in the League.[109] In both these cases, however, they began with something—either a club that was broke but still had had its ground or an established body of fans, albeit ones who had had their club taken away from them. It is the absence of either of these advantages that makes the development of FC United of Manchester all the more remarkable, for it truly is a club and a community built from thin air.

The club was formed in 2005 out of conversations in traditional United pubs and at Manchester Methodist Hall, locations which neatly displayed the two streams of fan culture that came together to launch the club: on the one hand a body of fans who were looking for something like the old match-day experiences of standing, singing, drinking and camaraderie; on the other hand, the organized and politicized members of the fanzine cultures and independent supporters' association whose networks had been forged in the struggles with Edwards, BSkyB and Coolmore. Of course, many fans fell into both categories, and there was from the start a conscious diversity of groups within FCUM.[110] While some watched and continue to watch Manchester United at the stadium and on TV, others have entirely broken with Old Trafford—but for all of them the Glazers' leveraged buyout was the final straw. Seven years later, the club is a few levels below the Football League and continues to attract a regular crowd of over 3,000. It has had to play at Bury's Gigg Lane but there are now plans to move into a new community stadium in Moston in 2014—a north Manchester neighborhood just a stone's throw from Newton Heath where United originally sprang from. The sheer level of voluntary labor required to make this happen by over 300 regulars, supplemented by the networks of friendships and associations drawn from Old Trafford, has created a new functioning football community in Manchester. The volume of singing, chanting, and lyrical invention, not to mention hard drinking, that has emerged at FC United suggests almost a performance, a recreation and reinvention that attempts to capture the best of the old football and its civic identities, but grafts that onto a distinct culture of community engagement and participatory democracy. "Won't pay for Glazer/Won't work for Sky/Still sing City's gonna die."[111] Perhaps, more pointedly, FC United sing, "This is how it feels to be FC/ this is how it feels to be home," and demonstrate that it is possible, in an English city where the best real estate has been sold off to the super-rich and the worst is left to rot, to find others who share your values and to build your own Jerusalem.

# CHAPTER 4

# Playing the Race Game
## Migration, Ethnicity, and Identity

The amount of racist abuse that came from the Millwall fans in the lower stand was incredible, "Black this, black that," monkey chants and the rest. Basically I am standing not more than five feet away from Ian. I sort of looked at them, looked at Ian and Ian shrugged his shoulders. Then I hear this voice from the crowd— "not you Tone, you're alright—It's Wrighty." I think that they just see a blue shirt when they look at me . . . But do they not see my color? Do I wear this shirt over my head?

**TONY WITTER**

I.

Millwall, England, 1991.[1] The incident would almost be funny if it weren't for the fact that Afro-Caribbean men suffer a rate of schizophrenia significantly higher than that of white males. Such were the ambiguities of race, identity, and belonging in English football at the beginning of the 1990s. Witter and Wright were part of the generation of black players, mainly born in Britain to migrant parents, who had forced their way into English professional football over the previous two decades and now comprised around a fifth of the players in the leagues. It was a project that was among the most successful acts of social mobility achieved by the community and it had been done against a background of often overt racism.

Tony Witter's acceptance, indeed minor cult status, at Millwall appears particularly remarkable, given that both club and neighborhood had come to represent the enduring bastion of an urban white working class that remained clannish at best and hostile to immigrants at worst. In that regard, Witter was emblematic of one strategy available to the wider black community: integration through a combination of talent, graft, and a mastery of the codes of the white working-class culture that occupied both the urban streets and the dressing rooms of professional football. He "wore the shirt" with pride and played robust, physical football, thus occupying a place where the bonds of class, gender and locality trumped the divisions of ethnicity. If Witter represented one mode of integration, more typical of the Afro-Caribbeans who have staked their place in the traditional working-class strongholds of industrial and municipal employment, Arsenal's Ian Wright represented a different strategy: one born of the day-to-day, face-to-face encounters of the street. Here, the older conflicts over space and status that had divided urban youth along ethnic lines was modulated by new alliances and friendships born of the shared experience of brutal policing, urban riots and social mixing in the cross-over cultural zones of music, slang, fashion and recreational drugs.

Ian Wright was no journeyman or stalwart defender; he was 100 percent London flash. Gold teeth, fleet of foot, sharply dressed for the dance hall or the disco and nobody's fool, he'd scored over a hundred goals for Crystal Palace in just three seasons. That might have provided ammunition for the crowd at Millwall, but at Crystal Palace he was loved. While Tony Witter's blackness became invisible at Millwall, at Crystal Palace Ian Wright's blackness delivered authenticity. As one white fan put it, "We had our own little quartet of black players who took Palace to the highest heights they'd ever been . . . I like the fact that these were lads that could probably have been on the streets of Tulse Hill . . . I could have gone to school with them and that was good." Another fan commented, "I always felt proud of the fact that we had these six black players at Palace . . . and black's cool as well . . . I remember like one time that the players were training and . . . the deejay . . . was, 'Oh and Ian Wright's requested this one' and it was a reggae tune and you saw Ian Wright dancing and you think oh that's wicked."[2] But even here, the place of the black footballer was paradoxical. Just as the Millwall crowd could sing, "Walking along, singing a song, walking in a Witter wonderland" and then give Ian Wright an extraordinary wall of abuse, so too at Crystal Palace. Even at a club that had a critical mass of black players, new black fans and a kind of cross-over black cachet among white fans, the chairman Ron Noades could, without any sense of unease, go on national television and say, "The black players at this club lend a lot of skill and flair, but you need white players in there to balance things up and give the team some brains and common sense."[3] Afro-Caribbeans had found and staked their place in English football as they had done in the wider society, where a few revelled in their presence, more found it uncomfortable, even threatening, and most viewed the whole experience through a lens still badly distorted by ignorance and prejudice.[4]

More than twenty years later, reading the state of race relations from the state of English football is not just the preserve of sociologists. It is a notion that has become mainstream. It is one of the stories that we like to tell about ourselves, about the way in which the country has changed since the end of Thatcherism. Football, after all, has been transformed since 1991. The baying crowds, monkey chants and bananas of the old era have been banished from the nation's football stadiums by an apparently successful raft of anti-racism campaigns; the progress of the far right, who have consistently orbited the world of football looking for trouble, has been stymied; no England team would be imaginable without a large contingent of black and dual heritage players. So, too, in our wider culture. Overt forms of racism are not merely illegal but widely deemed unacceptable; the far right, from the National Front to the British National Party to the English Defense League, while busy has yet to achieve any significant electoral success. Notions of an ethnic Englishness or Britishness tied exclusively to whiteness seem with each passing year ever more implausible.

In 2012 the Conservative Secretary of State for Culture, Jeremy Hunt, went as far as to argue that, "One of the main reasons we have made huge strides in changing attitudes to racial discrimination is because of the changes in football."[5] No longer mere metaphor or moral example, football appeared to have become a decisive causal force in shaping attitudes to race and ethnicity. Hunt was responding, with some alarm, to the furore that surrounded John Terry, England and Chelsea captain, who had been caught on camera saying, "You fucking black cunt" to Anton Ferdinand of QPR. The overt racism of the event punched a hole through the popular narrative of football and race, damaging enough for both political and football elites that Prime Minister David Cameron felt impelled to call a one-day Downing Street conference on Discrimination in Sport.

In fact football's relationship to the wider politics of race was, in the official version, never more than a partial account of the story. That is not to suggest that we abandon football as a way of grasping the politics of race and identity in modern Britain, or that we take no pride in the massive changes that have occurred. Rather, we need to tell ourselves different, more complex and more candid stories. Those stories begin, long before the Windrush generation of players, with the thin trickle of black players, overseas and domestic, who played in England, as well as the footballing career of the new Jewish communities of the early twentieth century. Within the conventional narrative the racism faced by the first generation of English black players and fans has been underplayed. Because the football world has clung for so long to the simple equation of hooligan and racist, the sheer ubiquity of racism on and off the football pitch has been missed. Nor has the considerable dignity with which black players dealt with it always been remembered.

The story of player integration followed by the transformation of the crowd has also managed to completely write out the role of football's owners, managers, administrators and broadcasters, both as individuals and institutions. In the real world it took the murder of Stephen Lawrence—a Black teen from south London—and the Macpherson Report to name the institutional racism at the heart of the British establishment. Football, which claims to have led the process of change, remains in its wake. The achievements of the last decade in terms of crowd behavior have yet to be matched by reform of football's coaching, administrative and economic elites. The silencing of overt public racism has come at the price that other forms of stereotyping and discrimination can be overlooked.

Football's story has chimed with the popular historical memory of postwar migration which had tended to privilege the experience of the Afro-Caribbean Windrush migrants over the South Asian migrations from India, Pakistan, Bangladesh, and East Africa. The absence of British South Asians from professional football served to reinforce this, though it hardly makes the history of the game an inclusive national metaphor. The late emergence of the first Anglo-Asian professionals, the entrenchment of Asian amateur leagues and fan groups and the appearance of the Islamophobic English Defense League (EDL) in football all demand inclusion in football's story. Even then, we would only be making up for lost time. For while Asian migrations peaked in the 1970s and 1980s they have been surpassed by the new migrations of the twenty-first century: on the one hand, the globally recruited pool of highly skilled and highly paid foreign labor in finance and football alike; on the other, the waves of asylum seekers and economic migrants from Somalia, West Africa, and Eastern Europe. The world of football like the rest of the country is only just waking up to their presence.

## II.

By the late nineteenth century sport had assumed an ambiguous position within the British imperial project. On the one hand, it was an essential tool of imperial rule. As a central component of the curriculum of the public schools, Oxbridge and the officer class, sport nurtured the battle-hardened masculine bodies and elite esprit de corps that a muscular Christian gentleman, destined to rule the empire, needed to possess. The Sudanese civil service was so partial to successful Oxbridge sportsmen that it was known around the Foreign Office as "The land of blacks ruled by blues."[6] On the other hand, sport provided the most powerful instruments of engagement with colonized peoples. In Egypt, the Gold Coast, South Africa and India football was spreading from the feet of soldiers, clerics and administrators to local elites, military recruits and missionary schoolboys. Playing sport together was part of the civilizing mission. It provided a tangible example of the Empire as a family, albeit a hierarchical family, rather than just an extortion racket. The game created a space in which, for ninety minutes at any rate, colonizer and colonized faced each other under formally equal conditions, the same rule of law. Although the balance of athletic power remained with British football this was a place where the hegemony of the colonizer could be openly challenged. Unencumbered by a large domestic black population and supremely confident in its theories of racial superiority, British football did not fear competition from the colonials, nor did it feel impelled to impose a color bar as happened in American baseball. Indeed, it proved porous enough that the sons of mixed marriages who had access to the trans-imperial institutions of the church, the military and the education system could become the first black players in British football.

Andrew Watson, the son of a Scottish-Jamaican planter and an Afro-Caribbean woman, was born in Georgetown, Guyana but sent "home" for his elite education at Rugby School and Glasgow University. In the early 1880s he played for the prestigious amateur side Queen's Park, served as club secretary and captained Scotland in games against Wales and England. Arthur Wharton, the son of a mixed-race relationship, was born in Accra, then the capital of the Gold Coast colony. He came to England in the 1880s to train as a Methodist missionary but ended up playing in goal for the leading professional club of the era, Preston North End. A decade later Hassan Hegazi, scion of a rich Cairo family, was sent to Dulwich College. In 1913 he dallied a year at Fulham as a striker, then played a few games for Millwall before going up to Cambridge University to read History and Arabic. Walter Tull, by contrast, came from the other end of the social spectrum, growing up in a children's home in Bethnal Green after the deaths of his Jamaican father and English mother. For Tull, football and the army were the route to social mobility. He first played for Tottenham Hotspur in 1909 before moving to Northampton Town. On the outbreak of war, he followed many of his fellow professionals into the army's special 1st Football Battalion where he was made a sergeant and served at the Battle of the Somme. In 1917 he returned to the Italian front as the British Army's first black officer, before dying on the Western Front in March 1918.

There is no record of racist comments directed toward either Watson or Hegazi during their football careers and both moved comfortably in elite football circles; Watson went on to be a member of the aristocratic amateur club Corinthians, while Hegazi was a football blue at Cambridge. Wharton and Tull were less fortunate. On the eve of an FA Cup tie in 1887 the *Athletic Journal* believed Wharton's goalkeeping to be a major drag on Preston's chances, asking, "Is the darkie's pate too thick for it to dawn upon him that between the sticks is no place of skylark?"[7] On his arrival at Stalybridge Rovers in 1896 the local paper remarked that the club had "bagged itself a real nigger, none other than the Darkie who used to guard the North End Citadel." Tull, most famously, was barracked when playing for Tottenham at Bristol City in 1909: "A section of the spectators made a cowardly attack upon him in language lower than Billingsgate."[8] It may have been a small section of the public on this occasion at Ashton Gate, but later under conditions of postwar austerity, unemployment and desperation, the casual racism of the press and vulgar abuse of the crowd drove a wave of violence. In the summer of 1919 race riots broke out across England and Wales, from Cardiff and Liverpool to South Shields and London, and white mobs viciously attacked the small black and Chinese communities of these port cities.

While the achievement of the prewar generation was remarkable, they were for the most part the products of elite imperial migrations rather than the product of the upward mobility of a newly arrived working-class immigrant community. For this, we must turn to the Jewish experience. Towards the end of the nineteenth century the quiet life of the longstanding and well-heeled Sephardic community in Britain was disrupted by the arrival of a wave of poor Ashkenazim Jews, workers and peasants, escaping from Russia's pogroms. Horrified by their backwardness and obvious foreignness, the English Jewish elite embarked on a program of collective Anglicization. What could be more English than the embrace of sports in general and football in particular? The boys brigades, youth clubs, and Jewish sporting organizations that emerged were fortified by the new ideology of the muscular Jew developed in central Europe—an ethnic identity that rejected the stereotype of the weak and bookish scholar. What followed was an explosion of grassroots Jewish football, successful Jewish boxers and the first Jewish professional footballers. Louis Bookman, an

Irish-Lithuanian Jew, played for Bradford City before the First World War, while Les Goldberg was the poster boy of the Jewish athletic renaissance, playing for Leeds United and the first Jew to play for England Schoolboys just before the Second World War. Anxious to move on from the past and acutely aware of the low-level anti-Semitism of English culture, he finished his career as Les Gaunt playing for Swindon Town.[9]

For the half century after the First World War, two tiny streams of black players entered the football mainstream: mixed-race sons of the still small but permanent black migrations of the late imperial era and sporting migrants from the edge of the Empire where football had become a hugely popular game. Jack Leslie, son of a Jamaican father and English mother, made it out of Canning Town and embarked on a long professional career with Plymouth Argyle in the 1920s. Frank Soo, born in Derbyshire, the son of English and Chinese parents, played for Stoke City in the 1930s. Roy Brown, also born in Stoke, had English and Nigerian parents and went on to play for his hometown team in the 1940s. Charlie Williams, who was born in Barnsley in the 1920s, made it via the local colliery team to Doncaster Rovers. He played for over a decade before making a new and more successful career as a stand-up comic and TV quiz show presenter. Tony Collins lasted even longer, playing for fifteen years until he became the first black manager in British football, running Rochdale between 1960 and 1967.

Imperial migrants were both rarer and less successful. Alfred Charles made the journey all the way from Trinidad in the 1930s with the West Indies cricket team, serving as valet to the star of the squad, Learie Constantine. He stayed on in England, drifted among a number of clubs, but only managed to get himself a single first-team game with Southampton. Mohammed Salim was among India's best footballers of the 1930s, scoring goals for Mohammed Sporting in Calcutta. Through a cousin already based in Britain, he managed to get himself a trial at Celtic and despite playing barefoot got himself into the team in 1937 before returning home. Egypt's young elite continued to provide players, with Tewfik Abdullah going to Derby County and Cowdenbeath in the early 1920s and Mohamed Latif taking the field for Glasgow Rangers in the 1930s. After the war they remained a rarity. There were short-lived stays for the Nigerian Teselimi Blogun at Peterborough United, the Iraqi Youra Ashaya who made his way via the RAF in the Middle East to Bristol Rovers, and the Jamaicans Giles Heron who played for Celtic in the early 1950s and Lindy Delaphenha who played for Middlesbrough and Mansfield Town.

In the postwar era, the Jewish community began to shrink, marry out, secularize and be socially mobile. Not surprisingly professional players were few and far between, but those that did play remained emblematic of a wider communal history. Mark Lazarus, who scored the winning goal for QPR in their 1967 League Cup triumph, was the archetypal tough East End Jew, and thus a dying breed; while David Pleat, who has had a long career as a player, manager and pundit, made his Jewishness almost invisible like many in his generation. Invisibility was not an option for the two most notable black players of the 1960s, the South African Albert Johanneson at Leeds United and the Bermudian Clyde Best, who played for West Ham from 1969 until the mid-1970s. Both met more orchestrated racism from the crowd than earlier generations. They were booed when on the ball, subjected to monkey chanting and insulted. Johanneson in particular was roughed up by his opposing full backs. When he complained to manager Don Revie that an Everton defender had called him a black bastard, Revie replied, "Well, call him a white bastard!"[10] Johanneson didn't have the psychological resources for that kind of riposte. Brought up under the debilitating cruelty of apartheid, he found the Leeds United dressing room alien and threatening enough. The bile of the crowd and the cold indifference of Yorkshire were too much and ate what little self-confidence he had managed to bring with him. By the end of the decade his slide into alcoholism had already begun and he would be found dead in his public housing apartment at the age of fifty-five.

Why in the 1960s and 1970s did Johanneson and Best face much more hostile crowds than Williams or Delephena had in the 1940s and 1950s? Why did they appear as a threat rather than as exotic strangers? In short, because Britain, or rather England, had acquired its first large black immigrant communities: between 1948 and the early 1960s, nearly 300,000 had made the journey from the Caribbean; while around 200,000 Sikhs, Hindus, and Muslims had migrated from post-Independence India and Pakistan. Over the next decade family reunions, the wave of East African Asians expelled from Uganda and scared out of Kenya, and new Bangladeshi and Pakistani migrations saw Britain's black and minority ethnic population swell from the low tens of thousands in the late 1940s to over 1.5 million in 1975. Compressed by mutual attraction, sources of employment and restrictive housing policies, their presence was even clearer in the urban strongholds of Liverpool, Manchester, South Yorkshire, the West Midlands, Leicester, London and Bristol.

It had not been an easy journey. Higher wages and broader horizons than were available at home were only part compensation for personal slights and systemic discrimination. In the late 1960s life became more uncomfortable. The simmering discontent that existed among right-wing Conservatives and the white working-class communities of urban England over their presence finally found political expression when Enoch Powell made his Rivers of Blood speech in 1968. Declaring that the future of the English-speaking Christian nation was profoundly threatened by the arrival of people of color, Powell called not only for immigration to cease but for repatriation to begin as an alternative to an inevitable race war. This, just a year before Clyde Best's arrival in the East End of London, where dock workers had marched in support of Powell. Before his debut for West Ham Best received a threatening note: "The letter stated that, as I ran through the tunnel, they were going to throw acid in my face. I was petrified and I probably never moved so much and so fast on a soccer field in my life."[11] No acid was thrown but Best played for six years under a hail of abuse, yet still he went on to demonstrate that the stereotypes of black players—foreigners who were unable to cope with the weather, the banter or the physicality of the English game, gifted athletes but ill-disciplined, hopeless thinkers—were all wrong. Eventually idolized at Upton Park, Best would take the field with two other black players—the Nigerian Ade Coker and Londoner Clive Charles—as for a short while in the early 1970s Ron Greenwood's West Ham became the most diverse in the land. Best was not only winning hearts and minds in a stronghold of Powellism, he was inspiring the generation of Afro-Caribbean players who were about to break through. "It was important for me to see Clyde Best, a black man," says one interviewee quoted in a recent oral history project. "I was proud to be black. I couldn't wait for West Ham to come down here to see this big, black man, as a center forward playing. The guy was a legend, a hero. Seeing a black man out there was tremendous. It was [a] good feeling to see one of you and be able to say, 'If he can do it, I can do it'."[12] And from the early 1970s that is precisely what the new generation of black British players did.

## III.

If English football proved an inhospitable climate for foreigners like Johanneson, it didn't seem to suit the handful of black British players in the 1960s either. Cornish-born Mike Trebilcock scored two goals for Everton in their amazing 1966 FA Cup final comeback just weeks before England won the World Cup on the same turf. Five years later he had slid down the leagues and out of historical memory, as he dropped from Portsmouth to Torquay United to Western Suburbs FC of Sydney, Australia. Clive Charles played just three seasons for West Ham before he headed for the El Dorado of the North American Soccer League (NASL) in America. However, by the mid-1970s the number of professional black players had risen into double figures and was growing fast. The first generation of Windrush migrants, either born or schooled in Britain, came of age. Football was not at the time an obvious move for the children of immigrants. Whereas Anglo-Jewry, a generation earlier, had seen football as a route to assimilation, many Afro-Caribbeans thought it a zone of exclusion. Darren Smith remembered, "My parents didn't want me to go into soccer because they felt that black players weren't treated right at that time."[13] It wasn't just a question of racism, there were economic calculations to be made as well: "My Dad was always big up on having a trade; my brother said you have got to have a trade. All I wanted to do was play football but they didn't take it seriously, because there weren't a lot of black players playing football. And my older brother looked at me and said what do you want to play football for, that's a white man's game?"[14]

However, there were other voices and pressures at work. At the grassroots football had proved an invaluable source of friendship and solidarity for the first wave of predominantly male migrants. As one old timer from Highfield in Leicester put it, "I think, during the early days, Highfield Rangers was a very important part of the black community. The only real thing that the Afro-Caribbean Community had were the football teams."[15] More widely, English Afro-Caribbeans lived and worked in close contact with the white working class of the now declining inner cities, who remained football's core constituency in the 1950s and 1960s. The huge number of black kids playing football and their successful progress was testament not to their special abilities, but the degree to which they were becoming integrated with working-class life and culture.

The kids that made it offer a good cross-section of the main routes of migration and zones of settlement of the Afro-Caribbean community across urban England. Ces Podd came from St. Kitts via Leeds to the back four of Bradford City. Nottingham produced Viv Anderson, Manchester produced Remi Moses, and they went on to play for Forest and United respectively. Londoners Phil Walker and Vince Hilaire played for Millwall and Crystal Palace. Garth Crooks was born in and debuted with Stoke. Liverpool produced Howard Gayle and Cliff Marshall, who were the first homegrown black players at Liverpool and Everton respectively. Laurie Cunningham made the journey from North London to West Bromwich to Real Madrid. Luther Blissett and John Barnes were born in Jamaica, raised in Watford and went on to Milan and Liverpool. From the wider Caribbean Brendon Batson came from Grenada, Cyrille Regis was born in French Guiana, both grew up in London, and played together at West Bromwich in the late 1970s. They were joined there by Laurie Cunningham and christened "The Three Degrees" by manager Ron Atkinson. West Bromwich wasn't quite Motown, and the team wasn't quite young America. They weren't even the first side to field three prominent black players, but it was the moment when the wider public began to register the unmistakable and growing presence of black British footballers. Players with Nigerian roots completed the picture, like the Fashanu brothers, John and Justin, who began their careers at Norwich in the late 1970s.

By 1985 there were 112 black players at 66 of the 92 League clubs. By 1993, the first year of the Premier League, there were 244 black players in English professional football making up 12 percent of the total workforce and present at 88 percent of clubs; and they were playing at a higher level on average than their white colleagues: 23 percent of white professionals were in the Premiership compared to 36 percent of black players.[16] In 1978 Viv Anderson became England's first black player. By the time that the England team were redefining the popular appeal of the game at the 1990 World Cup, its leading figures included Des Walker, Paul Ince and John Barnes.

How should we measure their collective achievement? Occupying 15 to 20 percent of the professional labor pool through the 1990s from perhaps 2 to 3 percent of the population is an overachievement by anyone's measure. But what of its wider cultural resonance? The closest equivalent, perhaps, is the breaking of the color bar in American baseball in the 1940s by Jackie Robinson and the wave of African-American players that came into the game after him. Robinson is a kind of secular saint in the US and the generation that followed him inscribed African-Americans into the mainstream of the nation's popular narrative. The breakthrough of Afro-Caribbeans into English football was never likely to match this epic, narrative weight. It was not a struggle fought out in the context of institutionalized segregation nor did it anticipate a liberation movement of the immensity of the Civil Rights movement. Nonetheless, it had its own smaller, but real, hurts, struggles, and triumphs. Without them there would have been no anti-racism movement in football, no well-behaved crowds, no air of successful multiculturalism for the country to bask in. This generation of players began their careers in an era when the *Black and White Minstrel Show* was still considered wholesome Saturday night family entertainment and the most likely place to see a black face in the national media. The black presence in boxing and athletics was still in its infancy, the appeal of reggae music and ska artists had barely begun to cross over, and no person of color had been elected to parliament since the 1920s. Professional footballers were the most visible black men in British public life. They walked out into a culture where young Afro-Caribbeans were increasingly perceived as a threat to personal, sexual and national security—an old trope given new life by the moral panic over mugging in the 1970s. Thus they began their careers against a background of pervasive racial stereotyping and everyday unreflective racism expressed throughout the period in the football stadiums of England.

Alongside the quotidian disdain, black players like the rest of the community had to contend with the political and emotional aftermath of Powell. Powell had given articulate voice to the ethnic nationalism that underwrote the new activists of the far right in Britain. The National Front, in particular, mobilized anti-immigrant sentiments and made its presence felt in and around English football stadiums in the 1970s. From as early as 1972 in Leeds and 1975 at Chelsea, the occasional racist epithet was now joined by Nazi slogans, collective racist chants and the systematic abuse of black players on the ball. These continued throughout the 1980s among other clubs such as Chelsea, Walsall, and Oxford United. In the late 1980s the Front began to fall apart and was replaced as the main organized force on the far right by the British National Party and its offshoot Combat 18. Both made their presence felt in club and international football crowds.

Simultaneously this generation of players had to carve out their space inside the hitherto exclusively white working-class culture of the professional dressing room. The overt abuse of the terraces was not reproduced inside the dressing rooms of professional football, but racist abuse, on the pitch, at any rate was considered an acceptable norm in the industry's code of competitive banter. Tony Davis who played at Manchester United remembered it this way.

> You've got players saying, "You black bastard" and "I will break your legs." It went on right through my career. The irony of it is that you will get this and they want to apologize afterwards. You would see them in the bar afterwards and they would say, "Sorry about calling you a black bastard."[17]

Finally, while black footballers and fans received some support from organizations like the Anti Nazi League and local anti-fascist action groups in Leeds and Newcastle, they received almost no support from the football authorities or their own trade union, the PFA. Despite every indication to the contrary in the early 1980s, the Commission for Racial Equality and the FA agreed that the problem of racism was too small to be worried about. Consequently, they had to make the journey by themselves and despite the occasional lapse, and in the face of relentless provocation, they did it with great dignity and some style.

The racism of the English football crowd in the 1970s and 1980s was a complex, poisonous hydra. It could be roused by a single voice or incident, and it fed on existing football antipathies. It could take the form of a single slur or abusive epithet or it could be a wall of noise and booing, it could be a cheer from a stand as a player was sharply bundled over the line or it could be all 40,000 people screaming, "Nigger, nigger lick my boots" or "Get back on your jam jar!" Players were on the end of monkey chants, crude racial ditties, sharp but subtle digs and jokes, and bananas were thrown at their feet. As Vince Hilaire put it:

> It's a public order offense to do something like that. If that was the case ...up to the mid-1980s, there'd probably be no one left watching football, they'd all be in like prison or banned from the grounds for life . . . it was unmerciful . . . the black players that played then . . . the players playing now owe them a bit because they did take merciless stick . . . and it was malicious and nasty . . . and you had to turn a deaf'un.[18]

Brian Holland, in an act of heroic sociological geekery, stood on the terraces of Newcastle United and Leeds United for two godforsaken seasons between 1989 and 1993.[19] While observing the presence of the far right and racist literature in the stadium (usually concentrated in small pockets of young men with tattoos and leaflets), he meticulously counted the form and frequency of abuse given by the crowd to the players. He managed to distinguish between non-racial and racialized abuse; booing, chanting and singing; home and away players and black and white players. The typical burden of abuse in a game was that white home players got off most lightly; away white players got about eight times more abuse than they did and home black players double that again. However, away black players received, staggeringly, eighty times as much flak as the white home players, and of that around a third of the abuse was clearly racial in character.

Faced with all of this, players adopted a range of strategies. Many, relieved to have made it into the professional world and wary of losing their precarious position, kept a low profile. Frank Lee at Millwall argued, "When I got my contract I felt part of the family, I had been classed as an equal under the same badge as a family . . . I was a pretty easy person to get on with, pretty polite and as a black person you had to be double polite. To be accepted you had to keep people happy."[20] Similarly John Barnes saw it as a responsibility: "If the first black player had been ranting and raving and carrying on and not being able to take the abuse . . . he wouldn't have lasted the game [and] the emergence of black players would have been put back . . . because who would have been willing to take a chance on another black player?"[21] There were limits to this strategy of politeness.

On occasion, players would lash out at abusive members of the crowd. Ces Podd remembered, "I was coming off the field . . . and somebody called me a black bastard and spat at me and it caught me in the mouth . . . I can remember jumping up at this guy . . . and a policeman grabbed me as though I was the one to blame and I thought this can't be right."[22] On the pitch, abuse could be returned with interest.

> They would say . . . "fucking nigger" and I always said, "that's what your wife says when I'm shagging her" . . . then the white boy would have a problem . . . I found that always had the desired effect. [If that didn't work, there were other options.] There was always a nice tackle you could get into . . . Then we would say if you've got a problem then I will see you in the fucking car park . . . if you've got a problem then I will see you outside where the referee can't protect your arse.[23]

As one prominent defender of the 1980s put it, this boxed black players into a limited and stereotypical range of acceptable responses: ". . . you've got to be thick skinned or a bad bastard."[24]

Football was not an environment in which other forms of black masculinity could find a comfortable place. Richie Moran, who considered his dreads a reaffirmation of his African heritage, was asked by his Scottish manager at Birmingham City to shave them off. "I told him . . . If I should have my hair cut he should have elocution lessons to change his Glaswegian accent . . . I didn't play in the first team again strangely enough."[25] Justin Fashanu presented an even greater challenge; he remains one of the very few gay footballers globally to have come out. He made an announcement in the press in 1990 just after retiring, but throughout his career fans and players had alluded to his sexual orientation. Despite being the first million-pound black player in Britain, his legacy is bitter. Accused of non-consensual sex with a young man, and threatened with exposure in the tabloid press, he committed suicide in 1998. In an interview before his brother's death, John Fashanu made clear how problematic his brother had become: "Football is like the mafia, we all move together and set the rules. They say your brother's gay but you can't choose your family. I wouldn't like to play or get changed in the vicinity of one. That's how I feel, so you can imagine how other players feel."[26]

Given the attitudes of the English football crowds to black players, their own included, it is hardly surprising that black fans were rare on the ground. They, too, entered a world in which their race would be both visible and invisible, and where their status as insiders remained contingent. Paradoxically, hooligan firms were among the most mixed parts of the crowd. In the early 1970s significant numbers of young black men from Moss Side started supporting Manchester City at Maine Road and created the Cool Cats, an overwhelmingly black crew that traveled in its own coaches to away games and was a known presence in and around football stadiums all over the country. Able to mobilize up to 400 boys, they drove the National Front presence out of Maine Road by the time they fizzled out in the early 1980s. In the West Midlands black fans drifted into a multi-ethnic fighting crew that came to be known as the Birmingham Zulus where violence, or the capacity to threaten violence, was the currency of integration. In London individual black fans and small groups could be found at West Ham, Millwall, Crystal Palace, Arsenal and Tottenham. As Tony Witter implied, the price of admission here was both mastery of the white working-class milieu and a strange double life as the invisible man. As a black Millwall fan of the era described: "What has happened is that these guys don't see us as black . . . John Fashanu was playing for us and they were shouting, 'You black bastard, get off your arse and do something, you fucking nigger.' Then they turn round and say, 'Sorry mate, no offense I am talking to that black bastard on the pitch!'"[27]

## IV.

The tone of the crowd, however two-faced and contradictory, was instantly understood by any black player or fan in English football. It took rather longer for it to reach the ears of government and the criminal justice system. Lord Justice Popplewell's report on crowd safety was published in 1986 after a succession of football disasters and very public fights: the Bradford City fire, the disaster at Heysel, and major outbreaks of disorder at games in Luton and Birmingham. While the main concern of the report was a more general hooliganism, it noted the role of the far right in orchestrating racist chants and recommended that a specific offense of racial abuse at sports grounds be created. Lord Justice Taylor's report, published five years later in the aftermath of the Hillsborough disaster, endorsed this view and the offense was duly legislated for in the Football Offenses Act 1991.[28]

Unsurprisingly the legislation, initially, made almost no difference at all. In the early 1990s racist chanting and singing remained a standard feature of almost every football ground in the country. Neither the clubs nor the police nor the FA made much use of the law, and all these constituencies remained wedded to the notion of racism as a subset of hooliganism, rather than a more widespread phenomenon performed by much larger swathes of the crowd than those engaged in fighting. As in the 1970s and 1980s, racism still came as crude abuse and insult but it could also be recoded as a joke, its mendacity hidden by a linguistic sleight of hand. At Millwall, where Tony Witter was lionized, his slim-framed, wiry black contemporary Bobby Bowry was hailed with the malicious, "Bobby Bowry's an Ethiopian." A similar metonymic slippage, this time from blackness to predatory criminality, was encoded in the chants of, "Oi! OJ!" and "OJ, where's your gloves," from white fans to black stewards. The stereotypical connection of black men to low-wage, low-status labor was made every time a crowd chanted, "Cab! Cab! Cab!" as black players ran past them.[29]

A transparent example of the form and scale of racist abuse was the treatment meted out to Ruud Gullit when playing for Chelsea against Everton as late as 1996.[30] On the one hand his every move was met by boos, jeers, whistles and barracking; from the announcement of his name before the game to the final whistle. On the other hand, Chelsea's other black players, Duberry, Newton, and Phelan, did not receive the same treatment at all. Gullit was perceived as an alien and as a threat for a myriad of reasons. Foreign, well-spoken, even erudite, his stylish continental masculinity, with football skills to match, ran against the grain of almost every unspoken social and sporting norm of the Everton crowd. Yet while they abused him for having long hair, and threatening the Everton goal, his race became visible. For the record the day's epithets, from fans of all ages, included: "Get off the pitch ya fuckin' gollywog! Fuck off the pitch ya fuckin' nigger! Fuck of ya' hippy! Fuck off ya' black cunt! Fuckin' cheatin' divin' black cunt! Knob'ead! Wog'ead! Gollywog! Nigger!" No one, needless to say, was arrested that day under the Football Offenses Act 1991.

Relations were no more harmonious on the pitch in the mid-1990s. Darren Beckford was spat on while playing for Port Vale, Stan Collymore complained bitterly of the constant racial abuse he received from Liverpool's Steve Harkness and got sent off the following season for a two-footed lunge on the defender. Manchester United's goalkeeper Peter Schmeichel was alleged to have called Ian Wright a "black bastard" and received a similar tackle from the Arsenal striker the next year. Both incidents were investigated by the FA, but like the hundreds of other clashes and harsh words spoken no further action was taken.

However, in the 1990s two things transformed the relationship between racism and football. First, the murder of Stephen Lawrence, a black teenager from South London, was followed by a hapless investigation. This not only failed to produce convictions but demonstrated a shocking level of casual racism and unreflective stereotyping by the police. The Macpherson Report on the matter, published in 1999, transformed permanently the landscape of race issues in the criminal justice system and beyond to every public and private sector institution. The report's definition of institutional racism is worth recalling:

> The collective failure of an organisation to provide an appropriate and professional service to people because of their color, culture or ethnic origin [which] can be seen or detected in processes, attitudes and behavior which amount to discrimination through unwitting prejudice, ignorance, thoughtlessness, and racist stereotyping which disadvantages minority ethnic people.[31]

Henceforth neither homicide investigations nor matters of public order in football stadiums could be policed without reference to issues of race and racism. Although it has been uneven, police forces across Britain have responded to issues of racist abuse with an altogether different level of seriousness.

Second, an anti-racist coalition emerged in English football over the following decade, which was able to transform successfully the norms that governed crowd behavior. It drew support from many strands of the wider football culture and acquired the tacit and then explicit support of the police and football authorities; a process aided by the arrival of the new

Labour government of 1997, which brought a new seriousness to issues of racial injustice in Westminster and Whitehall. It was not, however, a coalition of sufficient strength and perhaps vision to apply the arguments of the Macpherson Report to the institutions beyond the crowd.

Football's anti-racism movement grew from a number of sources. In the 1980s the issue of racism had been aired for some time in the fanzine cultures and fused with anti-fascist groups to produce local initiatives like Leeds Fans United against Racism and Fascism and their 1987 fanzine *Marching Altogether*. The Football Supporters Association went down a similar route publishing the anti-racist *United Colours of Football*. Initiatives to counter a local National Front presence were started by fans at Leicester, Newcastle, West Ham and Charlton. The Commission for Racial Equality finally considered the situation important enough to be worth intervening. The PFA, likewise, recognized it was time to pay attention to the needs of a growing part of their membership. In 1993 they put time and money behind a new initiative called "Let's Kick Racism Out of Football."[32]

The initial campaign asked the professional clubs to sign up to a program of action: publicly stating their opposition to racism through the match-day program, advertising hoardings and over the public address system before matches. More seriously, it asked the clubs to make compliance with the policy of no racist chanting a condition of holding a season ticket and to take action with the police to remove and prosecute offenders guilty of racist abuse or singing. The FA, initially distant from the campaign, started worrying about the blanket media coverage of neo-Nazi violence at the England game in Dublin in 1995 and Eric Cantona's kung fu kick at a fan who racially abused him from the terrace at Crystal Palace. As Kick It Out acquired some popular traction, the FA gave its support to the program. Despite the uniformly positive media coverage of the campaign and the near total public support it received from clubs, players and officials, there remained considerable local and hidden resistance. In response to the Kick It Out banner being paraded at one ground, fans were heard to sing, "You can stick your fucking banner up your arse."[33]

Yet despite this kind of cynicism, and the reluctance with which many clubs actually put their pledges into action, there was change. Kick It Out publicly set a new norm of behavior in English football, and while many didn't want to know, slowly the pressure of example mounted. Racist chanting began to decline.

Perhaps most important of all, clubs and the police using CCTV and other means began to conduct a steady flow of arrests, prosecutions and bans on fans who made racist remarks. At the same time the case against racism became stronger as the England team came to publicly embody the multi-ethnic reality of the country, in which black players were not peripheral actors but the living embodiment of the patriotic nation. In 1998, before a friendly game with Morocco, it became apparent that the locals had no recorded version of the National Anthem, leaving the team to sing it unaccompanied. In pictures splashed across the back of the tabloids Ian Wright could be seen leading the lusty singing alongside Sol Campbell, Paul Ince, and Paul Gascoigne. There might not be any black in the Union Jack, but now there was in the red cross of St. George. Unable to attend the 1998 World Cup due to injury, Wright became a fixture of the BBC's coverage, appearing emotionally and literally draped in the flag.

While domestic incidences of racism remained under-reported, the tone of the press coverage of racism when it occurred safely abroad began to change. In a notably unpleasant Champions League encounter between Arsenal and Lazio in Rome in 2000, the French-Senegalese midfielder Patrick Vieira accused Serbian Siniša Mihajlović of relentless racial abuse and was widely supported in the English press. By 2002 the *Daily Telegraph*, not noted for its closeness to the anti-racist movement in Britain, reported on the aftermath of England's game against Slovakia, thundering, "If UEFA, the governing body of European football, needed any firsthand witness accounts of the scourge of racism staining their competitions, they should have listened in yesterday to the powerful testimony of Ashley Cole and Emile Heskey." Both had been subjected to stadium-wide monkey chanting, even from the stretcher bearers.[35]

It was in this context in late 2004 that England were scheduled to play a friendly against Spain in Madrid. In a prematch training session, cameras caught the Spanish coach Luis Aragonés attempting to motivate his forward José Antonio Reyes by claiming he was better than his Arsenal teammate Thierry Henry, "that black shit." An outpouring of criticism in the English press rained down on the Spanish. The England team trained in "Let's Kick Racism Out" T-shirts. During the game itself England's black players were given the monkey-chant treatment by the ultras Sur, a small group of Real Madrid fans with known far-right wing sympathies. They were soon joined by the whole stadium, including police officers. Bobbing in unison they sang, "Whoever doesn't bounce is a fucking black."[36] The English press wanted blood but had to make do with a very formal apology extracted from the Spanish football authorities. FIFA issued them with a nugatory fine of £44,000. Uniformly negative coverage of the Spanish crowds and authorities was paired with a collective self-righteousness that contrasted Britain's new confident multiculturalism with the barbaric attitudes of continental Europe; a tone not dissimilar to that used to describe the car burnings and disorder that racked France's *banlieues* the following year.

Given such impeccable credentials when it came to scolding foreigners for their racism, one might imagine that English football had tackled racism at home in a comprehensive manner, especially after the incontestable account of institutional racism in the Metropolitan Police had been delivered by the Macpherson Report. However, the standard trope in the game remained, as in many other institutions, that football was self-evidently meritocratic and color-blind. As one club director put it of his staff, "I couldn't care less if they come from bloody Mars or Jupiter, as long as they can play football."[37] This was an argument from people who seemed unperturbed that their clubs' grounds had served as public theaters of the most obvious racism through the 1980s and 1990s. Where disingenuousness wouldn't wash, football responded with outright denial. As Jimmy Hill said in 1999 of the football world beyond the terraces; "There is no racism in football." In some respects the anti-racism campaigns of the 1990s and early twenty-first century provided the perfect cover for the football industry. By linking the antisocial hooligan and the racist so explicitly and exclusively together, the deeply ingrained institutional racism of the rest of the industry could remain unexamined.

Despite the remarkable presence of black players in English football, both British and foreign, the unreflexive norm of football club cultures from the board to the groundstaff to the dressing room was white. As late as 2005, all 103 members of the FA Council were white. It was only in

2011 with the appointment of Heather Rabbatts as a director that the FA Board ceased to be a wholly male and white affair.[38] In 2014 Greg Dyke established a high-profile commission on the future of the England team without a single black or minority ethnic member. Within the domain of coaching, scouting and player development it was apparent in the late 1980s and early 1990s that black and white players were concentrated in different positions and that until at least until the mid-1990s there were discriminatory wage levels.[39] The fact that so many of the leading black players of the era started their professional careers late after languishing in industrial jobs and semi-professional football suggests that the scouting networks of English football were at the very least not looking in the right places for talent. And there persists a disquieting sense of discrimination against black players at the highest level. Sol Campbell has argued that he would have captained England for ten years had he been white, lambasting the FA as "institutionally racist."[40]

Even when they did manage to get to the right place, white scouts and coaches brought a whole range of unspoken stereotypes and prejudices that shaped the encounter. The myths of the 1950s and 1960s, of uncontrollable and unfocused jokers, flakes who couldn't handle the rain, had been thoroughly disproven on the pitch. In their place, new spectres arose of the perennially disaffected black youth. As one player of the era recalled, "When I first started playing the cliché was that they were not disciplined and all they wanted to do was run and go out dancing and to go to a night club and anytime they told you anything they put it down to having a chip on your shoulder."[41] The "chip on the shoulder" was the ubiquitous code for a kid's refusal to conform to the hierarchies of age and ethnicity. "When I first started at QPR there were a couple of black lads," the player continued. "I would often hear the Youth Development officer say, I don't know why they have got a 'chip on their shoulder'. We did have this white goalkeeper who had the same attitude as this black fellow. I used to say, 'Why hasn't he got a chip on his shoulder?' And they used to say he's all right he just takes it hard."[42] Les Ferdinand remembers this stereotyping of young black players with a twinge of anger: "When I was a kid there was a definite reluctance to look at black kids. Those words I hate and despise: 'They've got a chip on their shoulder.' You'd hear that all the time. No one tried to understand or work with us; the moment there was a hint of anything, we got dismissed as having an attitude problem."[43]

Stereotyping did not cease once players had made it, but continued in different guises. As we noted, the first generation of black players found themselves painted as ill-disciplined or naive on the ball and this attitude carried over into the employment of professional coaches and managers.[44] Given that the labor pool for professional football managers is almost exclusively ex-professional players, one might have expected the demographic bulge of black players in the 1980s and 1990s to turn into a similar shift in the ethnic balance of the managerial workforce. However, since Tony Collins' appointment at Rochdale in the early 1960s, black managers have been few and far between in England. From among the Windrush generation of black players only Keith Alexander carved out an enduring coaching career, and all of that in the lower leagues. Cyrille Regis and Viv Anderson had short-lived or junior coaching appointments, Garth Crooks headed for the media and Brendon Batson into administration. In the mid-1990s, high-profile appointments of foreign black managers Ruud Gullit at Chelsea and Jean Tigana at Fulham suggested that a shift in attitude might be coming. Curiously, while Gullit's race became highly visible when he was an opposing player, it became invisible when he was a manager. Leslie Silver, chairman of Leeds United, thought it "an interesting one. I haven't even thought of him as black, I thought of him as a Dutchman."[45] Between 2007 and 2011 black managers made up from 1 to 4 percent of the leagues' totals. In April 2011 when Paul Ince left Notts County, Chris Powell at Charlton Athletic was the only black manager at any of the 92 League clubs. In the next two years he was rejoined in league management by Chris Hughton at Norwich City, Ince at Blackpool, and Chris Kiwomya (Notts County). By the end of the 2013–14 season, all had been sacked.

Explanations of Afro-Caribbean under-representation in other managerial sectors and white-collar occupations can in large part be explained by issues of class. Factoring in the educational and economic profile of Britain's Afro-Caribbean community accounts for much of the enduring and apparently ethnic inequalities they endure in the labor market. However, in football a working-class background is no bar to achieving a managerial position; indeed, it is almost a sine qua non. Nor is there any kind of premium of formal education in English football. So what can explain the gap between the 20 percent of black players who produce only 4 percent or less of the managers? Even taking into account the existence of longer established networks of kin and friendships among white players, it is hard not to agree with Cyrille Regis. Reflecting on his own coaching career, he believed decision-makers simply do not trust black managers: "The real power . . . is where you are dictating policy, commanding players and dealings with budgets. There are still questions being asked about black British managers and whether or not they will be able . . . to produce the goods . . . I think a number of chairmen are hesitant about appointing a black manager."[46]

If this is not institutional racism, in precisely the terms Macpherson laid down, then what is?

## V.

Until the beginning of the twenty-first century, the cultural politics of ethnicity and racism in English football and society had been dominated by the Afro-Caribbean experience. In actual fact, Afro-Caribbeans had long ceased to be the majority immigrant group, and by 2001, demographically and culturally, they were just one strand in a much more variegated tapestry of communities. Over the next decade, football cultures would begin to reflect that shift and on occasion shape the new cultural landscape in a number of ways. The arrival of the first British Asian professionals bore testament to a long-standing but little-known hinterland of Asian grassroots football. For over thirty years Asian players and clubs had fought a quiet struggle against a unique set of racist assumptions about their masculinity. However, the arrival of Anglo-Asian professionals was the last act in football's relationship with the first wave of new Commonwealth migrants. From the mid-1990s, football more closely reflected the new texture of race relations and the new waves of migration that took place under the Labour governments of Blair and Brown.

For over a decade, the top of the labor market in finance and football alike was open to a global pool of very highly paid talent. At the bottom end—in cleaning, child care, construction, shift work, and fruit picking—the market was open to those prepared to take on the wages and conditions that others wouldn't. There were plenty ready to do so, from poor Chinese peasants illegally smuggled into the country to the millions of

Eastern Europeans who came after their countries' accession to the European Union. Both foreign footballers and plumbers helped fuel the long boom of the Blair years, but at the same time became the objects of caricature and xenophobia, accusations of job stealing from a displaced white working class, and, on occasion, threats, violence and intimidation.

The experience of British Asians in football had, so far, been one that turned on ethnic and color differences rather than religion. The riots that broke out in 2001 across northern English mill towns followed by the events of 9/11 changed this. In time the language and the politics of the War on Terror would mutate into a popular domestic Islamophobia. After the home-grown Jihadist bombings of July 2005, it found expression in football chants and the emergence of a scattered archipelago of tiny far-right groups that mixed the English Defense League (EDL) with a network of old boys and retro hooligans called Casuals United. At the same time, there were small signs of a new and more complex multiculturalism emerging in football.

In the early 1950s the first waves of migration from India and Pakistan included Sikhs, Hindus and Muslims, Punjabis and Gujaratis, middle-class high-caste professionals and untouchable peasants. The earliest South Asian football clubs in the UK were formed in the early 1950s by the Punjabi Sikhs, who played football at home and arrived with more of their own social organization. The demand for football as a source of pleasure, socializing and escape was immense. Teams emerged like the Bradford-based Albion Sports, Guru Naak in Gravesend, Supnaa in Leicester, Paak United in Nelson, and Punjab United and Punjab Rovers from Wolverhampton. Excluded from many established facilities and unable to build their own, many clubs began life in the tough environment of urban green spaces like London's Hackney Marshes and Leicester's Victoria Park. Exposure to open racism when playing local white teams and hidden racism from those that avoided fixtures with them were widespread.[47]

Despite the strength of grassroots South Asian football and a population initially similar to, then larger than, the Afro-Caribbean community, the British Asian presence in professional football has been minuscule. In the late nineteenth century two Anglo-Indian brothers, Jack and Eddie Cotter, played for Watford. The Anglo-Pakistani Roy Smith was at West Ham in the 1950s, while in the 1970s the Anglo-Indian trio of Bud

Houghton, Ricky Heppolette and Kevin Keelan played all across the lower leagues. Rahinder Singh Verdee, a Kenyan-born Indian, moved to Britain as a child and had a short-lived youth career with Wolves and Ipswich as Roger Verdi before moving on to North America. It's only in this century that South Asian players have begun to break through. Michael Chopra, of Anglo-Indian parentage, played for his hometown team Newcastle United before moving on to Cardiff and a spell in the Premiership with Sunderland. Anglo-Bangladeshi Anwar Uddin made a career with Dagenham and Redbridge. More recently players with two Asian parents have made it into professional football. Zesh Rehman, for example, from Birmingham was the first British Pakistani to play in the Premiership.

British South Asians' slow progress is attributable in part to competition from cricket, and in part from the lack of networks required to steer a promising player from a youth side to a professional career. However, British South Asians have also had to negotiate the imperial anthropologies of race; invented by the British Raj, they came home with the Empire. Bengalis—and by extension most Indians—were excluded from military roles after the Indian Mutiny of 1857, and were reimagined as limp-wristed subservient bureaucrats. While Afro-Caribbean men have been cast as feckless or dangerous, characterized by a hyper-masculine taste for violence and sexually predatory behavior, South Asian men have been cast as effete, menial and physically feeble. In the world of British football in the late twentieth century these ideas underwrote a whole series of myths and stereotypes: that South Asians didn't play football, that they were too small or weak for the game, that their diet was insufficiently hearty to ensure development. Dave Bassett, for example, when manager of Sheffield United, thought that "The Asian build is not that of a footballer . . . It may well be that Asian ingredients in food, or the nutrition they take . . . are not ideal."[48] A senior official at West Ham thought them liable, at the drop of a hat, to stop playing and start praying. While these notions are beginning to break down in the face of Asian players' development, it remains the case that less than 1 percent of players in the Premiership's academies are of Asian origin.

At the turn of the century, it looked as if a new popular rapprochement between mainstream and British South Asian cultures was in progress, an encounter typified by the ubiquitous consumption of the hybrid

British–North Indian–Bangladeshi curries. Crossover musical forms merged Bollywood, Bhangra, hip-hop, and electronica; the first Asian sitcoms appeared on radio and television, a trend that coalesced in the hugely popular movie *Bend It Like Beckham*, in which a British Sikh girl scores the team's winning goal and escapes on a football scholarship to California. The easy cosmopolitanism of this culture of consumption was brought up short in 2001. The daily television coverage of asylum seekers queuing up in Sangatte, on France's northern coast, to make their way across the Channel heightened an already palpable moral panic about illegal immigration. That summer, rioting with a distinct racial component broke out in the mill towns of Lancashire, a mere prelude to the global fallout for all Muslims in the West after the Jihadist attacks of 9/11. In this context football looked less like an arena for integration and more like a public stage for the expression of the new antipathies towards Muslims.

The relationship of football culture to anti-Islamic sentiments can be traced back to the late 1980s when Leeds United fans would chant, "Rushdie is a Leeds fan, Rushdie is a Leeds fan." Radical Muslims in Yorkshire had burnt Salman Rushdie's book *The Satanic Verses*, and given tacit support to the global fatwa declared against the author by Ayatollah Khomeini, the supreme religious leader of Iran.[49] These attitudes were given a new lease of life when two Leeds fans, following the team in the Champions League, were murdered by a Turk in Istanbul in 2000. At the England–Turkey game played in Sunderland in 2002, part of the crowd chanted, "Die Muslims! Die!" Some football supporters' antipathy towards Islam and the Muslim communities of northern England acquired its clearest expression during the riots of summer 2001.

The street fighting in Oldham was preceded by months of agitation as right-wing groups attempted to march through the Asian areas of the town; those groups included the remnants of the old and now defunct National Front with a new generation of Oldham Athletic Casuals. In the days before the riots proper the atmosphere was supercharged by visiting Stoke fans who started trouble with local Bangladeshi youths who responded, in part, with petrol bombs. The following day Oldham Casuals were joined by contingents from Stockport County, Shrewsbury and Huddersfield Town who were at the center of the rioting in the city.[50] The riots in Burnley started as nightclub fights and turf wars between Asian and white drug gangs, but soon escalated to the wider public. The Asian taxi networks mobilized in support of their gangs and white Burnley football crews joined in on the other side. While the events of 9/11 and the global response exposed the fault lines between Islam and the West, the street-level encounter in the North of England was best dramatized by the trial of Leeds United players Lee Bowyer and Jonathan Woodgate.

In January 2000 Sarfraz Najeib, a student at Leeds Metropolitan University, went to the Majestyk night club in Leeds City Square with his brother Shazad and three friends. On arrival they met a man who was drunk and raging at his recent eviction from the establishment. A conversation followed, no doubt peppered with a lot of wind-up, and then blows were exchanged. Najeib ran and his assailant gave chase; friends of the ejected drunk tripped the student. Two days later Najeib awoke from the coma that had resulted from the beating he had received. Jonathan Woodgate, Lee Bowyer, and friends Paul Clifford, Neale Caveney, and Tony Hackworth were charged and put on trial. The first run of the soap opera ended in April 2001 after the *Daily Mirror* published an interview with Najeib's father prejudicing the jury and thus requiring a retrial in November 2001. Woodgate was cast as the remorseful penitent, face permanently furrowed, enveloped in gloom, his football form collapsing. Lee Bowyer was dressed all in black and cast as the swaggering, impertinent bully. The tabloids subjected his past to a ruthless going-over and unearthed plenty of stories of racist abuse, drug taking, and teenage fighting. His demeanor in court was brash and uncontrite, his performances on the pitch for Leeds seeming to soar as more pressure was applied off it. The prosecution case turned on the evidence of their black Leeds teammate, Michael Duberry. Initially he denied that his colleagues had had any involvement in the fight before changing his story and reporting that Woodgate had said to him on the night of the assault that "There had been a fight with some Asians." Crowds took sides. At Anfield, Bowyer was greeted with the chant of "There's only one racist bastard," while Woodgate was praised at home to the tune of "London Bridge" "Johnny Woodgate is our friend. He hates Pakis." In the end Paul Clifford took the main rap and was sentenced to six years for grievous bodily harm. Woodgate and Caveney were convicted of affray and sentenced to one hundred hours' community service. No charges of racial assault were brought. Lee Bowyer walked free.[51]

Unpleasant as the attack on Sarfraz Najeib had been, it was merely one example of the many thousands of street-level fights, slights, and drunken brawling between Asian and white youths in northern cities. However, race relations had not yet been poisoned by the language of the War on Terror that would come. The already powerful coupling of Muslim and terrorist was made even more so in the popular imagination by the London bombings of 7/7/2005. When in 2007 the Egyptian striker Mido took the field for Spurs he was met by chants of "shoe bomber" and "your mother is a terrorist."[52] Later, in Middlesbrough, he was embraced by the home crowd after unforgettably scoring against Newcastle in only his second game, and putting his fingers to his lips to hush the hail of Islamophobic abuse that had been coming his way.

The affiliation of older football firms with small far-right groups and their embrace of this new language of explicit anti-Islamic beliefs was given tangible form in the summer of 2009 as recently formed micro-groups like the English Defense League, Stop the Islamification of Europe, British Citizens against Islamic Extremists, and Casuals United came together in regular city-center clashes with police and counter-demonstrators. The EDL began life as the United People of Luton, a small group that gathered to protest against a radical Islamic crew called Ahle Sunnah Wal Jammat who had abused soldiers marching through the town on their return from Iraq in 2006. At the same time Casuals United was formed: an online network of football supporters opposed to the Islamic presence in Britain. It boasted a membership that included businessmen, women, and ethnic minorities, but at its core were the old boys. As one of the founders put it, "There are a lot of people in their forties and fifties who used to be football hooligans but went on to settle down."[53] In May 2009 the fledgling EDL and Casuals United held their first demonstration in Luton, including a breakaway march that headed straight for the Asian neighborhood of Bury Park and set about lighting fires and burning cars. The same pattern was repeated in Birmingham, Nottingham, Manchester, and Leeds, and quickly attracted increasing numbers of protestors (up to 1,000 in some cases) as well as a huge media and online presence. Since then members of both organizations have been involved in football brawls, got themselves banned from grounds, and posted some malicious stuff online. They have not, however, been able to make their presence felt inside football stadiums in any organized way.

If English football appears to be a place in which racial and religious tension has acquired a worryingly public platform, there are also signs of a new multiculturalism emerging within the sport. When Sporting Bengal played London ASPA in 2009 in the extra preliminary round of the FA Cup, it was the first tie between two British Asian sides in almost a century and a half of the competition, a fact that contributed to the highest level of media coverage ever accorded such a lowly fixture. ASPA drew mainly on those with Pakistani roots. Sporting Bengal were the select team of the Bangladeshi Football Association, which ran a summer league in Victoria Park in Hackney and whose ethnic make-up was testimony to the super-diversity of the neighborhood and the openness of the association: 51 percent British Bangladeshi, 16 percent other British Asians, 12 percent white, 11 percent black, 4 percent Somali, and 6 percent others.[54]

While the make-up of football crowds does not parallel the ethnic make-up of the country, some of the under-representation of minority groups is based on class and income. Where minority groups have been more economically successful, British Indians and Jews for example, there is ample evidence of their presence. Less well-off but equally organized British Sikhs have formed their own fan clubs at Sunderland—the Punjab Army—and at Wolverhampton, where the Punjab Wolves have up to 500 members. If football has allowed Sikhs to become Wearsiders and white East Enders entry into the Bangladeshi leagues, it has offered equally fluid identities and allegiances in the international realm. Visits from South Asian and Caribbean national teams have become an occasion for the celebration of diasporic identities. Jamaica's appearance at the 1998 World Cup and Trinidad and Tobago's in 2006 occasioned very public displays of Caribbean celebration and support. When Jamaica played a friendly at Loftus Road in West London in the run-up to the World Cup, almost the entirety of the stadium was drawn from London's black communities. *The Gleaner* reported: "Never . . . had I seen so many black people inside one ground. Generations of Jamaicans had come to watch the game. The most emotional moment for me was witnessing grandmothers at a site that they would never have dreamed of entering . . . steel band and reggae music blaring out of the PA system, Jamaican patties on sale and even the odd 'FUNNY' cigarette being passively smoked."[55]

When in 2005 Australia played South Africa in a friendly at a packed Loftus Road the enormous scale of southern hemisphere migration to West London was given tangible form. At the grassroots a host of local initiatives have produced clubs like Bradford's Albion Sports and Leicester's Nirvana whose core is Asian but whose membership is truly diverse.[56] But even they cannot compete with the super diversity of the Unity Cup annual competition among teams made up of refugees and asylum seekers. In Ipswich, not usually considered the most variegated of English cities, the 2007 tournament featured Bulgarian, Bangladeshi, Kurdish, Czech, Iraqi, Polish and Zimbabwean teams. Here at least football is taking on the complexion of the nation's newest arrivals.[57]

If the Unity Cup is the first sign of the new low-skill migrations to Britain, the make-up of Premiership squads reflects the high-skill migrations from all over the world that have been staffing the upper echelons of finance and medicine in the UK. The demographic transformation of English football accomplished by British black players in the 1970s and 1980s was, numerically at any rate, eclipsed by the arrival of foreign players from the early 1990s. In the first season of the Premiership there were just eleven of them in the top flight. Ten years later they made up over a third of the playing staff and another decade later they had become the majority by some way. European Union labor law was adjudged to be superior to UEFA's rules and so the limits that had existed on the number of foreigners playing in a team were abandoned. European Union citizens, the majority, had complete freedom of movement and players from the rest of the world could obtain work visas relatively easily. Clubs plugged into the new global networks of agents, scouts and academies, and with access to more funds than ever, English football went shopping.

The foreign legion have received, individually and collectively, a mixed response. On the one hand there is a clear consensus that the quality of football on offer is immeasurably better since their arrival. As players and coaches, foreigners have brought seriousness about nutrition, drinking, technique and tactical thinking that has raised the level of every footballer in the league. Individually, the best have been embraced with a rare passion and fervor: Dennis Bergkamp and Thierry Henry at

Arsenal; Gianfranco Zola at Chelsea; Eric Cantona at Manchester United; David Ginola at Spurs and Newcastle. The presence of foreign stars in a local team has opened up the world of global football cultures to English fans, and helped build a small culture of connoisseurship and cosmopolitanism among some. Indeed, football in the form of the Champions League is one of the very few areas of public life in Britain where membership of a wider European community is seen to be both practically advantageous and a source of status and pride.

On the other hand there remains a pool of withering contempt and a host of stereotypes reserved by both crowds and the media for those less gifted, enthusiastic or lucky. Foreigners, particularly suspect Latins, are often cast as the source of prevalent diving, cheating and simulation or as soulless mercenaries. David Ginola was often cast as an over-flamboyant and selfish individualist, his groomed even effete demeanor an affront to the rough masculine norms of an English footballer. Consequently he received a lot of abuse, much of it expressed in Francophobe terms. Eric Cantona received the same treatment from Crystal Palace fan Matthew Simmons in 1995. Cantona responded with a flying kung fu kick. A decade later, after fielding an all-foreign Arsenal XI Arsène Wenger received a hail of criticism in the press and felt compelled to defend himself: "It's really disappointing . . . First we kick racism out of football and the racism starts there . . . It's a regressive way of thinking and I would never want to say to a player, 'You are better but you do not have the right passport'."[58]

## VI.

Enduring forms of institutionalized racism, the uncomfortable place of British Asians in the game, the lingering association of football crews with the far right; all suggest that the anti-racist credentials of football are, at best, an unfinished project. However, the unacceptability of overt racism is now entrenched in football, a change underlined by the events of October 2004 when Ron Atkinson, after commentating on a Champions League game between Chelsea and Monaco, was caught off-camera but on-mic describing the Chelsea defender Marcel Desailly as a "lazy, fucking thick nigger." There was almost no debate on the subject: Atkinson had to resign from ITV and a host of other media gigs, and has since lived a half-life in the seventh circle of minor media hell as a contestant on *Celebrity Wife Swap*.

One of the very few to defend Atkinson at the time was Jimmy Hill whose comments are worth examining at some length. After all, few people can claim such a life-long devotion to the game of football, contributing to it at so many different levels. A player in the 1950s, he led the union that broke the maximum wage in the 1960s before going on to be a club director, the BBC's leading football presenter and the man who introduced the panel of pundits to British football coverage. He had interpreted Ron Atkinson's description of the Chelsea defender Marcel Desailly as merely "the language of the football field," which had temporarily migrated to the commentary box. In a newspaper interview he said, "In that context you wouldn't think that words like nigger were particularly insulting; it would be funny. Without meaning to insult any black man, it's us having fun"; and on the subject of humor, he retorted: "What about jokes about my long chin? I mean nigger is black—so we have jokes where we call them nigger because they are black. Why should that be any more of an offense than someone calling me chinny?"[59] Over the next few years it appeared that Hill and Atkinson, both past retirement age, represented the unreflective, engrained racism of an older generation in football; their contorted self-defense appeared pitiable and their ignorance could be written off as the last of the old order.

At the same time black players were increasingly prepared to directly challenge racism in the game and the criminal justice system was prepared to enforce the law. Nathan Blake refused to play for Wales under manager Bobby Gould after accusing him of using racist language in a prematch training session. Gould's version was incredulous: "All I said was, in a situation where we have conceded three goals against Holland, 'Why didn't somebody pick up the big black bastard,' something like that . . ."[60] Jason Euell was verbally abused by a Stoke fan when sitting on the Blackpool subs' bench and reacted by getting right back in the man's face. He received huge public support from his club and across the football world, while the Stoke fan, after pleading a schizophrenic condition, was sentenced, fined, and served a three-year banning order from football.

Social media proved to be a new arena for racist abuse. Manchester City defender Micah Richards closed down his Twitter account after Internet trolls posted regular racist comments. He refused to involve the police, but a man from Pontypridd was arrested and given an eight-week prison sentence for tweeting racist comments about Fabrice Muamba, the Bolton defender who had collapsed with a heart attack during the team's FA Cup tie against Tottenham. However, "the language of the football field" that Hill had described, what was said on the pitch, remained out of bounds. Until 2011, that is.

After a match between Liverpool and Manchester United, Patrice Evra, a black Frenchman, accused Uruguayan striker Luis Suárez of racist abuse. Just a week later, QPR's Anton Ferdinand made the same accusation against John Terry, the England and Chelsea captain. In both cases the video evidence is pretty compelling. Suárez can be seen calling Evra "*negrito*" with a tone and demeanor that is clearly derogatory, whatever the more diminutive or affectionate version of the word is in South America. Terry was captured screaming, "You fucking black cunt!" at Ferdinand, a fact he did not deny but argued that he was merely repeating back Ferdinand's own words to him. If that does sound plausible to you, take a look at the footage and see if Terry's body language suggests he is quizzically returning a comment.[61]

The FA found Suárez guilty, fined him £40,000 and suspended him for eight matches. The following February, in a rematch between the teams, Suárez refused to shake Evra's hand. Initially Liverpool manager Kenny Dalglish defended Suarez, but both coach and player were slapped down when the club's new American owners took charge and insisted on an unconditional apology from Suarez. In the case of Terry and Ferdinand the file was passed to the Crown Prosecution Service who decided that there was a criminal charge to be answered. The FA then stripped Terry of the England captaincy, though they seemed happy enough that the case would not actually come to court until the summer, after England and Terry had competed at Euro 2012. Given the exceptionally high standards of proof demanded in a criminal trial, Terry was acquitted; but a few months later the FA's own inquest had no doubt at all, finding him guilty of racist abuse, fining him £220,000 and banning him for four matches.

The twenty-first-century experience of Jews in contemporary English football is, in some senses, a strange mirror image of the experience of

Afro-Caribbeans. While the latter no longer suffer the same kind of crude abuse that they once did in football stadiums, the institutionalized racism of the rest of the game, from dressing room to boardroom, has limited their advance. By contrast, for Jews, the institutional racism of the game has ceased to affect them in any obvious way, as they have come to occupy positions of power and authority, but the anti-Semitic ire of the crowd seems to be rising. The new wealth and professional networks of the second and third generation of English Jews began to open up the boardrooms of English football in the 1960s and 1970s. Manny Cussins stood behind Don Revie's Leeds United, while at the other end of the league Harry Zussman ran Leyton Orient with irrepressible chutzpah. Morris Keston, a hugely successful coats and dresses man, made himself indispensable at Spurs, the first celebrity super-fan whose victory parties overshadowed the club's official celebrations. In the last quarter of a century English Jewish players have all but disappeared from the leagues, but there has been a steady trickle of Israelis—from Avi Cohen to Yossi Benayoun—to replace them. The provincial businessmen in the boardrooms of the 1960s have been replaced by a new generation of the globally connected and very rich—from Irving Scholar and Alan Sugar to David Dein and Roman Abramovich. The last bastions of the old order—the upper reaches of the FA and the judiciary—have been taken: Lord Justice Taylor, whose report set in train so many of the post-Hillsborough changes in the game, David Triesman, the first independent chairman of the FA, and his successor and Manchester City director, David Bernstein, are all Jewish.

In the 1980s anti-Semitic and pro-Nazi chanting could be heard in English football, especially in connection with small pockets of far-right supporters. However, over the last decade there seems to have been a marked increase in the volume of these voices, especially in London. At the center of this shift has been the large section of the Tottenham crowd, both Jewish and gentile, which has actively embraced the Jewish identity that they first acquired in the inter-war era. Although there are very significant blocks of Jewish support at Leeds, at both Manchester clubs as well as at the other big London teams—Arsenal, West Ham and Chelsea—it is only Spurs where this has gone public.[62] From the late 1980s onwards they began to reclaim the slurs Yid and Yiddo, referring to themselves as the Yid Army.

In 2002 the comedian and writer David Baddiel described the state of affairs at Stamford Bridge where the crowd sang of Tottenham Hotspurs fans, "He's only a poor little yiddo/He stands all alone on the shelf/He goes to the bar/To buy a lager/And only buys one for himself."[63] As Baddiel argues, it is at one level amusing, even endearing, that the depths of English anti-Semitic caricature concern not punting up for your round rather than the usual global conspiracy theories. However, it is much less endearing that Yiddo was not reserved for Spurs alone but had come to apply to ex-Spurs players on other teams, Israeli players in England, Israeli teams in European competition, in short to Jews. Mark Bosnich, goalkeeper with Aston Villa, gave a Hitler salute to the Tottenham end in 1996. Moreover, as early as 2002 Spurs were being met with the elongated hissing that stands for the release of Zyklon B in the gas chambers of the Holocaust. Arsenal fans celebrated their acquisition of Spurs captain Sol Campbell in 2004 singing, "Hey, hey yiddo—you scum—I wanna know where your captain's gone."[64] Southend fans opted for, "I'd rather be a Pikey than a Jew"; Arsenal sang, "We've got Cesc Fabregas, you Yids are scared of gas." By 2007 Baddiel was reporting anti-Semitic chants on a weekly basis at Stamford Bridge and the club's Israeli manager Avram Grant was sent anti-Semitic hate mail and death threats. A Jewish West Ham fan wrote, "I cannot recall a . . . game against Spurs when I have not heard some anti-Semitic abuse, comment or chanting."[65]

The FA's response to the debate was to set guidelines that outlawed the term of the word in English stadiums and made those convicted of its use subject to stadium. Tottenham fans at their next home game replied with: "We'll sing what we want. Yid Army! Yid Army!" To date, no one has been prosecuted or banned under these regulations. Nicolas Anelka was dealt with differently. In late 2013 the French striker celebrated a goal for West Bromwich Albion by performing the *quenelle*—a gesture deemed to be anti-Semitic that is illegal in France, but hitherto barely known in England—an act for which he was given a five-match ban and a hefty fine by the FA. One of West Bromwich's sponsors withdrew their support from the club and Anelka was sacked.

In 2005, French comedian and political activist Dieudonne M'bala M'bala first made the *quenelle* in a satirical sketch—touching his hand to his opposite shoulder while pointing the arm down. He has described it as being a "kind of up yours gesture to the establishment with an in the ass direction." While he used it in association with an anti-Zionist political campaign, a term he has always been careful to distinguish from anti-Semitism, many others used the gesture in photographs in front of Jewish memorials and synagogues which then went viral on social media. The French and Jewish establishments have insisted that the gesture is an inverted Nazi salute and have passed legislation to ban it. Anelka said, "Because some people have performed [the *quenelle*] in front of a synagogue, then the gesture is suddenly meant to be racist and anti-Semitic in any place and in any situation? My *quenelle* was very misunderstood. I have no record of racism or anti-Semitism, there is no evidence to support it, not even a shred of evidence. I have never had a problem with the Jewish community, and besides why would I have?"[66]

None of this constituted the "huge strides in changing attitudes to racial discrimination . . . because of the changes in football" that Secretary of State for Culture Jeremy Hunt was thinking of. It is not that Hunt and the popular narrative of progress is entirely wrong. There have been real gains: the success of Afro-Caribbean and now Asian players; the indefensibility of overt and public racism; the transformation of the relationship between Englishness and ethnicity; the emergence of new complex forms of cultural and ethnic hybridity that have challenged narrow stereotypes. However, the fact that England's Jews, probably the most economically and culturally successful minority, and longstanding devotees of football, are addressed, through the simulacrum of Tottenham Hotspur, with the sounds of a genocide should give us all pause for thought.

# CHAPTER 5

# Football at Twilight

## Britain's Endgame

The crisis consists precisely in the fact that the old is dying and the new cannot be born; in this interregnum a great variety of morbid symptoms appear.

**ANTONIO GRAMSCI**

JOURNALIST: Prime Minister, what would you like for Christmas?
GORDON BROWN: That we have . . . for the 2012 Olympics . . . a football team from Britain.

**DOWNING STREET PRESS CONFERENCE, 2008**

I.

In the dying days of the Hapsburg Empire, Bohemia applied to join FIFA as a separate nation, looking for international recognition of its sporting sovereignty as a conscious prelude to Czech national independence. For over a century FC Barcelona and Athletic Bilbao have been central actors in the formation of modern Catalan and Basque national identities and the wider struggle with the Spanish state. In 1991, as Yugoslavia burst apart, Dinamo Zagreb and Red Star Belgrade played out literally rather than metaphorically the opening salvoes of the Serbo-Croat war; their game descended into a violent brawl pitting Croat ultras against their Serbian counterparts and the Federal Yugoslav police. There have been other theaters of public expression and more formal occasions for staging the imagined community, but few as large and spontaneous as football matches. Historians and linguists have conducted more conscious cultural interventions and projects but nations at some level must be lived and invented in truly popular guise.

In the twilight years of the British state, the new politics of national identity was played out in the football stadiums of the isles. Not all the signs were morbid; there were glimpses of the new. But there were unmistakable signs of mortality, too. How could it be that the host nation of an Olympic Games should struggle to field a national team in its national sport? More alarming for the patient was the fact that it should top the prime minister's political wish list. In part this was testament to Gordon Brown's affection for football as well as his relentless workaholic obsession with detail. But his remark was no mere frippery. It was a matter of high strategic politics. As Brown himself had argued, "Almost every question that we have to deal with about the future of Britain revolves around what we mean by British."[1]

The issue arose in the first place because the sporting geography of global football and the Olympic movement are not the same. The football associations of the British Isles were established between 1863 and 1880. At the time, there doesn't appear to have been any suggestion that football should be administered on a British basis; like the Anglican Church, the new football associations were organized along cultural-national lines. International football, for the entirety of the nineteenth century, consisted of games between the home nations as they were quaintly referred to. In 1886 they created among themselves the International Football Association Board (IFAB), the international rule-making body for football. FIFA, now the game's global governing body, was not created until 1904 and without the British. The home nations were at best uninterested, at worst hostile to an irksome project hatched by seven fledging European football associations. Unlike the current incarnation of FIFA, the embryonic version was desperate for all the British nations to take a full role in the organization. It was always assumed that the four home nations would join individually rather than as one British FA. However, not everyone got this treatment: a bid from Bohemia to join separately from the Austro-Hungarian Empire was rejected, as was a demand from the Germans that every *Land* should get a seat at the table.

In 1947 a game was played between Great Britain and the Rest of Europe as a fundraiser for the penurious postwar FIFA and a celebration of the home nations' return to the FIFA fold—they had walked out of the institution twice during the inter-war era and stayed away from both FIFA and its World Cup through the 1930s. The quid pro quo for the gate money was that the newly written FIFA statutes made the United Kingdom's four home nations the only permissible exception to the one-state, one-team rule. Since then Team GB has only been seen once: in 1955 they played in Northern Irish colors against the Rest of Europe to celebrate the Irish FA's seventy-fifth anniversary.

The International Olympic Committee (IOC), which was founded in 1894, did not have to negotiate with preestablished Olympic committees or accommodate older more powerful institutions—in fact it virtually called them into being. While FIFA had to deal with just football, the IOC was dealing with a much wider range of sports, many of which had taken on a British level of organization. More closely aligned, at the time of its creation, with the world of international politics, the IOC has always had to tread more carefully on questions of national recognition. Consequently, as it established a global sporting order from above it was always a British Olympic Committee, rather than English or Scottish, that took a team to the Games. Great Britain teams, run by the FA with the acquiescence of the other football associations, were fielded, but as the competition was still a formally amateur affair and the status of the tournament so low, there was little to worry any football administrator. In fact the British teams were so poor that they last qualified in 1960 and gave up trying to qualify altogether in 1972.

While the FA was cautiously supportive of the idea of fielding a British team at London 2012, the football associations of Scotland, Wales, and Northern Ireland were not. In fact they were adamantly opposed to the notion and with good reason. Over the last thirty years, the FIFA hierarchy has both publicly and privately made plain its distaste for the over-representation of Britain in the game's ruling councils: not only were there four nations and teams for one state, but the home nations were guaranteed a vice-presidency and four seats out of eight on the IFAB, which remains the custodian of the rules of the game. The British FAs were so wary of this sentiment that when in 1984 professionals were allowed to return to the Olympic Games, albeit in under-23 sides, the home nations agreed not to compete at all. Scotland, who qualified via the performance of their under-21 team in European competition, refused to take up the spot at either the 1992 or 1996 Olympics. England did the same in 2008.

Despite protestations to the contrary from FIFA and assurances actively sought and gained by Brown when prime minister, the Celtic FAs were having none of it, believing that were they to submerge themselves in a British Olympic football team, the pressure would be ratcheted up for this to apply outside of the Olympics. For some there appeared to be more than the mere survival of an independent football association at stake. Former Scotland manager Craig Brown said he would "rather lose as Scotland than win as Great Britain." The Scottish FA made it clear that it would not prevent any Scottish players joining the squad but they would be "educated . . . made aware that in the eyes of the fans it would be an act of treachery for personal gain over collective interest."[2]

In the half century since Great Britain last played football at the Olympic Games a lot has changed. Not only has the position of the home nations within FIFA become more perilous, making a British team a Trojan horse for the Celtic FAs, but the expression of Britishness has become more deeply politicized and problematic than at any time since the division of Ireland. Having unleashed the process of devolution in Scotland and Wales, and nurtured the Irish peace process to the point that devolved government could return to Stormont, the Labour governments of Blair and Brown found themselves in charge of a formally British state that demographically and institutionally was more and more English. Fearful of the small but active ethnic and extremist versions of English nationalism, and knowing full well that Labour would be massively disadvantaged in English-only political institutions shorn of their large

Welsh and Scottish support, both Blair and Brown actively championed expressions of Britishness. Their most successful venture was their relationship with the royal family; from the PR operation they put into effect after Diana's death to their enthusiasm for the 2002 Golden Jubilee. Less successful was their clumsy embrace of the short-lived Cool Britannia and the attempt to rebrand Britain in the garb of its commercially successful culture industries. Worse still was the vacuity of the millennium celebrations, which served mainly to highlight London's disproportionate wealth and power. In this context, the idea of a British football team at a British Olympics was a late throw of the ideological dice.

Brown, though now out of power, got his Christmas present. In 2011 the British Olympic Association announced an "historic agreement" among the four football nations that would see British men's and women's teams compete at the 2012 games. Be careful what you wish for. The Scots, Welsh, and Northern Irish FAs immediately replied, saying, "No discussions took place with us, far less any historic agreement."[3] In fact, Team GB was the responsibility of the FA alone—a move sanctioned by both the IOC and FIFA. Its institutionally English character was given a big public face by the appointment of Stuart Pearce as the manager; a footballer whose career was defined by his mad dog displays of bravery in an England shirt and who was known to regularly fly a large St. George's flag from a pole in his garden. Hope Powell, the women's coach, is a gay black Londoner. This is England. Hugh Robertson, the Conservative minister of sport, was reduced to begging, "I understand the politics, I understand the sensibilities, but please, please, please, let's put the politics aside and concentrate on the athletes."[4] His plea was not heard. The organized fan groups of each home nation vigorously opposed the plan as well. Support could be heard in some quarters, particularly from Anglo-Scots who found England a distasteful footballing identity and saw a British team as a much more comfortable refuge, but they were few and far between.[5]

The London 2012 Olympics would deliver collective moments of imagined British community, but they would not be delivered by the British football teams. In fact the event that managed to fracture the detached irony, studied non-interest and active cynicism of much of the British public and open up the emotional and nationalist potential of the

Games, was not a sporting event at all. As Simon Kuper, watching the Opening Ceremony, described it: "I felt a strange stirring inside. At first I thought it was the dodgy chicken sandwich bought in the stadium, but I eventually identified the feeling: British patriotism. This was new to me."[6] Danny Boyle had choreographed a collage made from a whimsical tableaux of pop British history. The spectacle drew on the visual language of the cinema, cable television, and the circus; it was part gargantuan West End musical, part stadium rock spectacular. The ceremony opened with an irony-drenched staging of the English countryside as seen in children's television, then moved on to an enactment of the toil and wonder of the world's first industrial revolution by way of *Oliver!* the musical, it threw in a quick dash of war and remembrance, cameos for the Celtic nations and a spot for Britain's eggheads in the form of Tim Berners-Lee. However, the greatest emotional rush was reserved for royalty and celebrity, pop music and socialized medicine. Mary Poppins met the NHS, James Bond brought the Queen to the stadium by parachute, David Beckham brought the torch on a boat, and Paul McCartney played straight man to Mister Bean. In the end it wasn't clear at all what it meant, but it looked and sounded enough like the public's own fragmented vernacular sense of Britishness that it worked. The nation was ready to see itself through the Games. It only required sporting success to ignite the patriotism that had been kindled. Over the next two weeks British athletes achieved the nation's biggest haul of Olympic medals since 1908, including twenty-nine golds. BBC Sport was in such a state of patriotic delirium that Mark Thompson, the Director-General of the corporation, suggested they might consider focusing a little more on what everyone else at the 205-nation festival was doing.

For most commentators however this surge of popular Britishness was a reason for celebration. Among the most celebratory was Dominic Sandbrook who, writing in the *Daily Mail*, was really feeling it: "To see so many British athletes wiping away the tears as the national anthem plays, so many Union Jacks flying with unashamed enthusiasm, has been a tremendously moving experience."[7] Across many similar pieces from both left and right in the media, the Games and their Britishness were lauded in a variety of ways. The bonhomie and unpaid labor of Olympic volunteers and the army exemplified the nation's community and public spirit, in contrast to the lamentable and avaricious private security firm G4S—the pantomime villain of the summer who had spectacularly failed to fulfil their contracts with the organizers. Sporting success was attributed to a combination of scientific innovation, technocratic professionalism and individual dedication, sometimes cast as virtues that had made Britain's manufacturing fortunes. Of all the British triumphs it was the gold medal in the 10,000-meters won by Mo Farrah, a Somali-born Londoner, that was most closely aligned to a new sense of Britishness. Sandbrook put the moment to immediate political use: "What better symbol could there be of a united inclusive country in the postimperial age? What better answer to those who insist Britishness is dead, and multiculturalism is the future? And what better rebuke to the narrow-minded nationalists who want to break up our country and reduce it to a hand of petty fragments?"[8]

In the midst of this orgy of self-congratulation the Olympic football tournament, although attended by over a million people, barely registered in the mainstream coverage of the Games. Both the men's and the women's teams made it through their groups to the quarter-finals, lost and then football disappeared off the Olympic news and sports agenda. It was only as the first postgames retrospectives were being written, and the Premier League season was beginning, that football became part of the Olympic story. Now, rather than a herald of Britishness, it was cast as Sodom and Gomorrah.[9] Geoffrey Wheatcroft was garrulous and splenetic: "We returned from the loyalty and fair play of our cyclists, rowers and runners to the vast carnival of cheating brutality and avarice known as the Premier League."[10] The accusatory questions asked in dozens of articles were: Why couldn't footballers be more like Olympians? Why couldn't football crowds be more like Olympic crowds?

The unspoken assumptions of so much of this conversation were made clearer by a parallel debate unleashed during the Olympics when the Sutton Trust published research showing that just under 40 percent of Team GB had been to fee-paying schools. The Olympic nation, for all its ethnic diversity and occasional working-class hero, was a middle- and upper-middle-class affair. Football, its crowds, but above all its players, was working-class, and according to Wheatcroft neither civil nor patriotic: "Few of our grotesquely overpaid and overindulged footballers have any sense of loyalty to club, let alone country, where the Olympics have burnished anew the tainted name of patriotism." The pervasive demonization of the working class in modern Britain had seen them condemned for their fecklessness and their crudity; now they were being accused of treachery. Defenders of the game and players were rare. Sam Wallace in the *Independent* was one of the few to dwell on the complexities and difficulties of life for kids, recruited from among the most disadvantaged communities in the nation, negotiating their personal and professional course through the madness of modern football.[11] The London Olympics had, as Gordon Brown had hoped, helped frame a new sense of Britishness, but it was a Britain whose demographics were closer to the supporters of the Conservative and Liberal coalition than the New Labour government. Britishness was not dead, but in this form football was not going to nourish it. A glance across the national football identities of the home nations over the last couple of decades would have made that abundantly clear.

## II.

In Northern Ireland sport has been enmeshed in the same interlocking ethnic, religious and national conflicts that have wracked the rest of society for over a century. In the years since partition, Gaelic football and hurling were the preserve of Nationalists ensconced in the Gaelic Athletic Association (GAA), who by statute banned the playing of British games, and playing with members of the British security forces. The popularity and exclusivity of these sports made them important redoubts of political Irish nationalism. Rugby and cricket, organized on an all-Ireland basis, were the games of the middle and professional classes, small town and suburban, north and south of the border; they were a measure of the tiny strand of opinion that attempted to stand outside of the enduring nationalist-Unionist conflict. Football, by contrast to both Gaelic games and rugby, offers a reasonable proxy of a wider swathe of civil society. It was the one game primarily organized on a Northern Irish basis—rather than at a UK or all-Ireland level—and the game starkly highlighted the fundamental issues of inequality and identity, symbol and statehood that fueled the conflict in the north. Both Nationalists and Unionists played the football in significant numbers. At the grassroots level of the game it was a rare area of cultural life in which cross-community encounters occurred. They were not always cordial ones.

Twice in the postwar era, the leading Catholic-nationalist club, Belfast Celtic in 1949 and Derry City in 1972, were forced to withdraw from the League of Ireland, in Belfast Celtic's case because the level of Loyalist-organized violence at their games made life impossible. It was a campaign that culminated with a pitch invasion by Linfield fans who then attacked and injured the Celtic players while the Royal Ulster Constabulary stood by. The club, acknowledging the implacable reality of state-endorsed unionist hegemony, simply folded. By 1972 nationalist Northern Ireland was not ready to quit so easily. Derry City's Brandywell ground was located in a fiercely nationalist area of the city. After the persistent outbreaks of protest and disorder in Derry that followed internment, Bloody Sunday and the suspension of the Northern Ireland's parliament, it was deemed a no-go zone for the rest of the league by the Irish FA and the RUC. The club played on for half a season in the Unionist town of Coleraine before leaving the league. Indicative of the new militancy and confidence of nationalist civil society though, Derry didn't fold, but in 1985, after years in the junior leagues, took itself off to play league football in the Republic. By 1989 it could attract 14,000 fans down to Dublin for the FAI Cup final. Writing at the time Eamonn McCann claimed they were "celebrating an all-Ireland dimension of existence, broke away, free from the bastards 'up there'." It was the kind of cross-border initiative that would become a hallmark of the wider politics of nationalism on the island.[12]

While football continued to attract its small but fair share of sectarian incidents and violent encounters over the next twenty years, it also suffered from the same structural economic pressures that were eating away at the whole of Northern Ireland. The economy had been as dependent on the old heavy industries as the North of England or the West of Scotland, and the Troubles were played out against a backdrop of remorseless deindustrialization. While Northern Ireland's decline, paradoxically, was cushioned by the high levels of public expenditure and employment that accompanied the Troubles, almost three decades of insecurity saw a collapse in new investment, a huge outflow of the most skilled and educated to the mainland, and the declining competitiveness of the companies that remained. The best footballers of the 1950s and 1960s, from Billy Bingham to Danny Blanchflower to George Best, made their careers in England. The outflow was even greater twenty years later. Only four of the 1982 World Cup squad played their club football at home. In 1986 it was just two out of twenty-two. Many fans made a similar move. The sectarian magnetism of Rangers and Celtic drew upon long-established and large fan bases in Northern Ireland. English football had always had its adherents and when in the early 1990s regular live Premier League football arrived, the spiritual and emotional exodus got larger: Manchester United, Liverpool, Tottenham and Leeds could probably claim a bigger support in Northern Ireland than most of the local clubs.

What was left for the players and supporters that remained engaged with local football in the 1980s and 1990s was a semi-professional competition played in increasingly dilapidated stadiums, where an air of paranoia, mistrust and fear had become the norm. Football itself made a small direct contribution to this with sporadic outbreaks of violence and sectarian chanting around individual games, including widespread fighting at the 1979 Cup final between Clintonville and Portadown. But this was small beer compared to the pervasive sense of sectarian threat in everyday life and the vicious circle of segregation and mistrust that followed. The 1980s and 1990s saw a steady demographic and geographical shift. Catholics and Protestants became more and more concentrated in their own areas and more explicitly separated by peace walls, checkpoints and strategically placed roads. North Belfast side Cliftonville had begun life in a mixed part of the city but acquired a nationalist identity as the steady separation of ethnic groups made the area overwhelmingly Catholic. At the same time their near neighbors Crusaders took on a more aggressively Protestant identity. As Marc Langhammer, a member of the Crusaders board, put it in 2011, "This club was a very unwelcoming place during the Troubles . . . If a Roman Catholic had walked into our bar just ten years ago he would have been shot dead."[13]

The last glimmer of football as a truly cross-community enterprise, rather than an arena of conflict, was the Northern Irish national team of the early 1980s. Recalling the era, Frank Curran, editor of the *Derry Journal*, said, "Before most of the 'Troubles' a majority of people in Derry would have supported the Northern Ireland soccer team."[14] It was, like its predecessors, a mixed side, drawing players from both traditions: Pat Jennings, Martin O'Neill and Gerry Armstrong were all Catholics; David McCreery and Norman Whiteside were Protestants. Unlike its predecessors it was very good, qualifying for both the 1982 and 1986 World Cups and this side could count on support across the ethnic-national divide. In other circumstances this might have been a moment at which a successful football team became a vehicle for expressing a common Northern Irish identity. But these were not the circumstances of the mid-1980s.

The rising pitch of communal conflict directly entered the world of Northern Irish football in 1981 when the Home Championships were left incomplete. The IRA hunger striker, Bobby Sands, after refusing food for five months, died in his prison cell in the Maze in early May. He was the first of ten Republican prisoners to die in the protest. Belfast was on fire and the English and Welsh FAs, scheduled to play there in late May, refused to make the journey. In 1982 Northern Ireland won the now re-sumed competition, but it was a pyrrhic victory. The championships, founded in 1884, were abandoned in their centenary year. The English FA had announced in 1983 that it would not be competing again: a decision driven by persistent trouble at England–Scotland games, the problems of Northern Ireland and the search in an already crowded international schedule for stronger opposition and more lucrative, easy-going crowd pleasers than a night out at Windsor Park.

Windsor Park was the threadbare ground where the national team had played. Located in a densely packed working-class Protestant area of the city, it has always been considered a Unionist zone. It also served as the home ground for Linfield, the biggest club in Northern Ireland and the side most closely and publicly aligned with the Orange Order and militant Loyalism. Their spiritual occupation of the national stadium was made material when in 1985 the IFA agreed to give them a share of the box office at every Northern Ireland home game; not a cause that even the most apolitical Catholic fan would want to be supporting. The same year the INLA, a small Republican terrorist group, planted a bomb close to the stadium, before a Northern Ireland game against England. What had been merely a fortress became a bunker. Inside Windsor Park the scale and volume of sectarian chanting began to rise, peaking in 1988 when Anton Rogan, a Catholic midfielder with Celtic, was loudly and mercilessly booed when playing for the national team. "God Save the Queen" was barely acceptable to moderate opinion, the chorus "Up to our necks in Fenian blood" was intolerable. For most nationalists, the stadium now acquired the status of a no-go area. What Catholic-nationalist support there had been for Northern Ireland slipped away.[15]

In 1998, after four years of endless talks, ceasefires, breakdowns and restarts, the Good Friday Agreement was signed and then ratified by referendum. It was an agreement across the ethno-nationalist divide to share devolved political power and to live together in a society that had become very used to living apart. While Northern Ireland's political parties inched their way towards self-government, the Northern Ireland Office busied itself looking for ways to refashion Belfast's rustbelt economy and build cross-community institutions and identities. Among other initiatives they seriously contemplated inviting Sam Hammam and his then itinerant Wimbledon to relocate themselves from Crystal Palace to Belfast. Wimbledon were still a Premiership club, and, perhaps, the official thinking went, if they were offered a subsidized stadium on a strip of Belfast brownfield land and renamed as Belfast United they might lure football fans from both sides of the divide. Visits from Manchester United and Arsenal might be enough of a draw to remake football as at least a neutral shared arena rather than an expression of division.[16]

The plan came to nothing but the idea that Northern Ireland could build its way to football unity persisted. Windsor Park—the heartland of Unionist control of Northern Irish football—was to be abandoned and a national multisports stadium built on the site of the H Blocks at the Maze prison.[17] With ample government funds available for the redevelopment of sites connected with the conflict, the plan was to build a 30–40,000 seat stadium in which the Irish RFU and the GAA would have a stake and play some games, while the Irish FA would play all its home games there. Demolition of the prison would also create the space for a retail and residential complex, all conveniently located on a motorway intersection closer to the center of Northern Ireland than Belfast. Republicans extracted an agreement that one H Block was to be preserved as a site of memory, mourning and education though it was considered by many Unionists to be, in the ever inflammatory language of political discourse, a terrorist's shrine. But the promise of construction and retail jobs, and almost £1 billion of investment in housing, retail and leisure facilities, were enough to persuade many Unionist politicians to back the scheme. However, there was almost universal opposition to the scheme among regular attendees at Windsor Park, who "weren't keen to swap the cozy match day experience for a trip to a soulless self-contained site." With the implosion of government finances after 2008 the plan died a quiet death.[18]

If football in Northern Ireland has demonstrated the limits of community building from above it has had more success when working from the grassroots up. However, despite widespread agreement in political circles that the Irish FA needed to take the lead in making these changes happen, there was no rush to institute reform. Change was finally forced on the authorities by the treatment of Neil Lennon, a Catholic from Lurgan, who had played without incident for Leicester City and the Northern Irish national team through the 1990s. In 2001 he moved to Celtic and a torrent of hate mail and death threats came his way. Graffiti in his home town read "Neil Lennon RIP" and Windsor Park booed him with renewed energy. The following year on the eve of a game against Cyprus, Lennon, now captain of Northern Ireland, received a bullet in the post and announced his retirement from international football. Finally the Irish FA, the local political parties and the leading clubs had to act. To its credit the Irish FA instituted a serious policy of anti-sectarianism in Northern Irish football, issuing and implementing new codes of acceptable crowd behavior. More imaginatively, a segment of the organized support for the Northern Irish team took to actively opposing the sectarian chanters in the crowd and with humor rather than rancor, drowning out old Loyalist tunes with the sardonic strains of "It's just like watching Brazil." By 2008 the Northern Irish fans had become known as among the most carnivalesque and friendly on the road.[19]

The anti-sectarian work pioneered around the national football team has been finding its way into club football too. There have been truly notable shifts, with Linfield actively fielding Catholics and beginning to cut its previously umbilical connection to militant Loyalism. Crusaders, in the north of Belfast, have shared facilities with local nationalist sides like Newington. Grassroots schemes that seek to bring children from the otherwise separate communities together have been actively pursued.

Cross-border initiatives have multiplied with the Setanta Cup pitting the best of the club sides north and south of the border.

However, there are real limits to these kinds of intervention. The single most important fact about the fans of the Northern Irish national team is that from a population that is just over 40 percent Catholic, they make up less than 6 percent of the crowd at Windsor Park. The national football affiliation of the nationalist community has long since switched to the Republic. It was a shift quickened, no doubt, by their markedly better international form; since Northern Ireland last appeared in an international tournament, the Republic has been to three World Cups and two European Championships. As enshrined in the Good Friday Agreement, everybody in Northern Ireland has the choice as to whether they are British or Irish. Nationalist football fans have taken the latter option and so increasingly have the players. At one time the Irish FA considered its prerogative to pick players from across the whole island. Now, many young Catholic players, born in the North and sometimes trained and developed in the North as well, have declared for the Republic. In fact a trickle seems to have become a flood, with players like Darron Gibson, Marc Wilson, Daniel Devine and James McClean all taking the route south.[20] A long legal challenge was mounted by the Irish FA in the Court of Arbitration for Sport and was defeated, and repeated protests to FIFA went nowhere. Even those Catholics who have played for Northern Ireland seem to do so with their heads and not their hearts. In late 2011 Nial McGinn played for a Northern Ireland team demolished five-nil by the Republic. Afterwards he tweeted, "It's always good to feature in games like that. I'm a Republic of Ireland fan and it's obviously good to play against them. I think the only good thing to come out of tonight is that I got Robbie Keane's jersey."[21]

In the new political and footballing spaces created by the Good Friday Agreement, Northern Irish nationalists have pursued a variety of options. They have built new cross-border alliances and identities, selectively opted out of some Northern Irish institutions, and taken a more powerful and secure place in others. For example, the number of nationalist teams in the Irish League has increased. As Stephen McKillop, a board member of Cliftonville, put it: "What's the alternative? Do we pack up and say, 'we're going home.' Playing in the League of Ireland isn't a viable option. And there's a thing—we're the oldest club in Ireland, we were founder members of the IFA . . . we were playing before any of the rest of them, fucking sure we are not going to be the ones to leave."[22]

At the same time Unionists have retained their leading position in Stormont, the IFA and the wider game in Northern Ireland. They retain a veto, for the moment, over the issue of sovereignty—the IFA will not contemplate replacing "God Save the Queen" as the national team anthem. On the other hand they have been forced to address the worst of sectarianism. In its most progressive forms football in Northern Ireland offers a glimmer of a less divided society. However, there remains an unstable minority in Northern Irish football and enough tinder, alcohol and anger to ignite both older forms of sectarianism and new forms of xenophobia.

Old school sectarianism still erupts at games. As recently as 2011 the final of the Belfast School Cup descended into a huge fight between players and supporters of Belfast Boys Model School and St. Mary Christian Brothers Grammar. On Boxing Day the same year, five Loughgall fans stormed the field carrying Union flags and started heading for the dugout of their opponents, Lurgan Celtics—a team with obvious nationalist affiliations. Altogether more serious was the final day of the Scottish Premier League in May 2009, when Rangers pipped Celtic for the title. In Coleraine Loyalists took to the streets in an angrily celebratory mode. Kevin McDaid, a Catholic, was killed on his own doorstep by a mob wielding homemade weapons.[23]

In the years since the Good Friday Agreement and on the back of the long economic boom, Northern Ireland received a wave of economic migrants. Poles in particular came to find work. In 2009 their national team and a large contingent of their trouble-seeking fans came to Belfast for a World Cup qualifier. Polish football has been racked by its own forms of violence and xenophobia for the last two decades; a wider culture of wild drinking and organized violence in club football had spilled over into the national team's support. The encounter was given an additional edge by the presence in the Polish side of the Celtic goalkeeper, Artur Boruc. Loyalists had spent the previous week painting his name and a hangman's noose on a wall in Sandy Row. Supporters of both sides spent the afternoon drinking and setting off fireworks in the city center, which soon turned to violence. Fighting continued with police across the city through the night. The Loyalist element on the streets never got to Boruc, but in the following days a rash of attacks on Polish households in South Belfast saw as many as forty flee their homes.[24]

Paradoxically, the most troubled fixture in Northern Irish football remains Linfield against Glentoran, both clubs whose past identities have been closely linked to the Unionist communities that support them. A game in 2005 descended into a complete on-field riot after Linfield had scored a late winner. The annual Boxing Day game became particularly volatile. Fighting broke out in 2008 with Glentoran fans throwing missiles and launching fireworks into the Linfield stands. The loathing of some Glentoran supporters for Linfield reached the point where they have abandoned the national team because they cannot bear to see their money go, via the Windsor Park box office, to Linfield. Even more extreme, some have taken to wearing Celtic's colors at games against Linfield on the principle that my enemy's enemy is my friend.[25]

But then Northern Ireland has become accustomed to unusual bedfellows and alliances. Stormont is now run by a coalition of the Democratic Unionist Party (DUP) and Sinn Fein, whose hard-line unionism and nationalism have squeezed out their more moderate competitors. Peter Robinson, the DUP leader, has attended his first GAA game, and the organization has formally lifted its anti-British bylaws. Sinn Fein's Martin McGuiness revealed that he loved football so much that he personally helped defuse an unexploded bomb found near Derry City's Brandywell ground back in 1989—thus preventing the cancellation of a key European fixture against Benfica. He says he looks forward to going to see his first match of the Northern Ireland team at a newly refurbished Windsor Park, for which money has finally been found. It is tempting to see all of this as a sign of the depoliticization of Northern Ireland's contested institutions, perhaps even the creation of new cross-tradition identities. Given the course of Northern Irish football in the last forty years, it is more plausible to see them as polite ambassadorial visits of one nation's representatives to another's festivities.

## III.

Politics in Northern Ireland had become closely associated with identity and citizenship since the province's inception, but in Wales nationalism had only become a significant organized political force in the 1960s and 1970s. In 1979, when offered a referendum on a modicum of political devolution the Welsh electorate decisively said no. It would take a long period of Conservative rule and ruinous deindustrialization to change their minds. Even then in 1997 after Labour returned to power, they only just voted in favor of a devolved Welsh assembly, somewhat short of a law-making parliament. Over the next decade a new and more confident Welsh identity was expressed through rugby union, a short burst of locally generated pop and indie rock innovation and, inevitably through football.

"Wales and Welsh people are not an appendage and it is through football, and specifically through Cardiff City FC, that we are going to establish Welsh identity and pride."[26] It is one of the curiosities of cultural life in post-devolution Wales that this call to football arms was not issued by an ambitious politician or a populist local business tycoon. The unlikely herald of the new Welsh football nationalism was Sam Hammam, the mercurial Lebanese businessman who had made his name in football as chairman of Wimbledon FC. However, Hammam had trod this path before. He had flirted with English nationalism, once describing Wimbledon as "the English bulldog SAS club. We have to sustain ourselves by power and the attitude that we kick ass." He had also considered taking the club to both Dublin and Belfast in pursuit of bigger audiences and a nationalist presence in the Premiership. Now it was Cardiff's turn.

Sam may have been just turning a blind eye, maybe he hadn't noticed, but there had been no shortage of efforts to use sport as a way of establishing national identity and pride in Wales. It just hadn't been football. Rugby union, despite being played by a very small percentage of the population, and almost none at all in the north of the country, was long established as the defining national sport. Thatcherism's economic assault on the game's traditional heartlands in mining and manufacturing communities, small and mid-sized industrial towns, made the sport an ever more precious marker; the surviving remnant of a Welsh culture and life all but eradicated.

In the autumn of 1999, a few months after the first Welsh Assembly had been elected, Wales hosted the Rugby Union World Cup and realigned the sport of the valleys and the old Wales with the new Wales of devolved government, indigenous pop cultures and service-led urban redevelopment. The opening ceremony was held in the brand new Millennium Stadium. The Welsh RFU and Cardiff City Council had bulldozed the old Cardiff Arms Park and spent a huge lottery grant on the city's biggest exercise in architectural branding. Towering over the buildings that lined the Victorian red-brick streets around it, the stadium was a statement of metal-lattice modernity, hi-tech and flexible, home to sport, music and corporate entertainment. It promised regeneration through retractable roofs and a new Cardiff built on sport and shopping, tourism and government. Official publicity videos for the World Cup intercut Plantagenet border fortresses, high moors and mountains and the Manic Street Preachers. Shirley Bassey sang the official theme song in a Welsh-flag dress, Cerys Matthews of Catatonia sang, "Every day I wake up and thank the Lord I'm Welsh." Even BBC Wales, normally timid about such expressions of overt nationalism, in their World Cup coverage featured the Stereophonics singing, "As long as we beat England I'm happy." Much of the tournament was in fact played outside of Wales, where stadiums large enough for the occasion were thin on the ground. The Welsh team did not make it past the quarterfinals but there were other measures of success. Over four thousand journalists covered the World Cup; rather more one suspects than covered the Welsh elections earlier in the year and indeed rather more than covered the Welsh football team.[27]

Although not without players of considerable talent and despite some respectable runs of form and near misses, the Welsh national football team was unlikely to attract the energies of conventional or ambitious cultural nationalism of any kind. Attendances at Cardiff's Ninian Park in the 1990s were dispiritingly small in a small stadium. For the games at the Millennium Stadium they have dipped as low as 15,000, while the rugby team has filled the place to its 75,000 capacity. Bobby Gould's reign as manager was marked by unpleasant accusations of racism and endless spats with his players. He certainly didn't endear himself to the Welsh nation, choosing to live across the Severn in England and remarking, on seeing the qualifying draw for Euro 2000, that they had "No chance." Mark Hughes' tenure was an improvement. The football was better and Hughes was unmistakably Welsh, but he was lost to the glamour and the money of the English Premiership.

The relationship between fans and team is perhaps best captured by the story of their flight to Belarus in 1999 which was loaded with more team baggage than was legally allowed. Twelve supporters were ejected from the plane. Speaking to Radio 5 Live one of them suggested they should have left Ryan Giggs behind. The reporter countered, "You can't leave your best player behind." To which he replied, "Why not? We're here for Wales every time, he isn't."

If rugby union occupied all the emotional space in international competition, a niche did remain, as Hammam realized, below this. Welsh club-level rugby never received the same support as the national team. With only a small number of clubs viable in the professional era that began in 1995, Welsh rugby was just one element of a relatively poorly attended league that stretched across Scotland and Ireland. Welsh club football by contrast could attract bigger crowds in the bigger cities. More importantly, they could acquire a nationalist edge because the leading teams played in England.

For over a century Welsh football had been too thinly spread to sustain a national professional league. Poor communication and transport links between the north and south of the country made it impossible to link up the strongholds of football: Wrexham and the towns on the border near Liverpool and Manchester and the big city clubs of the south— Swansea, Newport and Cardiff. By contrast links to England were better and of course, the football economy was larger and richer across the border. Consequently, the clubs that could do so made their way to England, the Football League and the FA Cup. Cardiff City had won the Cup in 1927 cementing their place in the English game, and the enduring significance of being in England.[28] Despite the best efforts of the Welsh FA and UEFA to detach the leading clubs from England, little has changed. It was only in 1992 that the Welsh FA tried to establish a professional national league, insisting that the smaller Welsh clubs playing in lower English leagues must return to the national fold. The professional clubs stayed away. When UEFA insisted that Welsh teams could qualify for Europe only through Welsh competitions if they played all their football in Wales, teams like Cardiff and Swansea were forced to choose between staying in the English league game and losing the chance of European qualification through the Welsh Cup. There was no real choice, and the Welsh Cup lost its biggest teams.

It was this ambiguous position of being both in English football and yet not fully part of it that Hammam relished. There had been a current of anti-Englishness running through Cardiff's support, especially its small but rough traveling ultras. However, no one had tried to mobilize this into a consciously Welsh project. Hammam changed all of that, announcing in his plans for the club that "There should be a feeling that every second week the 'Welsh army' is crossing the border carrying the flag, proud and high."[29] He changed the club's away kit to red, white and green, and mooted that the traditional blue strip be switched to the unambiguously Welsh scarlet. He also toyed with renaming the whole show Cardiff Celts, planned to switch the nickname from the Bluebirds to the Dragons and rename the stadium in Welsh. He never quite got to that, but he did institute the opening bars of "Men of Harlech" as the prematch song, a practice that has endured. Hammam, to his credit, was more than mere rhetoric: he recruited Welsh managers, brought Welsh internationals to the club and invested heavily in an academy that he hoped would produce a whole squad of local stars.

Under Hammam the club rose from the bottom of the league to the upper reaches of the Championship, attendances tripled and media coverage in Wales boomed. Leading from the front, Hammam reprised his touchline parades and tirades from Wimbledon days. At an FA Cup tie against Leeds United in 2003 he joined the home crowd behind the goal in the second half to celebrate the downfall of the visitors. On the final whistle he was carried onto the pitch by fans before parading around with a huge Welsh flag. The Leeds players had to flee for the tunnel while their fans were cornered by the home crowd until the riot police dispersed them. In the semifinals of the second division promotion playoffs in 2003, Cardiff were drawn with Bristol City, just across the border. Hammam must have been delighted to hear his own rhetorical tropes now part of the mainstream media's vocabulary. Sky's Martin Tyler described the clash as "A battle between two cities, Cardiff and Bristol. It's a tale of two countries, England and Wales, two countries, two cities, one winner."[30]

If Hammam had tapped into the nationalist potential of Cardiff City, he completely misread the internal football politics of Wales. In 2002, in the lead-up to a cup game against Swansea, he said, "As far as I am concerned this is a Welsh thing, a Cymru thing, a Celtic thing, not a Cardiff thing . . . Swansea and Cardiff should join together in giving Welsh people the chance of something."[31] His offer to pay for Swansea fans to come to Ninian Park was met with horror. He might have been forgiven for thinking that anti-Englishness would be enough common ground to bind these Welsh fans together. After all, throughout the decade anti-English chanting could be heard from the hard core at Vetch Field and among Swansea's voluble traveling support. "We'll never be mastered by no English bastard, Wales! Wales! Wales!" was sung to English opposition at home, while away to Chester on the Anglo-Welsh border the taunts rang out, "You're Welsh and you know you are."[32] What Sam failed to notice was, once again obeying the principle that my enemy's enemy is my friend, the regular appearance of English flags among Swansea fans when playing Cardiff. He didn't appear to be listening to his own fans either. As one Cardiff fan wrote, "What Hammam doesn't understand is we hate the Jacks [Swansea] more than anyone. North Wales clubs like Wrexham don't really bother us, but we hate the Jacks. We hate them much more than we hate the English."[33] The feeling went the other way too. After beating Carlisle at the Millennium Stadium in the 2006 Football League Trophy final, fans handed Swansea players Lee Trundle and Alan Tate a Welsh flag that said "FUCK OFF Cardiff" which they paraded in front of the stands. Trundle wore a T-shirt that pictured a Swansea player urinating all over a Cardiff shirt. It was tasteless but popular.

Hammam's adventures in Welsh nationalism never quite recovered from the Swansea incident. A couple of seasons later, unable to get the team into the Premiership or Cardiff City Council to agree to his stadium plans, he sold the club to the ex-chairman of Leeds United Peter Ridsdale and a group of investors who kept the club afloat by bringing in a new Malaysian owner. Vincent Tan, a billionaire businessman and eccentric philanthropist, who by his own admission knew almost nothing about football, did what not even Hammam or anyone else had the gall to do. He changed the team's strip from blue to red and put a dragon on the crest (good for east Asian markets and Welsh nationalists alike), abandoning the club's venerable bluebird, claiming "it was frightened by much bigger and stronger symbols, the wren and what not."[34] Yet Tan also spent enough money, all of it borrowed, to get the club into the Premier League in 2013 and attendances continued to climb. The Bluebirds United support group, with over 10,000 members, have opposed the changes, and sing "We're Cardiff City, we'll always be blue" but they do so at home games. They certainly were. Tan sacked the chief scout, installed a young Kazakh, a friend of his son's, for a few weeks until he ran into work permit issues,[35] sacked manager Malky Mackay with whom he pursued a nasty legal spat and watched impassively from his box as the team were relegated.

If Cardiff required the financial connections and football acumen of a foreign billionaire to win and lose Premier League status, Swansea City came at it a very different way. They had spent much of the early twenty-first century broke and at the bottom of the Football League, but then staged a sensational rise that took them all the way to the Premiership in 2011, bringing top flight English football to Wales for the first time in nearly thirty years. The club's success appeared rooted in a large coalition of local business people and the supporters' trust who retained a seat on the board, and in a sustained commitment to playing their own style of football with rational and consistent appointments to match.[36] In 2013, they finished ninth, won the League Cup and made a profit.

Globalist or localist, both clubs had to bend to the forces of national politics. In order to secure their place in English football both Swansea and Cardiff have accepted that, after always having been regulated on disciplinary and other matters by the Welsh FA, they must now come under the jurisdiction of the FA as well. Such is the fractured nature of Welsh allegiances, and perhaps there lies the political limits of Welsh nationalism. The Scots have invented their modern nationalism on the basis of long-standing separate national civic institutions, including the administration of football. Wales, by contrast, has remained much more closely enmeshed with England, constitutionally and economically. The vote for devolution was less than overwhelming, a majority of just 6,000 on a 50 percent turnout. The case for full independence has rarely been raised, even by Plaid Cymru. At the same time the country is more divided internally by the sharp contrasts of urban, suburban and rural

Wales, the geographical separation of north and south and the contentious politics of the Welsh language. Anti-Englishness is an element of that identity, but as the fan chat rooms of the leading clubs suggest, there are real limits to its appeal in a country that is still majority English-speaking, has a significant English minority and has a professional football culture that has thrown in its lot with its bigger neighbor. The crowd are still slaying the English, but one suspects, like the overwhelming majorities that oppose independence, they wouldn't consider leaving them for a moment.

## IV.

In the summer of 1997 Scotland's mass circulation tabloid the *Daily Record* announced the publication of the Home Rule Bill, the legislation that would pave the way for a referendum on Scottish devolution and the re-establishment of the Scottish Parliament after an interval of nearly three hundred years. The headline on the front page read, "Scottish and Proud of It" and next to that was a picture of the Tartan Army, in full regalia, partying in Trafalgar Square. Had this loose band of costumed football fans become the most characteristic visual expression of the stateless nation in waiting? It was not as if Scotland was short of institutions around which its contemporary civic nationalism could be constructed. To its long-standing legal, educational and ecclesiastical institutions could now be added the increasingly Scottish political parties, voluntary organizations, trade unions and culture industries. While these interconnected Scottish elites could stand for some aspects of the imagined nation—urban, upper middle-class, university educated—there were limits. Their style was avuncular but strait-laced and serious, perhaps even a touch patrician. The national football and rugby union teams themselves were another option but their performances while often heroic, even occasionally successful, did not quite match the self-image of a rising nation. Scotland created a fan culture that could do the job instead.

No one was ever under the illusion that the Tartan Army, demographically or politically, really stood proxy for the nation, but it did bring something missing from the imagery and ideas of the Scottish elite. They were overwhelmingly male and working-class, gruff but surprisingly gracious, representatives of canny, bacchanalian Scotland. There were elements of violent anti-Englishness among Scotland's traveling support in the late 1970s and early 1980s. The Scots had been booing "God Save the Queen" before games against England since 1967, a rancorous trajectory that peaked at Wembley in 1977, the year of the Queen's Jubilee. Having beaten England 2–0 the Scots invaded the pitch, draped themselves over the crossbars, dug up the pitch to take home and chanted, "Give us an Assembly, and we'll give back your Wembley."[37] A decade later the whole demeanor of Scotland's fans had switched. The small crews of young Scottish casuals that had been at the heart of past troubles were marginalized and then overwhelmed by the bonhomie of mainstream, older fans.[38] At the 1990 World Cup and the 1992 European Championships the world was introduced to the great shambling, drunken carnival that the Tartan Army had become. While England's traveling support continued to cause trouble, the Tartan Army was acquiring an unofficial ambassadorial role for the stateless nation. Drunk but happy, self-confident but self-mocking, they threatened the Italians, to the tune of "Guatanamera," with the prospect that, "We're gonna deep fry your pizza." The "Hokey Cokey" was versioned to taunt the English: "Oh, Diego Maradona. He put the English OUT, OUT, OUT!" In 1992 UEFA deemed them the fans of the tournament; a Scottish success off the field if not on it.

In 1997 Scotland began the process of putting the English out for real, voting three to one to create a Scottish Parliament with tax-raising powers and significant control over home affairs. The 1998 World Cup in France was the party; Scotland looked forward to its newly acquired devolved government and the Tartan Army defined their Scottishness by not being the English. As the England fans battled French-Tunisian youth and the French riot police in Marseille, the Tartan Army was pulling out all the stops. Against Brazil they decked themselves out in the other side's shirts, against the Norwegians they added horned Viking helmets and charmed the opposition singing, "We're the Tartan Army and we are here to save the whale." In the hours before the game against Morocco, and the team's inevitable and ignominious exit, they occupied large zones of central Paris where their flags read, "Jacques Chirac is a Scotsman."[39] Once inside the stadium the crowd drove the point home.

For the first time at a World Cup, instead of "God Save the Queen" they sang the Corries' 1965 folk dirge "Flower of Scotland": a mournful commemoration of the fourteenth-century battle of Bannockburn, when Robert the Bruce defeated the invasion led by Edward II.

France 1998 was the last major football tournament for which Scotland has qualified. Devolution has not been accompanied by any football renaissance. The consensus, among the commentators at least, is that the arrival of devolved government has, so far, taken the sting out of the politics of football nationalism. The playoff game between England and Scotland for a place at the 2000 European Championships was reported in Scotland as a sporting defeat, self-consciously one without political ramifications. The Tartan Army is still singing and drinking its way around Europe, but it appears less bellicose. Many older fans complain of the over-organization that accompanies today's missions. The sense of Scottishness that has emerged certainly did not necessarily translate into a commitment to independence. Anti-Britishness was not as widespread as one might imagine; one researcher found a significant section of the fans to be comfortable with at least a partial British identity. A Rangers and Scotland fan said, "I'm certainly British, but first and foremost Scottish . . . British by birth, Scottish by the grace of God."[40]

Simultaneously, the Tartan Army's playful anti-Englishness and romantic medieval revivalism have had to contend with harsher and more complex cultural undercurrents that have threatened to disturb its apparently benign modern nationalism. While the Tartan Army could accommodate both unionists and nationalists peacefully, the accommodation of Celtic and Rangers fans, in particular, was harder. Both clubs attracted animosity from other teams' supporters because of their domination of the game, but more importantly there was and is a significant part of each club's support whose national allegiances lie elsewhere. The more extreme elements of Rangers' support can be found backing England, while many Celtic supporters back the Republic of Ireland. Thus among the unwritten rules of the Tartan Army in the field is that club and religious affiliations are kept to a minimum, rather they are actively discouraged. As one fan put it, despite the public unity, "There is still a great divide, but in the Tartan Army it is swept under the carpet quite well."[41]

The Tartan Army has not been without its domestic critics. On the one hand, the unionists in Scottish politics have always feared that the anti-Englishness that is at the heart of the army's self-perception would tip over into outright hostility to the union itself. During the 1998 and 2002 World Cups, Scottish politicians and commentators deplored the "anyone but England" attitude that appeared to grip the sporting nation. The *Daily Record* called for its readers at least not to wish ill on the English. In 2002 the admittedly iconoclastic Scottish nationalist MSP Andrew Wilson actually called for the Tartan Army to support England in the competition.[42] Others have wondered whether the tartanry has descended to the level of embarrassing kitsch and whether in a post-devolution Scotland quite so much emotional energy should be expended on recycling national stereotypes and more on playing better football. The critic Stuart Cosgrove, for example, wrote, "Does another generation have to come and go before Scotland and its clubs make an impact at a major tournament? Even more depressing is the thought the Tartan Army have become our equivalent of Morris Dancers—grown men in ridiculous outfits trying to conjure up enthusiasm for the good old days."[43] However, when the attack came from outside, Scotland was quick to defend its football fans. In 2006, during the World Cup, two assaults in Scotland, one on a seven-year-old boy, a second on an older man, both wearing England shirts, made the headlines. Prime Minister Tony Blair argued in the House of Commons that the events had besmirched the reputation of the Tartan Army, though there was no connection at all. Alex Salmond's acid response can stand proxy for Scotland's distaste . . . "Tony Blair knows next to nothing about football, nothing about the Tartan Army and very little about Scotland."[44]

If football still provided one of the most effective ways in which to distinguish Scotland from England, it was also a reminder of the unspoken interactions and dependencies on which the new devolved order rested. Since the emergence of professionalism in the last quarter of the nineteenth century, England has been the destination for the cream of Scottish talent. Scotland has traditionally run a football balance of payments surplus with the English. Being institutionally separate but economically connected was a system that had worked in football and Scotland wasn't doing too badly out of the new political and economic division of labor. Scotland had retained a higher per capita share of public expenditure than England and a higher level of representation at Westminster where Scottish MPs could vote on English legislation, without the English having a say in Scottish affairs. No wonder then that Labour's Scottish election campaign in 2007 featured Alex Ferguson, Walter Smith, Alex McLeish and nine other Scots making their living in English football with the strap line: "We are proud that Scotland has always stood on its own two feet, but we also believe that Scotland stands taller because we are part of the United Kingdom."[45]

There were some in Scottish football who would have liked to have made the connection a whole lot more explicit. Since the mid-1990s, the owners and the boards of Rangers and Celtic had been scheming and suggesting that they might abandon Scottish football altogether and join the infinitely richer Premiership if they could, or the Football League if necessary. All advances were rebuffed. As an alternative, an Atlantic league comprising teams from the Low Countries, Portugal, Scandinavia and Glasgow was contemplated and rejected. Stuck in their small domestic league, the clubs pursued plan B which was to use every possible method to extract more from the Scottish football economy. The top division was shrunk to exclude as many paupers from the table as was possible. Corporate boxes proliferated, both clubs' stadiums expanded, ticket prices rose and European success was made an ever-increasing priority. The clubs nurtured and tapped their respective Scots-Protestant, Catholic-Irish diasporas, but none of this could raise them above the level of even a mid-ranking Premiership team. That was enough however to destroy the last remnants of competitive balance in Scotland. Facing opposition whose budgets were closer to the bottom end of the English Championship, their structural stranglehold over Scottish football was more complete than ever. It is now twenty-seven years since anyone else has won the title. The financial meltdown of Rangers in 2012 is unlikely to do much for the league's competitive balance either.

The antics of the Old Firm —the collective term describing Celtic and Rangers—mirrored some of the problems of the Scottish economy, with its peripheral location and small domestic market. However, the enmeshment of both clubs with Scotland's sectarian division was not merely a symbolic contribution, but an active and often malign participant in its formation. For a short moment in the early 1990s it looked as if the long embedded sectarian identities and conflicts in Glasgow football were finally waning. Rangers' signing of Catholic Mo Johnston in 1989 was the most obvious herald of the new order. It was thought the super-corporate model that the David Murray regime brought to Ibrox would have no time for any kind of antediluvian behavior. Similarly the new Celtic board under Fergus McCann reiterated its opposition to the display of republican icons at Celtic Park and backed anti-sectarian campaigns like Bhoys against Bigotry. The impact of these early initiatives though was limited. Rangers' goalkeeper Andy Goram could still be found switching on the Christmas lights in the Loyalist Falls Road in Belfast, while board member Donald Findlay was forced to resign after being caught on video celebrating a Rangers win with sectarian tunes and a jig. From the Rangers crowd itself there was a steady chorus of notorious songs, particularly "Billy Boy," which celebrated the loyalist victory at the Battle of the Boyne, and "The Famine Song" of which the least poisonous lines in a cascade of vulgar abuse are "They've all their Papists in Rome/They have U2 and Bono/Well the famine is over, why don't they go home?"

Over the last twenty years, games between the Old Firm have been accompanied by skirmishing and fighting not just at the stadiums but across the city and in other cities too in Scotland and Northern Ireland. Between 1995 and 2001 at least five and possibly as many as eleven sectarian-related murders were recorded in Scotland.[46] In 2003 the Scottish Parliament passed legislation that made sectarian hate crimes a form of breach of the peace, making it much easier for the police to arrest and prosecute individuals. But matters only seemed to get worse. Occurrences of these crimes suddenly rose sharply, with nearly 700 reported in 2005 alone and nearly all of them tied to Old Firm games. Reports from emergency departments in hospitals that dealt with the aftermath of a match told of paramedics dressed in green being abused by Rangers supporters, while Celtic fans abused the nurses who were dressed in blue.[47] In 2004 a section of the Rangers away crowd at Celtic Park threw potatoes onto the field—a reference to the Irish potato famine of the nineteenth century. The 2005 Scottish Cup semifinal showed that the sectarian divide was alive and well beyond Glasgow when fans from the Edinburgh club

Hearts booed their way through a minute's silence held to honor the memory of the recently deceased Pope John Paul II.[48]

The wider public debate over sectarianism in Scotland has been at best spasmodic, at worst a collective case of denial. Furious outbursts and angry pleas for a serious engagement with the issue punctuated but did not dispel an uneasy acceptance of the situation among many Scottish institutions, not least of which was the Scottish FA. This state of affairs was made transparent in 2006 when UEFA announced that they were going to prosecute Rangers for tolerating sectarian chanting among their fans during two games against Villarreal in the Champions League. However, UEFA felt constrained in its approach by the extraordinarily lax, even negligent approach of the Scottish football authorities. UEFA wondered how they could act when this kind of behavior was tolerated, "without either the Scottish football or governmental authorities being able to intervene." UEFA concluded that, "in the social and historical context, we cannot demand an end to behavior that has been tolerated for years."[49] Yet still the Scottish FA failed to respond, arguing much to everyone's astonishment that they couldn't blame the whole club for these incidents so they couldn't punish the whole club, that the club had done everything it could to stop the chanting, and in any case it was all down to the Scottish Premier League. This kind of inaction and mealy-mouthed excuse-making was characteristic of a number of Scottish institutions on the issue of sectarianism. Labour First Minister Jack McConnell called not one but two football summits to discuss the problem in 2005 and 2006, with the result that absolutely nothing happened at all.

In 2011 the issue of sectarianism was reignited by James MacMillan, the Scottish composer. He was forthright in his public condemnation of the Scottish Executive, courts and police who had somehow managed to lose the official data on sectarian attacks in Scotland, attacks not just confined to football but including attacks on individuals and church property:

> The SNP administration, the police . . . are embarrassed and annoyed that the evidence points to Scotland's sectarian problems being specifically anti-Catholicism. This does not fit with the Nationalists'

rosy propaganda about a fine wee country being totally at ease with itself and lacking the kind of community tensions in which those nasty racist Sassenachs indulge.[50]

Scottish football seemed to be doing its best to make his point. In 2011 Rangers were punished again—twice—by UEFA for sectarian chanting in Europe. At the Scottish Youth Cup that year, the BBC recorded supporters of Rangers singing sectarian chants while the Celtic fans celebrated the IRA. The emotional temperature was further raised when one fan group, the Celtic Trust, defended the singing as part of a tradition of struggle, while another group calling themselves the Green Brigade unfurled a large banner at Celtic Park protesting the placing of the British Legion's red poppy on the team's strip. Finally, chants in support of the IRA were clearly heard at Celtic's SPL game against Hearts and again during the game against Rennes in the Europa League. The club was duly punished by UEFA but the Scottish FA remained aloof.

The eye of this gathering storm was Celtic manager Neil Lennon who had already occupied this unenviable place in Northern Irish football culture. At the beginning of 2011 a package containing bullets and addressed to Lennon was intercepted on its way from Northern Ireland. In April that year a viable parcel bomb destined for Lennon was found by the Post Office, and two more packages were stopped, both addressed to high-profile supporters of the club: senior lawyer Paul McBride and MSP Trish Goodman. Then, during a game at Hearts, home fans ran out of the stands, made a beeline for Lennon and attempted to assault him in the technical area.

The Scottish nationalist government at Hollyrood reacted by tabling the Offensive Behaviour at Football and Threatening Communication Bill—a law that was both draconian and ambiguous. The legislation proposed the banning of songs and the criminalization of almost any behavior in connection with football if it was "offensive or threatening," but fell short of specifying what songs and what insignia were prohibited. As Iain Macwhirter wrote in the *Herald*, "There is no list of proscribed songs because to compile one would invite ridicule."[51] The law also passed significant discretionary powers to the police. Despite broad opposition the bill was railroaded through Hollyrood by the SNP. The incendiary cultural politics of Scottish football had helped make the nation that the nationalists governed; now they feared it would expose its internal fault lines.

Scottish football sectarianism illuminated some of the most atavistic elements of the nation; the economic condition of the game in general and in particular of Glasgow Rangers pointed to other frailties. The case for an independent Scottish economy had already been damaged by the collapse of the nation's largest financial institution RBS and its rescue by the UK government and by the Euro crisis. It took a further blow when the perilous state of Rangers' finances was made clear.[52] In 2009 the club revealed that it owed £18 million to Lloyds TSB and had a tax bill, pending the outcome of a legal challenge, to the tune of £49 million for taxes not paid or illegally evaded by paying players through the unusual device of an employee benefit trust fund. Given the very limited size of the Scottish football economy, it was inconceivable that the club could raise sufficient funds to cover this. Owner David Murray cut his own losses and ran, selling the club and its debts for £1 to Craig White. White ran the club on borrowed money and mortgaged season-ticket income and went on to fail the Scottish FA's "fit and proper person test" for club directors due to his undeclared case of bankruptcy. He put the club into administration and bowed out.

Rival factions of Glasgow businessmen fought over the ashes of the old Rangers, while the rest of Scottish football argued over what league the new Rangers should be allowed to begin its life in. The big clubs, the SPL and the Scottish FA all preferred to see Rangers return to as high a league as possible, to ensure that the value of already meager TV contracts was maintained. Fans across Scotland differed, believing that the integrity of Scottish football required Rangers to go right to the bottom of the professional leagues. In an encouraging display of fan power, an online and social media campaign went into action calling on fans to tell their clubs—the votes of which would decide Rangers' fate—to send them down. This was backed up by widespread and credible plans of non-attendance, and as smaller Scottish clubs are almost entirely reliant on their match-day income for survival, this was no idle threat. When the votes came in they were almost entirely in favor of Rangers' demotion to the fourth level of Scottish football. This was not quite the "Scottish

Spring" as some commentators suggested, but a powerful demonstration of what organized and networked football fans might accomplish.[53]

Meantime, the Scottish national team's efforts to qualify for a major tournament looked more and more forlorn. Alex Salmond and the nationalists have wisely placed their affections and their bets elsewhere. At the Men's Final at Wimbledon in 2013, the First Minister pulled out a large Saltire and jigged behind David Cameron as Andy Murray became the first British man to win the competition since the 1930s. The independence referendum was timed to come just after Glasgow hosted the Commonwealth Games where a Scottish team were competing.

## V.

Lisbon 2004. A quiet crowd is gathering on the platform of the sparkling Lisbon Metro. We are waiting for the train that will take us to the game between England and Croatia. It comes rumbling into the station and instantly it is obvious that we are going nowhere; every carriage is packed to the gills with England fans. On the platform we are all silent and motionless, there's no point edging towards the doors. They open with a hiss, and on cue, as if we had just flicked the mute switch off, the whole train bursts into song; to the tune of "Knees Up Mother Brown," "you're not getting on, you're not getting on, you're not getting, you're not getting, you're not getting on." The doors snap shut. Silence. We all look at each other bemused and amused, and the show rolls out of town.

Bloemfontein 2010. We are standing on the rooftop parking lot of the city-center shopping mall where England fans have gathered before the game with Germany. Below, the bars and lawns, walkways and side roads are awash with red and white. Here and there one can make out a flash of black and gold where a few German fans have a flag and taken the odd table, but they are few and far between. Immediately below us a roving conga line of blokes is tumbling through the crowd. They are wearing an assortment of novelty hats—most seem to be blow-up balloon Spitfires. Suddenly, from around the corner, what appears to be a *Wehrmacht* staff car of World War II vintage pulls up with a uniformed driver and a German officer—but they are flying Union Jacks from the car aerial and one has been tied to the back of the boot. The boys immediately strike up, "There were ten German bombers in the air, ten German bombers in the air." My heart sinks, they've started with ten, this will go on forever. The "German officer" is conducting the chorus. I wonder what the real Germans are making of it. "And the RAF from England shot them down, the RAF from England shot them down." Since when did the RAF come from England rather than Britain?

Such were the contrasts and contortions of the English football nation in the twenty-first century. On the one hand, a riotously funny cavalcade, the real Carry on England, mining a distinctly English seam of music hall and comedy. On the other, a cultural farce in which only the English caricature of the Germans will do, while the royal house and its military are fancifully imagined as English rather than British institutions. Unintended, unplanned, and occasionally unsavoury, the England team and the fans that follow it have played out an unpredictable drama for the nation, one intensely covered by ever more forms of media and intensely followed by an ever wider slice of the public. At the peak moments of the story—England's climactic defeats in the knockout rounds of European Championships and World Cups—the spectacle has dominated the print media, infiltrated every spot on the radio spectrum, forced schools and businesses to shift their timetables and attracted television audiences of between twenty and twenty-six million people. This strange ensemble of team and fans, media and public has, in the context of the tectonic shifts in the United Kingdom's constitutional practices, been an experimental imagined community of the protean English nation.

The cultural significance of the England team was first registered in defeat. Hungary's 6–3 victory at Wembley in 1953 was not merely a footballing lesson and England's first defeat by a foreign team at home but unquestionable evidence of Britain's diminished power in the world—a fact that the Suez crisis three years later would reiterate. Tellingly, it was only England of the four home nations whose performances continued to be linked to the fate of the British imperial state. The elision between England and Britain peaked at the 1966 World Cup. It was hosted and won by England but its iconography was British. World Cup Willie, the tournament's leonine mascot, sported a Union Jack waistcoat, the publicity material and programs had the flag all over them and among the crowd at Wembley the Union Jack outnumbered the St. George's Cross by twenty to one. Self-appointed England mascot Ken Bailey, a perennial presence at international sporting events until his death in 1993, dressed in a red jacket with Union Jack waistcoat and the flag on his top hat as well. The defeat of West Germany in the final was personally experienced and subsequently recycled through the British prism of the Second World War. D. J. Taylor recalled how his father dealt with it:

> Having had five years of his early manhood spirited away, seen his house bombed out and several of his friends die, he hated Germans. The final, consequently, was invested with vast symbolic significance. I can remember him jumping out of his armchair in a paroxysm of delight, and such was his exultation, presenting me with a pound note, the first time I'd ever had such a thing.[54]

When Hurst's goal made it 3–2 the crowd spontaneously broke into "Rule, Britannia!" The victory party in London was likened to VE day, but not in Edinburgh or Cardiff. Denis Law remembered it as "the blackest day of my life." Unnoticed south of the border, the Scottish press gave little room to either the game or the celebrations. Hugh McIlvanney recalled that in the press center, "Scottish supporters sat in smoldering sulk . . . and insisted that they did not know what all the fuss was about."[55]

As late as the 1990 World Cup, England's turbulent ride through the tournament was accompanied by the Union Jack, but at Euro 96 English football and its fans looked different. Although the Union Jack was not entirely absent, it was, for the first time, completely overwhelmed by the St. George's Cross. Flags, homemade banners and face paint were red and white, but rarely blue. While the Union Jack can be found at England games today, it is rare, more often than not confined to the corner of a large St. George's flag on which is written something along the lines of "Bristol Rovers FC, the Gas on Tour." Not even a secondary identity, Britishness seemed to rank third behind England and city for the large numbers of fans who support small-town and lower-league clubs. In early 2012 yet another England kit was released, red and white but finally without a trace of blue.

If Euro 96 had demonstrated that the national team had become a public theater of embryonic English nationalism, it would require a Labour government and its very particular model of asymmetrical political devolution to force the English question. In opposition first John Smith and then Tony Blair had made referendums on Scottish and Welsh devolution a central element of Labour's agenda. However, neither showed any serious commitment to a systematic program of constitutional reform within which the ambiguous status of England in the new order would be clarified. Rejecting calls for a written constitution that might have rationalized and democratized the clutter and accretions of statute, precedent, tradition, and legal rulings that constituted the nations' unwritten constitution, Labour preferred piecemeal tinkering with the House of Lords and the judiciary, a half-hearted effort to think about regional government in England that was quickly shelved, and a range of dismal British cultural initiatives, from the Millennium Festival to the idea of a Team GB football squad, first mooted in 2000 by Jack Straw when Home Secretary. A number of prominent members of the Cabinet actively campaigned against any attempt to frame public life in English terms—fearing that it could only whip up forms of ethnically inclined nationalism. The English question was simply not to be asked, but it would become unavoidable. Under the new dispensation Scottish MPs, already over-represented at Westminster, could vote on legislation that affected England and Wales, while English and Welsh MPs did not have a vote on the laws passed by the Scottish Parliament. Similarly, the formula for divvying up public expenditure to the Scottish, Welsh and Northern Ireland Offices, crafted in the 1970s, ensured that Scotland received more per head of population than England. Nationalists on both sides of the border squabbled over the legislative and fiscal entrails of these imbalances and the wider English public finally took notice of the discrepancies. Scotland and Wales now began to look and sound different from England. Their political cultures, underwritten by proportional voting systems, appeared less adversarial than Westminster and significantly to the left of England. The last stateless nation of the United Kingdom finally had to take a look at itself. This proved harder than one might imagine.

The Scottish model of civic nationalism rested on there being distinct Scottish institutions of church, law and education. Where were their

English equivalents? The Crown, parliament, the BBC and the armed forces were British. The law was shared with the Welsh, the literary canon was considered English but the language was now used by most of the world. The Church of England was available, but was rendered redundant by the multi-ethnic and multifaith character of religious England and the indifference of the predominantly secular majority. Historians had begun the long, complex task of sifting English from British, but even in its most populist forms it was an elite conversation. English Heritage? English National Opera? The English national football team (and in a minor key its rugby union and cricket teams) offered one of the very few civic institutions where Englishness was publicly on display and up for grabs.

By 2006 the flag of St. George had left the stadium and gone mainstream. During the World Cup in Germany that year the *Guardian* reported that 20 percent of adults in England had bought a flag, around 10.5 million of them. In a step change of commercial energy the nation's retailers went to work. Supermarket chains, garages, pound shops and DIY stores began to sell not only flags, but a whole range of England themed tat—chocolate footballs, drinking cups and school lunch boxes. Party shops started stocking plastic chainmail for the full St. George look. Among the most ubiquitous innovations was the car flag. Spotted during earlier tournaments, often improvised around radio aerials, the 2006 model came off the shelf with easy clips to attach to your windows. The English public, in the midst of the country's longest credit-fuelled consumer binge, lapped it up. Sainsbury's, now the official England supermarket, shifted 400,000 flags on top of the 6,000 St. George foam wigs they had flogged. Sales of widescreen televisions, pizza, beer and barbecue kits increased by up to 40 percent. Marks & Spencer gave the team its seal of approval, stocking St. George Cross underpants.[56] The biggest winners of all were the bookmakers who by 2011 were taking more than £1 billion a year on football betting, reflecting a 10 percent boost in turnover when the World Cup came around.[57] The English put their money where their hope was, backing England so heavily that the shortened odds made them look like favorites. Another financial illusion, another unsustainable bubble buoyed up by unrealistic expectations and statistical sleights of hand. When the bust surely came around and England departed from the tournament, the bookmakers breathed their ritual sigh of relief, counted their winnings and started taking bets on who would be the next England manager.

## VI.

Like any imagined community, the English football nation is predominantly a mediated occasion. England's games are, for most, a television experience. But in a telling parallel with much of the nation's political conversation, the tone of media coverage has consistently been set by the tabloid press. Over the two decades since the 1990 World Cup the steady decline in newspaper sales, and the huge expansion of space for football in the broadsheet press as well as on TV, radio, and Internet, have diluted the impact of the tabloids, but they remain the most powerful voices. Their contribution has been fourfold. First and foremost they have consistently set the narrative arc of every tournament in which England have played. That arc runs from the generation of overinflated expectations to the splenetic recriminations and vacuous post mortems that follow defeat. Secondly, within that arc, the press have elevated the role of the England manager in the story and then pursued a highly personalized and vindictive agenda usually reserved for politicians in their sights. Thirdly, the tabloids have taken the lead in framing England's opponents in terms of comically antiquated stereotypes. And, fourthly, as sex and violence sell, the press have gone looking for such stories. In the 1990s they simultaneously pilloried and delighted in the violence that accompanied many of England's games, actively searching out trouble.

The England team, though often harshly criticized during qualifying competitions, has repeatedly been transmuted into potential winners by the time tournaments have begun. The 1966 World Cup remains the key ingredient in this alchemy, the historical stardust that allows, despite all evidence to the contrary, the press and the nation to consider England immutable global contenders. Forty years later in 2006 the *Daily Telegraph* opened its coverage of that year's tournament with the headline "14,560 days since Bobby Moore lifted the World Cup."[58] Members of the 1966 World Cup squad are wheeled out to offer their thoughts, suitably repackaged to sanctify the now rampant over-optimism. England's not infrequent poor starts to tournaments are compared to the similarly slow progress made by the team in 1966. The characteristic English virtues of hard running and hard tackling, grit and teamwork, which characterized the 1966 team, are offered as solutions to the current team's dilemmas. It has all been in vain. Since Euro 96, England has made just two World Cup quarterfinals. Defeat has rarely been explained by a lack of tactical acumen or a shortage of basic skills—despite the team's disastrous record in a task as simple as taking penalties. Often defeat has been seen as the result of the mendacity of opponents, freakish bad luck, individual failures and incompetent referees: the hand of Maradona, David Beckham's broken metatarsal, Ronaldo's Latino trickery that got Wayne Rooney sent off, Frank Lampard's goal that crossed the line in Bloemfontein—take your pick. When none of this will suffice to appease the gods, the England manager can be offered as sacrifice instead.

The promotion of the England manager to such a central role in the story was part of a wider shift in the reporting of football in which an analysis of players and the play took a back seat to reading the runes of gnomic managerial pronouncements and rumors of dressing-room conflicts. While the football press has never endeared itself to any England manager since Walter Winterbottom first took the job in the 1950s, the relationship took a step change under Bobby Robson, who was pursued with a new relentlessness, his private life becoming fair game for the press; he was derided as a "plonker" and implored "in the name of Allah" to go. The team's dramatic semifinal exit from the 1990 World Cup allowed him to leave merely battered but undiminished. The same fate did not await Graham Taylor.

Early relations with the press were reasonably cordial but when England were knocked out at the group stage of the 1992 European Championships by hosts Sweden, the *Sun* ran the headline "Swedes 2 Turnips 1." Taylor's face was superimposed on the vegetable, the image stuck and his dignity was fatally undermined. One incandescent England fan ran on a Sack Graham Taylor ticket in a by-election in 1993. When after a disastrous campaign, England failed to qualify for the 1994 World Cup his inevitable departure was gleefully announced by the *Sun* "That's your allotment." Terry Venables was lucky enough not to have faced a competitive game as England manager until they took the field as hosts at

Euro 96. In the meantime he offered enough quotable copy and cheeky bonhomie to keep the wolves at bay from both his team's performance and his own dubious financial dealings. He also knew when to quit and with court cases looming he got out after Euro 96 relatively unscathed. His successors were not so lucky or so fleet of foot.

Glenn Hoddle's tenure was already looking shaky after the press revealed the squad's disquiet over his use of faith-healer Eileen Drewery at England camps and his cold-hearted dismissal of Paul Gascoigne from the team on the eve of the 1998 World Cup. He might, perhaps, have ridden out the storm: Gascoigne was by now a liability and Hoddle's New Age mysticism was not so out of place in the new English landscape of urban Buddhists, crystal power and druidic revivals. However, the application of reincarnation to theories of social justice was a move too far. In an interview with the *Times* he was reported as saying, "You and I have been physically given two hands and two legs and a half decent brain. Some people have not been born like that for a reason. The karma is working from another lifetime."[59] The press closed in for the kill. The *coup de grâce* was delivered on daytime television by Prime Minister Tony Blair, who considered his comments beyond the pale and incompatible with his post.

Kevin Keegan came into the job on an avalanche of press and popular acclaim and a desire for an England team that would play with the élan of his club teams. But he, too, was hounded from the job after a dismal exit from the first round of the European Championship was compounded by defeat to Germany in the final competitive game to be played at the old Wembley Stadium. Common-sense English populism had been found sorely wanting as both a way of choosing managers and running the team. Even Keegan himself, speaking in the third person, knew he was over promoted and out of his depth: "Maybe Kevin Keegan hasn't got it at this level." The FA, undergoing a spasm of modernization under new Chief Executive Adam Crozier, took its chance and appointed for the first time a foreign manager—the Swede Sven-Göran Eriksson.

In an era when foreign players and coaches had perceptibly improved domestic football, it was less of a leap to appoint a Swede to the job, but there remained considerable disquiet in the press that the national team was now run by a foreigner, however well qualified he might be and however poor the domestic alternatives. One strand of opinion always found Sven too passionless to fit the usual mould in which England managers had been cast. His technocratic demeanor was alien, the *Telegraph* describing him as "monochrome and colorless," and the *Times* suggesting he had "the humor of the librarian." Jeff Powell in the *Mail* screamed, "We've sold our birthright down the fjord to a nation of seven million skiers and hammer throwers who spend half their lives in darkness!" Whatever the doubts, it seemed initially to have been a good call. Sven's England beat Germany 5–1 in Germany, qualified for the 2002 World Cup, and made it to the quarterfinals where they were dispatched by eventual champions Brazil.

This proved to be the calm before the storm. Footballing matters aside, the press quickly established Sven's insatiable appetite for women and money. His affair with FA secretary Faria Alam was just one of a series of infidelities catalogued by the tabloids in excruciating detail. More sensationally, journalist Mazher Mahmood, posing as the "Fake Sheikh," sat down with Sven in a Dubai hotel notionally to discuss a new football academy and recorded him saying that he would like more money and would consider leaving the England post to coach a Premiership team. It was hardly a case of high treason, but as a consequence Sven agreed to leave the job after the upcoming 2006 World Cup. His departure was met with bitter invective. Despite successfully qualifying for three successive tournaments and making the quarterfinals of all of them, performances that could reasonably be considered par for the course, he was demonized. The *Sun* was blunt, headlining the story "Goodbye Tosser" and describing Sven as "a passionless bungler who doesn't have the balls to make big decisions."[60]

Sven's departure gave full vent to the tabloids' capacity for national stereotyping, a skill sharpened by nearly two decades of brilliantly inventive wordplay in the service of the crudest of world views. Prior to playing Scotland at Euro 96 the *Sun* instructed the England team to "Blow their Jocks off" and, against the Dutch, to "Go Give 'Em a Clogging." After the quarter-final victory against Spain, the *News of the World* announced, "We Kicked them in the Castanets," while the more politically astute *Sun* referenced the bitter battles over European fishing quotas being fought out with the EU and Spain: "For the nation that nicked our fish there will be no plaice in the semi final." Not to be outdone, the BBC's Jonathan Pearce greeted the victory by exclaiming, "Salvador Dali, Pablo Picasso, Jose Carreras, El Cordobes, Don Quixote, your boys are out and they can stick it up your Julio Iglesi . . . ASS!"[61] The semifinal against the Germans raised the rhetorical bar. For once the *Mirror* lay at the cutting edge of national stereotyping: "Football War is Now Declared" announced the front page, accompanied by Stuart Pearce and Paul Gascoigne in Tommy helmets. "ACHTUNG SURRENDER—For You Fritz, Ze Euro 96 Championship is over." Inside editor Piers Morgan mimicked the voice of Chamberlain's 1939 declaration of war. Not content with mere words, the *Mirror* also hired an armoured car and sent it off to the German team's hotel. Thankfully the police intercepted it on the M25. Subject to repeated complaints and a Press Commission investigation, the *Mirror's* knuckles were lightly rapped.

While the press has not plumbed the same xenophobic depths as the *Mirror* in 1996, it has continued to offer up the same bizarre menu of military imagery. On the eve of the 2006 World Cup the *Daily Mail* opened the tournament with a football scarf around Nelson's neck and the headline "England Expects." Inside they put Wayne Rooney on a St. George's Cross poster, his index finger pointing and Kitchener's call for cannon fodder paraphrased for the TV age, "Your country needs YOU at 4:00 p.m. today." Actor Ray Winstone played rent-a-geezer for the tournament. He was contracted by the FA to travel to Germany and promote positive peaceful vibes among the fans. At the same time he was recording bellicose motivational messages for the *Sun* who sent his recording of Churchillian oratory and Shakespearian battle speeches to the team.

Coverage of fighting at England games had always hovered between moral outrage and a secret pleasure that there was so much juicy action to cover. As the incidence of violence diminished, and the papers searched for scuttlebutt more suited to spiteful celebrity culture, they turned to players' private lives and those of their wives and girlfriends—the WAGs. Hitherto their public profile had largely conformed to Alf Ramsey's patrician arcadia: "A footballer's wife needs to run the home completely so that he has no worries; give him the sort of food he likes . . . and to work only for his good and the good of his career."[62] Although she had notable predecessors, Posh Spice, now Victoria Beckham, rewrote the rules. A celebrity in her own right, she brought a new mode of doing business and new sorts of journalists into the England camp: the paparazzi and the gossip columnists. Their presence peaked at the 2006 World Cup when the England caravan holed up in the up-market spa town of Baden-Baden. While the team itself was virtually inaccessible, the FA had contrived to place the players' families in the same hotel as the journalists. While the team struggled, the WAGs went on the town—staged hotel exits and entrances, opulent shopping trips and fabulously expensive bar bills. The press had a morality tale they were looking for: wastrel women and gold diggers, living it up and stealing the stage, while the nation's football team went to pot.

## VII.

During the 1980s and 1990s England's traveling support confirmed all the reasons why unionists of both the left and the right preferred to keep the English question unanswered. Jack Straw, while Home Secretary, argued that English nationalism was "potentially very aggressive, very violent." William Hague considered it "the most dangerous of all nationalisms," expressed by what Peter Hitchens called "mobs of fat, beery men."[63] Over the last twenty years the fat beery men have stayed but the behavior and the composition of the England crowd have changed. Prior to the 1980s England away support could be counted in the hundreds rather than the thousands, but by the early 1980s they were making their presence felt. There were outbreaks of fighting at both the 1980 European Championships in Italy and the 1982 World Cup in Spain. After the Heysel disaster in 1985, UEFA banned English clubs from European football. Without the option of a club jolly abroad, the hard core and the adventurous switched their travel arrangements: there was a perceptible growth in the numbers and volatility of the England team's away fans. The English disease, as it was commonly referred to at home and abroad, had merely been diverted rather than eradicated. The team went to the 1988 European Championships in Germany and played dismally. Around 7,000 England fans went with them and fought running battles with German fans and police in the medieval warrens of old Düsseldorf.

It was with these events in mind that Italian security forces took a corral-and-charge-first, ask-questions-later policy when policing the larger contingent of England fans that followed the team at the 1990 World Cup. Deliberately located on the periphery in the opening rounds, England played their games in Cagliari on Sardinia while the rest of their group were based in Sicily. They scraped their way into the knock-out rounds while their fans got themselves involved in chair-throwing competitions on the piazzas, endured closely policed marches to and from the stadiums, and took a series of beatings from the carabineiri. They were rough and drunk, but the viciousness of the Italian police and their premeditated aggression managed to make England fans look more sinned against than sinning.

On the fringes England's support remained a recruiting ground for right-wing organizations like the recently formed British National Party. Matches against the Republic of Ireland provided the perfect stage for a particularly vicious display of British/Unionist anger. In 1995 England played the Republic in Dublin. When Ireland went 1–0 up in the twenty-first minute a group of England fans in the upper level of the main stand started hurling objects into the stand below. A phalanx of Nazi-saluting men formed up towards the front; they were later revealed to be members of the BNP splinter group Combat 18 who had come planning trouble. Fights broke out on the edges where Irish and English fans were not segregated, and progressively larger chunks of jagged wood from the old stadium were chucked into the terraces beneath them while they chanted "No Surrender to the IRA." Understaffed and underprepared, stadium security could no more than hold its lines, get people out of the way of the missiles and prevent Irish fans from storming the English section. Eventually the riot squad arrived and the stadium was cleared.

Euro 96 was almost entirely free of disorder within or around the stadiums. The tournament and the behavior of the England crowds provided a public rehabilitation of English football. Nonetheless, a toxic combination of xenophobia and alcohol remained on the fringe. After England's defeat to Germany on penalties in the semifinal there was a night of small-scale rioting in Trafalgar Square, with German cars targeted for burning. The 1998 World Cup in France and Euro 2000 saw both the biggest English traveling support ever and street fighting broadcast on television news. England fans in Marseille clashed with both local youths and the riot police. In 2000 in Charleroi in Belgium they first fought with German fans before the Belgian police moved in with water cannons and riot gear. In both cases the failure of local police forces to anticipate the sheer size of the English contingent created a public-order nightmare. Over-zealous policing played its part as well. The foreign correspondent of the *Washington Post* was in the main square of Charleroi in 2000 and reported that while there were perhaps a hundred England fans who were looking for trouble, "a good portion of the hooligan problem was a UEFA creation." The authorities had steered the ticketless England fans into a square with no big screen and no loudspeaker, where the only place to watch the game was a bar and the only way to hold your place was to drink all day. Heat, drink and frustration turned into small-scale stand-offs and jeering, The Belgian police converted it into an urban battleground. The verdict of the National Criminal Intelligence Services was not dissimilar from that of the *Post*'s correspondent. Although a smattering of known far-right activists were present, the whole thing was more piss-up that conspiracy: "A load of lads decided to get drunk and go on the rampage . . . probably just fairly normal lads who [get] on a ferry with their mates, drink too much and then let themselves get caught up in the trouble."[64] It was a report that could have applied to most outbreaks of trouble on most weekend nights in the center of most English provincial towns.

The new majority got their turn in the limelight at the 2002 World Cup in Japan and South Korea. Dissuaded or debarred by police bans, much of the old hardcore stayed at home. Others were put off by a very expensive itinerary with the result that fewer than 10,000 England fans traveled to Japan. Once there they were surprised to find considerable support, even affection, for them and their team. Alongside the official Japanese-English fans, delegated to support the honored visitors, the popularity of English music and David Beckham in the country gave the whole chorus an unexpected sheen of contemporary youth cool. With barely any kind of trouble reported at all, England fans dipped their toes in the water of the carnivalesque, celebrating the defeat of Denmark in the knock-out rounds with a thousand-person conga around Niigata Stadium. Unencumbered by media-magnified visions of thuggery, the nation at home embraced the moment more comfortably than ever. When England walked out to face Brazil at breakfast time in Europe, the TV nation had ground to a halt, streets emptied, traffic disappeared and schools and offices made special arrangements to show the game. As *When Saturday Comes* put it retrospectively, "England were just OK and for once it seems the country as a whole pretty much accepted that . . . more people felt comfortable about supporting England this time around than before . . . it did seem as though Sven's England was one that appealed to (or at least didn't alienate) a lot of groups who previously found it impossible to support the national team."[65]

What brought about this shift? In part it reflected the broader trends underway in domestic football, where a combination of all-seater stadiums, stewarding and an older more middle-class crowd had made violence at football a much rarer occurrence. Secondly, under pressure from UEFA and the public, the Home Office introduced tougher legislation to control the international travel of known hooligans. Perhaps most importantly the idea that one could hitch the notion of a white racial nationalism to the England football team and its fans became simply ridiculous, stripping ultra-nationalists and old-school racist firms of their niche in the crowd.

The challenge to the idea of an unambiguously white England was of course the work of two generations of black players, both foreign and English, who had fought their way past the institutionalized racism of the clubs and the public racism of the stands, and broken into the upper echelons of the game. Viv Anderson's first cap for England in 1978 broke the equation of Englishness and whiteness, and the prominent role of players like John Barnes, Des Walker and Paul Ince in the late 1980s and early 1990s rendered it meaningless. By the twenty-first century England would field a team that had a majority of black players. If the presence of black players in the squad rendered the team a poor place for expressing a racist political nationalism, it wasn't clear, at first, that it made Englishness more appealing to the country's minority publics. The widespread appearance of the St. George's Cross in 1996 sent ripples of anxiety through the black press, where there remained considerable unease with the notion of Englishness. The lingering air of racist chants in football stadiums saw few new black faces arrive in the crowd in the early 1990s, but even this began to change. Sarfraz Manzoor captured the ambiguity of the shift after celebrating England's victory over Argentina at the 2002 World Cup:

That night, as Asians, blacks and whites joined together . . . I remember thinking: this is what patriotism could be like if we could defang it of its nastier elements . . . But I also remember an Asian friend laughing at the sight of us all singing for England. When I asked him what he found funny, he replied: "It's as if, by wearing the flag, we're saying, 'See, we're not that different from you, please don't beat us up.'"[66]

Two years later, Leon Mann from the anti-racist campaign Kick It Out was less ambiguous when describing his trip to Euro 2004: "The first fans I saw were a group of 10 to 15 Asian lads who were draped in the flag of St. George—I thought 'wow'."[67] Perhaps, at last, the flag came with less baggage. Speaking of the 2006 World Cup, John Sentamu, the Archbishop of York, recalled: "In the city of Birmingham, where a good number of taxi cabs are operated by Asians, often Muslims, the flag of St. George became an addition to every cab."[68]

In late 2003 England played Turkey at the Stadium of Light in Sunderland accompanied by the last major spasm of violence and disorder at an England game. Sections of the crowd booed the Turkish national anthem, to which parts of the Turkish support responded by hurling racist abuse at England's black players. The frenetic nature of the crowd boiled over during the game as England's two goals were met by minor but maniacal pitch invasions. Into the night fighting was reported among English and Turkish fans in Sunderland city center.[69] While there continue to be minor scuffles and arrests around the England team, this was the last significant violence to occur, and this has been the precondition of the truly explosive growth of sentiment and public pageantry around the football team.

If the English carnival in East Asia in 2002 had been available only to the wealthier and more adventurous of England's fans, Euro 2004 in Portugal was truly cross-class and mass-market. It wasn't a hard sell. It was the peak of the boom in an era of cut-price air lines and easy credit. This was the same sun-drenched, Iberian beer or ecstasy fest that English holidaymakers had been going on for almost a decade, but with football thrown in as well. At around 150,000 it was easily the biggest contingent of England fans, overseas, ever. In and around stadiums on match days, England fans were the backdrop to the tournament, occupying public space in large numbers and not just at England games. At the quarter-final between France and Greece in Lisbon, during the quiet opening twenty minutes when the small visible contingents of both sets of fans had been virtually silent, the stadium was spontaneously filled by a chant of "Ingerland"—which revealed that they made up perhaps a quarter of the audience. Fighting and arrests were entirely confined to the very drunk and badly behaved at their holiday chalets.

Portugal though was an easy test of the change in England's support. The country was a long-established ally and known holiday destination, for which even the British press had difficulty in whipping up antipathy. The World Cup in Germany in 2006 was another matter. Perhaps as many as 170,000 England fans headed to the tournament or, as the *Sun* put it, "invaded." However, contrary to most expectations the Germans proved friendly and the English reciprocated. Indeed, the delirious enthusiasm of the English for beer and questionable meat products, football and song found a second home, forcing many to recognize just how similar the Germans and the English are. Caught up in the nationwide street party and cosmopolitan love fest that engulfed the normally strait-laced Germans, the English fell in.[70] As they had in Portugal, organized groups of English fans played football with local schoolchildren and visited hospitals. They also led a visit to the Dachau concentration camp where together with German football supporters they laid a St. George's wreath. The tournament passed without any serious incident. An outbreak of drunken chair-throwing in Stuttgart was seen as a regrettable aberration rather than the norm. Even the *Sun* was forced to report, "Love is in the Herr."[71]

## VIII.

At a distance, united in the stadium, the English football nation appears a simple homogeneous collective. On closer examination, its structure and its identities are multifaceted and complex. There are at least half a dozen elements to the crowd.[72] First, the old crowd has not entirely disappeared, they've just got older. The now middle-aged remnants of the old firms, now with families and caravan, are still there. Much more numerous these days are the official fans who, due to their dedication in attending England qualifiers, get the first shot at tournament tickets. Of the 25,000 members of the official supporters' club in 2006, 4,000 were women; a quadrupling in just four years. Reports from the campsites and stadiums revealed that many women of all ages had made the journey.[73] A significant section of England's support, increasingly so in the last two decades, is the corporate brigade, arriving on work-funded jollies, taking advantage of hospitality packages provided by a sponsor. Beyond this core of officially ticketed supporters there is a great mass of fans that have come with tickets for just some games or no games at all. Perhaps the largest new group are the independents and internationalists. They include small groups of friends, networks of tournament junkies and great stag-party posses. Some will have planned itineraries, others will have taken pot luck on the official website and landed tickets for a whole variety of non-England games; in between they are following England when and however they can.

In terms of identity politics, the picture is equally complex. The English have not quite decided yet where they stand. Though there is a small drift from Britishness to Englishness as the leading identity, the English have not abandoned Britishness en masse.[74] The continuing popularity of British songs and imagery, if not the British flag, among England fans underlines this. "Rule Britannia" remains a crowd favorite. The Second World War, or rather its cinematic versions, provides an important part of the soundtrack. The Hillsborough band from Sheffield, now officially promoted to be the England Supporters Band, has been a fixture at games since 1996, relentlessly churning their way through the music from *The Dambusters* and *The Great Escape*. The crowd still belts out "God Save the Queen" with unproblematic gusto. The first mutterings have been heard that the English, like the Welsh and Scots, should have their own anthem on sporting occasions, but there is no consensus for change. Surveys of the fans suggest that they are more inclined to describe their national identity as English rather than British by comparison to the general population, but they are by no means convinced of the need of an independent England.[75] There remains a significant minority who are shy of all forms of patriotism and nationalism, while among fans from the North of England there is a sense that the team and its base at Wembley are too closely linked to London and the South.

English or British: how did the nation imagine itself? Since Lonnie Donegan's skiffle novelty song "World Cup Willy" was released in 1966, over one hundred official and unofficial England singles have been released, and three in particular help answer that question.[76] New Order's "World in Motion" was released as England's official song for the 1990 World Cup, and for the first time in twenty years England were back at number one. England now looked and sounded different. In the place of amateurish tub thumpers of the 1970s and 1980s, English football was aligned with a highly crafted piece of pop electronica, melodic and danceable; the kind of tune you were more likely to hear at an illegal ecstasy-fueled rave than in the back room of a boozer. While the old England had been all about winning and reclaiming, "World in Motion" wanted style: "Express yourself, create the space." This was an England that preferred making love to making war. Most startling of all, the beery back-of-the-coach drone of the England squad was replaced by a black man who could rap. In the video version, John Barnes stood on the empty lawns of a windswept housing estate, and, sounding like a tentative Grandmaster Flash, offered a glimpse of what the English football nation was becoming:

Catch me if you can, because I'm the England man
And what you're looking at is the master plan
We aint' no Hooligan. This ain't no football song
Three lions on our chest, you know we can't go wrong.

While "World in Motion" is affectionately remembered it was never a song that was going to work on the terraces. The official song for Euro 96 certainly did. Not only did "Three Lions" make number one, but it was the song of choice during the tournament, including for the eventual winners Germany who sang it at their own victory parade in Berlin. Since then it has become a staple of the England crowd's repertoire. Written and performed by the blokeish comedy duo David Baddiel and Frank

Skinner and Ian Broudie, lead singer of the Lightning Seeds, the song's success rests on the infectious simplicity of its main refrain, "Football's coming home." Instantly and easily singable, the phrase connected on many levels: the return of English football to Europe after the post-Heysel ban; the end of the game's pariah status in English culture; the claim that despite its global reach the English could still claim to be the game's inventors.

The third and last song that has left a significant trace was "Vindaloo." While "Three Lions" encapsulated the unresolved postimperial nostalgia of English football and replaced an aggressive English macho with a more mawkish and sentimental masculinity, "Vindaloo" shone a light on an altogether more eccentric side of the nation. The song's video was a spoof of the video that accompanied the Verve's 1997 hit "Bitter Sweet Symphony," in which moody lead singer Richard Ashcroft rudely barged his way down the pavement of a busy market street in Hoxton. While Ashcroft bangs shoulders with a recognizable cross-section of inner city folks, his avatar in "Vindaloo" encounters an altogether more surreal England. On the street and in the ever-growing crowd following the Goth we see chalk-dusted Sumo wrestlers, kids in ice hockey kits, characters drawn from saucy seaside postcards and the Benny Hill show, naughty schoolgirls, strumpet nurses and cleaners and a tart in a leather skirt and leopard-print top. They are joined by a dreadlocked pearly king and queen, a drunk in tweeds, and the strutting duck walk of the long gone and much lamented music hall and TV comedian, Max Wall. Keith Allen, who had also featured in the video of "World in Motion," serves as the maniacal pied piper, an ageing artful dodger who speaks to the throng, rallies the crowd, leads the song and makes the case for a mongrel nation bound by its love of football, family and food—especially Indian takeaways.

Since 1998, the official songs have been, at best, anodyne. Ant and Dec's "We're on the Ball" looked and sounded like a second-rate sketch from kids' television while the Farm's old song "All Together Now" reissued for Euro 2004 dripped with worthy sentiment. The FA, perhaps wisely, got out of the music business and no official song was released in 2010.

There have been no shortage of unofficial songs, but England fans have proved resistant to the charms of these efforts. The 2006 World

Cup in Germany gave John Cleese another opportunity to reprise his Basil Fawlty "Don't mention the war" routine as an unofficial anthem for the team. Hard as they plugged it, no one could quite go there. Similarly radio station Talk Sport mobilized a chorus of Frank Bruno, Martin Peters, Geoff Hurst and one of the last surviving members of the *Dad's Army* cast—Bill Pertwee—in a shameless rewrite of the sitcom's theme tune, "Who do you think you are kidding, Mr Klinsmann?" Plugged by the *Sun* and Talk Sport it crept up to number thirteen in the charts, but sold fewer records than a re-release of "Three Lions." Even "We Are the Champions," which featured a sampled Crazy Frog—the most infuriating ringtone of the decade—came in higher at number eleven. Slaves to nostalgia and their mobile phones the English may be, but perhaps the limits of Germanophobia and the myths of the finest hour had been reached. For the football nation, this surely counted as progress.

## IX.

If the 2006 World Cup demonstrated how far England's fans had come, it also demonstrated how far the team and the FA had to go. In 2001, not long into his term as the chief executive of the FA, Adam Crozier ill-advisedly argued that the new wave of players, nurtured in the elite clubs of the Premiership, were the golden generation. He pinpointed 2006, when in terms of age they would be around their collective peak, would be England's best chance to win the World Cup. In fact they were eliminated, again on penalties, in a quarterfinal after torpid performances in the early rounds, but Crozier was right in one sense: this was their peak. England failed to even qualify for the European Championships in 2008, were knocked out of the World Cup even quicker in 2010 and departed in the same way at Euro 2012. At precisely the moment that the boom years of New Labour came to an end and the inflated bubble of property values was popped, the stock of the golden generation was properly evaluated and found to be oversold and overrated.

Despite the inevitable clamour for the job to go to an Englishman after Eriksson's resignation, the FA first approached the Brazilian Luiz Felipe Scolari, who turned down the job down. They then rejected Northern Irishman Martin O'Neill after he failed to show up at the interview with a decent PowerPoint presentation. There was nowhere to go but to follow the popular sentiment and appoint the only Englishman who seemed to want the post, Sven's part-time henchman and Middlesbrough's manager, Steve McLaren. His time in the job is best remembered for a stuttering lack of authority and confidence, highlighted by his wincingly embarrassing use of players' nicknames and his prickliness at the slightest criticism. Harry Pearson's assessment was cruel but true: "McLaren, with his fifties quiff and rosy-cheeked complexion, had the air of the coach driver rather than the boss."[77] McLaren called on Terry Venables to help him with the team and Max Clifford to help with the media. But there was nothing that these highly paid consultants could do to stop the rot. England played without heart or wit, reaching their lowest point in the first half of the qualifying game against Andorra. As the *Guardian* live blog reported from the game, "England are playing miserably, devoid of wit, confidence, class and, most exasperatingly of all in many ways, aggression. And the fans, who were full of bravado and all that guff before the start, are already into a chorus of: 'Steve McLaren is a banker'."[78] Despite this kind of setback, England needed only not to lose against Croatia in order to qualify for the European Championships. This proved too much for the golden generation. In gruesome weather, Croatia took them apart; 2–0 ahead after less than a quarter of an hour. A late England rally in the second half brought the score back 2–2, but a third goal from the Croats finished England and McLaren off. In an act of public pathos, he stood alone on the touchline, mute and broken beneath a golf umbrella that seemed to barely keep the driving rain off his padded anorak.

With even the most bellicose columnists muted in support of another English England manager, the FA went shopping again and got themselves Fabio Capello. The stern Italian seemed to offer everything that McLaren had not. Parsimonious with his opinions rather than garrulous, his limited English seemed at first to make him a man of few but wise words. His widely touted interest in modern art spoke of a manager with an intellectual hinterland, in contrast to the closeted one-dimensional football man that had preceded him. Where informality bordering on insolence had once been the norm, Capello spoke formally, if at all, to players, and made strict rules on dress, attendance at meals and the use of mobile phones. The WAGs, it was made clear, would not be welcome.

Under Capello England qualified for the 2010 World Cup but were awful, squeaking into the knock-out phase only to be summarily dispatched by Germany 4-1 in Bloemfontein. England were simply not good enough and that was it. In the years since South Africa the team stuttered its way toward qualification for the European Championships but never raised itself above the pedestrian. Even at home, a team of players used to competition at the highest level in the club game appeared overawed. For all his authoritarian bluster and supposed man-management skills Capello never seemed to be able to coax England out of their shell.[79] The pendulum of opinion swung from foreign expertise to homegrown wisdom. Capello was replaced by Roy Hodgson. Neither exotic nor charismatic, conservative in his tactics, he brought a degree of dignified calm to the circus and made England's early exit from the European Championships in 2012 look like the plausible but disappointing result that it was; it was a degree of realism in the assessment of England's chances not seen for decades. The home front was equally sober in 2012. Television viewing figures of England's games remained very high, but the press were muted and sales of flags and flat-screen televisions were down.

In this more sombre light, stripped of the hysteria and hyperbole of the boom years, what is the state of the English football nation? Like the nation itself its identity shuttles between Britishness and Englishness, still tied to a popular historical trajectory of empire and war. Either way both nations have, by and large, rejected the notion of an ethnic or a white identity, now borne out by its cross ethnic appeal, and the make-up of both crowd and team. It is predominantly conservative, with a taste for safe rather than adventurous traveling, but it has a radical cosmopolitan wing and a small rump of unreformed xenophobes.

More promisingly the football nation has continued to embrace the carnivalesque. England fans in South Africa were predictably a small fraction of the caravan that made its way to Germany. They were, however, more mixed than ever before. As one observer noted, "I was struck by how many women and families were at the England games and people were there for a party. Most were dressed up from basic England kit to knights and groups of Capellos with curly wigs and blazers."[80] Building on the success of similar initiatives in Portugal and Germany, English fans played in schools, supported grassroots football projects and visited

Robben Island and the townships.[81] By contrast, the England team's engagement with the South African public was microscopic.[82] Among those who had the misfortune to watch England's destruction at the hands of the Germans in Bloemfontein there was a new hard-eyed realism: "I've been here three weeks, spent too much money and seen too much atrocious football . . . England didn't deserve to win."

Consequently England's campaign at the 2014 World Cup was accompanied by an almost total absence of St. Georges flags on the cars and houses of the nation and the most down beat of expectations. Shorn of most of the "Golden Generation," the team certainly appeared more likeable while the appointment of Roy Hodgson as England manager has brought a welcome degree of moderation and calm to the circus. It was just as well for one point from three games, defeats by Italy and Uruguay was the poorest performance at a World Cup for over half a century. The players apologized, but as Barney Ronay suggested, maybe the nation needed to apologize to them; apologize for the desperate state of England's grassroots infrastructure and coaching. For all its contradictions and limitations, the England football nation has become a more attractive symbol of the stateless nation than its football team.

# CHAPTER 6

# You Don't Know What You're Doing

## The Misgovernance of English Football

There is more politics in football than in politics.

SVEN-GÖRAN ERIKSSON, 2004

## I.

Perhaps it takes the eye of a foreigner to see what is staring us in the face: football is a political game. Wherever there is power, money, and status at stake—and football offers all three—there is going to be a struggle over who makes the rules, who gets the loot, and who takes the glory. English football, which had thought of itself as studiously apolitical, has in the last twenty years become highly politicized. It has not been an edifying process. Hugh Robertson was one in a long line of government ministers responsible for sport, who were exasperated by the governance of English football. He declared in 2011 that "football was the worst governed sport in the country."[1] There has been competition. Horseracing and boxing and their relationship to the gambling industry have troubled governments; certainly the ruling bodies of the other popular sports, rugby union, cricket and tennis, have also been lampooned for their organizational sclerosis and amateurism. The Football Association (FA) has faced the same problems as most other sporting bodies in the country but with an outlook, an institutional structure, and a cadre of staff even more un-suited to the tasks in front of them and at an infinitely higher level of press coverage, if not scrutiny.

This is not what the FA went into business to do in 1863, and when the outside world came calling it was deeply reluctant to acknowledge its authority or its own inevitably political role in mediating among foot-ball's many stakeholders. First and foremost the FA saw itself as the cus-todian of football, the inventor and holder of the rules, devoted to the promotion and development of the game—a notion of development shorn of commercial or ideological interests. Thus the FA has always be-lieved itself a sovereign body within its own domain, the rightful and highest authority on football. On the inside cover of its own handbook the words read, "Published by order of the Football Association," an an-nouncement of independent authority like those that accompany parlia-mentary orders and command papers. But the FA was no leviathan. It always saw itself as a voluntary association and an amateur organization, free from formal structures of government or the pernicious influence of commercialism, run overwhelmingly on voluntary labor, organizing am-ateur competitions and coaching. Its conception of sovereignty and gov-ernance primarily concerned with keeping the institutions of both the state and the market out of the game.

With regard to the market, the FA made its uneasy peace with pro-fessionalism and the Football League in the 1880s. As we have seen, it did retain a measure of control over the economics of the professional game by restricting payments and dividends to club directors, but left much of the detail over transfers, pay and other matters to the Football League—a balance of power that would last almost a century.[2] But by the mid-1980s the FA's autonomy from both political and economic power was crumbling. The extent of disorder at games from the early 1970s on and the scale of the police response had already necessitated a wide range of government involvement. Heysel and Bradford made foot-ball a pressing matter of public policy. Hillsborough and its judicial af-termath drew the entire football industry into an extended and now semipermanent relationship with the state. Simultaneously the early commercialization of the biggest clubs, talks about super leagues and the promise of pay TV money were beginning to force the pace of change in English football. Grappling with these commercial and political changes alone would have been difficult enough for the FA, but the tasks of football governance were about to become infinitely more complex. The FA increasingly had to deal with international institutions like FIFA, UEFA and the European Commission, while it was challenged from below by grassroots activists including organized fan groups, a fan ownership movement and diversity activists who have attempted to address the patterns of inequality and exclusion in the game along the lines of gender, disability, ethnicity and sexuality. FA Secretary Frederick Wall never had to deal with the notion of gender budgeting, nor did Stanley Rous have to answer to the Equal Opportunities Commission. Now their successors had to. Agents, bookmakers, and sponsors, all once minor actors, acquired a new significance and brought the FA a new range of problems to deal with.

Above all, the FA had to deal with a football economy that was suddenly much larger, more volatile, and more global than ever before. Nothing illustrates the scale of change better than the changes in the FA's balance sheet. In the late 1980s the FA's turnover was around £3–4 million and nearly all its surplus came from selling tickets at Wembley. The shirt deals that had been signed for the England team, then considered vulgar by many, registered in the hundreds of thousands of pounds not millions. By 2011 the FA had a turnover of over £300 million, with sponsorship and broadcast deals for the FA Cup and England team close to a hundred million each, and a commercial debt on Wembley Stadium twice the size. That said, even this level of growth only made the FA about the same economic size as a single big club, and considerably smaller than the Premier League as a whole.

Problems of scale were matched by problems of complexity. Where once the FA had dealt with a small and relatively well-known set of print and broadcast journalists, with relations that were cozy at best and deferential at worst, the press pack and its demands began to change in the 1980s. In addition to the usual suspects the football press now included dirty-laundry merchants from the tabloids, relentless news hounds from the many new 24-hour sports and news channels, a steadily expanding foreign press corps, and occasional forays from the economics and business pages. The FA had long dealt with the Home Office and the police, but in the new environment it found itself talking to almost every other department of government. The Foreign Office, once indifferent to international football, was now closely consulted over bids for international tournaments. The FA found itself in conversation with the Treasury and the tax authorities over all manner of unsavory accounting practices in football; with the newly created Department of Culture, Media and Sport over national projects like Wembley and the Olympics; and with the Departments of Education, Health and Local Government who were interested in using football as an element in their social programs. Parliament took an increasing interest in the FA, too, with the Culture Media and Sport Select Committee publishing reports on some aspect of football governance almost every year from 2000 onwards. The all-party parliamentary football group was also prolific. Both reflected the fact that, for the first time, a significant tranche of the political class in Westminster were attuned to football and at some level engaged with it.

International politics was no easier for the FA to navigate. After rejoining FIFA in 1948, the FA had retained a degree of special influence and standing in the world governing body, sustained by Stanley Rous's term as president from 1963 to 1974. With the election of João Havelange to the presidency of FIFA, a new international order came into being in which the FA's small reserve of good will and political capital dwindled to nothing and its capacity to learn the new rules of football diplomacy was found sorely wanting. Politics at a European level was equally fraught as the FA attempted to navigate its way through the power networks of UEFA, massively empowered by the success of its Champions League. The European Union, European Parliament, European Council, and European Court of Justice have all ruled on football issues over the last twenty years, including interventions in the regulation of labor contracts, the operation of broadcast television markets and the probity of international football governance.

This would be a challenging agenda for the lithest, most adaptable of organizations. The FA was neither of these. Rather its culture and modus operandi—encapsulated in the metonym Lancaster Gate—were a hybrid of the punctilious provincial town hall and the clannish rotary club. Between 1910 and 1929, the FA had leased 42 Russell Square from the British Museum. Apparently haunted, the offices were too crepuscular and ancient even for the FA. In this context the move to 22 Lancaster Gate in West London, previously the dowdy Eden Court Hotel and the headquarters of the Association of British Launderers and Cleaners, looked like a step into the modern world; but not that modern. Stanley Rous was distinctly underwhelmed when he became secretary, writing that the FA was, "in many ways a quiet backwater when I arrived on 4 August 1934, to start my work . . . There was no problem parking my Hillman Minx as there was rarely another car in the road . . . There was a staff of five."[3] Under Rous and his successors Lancaster Gate was a world of mazy corridors and stuffy committee rooms; ink blotters and leather-bound registers; minutes, apologies, revisions to the minutes and any other business; the wooden balls and leather bag of the FA Cup draw and the ghost of Alf Ramsey drinking his mid-morning cup of tea. David Davies, newly arrived from the BBC, was aghast when he joined the FA as executive director:

> Entering . . . Lancaster Gate in 1994 was like stepping back into 1894 . . . I felt I'd been in more modern museums. A fading portrait of the Queen, painted when she was very young, stared down. Behind glass on rather dusty shelves stood silver trophies from bizarre places around the world, some of which no longer existed . . . the governing body of English football ran from nine to five, Monday to Friday, with an hour-off at lunchtime . . . football operated 24 hours a day, seven days a week, and was usually very busy at weekends.[4]

But then the FA of the early 1990s was an organization where the chief executive was opening other people's post as a matter of routine; where the head of the technical and coaching department was completely estranged from the professional game; and where the organization's press operations were simply laughable. Prior to Davies' appointment the FA relied on what were in effect junior press officers. The idea that it should have a communications department, and should think strategically about its interaction with the media, had not been entertained. This was an organization that despite becoming increasingly enmeshed in government initiatives and legislation had no dedicated political liaison or intelligence of any kind. Skills required to run the commercial and political dimensions of the FA were so thin on the ground that Ken Bates, the dogmatic and self-opinionated owner of Chelsea, was deemed a sensible choice to chair the new Wembley Stadium project.

In an era of such turbulence and complexity an organization designed to deal with a more clement social order was always going to experience stress and dysfunction and at the FA this surfaced as the increasingly rapid turnover of senior staff and officers. Between them Alf Ramsey, Ron Greenwood and Bobby Robson clocked up nearly thirty years as England manager. In just over two decades since Robson's departure, from Taylor to Hodgson, England has eaten up seven more. The chairman of the FA Board used to last longer, too, with just three men holding the post between 1966 and 1996: Andrew Stephens, a chain-smoking Scots doctor from Sheffield, Harold Thompson, an autocratic Oxford chemist, and Bert Millichip, a genial but dull solicitor from West Bromwich. In the years since Millichip's retirement the FA has been through five chairmen: Keith Wiseman, who resigned after his involvement in a secret payments scandal, the universally derided and largely invisible Geoff Thompson, and then in quick succession Lord Triesman, David Bernstein, and Greg Dyke.

The tenure of secretaries and chief executives has displayed a similar pattern. Frederick Wall and Stanley Rous account for nearly all of the first sixty years of the twentieth century. Denis Follows, Ted Croker, and Graham Kelly did around a decade each until Kelly was forced to resign along with Wiseman. Since then the axe had fallen rather more frequently. Adam Crozier lasted just two years before his reforming zeal came into conflict with the economic and political interests of the Premier League and he was driven out. His replacement, Mark Palios had a CV that included a professional career with Tranmere Rovers and Crewe Alexandra and a partnership at accountancy giants PricewaterhouseCoopers, not to mention being crowned "Turnaround Financier of the Year 2003." The perfect man for the job was gone in eighteen months after the revelation of an affair with a secretary at FA headquarters called Faria Alam, a fact made infinitely more problematic by the clumsy cover-up attempted by Palios's press team.[5] Brian Barwick, a seasoned TV sports executive, managed to last four years but was shown the door by the new chairman Lord Triesman, who doubted his political suitability. His successor, Ian Watmore, despite being able to cope with the nebulous complexities of Whitehall's e-government program and running the prime minister's delivery unit, lasted little more than a year before resigning in exasperation over the glacial pace of change and the scale of resistance to reform within the organization. Alex Horne's appointment in 2010 makes him the fifth chief executive—excluding David Davies' stints in the caretaker role—in just a decade.

Viewed in a certain light, one is almost tempted to argue that the FA hasn't done as badly as it might have. Encumbered by its own antiquated self-conception and hapless, compromised decision-making structures, the FA has been constantly playing organizational catch-up with wider changes in global football. One is only tempted though. As the political struggle over the governance of football shows, it was also the author of its own incompetence.

## II.

The misgovernance of English football has followed its own peculiar course, but it has often traced an uncannily similar arc to the misgovernance of the country as a whole. In the early 1990s the nation endured the long slow death of Conservative rule. John Major's administration, beset by internal conflict, was fatally tarnished by the notion of sleaze. At the same time the FA was overwhelmed by a wave of corruption and financial misdemeanors that made the status quo untenable. At the turn of the century, the newly elected Labour administration made good on some of its manifesto commitments to institutional reform, the governance of football included. But Labour's dismal attempt to reform the privatized utilities such as water, gas, and rail transit went the same way as the Football Task Force: projects that left private and corporate interests essentially undisturbed. In the second and third terms of the Labour administration, both government and football administrators rode a wave of unsustainable growth, a boom that saw money flood into banking, housing and football. In turn inequality grew, the space for malpractice expanded and levels of debt rose dangerously. Finally, under the coalition government elected in 2010, all reforming energies appear to have ground to a halt. Banking, the bubble-prone housing market and football all alike remain much as they were.

John Major's government was worn down by Europe and economic crisis, but it was swept aside by a collapse of legitimacy and plausibility. Major had inadvertently given his opponents a rhetorical stick with which to beat him. The government, he announced, was "going back to basics." His intended focus on mundane policy delivery was interpreted as a rallying call for Victorian values and propriety. At lightning speed *Back to Basics* became *Back to my Place* as the sexual adventures and entanglements of junior ministers took the limelight. Sexual scandal was compounded by more serious corruption and venality. Westminster City Council, the flagship of Thatcherite local government, was found guilty of gerrymandering and MP Neil Hamilton was shown to have taken cash for asking parliamentary questions. Kate Hoey, the backbench Labour MP, argued that football was cut of similar cloth and in 1995 used parliamentary privilege to denounce "the variety of allegations, scandals and corrupt practices that have surrounded the game in recent years." She named Brian Clough, Ron Atkinson, George Graham, and Terry Venables as perpetrators and declared that "millions of pounds are siphoned off from the game in backhanders, bungs and fixes."[6] As with much of the impropriety of the era, Ian Sproat, the Minister of Sport, declined to engage, preferring to leave football to regulate itself.

English football had its fair share of unconventional financial practices in the past. Before payments and professionalism was formalized, under-the-table cash, over-generous expenses and other inducements to players were the norm. In the 1960s and 1970s, stories relentlessly circulated about Tommy Docherty, manager of Manchester United, and his dealings in the transfer market; Don Revie at Leeds was accused of payments to opposition players to take it easy.[7] Docherty was sufficiently blasé about the system of regulation that he told the Football Writers Association after a long lunch, ". . . managers have to be cheats and liars. People say we tell lies. Of course we tell lies. We cheat. In our business the morals are all different."[8] The subculture of secret payments was fuelled by the new money that arrived in the early 1990s, an increasingly global labor market for players, and the rise of agents and intermediaries—and all of it lubricated by easy access to a deregulated offshore banking system. Perhaps, just as significantly, it was a culture that could operate in the secure knowledge that no one at their own clubs or at the FA would be monitoring them and their accounts. By the mid-1990s even the FA had to take a look as the press broke story after story in a blizzard of revelation, accusation, back-tracking and dissembling. Four long-running sagas dominated the news: a bitter financial, legal and media struggle between Alan Sugar, then chairman of Spurs, and his ex-manager and co-director at the club Terry Venables; the tax authorities' parallel investigation into Tottenham Hotspur's exotic accounting practices in the 1980s; the relationship between Norwegian football agent Rune Hauge and Arsenal manager George Graham; and Liverpool goalkeeper Bruce Grobbelaar's relationship with the East Asian gambling industry.

The case against Grobbelaar rested on a secret recording made of a conversation between him and an old friend at a hotel in Zimbabwe. He appeared to admit to taking a £40,000 payment for ensuring Liverpool lost a game against Newcastle in 1993 as well as losing money when he mistakenly saved a goal that should have been scored.[9] The money, it later transpired, could be traced back to betting syndicates in Malaysia. Rick Parry, then chief executive of the Premier League, spoke for much of the football world: "None of us want to believe it and I don't by the way, because that would be betraying the game more than any single act I could think of."[10] In the face of what appeared to be remarkably powerful evidence of corruption, the football world was ready to believe anything other than the idea that the game was, on their watch, subject to systemic manipulation. Two juries found Grobbelaar not guilty but their decisions were quashed by a ruling of the Court of Appeal, which was confirmed by the House of Lords. Grobbelaar was convicted of taking the money if not definitively proven to have actually influenced the outcome of games. His punishment from the FA, which only found him guilty of forecasting results for East Asian bookmakers, was a £10,000 fine and a ban from playing for six months.

This kind of collective denial was also in evidence around football's financial dealings. The lax standards of regulation and accounting that were the norm in English football were off the authorities' radar until the long-running fight between Sugar and Venables brought it into the open. The pair had bought Spurs in 1991 from the seriously indebted regime of Irving Scholar. Sugar had no shortage of capital to invest, but Venables it transpired had bought his share on the basis of loans secured against assets he didn't own or that didn't exist. It was a divergence of business practices that brought the two into open conflict, inflamed by Sugar's rage at what he regarded as Venables' cavalier use of his money in the transfer market and his installation of Eddie Ashby, recently bankrupt, as the effective general manager of the club.[11]

Simultaneously Britain's tax authorities were busy investigating dozens of contracts signed by the previous regime at Spurs. They concluded that the fictitious loans, and complimentary house and cars that came with many deals and remained invisible to the tax authorities, were illegal. Initially the FA's response was firm: a £600,000 fine, twelve points deducted in the Premiership and a one-year ban from the FA Cup. Two court appeals later the points deduction and cup ban were dropped, leaving a fine that barely dented Spurs' budget. More importantly there was no action to ensure that this kind of behavior would not be repeated, with club chairmen still notably reluctant to even consider outside scrutiny of their finances.

A similarly light-touch approach was applied to Rune Hauge and George Graham. In the early 1990s Hauge had cornered the market in Scandinavian football talent. He was able to buy cheap at home and sell dear in England, keeping the difference for himself and whoever at the English end had helped ensure that the deal went through. George Graham's role in this kind of transaction only came to light when he had to explain nearly half a million untaxed pounds in a foreign bank account. Graham ended up losing his job at Arsenal, getting fined £50,000, and being banned from football for a year, but by 1996 he had made the money back five times over by selling his story to the *Sun*, and was back managing Leeds. Hauge got a two-year ban from FIFA, but continued his business unhindered through a series of fronts.

Through all of these events, the Premier League's Reid Inquiry offered an ever shrinking fig leaf. Begun in 1993 and four years in the making, Robert Reid QC investigated what it could of the allegations and claims that were emerging about hundreds of transfers, but, limited in its powers and funds, it was not able to make the mysterious movements of so much money and so many players through so many bank accounts and clubs add up to an incontrovertible case. It was not able even to get a unanimous opinion out of its three-man panel. Reid reported and disappeared in a puff of indifference.[12]

The parallels between sleaze in government and sleaze in football were not difficult to see and both made a tempting target for the opposition. In July 1995 New Labour's leadership made its first intervention in the debate: an article in the *Mail on Sunday* in Tony Blair's name, but in his spokesman Alastair Campbell's voice. The hook was Andy Cole's expensive transfer from Newcastle to Manchester United at a price that now appears small change but at the time was another example of the exponential growth of income, wages and fees in the Premiership. Blair/Campbell worried about the corrosive consequences of the new money, the growth of inequality and the prevalence of backhanders. Another piece followed on the occasion of Stanley Matthews' sepia-drenched eightieth birthday, while Campbell engineered photo opportunities of Blair playing keepy-uppy with Kevin Keegan and sitting with his family in the royal box at Wembley. At the Labour Party conference later that year, the elision of football and politics was complete as Blair roused the crowd: "Seventeen years of hurt never stopped us dreaming, Labour's coming home."[13]

This was new territory. Among the previous generation of senior Labour figures Brian Walden had combined a parliamentary career with an Arsenal obsession and Tony Crosland liked to get away from politics by watching Grimsby Town, but neither ever made anything of it. Harold Wilson's embrace of England's 1966 World Cup triumph was a rare foray into clumsy football populism. Blair's Labour Party was different. In part the public engagement with football was part of the changing tenor of political communication, which required politicians to have more of a hinterland and to expose something of their demotic tastes. Football certainly offered this synthetic opportunity, but there was also a genuine body of fans among the party's MPs and political assistants. Campbell's fidelity to Burnley was unquestionable. Geoffrey Robinson, the businessman at the center of Gordon Brown's circle, was a director of Coventry City; Brown himself followed Scotland and Raith Rovers; Brian Wilson had actually written Celtic's centenary history; Kate Hoey and Iain Coleman were Arsenal regulars—indeed, in a set of leaked hand-over notes between Coleman's assistants, it was made clear that the diary was to be cleared and excuses prepared for any midweek Arsenal game in London. Despite an explicit order to Labour MPs not to be seen living it up at the 1998 World Cup, a number of Scots MPs defied the whip and went to Scotland's opening game with Brazil. The same interest could be found among many of the party's political advisers who would go on to form much of the top cadre of Labour leaders a decade hence: Ed Balls (Norwich City), David Miliband and James Purnell (Arsenal), Ed Miliband (Leeds United) and Andy Burnham (Everton). Even Peter Mandelson, now MP for Hartlepool, felt it necessary to serve as president of Hartlepool United. In 1997 Tony Benn asked workers to back Chesterfield on their unlikely FA Cup run as the anti-establishment ticket.[14]

Opportunism aside, Mandelson and Benn were tapping into a strong current of thought now running through the Labour Party: that football clubs were a working model of the kind of collective action and social solidarity they would like to nurture. Better, they were under attack from an unregulated market, precisely the scenario that required, indeed justified, new kinds of public intervention and regulation.[15] With the real policy work deferred until after an election, Labour drew up a manifesto which imagined a serious inquiry into football's financial and regulatory ills, and promised to examine the rising costs of going to the game. Once in power Labour moved quickly and established the Football Task Force under Conservative ex-minister David Mellor (a Chelsea supporter) and a membership drawn from the professional game, the grassroots game and independent activists and researchers. To begin with, the Task Force's work, which included a laudable process of outreach with public hearings across the country, focused on issues of racism, disability, ticket prices, supporters' involvement in running clubs and the clubs' relationship with their communities.

In the writing of the report and in the search for appropriate solutions these issues inevitably led back to bigger questions of governance and regulation. The hopeless state of football governance and the inadequacies of the FA were made all the more tangible during the Task Force's existence by a series of major court cases and legal rulings. The Monopolies and Mergers Commission blocked the BSkyB takeover of Manchester United. The Office of Fair Trading ruled against price fixing in the replica shirt market, while the Sky/BBC monopoly over live football rights was ruled illegal by the European court.[16] All of which demonstrated that whoever or whatever was regulating football it wasn't the FA any more. It was these issues and the proposal to create an independent regulator for the game that split the Task Force when it delivered its final report on commercial issues. The Independents were for a regulator with financial and legal teeth, the FA and football leagues were against. However, it was clear that the Labour government had no intention at this stage of proceedings to expend any political capital forcing a regulatory system onto the big clubs when they were clearly not prepared to cooperate with it. Having managed to extract from the Premier League an annual contribution to the grassroots projects of the newly established Football Foundation, ministers were minded not to push it any further.[17] After two years of dilution and diversion, the last remnants of the regulatory plan were resurrected as the Independent Football Commission (IFC), a quango of rare marginality, confined to adjudicating on complaints over ticketing, stewarding and rough policing.

If the fate of the Football Task Force and the independent regulator had not made the real balance of power in football governance clear, then the fate of Adam Crozier, chief executive of the FA, would. On fundamental questions of the powers of the FA and its relationship with the finances of the leading clubs, it was the clubs that ruled. Crozier, previously chief executive of Saatchi and Saatchi, came to the FA in 2000. In his two short years he moved the organization geographically and psychologically out of Lancaster Gate and into Soho Square; he created properly functioning commercial and marketing departments; excised the cancerous presence of Ken Bates from the Wembley Stadium project thereby keeping it alive; pushed for the appointment of the England team's first foreign manager, Sven-Göran Eriksson; and brought a degree of professionalism and organizational urgency to the FA that were quite unheralded. What he didn't do was make a lot of friends where it counted. Averse to socializing, he was a rare presence in football boardrooms and directors' boxes. He also showed too much interest in funnelling money to grassroots football and in the FA actually regulating football clubs for many chairmen's liking. When it was revealed that he had been signing FA contracts with sponsors, in effect on behalf of Premiership players, the chairmen had the stick they needed to beat him with. Premiership chairmen, led by two exemplars of good governance, Ken Bates and Peter Ridsdale at Leeds, used a meeting of the FA Board to mount an attack of sufficient vitriol that Crozier's position became impossible and he resigned.[18]

One might have thought that New Labour's zeal for institutional change in football would have been exhausted by the miserly returns its efforts to reform the game had yielded. However ministers and MPs were increasingly perturbed by the financial gyrations of the game and the steady drip of bankruptcies, frauds and wildly unsustainable debts. Ministers were buoyed by the success of the Foster Review into athletics, which sought to impose reform from outside and above the sport. So in late 2004, with the FA in another period of turmoil after the resignation of its chief executive Mark Palios, the government took the opportunity to establish the Burns Review. Terence Burns, previously a high-ranking Treasury civil servant, had already served on a number of tricky commissions for the Labour government, advising on the ban on fox hunting and the renewal of the BBC charter. The review's terms of reference asked Lord Burns to look at the FA's notoriously variable disciplinary processes and the interests of the grassroots game, but its central concerns were precisely the issues that the Football Task Force had identified and the IFC had failed to address: how was the FA itself to be governed and what was its role in the wider governance of football? And how could it be made independent from the vested interests that had hitherto controlled it?

Burns was brisk, dry, and to the point. His report, less than a dozen pages long, made three key sets of proposals.[19] First, that the FA Board should have an independent chair, brought in from outside, that the board should be smaller, that the professional game should have fewer votes and that an independent non-executive director should be added to the board. In truth this was no more than the most basic form of good governance existing in most of the private and voluntary sector, but at the FA they were considered positively revolutionary proposals. Secondly, the FA Council should be expanded to include representatives of the parts of the game hitherto unrepresented, notably coaches and supporters. And thirdly, the FA should establish a regulatory unit, semi-autonomous from its main work, which would have the authority and capacity to deal with issues of finance, governance, corruption and malpractice.

Published in early 2005 to a deafening chorus of consensus, the Burns Report, over nine years later, has still not been fully implemented. It has been an extraordinary display of institutional sclerosis, brought on occasion to a juddering halt by the key vetoes that some football actors were able to bring to bear on the process. It took over two years for the FA Council to agree to appoint an independent chairman, to reject the idea of independent directors or a smaller board and send many of the more detailed proposals on the reform of the board, sub-committees, club registration and financial regulation, into the lost labyrinthine world of its own committee structure.

For a brief moment in 2008 and 2009 it looked like further reform might be possible. The FA finally acquired its first independent chairman, the Labour appointee Lord Triesman. Simultaneously the reform party in football acquired its most vocal Secretary of State for Culture in Andy Burnham, who had served as secretary to the Football Task Force almost a decade before. Burnham sought to raise the stakes, calling for a response from the world of football not only to the Burns reforms but to the wave of financial malpractice and bankruptcies in the game: "Football needs to reassess its relationship with money," he argued, and called for greater transparency around the ownership of clubs, an end to the use of debt to finance takeovers, reform of football's shockingly unfair insolvency rules, and proper due diligence to be applied to club directors and major shareholders. He finished with a populist flourish calling for support of the national team and a reconsideration of the idea that club squads should include a minimum of national players.[20] Triesman had already been heading in this direction, speaking out about the level of debt in the English game and the dangerous consequences of leaving its finances and system of ownership unregulated.[21] Now, Burnham's speech and his request for a response offered Triesman the chance to take this agenda to the FA Board. He proposed that the FA should create a "fit-and-proper persons" test for club ownership, a domestic club-licensing scheme, enhanced financial regulations and a review of the level of debt in the game. Recalling the meeting he said:

> It took the Premier League two minutes to kick it out . . . The point was made by the Chairman of the Premier League [Sir Dave Richards] that this [submission] should be disregarded and to simply acknowledge the work done by the Premier League principally and the professional game, reminding the representatives of the amateur game where their money came from.[22]

By late 2010, Triesman had gone, resigning after the publication of the details of a private conversation in which he suggested that foreign FAs were liable to bribe referees.[23] David Bernstein was appointed as Triesman's successor; as a previous chairman of Manchester City he could hardly be considered an advance for the cause of independence from vested interests. Six years after Burns, the FA Board acquired its first independent directors—including Heather Rabbatts, the first woman on the FA Board ever—and minuscule changes were made to the composition of the already oversized FA Council.

In 2010 the parliamentary select committee that dealt with sport decided to enter the same quicksand that the Task Force and the Burns Review had sunk into. The Select Committee Inquiry into Football Governance conducted during 2010 and 2011 was part pantomime, part bloodletting. Lord Triesman dished the dirt on FIFA and the Premier League's representatives at the FA, and called it like it was: "the FA has given up on regulation." Mike Lee, consultant to the Qatar World Cup bid, did a slick see-no-evil, hear-no-evil routine. Richard Scudamore and Dave Richards from the Premier League denied that they were opposed to reforms or exercised any serious power. On the key question of why so little reform had been enacted, why above all there had been so little financial and regulatory reform, Lord Burns was as precise as ever: "It comes down to what you think the FA should do. If it is going to regulate the game, it needs to have people on the Board who do not have outside interests in the regulation that is taking place."[24]

To no one's surprise the committee said it was "very disappointed" by the football authorities' response to its proposals which included implementing the rest of the Burns Review as well putting fans' representatives on the FA Board and reducing the number of places for the Football League and the Premiership on the board to just one each. Indeed, the football authorities proved so slothful and recalcitrant in their response that the committee's chairman, John Whittingdale, a politician of impeccably mainstream conservative views and not given to outbursts of interventionism, argued: "If football cannot reform itself, the Government should introduce legislation as soon as practically possible." It was a view echoed by the Conservative Minister of Sport, Hugh Robertson: "If football does not deliver the reforms then we will look at bringing forward legislation."[25] Another few years have passed since then and the long list of proposals and reforms remains largely unfulfilled. Skeletally thin as the Coalition's Queen's Speeches have become, there never quite seems room for any legislation on this matter.

It is a story that has echoes of another economic sector. Lord Burns put it this way in his remarks to the Select Committee: "The present board is as if with the Financial Services Authority . . . had a controlling interest by the banks whom they are regulating."[26] As with the changes that swept through the financial world, the neo-liberal program of deregulation and commercialization in football produced a booming economic sector that delivered immense wealth to a small number of people, and created a regulatory environment in which any notion of the public interest and the public good was first decried and then resisted. Both banking and football had developed internal cultures of nonchalance, even disdain for the outside world and the rule of law, and both were blessed with systems of regulation in which powerful vested interests would look after themselves and block outside interference. Both have been subject to endless financial and legal scandals, calls for reform and committees of inquiry, threats of legislation and intervention, and yet both remain substantially untouched. Football's status as the national game may not be burnished by this but its office is more secure than ever.

## III.

When not embroiled in the interminable struggles over its own structure and regulatory role, the FA's remaining energies have been focused on five big projects: running the FA Cup; building the new Wembley stadium; bidding for two World Cups; running the England national teams; and developing grass roots and community football. The first three all demonstrate the ways in which the FA's capacity for effective governance has been compromised by both powerful social forces beyond its control and its own poor, occasionally disastrous, decision-making.

International football politics has been the FA's weakest suit, an environment in which it found itself competing with football associations that were more ruthless, better supported and less accident prone, and were playing a political game that the FA was not able to comprehend or engage with. The bid to host the 2006 World Cup was Bert Millichip's goodbye gift to English football. The chairman of the FA, emboldened by the success of Euro 96 and buoyed by football's newfound popularity and wealth, launched the idea of the bid just before stepping down after sixteen years in the post. In early 1997 Bobby Charlton and Geoff Hurst had been signed up on substantial retainers, and Downing Street was ready to host a launch for the bid. Among many invitations one found its way to UEFA headquarters in Nyon. A tart reply was faxed back informing the British government that UEFA's general secretary would not be attending. It appeared that UEFA had already agreed to collectively support a bid from Germany.[27] A joint response from the FA and leading politicians expressed itself deeply shocked. Shocked and dismayed that the world of football politics should be conducted through regional groupings, bloc votes, negotiated pacts and complex undocumented trade-offs and understandings? If the bid wasn't already dead, this degree of political naivety ensured that it would be slaughtered.

It became clear that UEFA, whatever the truth, believed Bert Millichip had tacitly agreed to precisely that kind of arrangement with senior UEFA and European football officials in 1993, trading support for England's bid for the 1996 European Championships with a reciprocal arrangement to support Germany's bid for the 2006 World Cup. Millichip's recollection of events was that, "At that time, Germany said that we would like to announce now our interest to run at 2006. All I have to say is that I may well have indicated we will support you, at that time, but there was no agreement." As Alan Tomlinson put it, "No agreement, but clearly an understanding and an arrangement."[28] It is hard to know whether Millichip failed to understand the exchange in those terms or was deceiving himself and others. Either way, naive or mendacious, it was certainly understood in European football as a "gentleman's agreement" and nothing shifted that perception. Undaunted, Graham Kelly and Keith Wiseman tried to laugh off the problem. Excruciatingly, they made light of the "gentleman's misunderstanding." The bid, enthusiastically supported by the newly elected Labour government, was set firmly on a course of failure. Whitehall played its part over the next two years by seconding senior staff from the Foreign Office to the bid. Tony Banks was allowed to stand down as Minister of Sport, then act as a virtually full-time ambassador. The FIFA technical team and the executive committee were wined and dined in the pomp of Hampton Court Palace, and the bid threw in Prime Minister Tony Blair and the Prince of Wales for good measure.

The FA's contribution was dismal. In a planned schmooze blitz on the FIFA executive in the high-end hospitality zones of France 98, the bid team managed face time with just two out of twenty-four committee members. In the bitterly contested elections for FIFA president that year, the FA burnt what was left of England's European credentials by supporting Sepp Blatter against UEFA's president Lennart Johannson. Blatter had dangled just enough promises in front of the FA for them to think he might be well disposed towards them during the decision-making process; promises that eventually amounted to nothing. Dabbling in the world of football as overseas aid, the FA pursued the Caribbean vote through Trinidad and Tobago, where it funded the building of a football academy, and sought the Asian vote through Thailand, where it sponsored a youth tournament.

What was already a forlorn situation was made worse by three events. First Graham Kelly and Keith Wiseman were forced to resign from their office after it was revealed that the pair had made secret payments to the Welsh FA; payments, it became clear, that were intended to secure Welsh support in electing Keith Wiseman onto the FIFA executive committee.[29] The following year England manager Glenn Hoddle was forced to resign after his comments about disability, cosmic justice and the afterlife. Then, just months before the final decision was to be made, a segment of the

England support in Charleroi at Euro 2000 indulged in a drunken brawl with the Belgian police, fans and themselves.

Tony Banks was ready to throw in the towel, and only the humiliation of conceding to these events kept the bid going. It was not a happy time and culminated in Banks giving a notoriously bitter and emotionally brittle presentation to UEFA officials on the night before the final vote.[30] In the dying moments of the contest, it appears that the FA went negative, whispering in the FIFA corridors that a split Germany–England vote would leave the way open for South Africa to come through the middle and what a nightmare security issue an African World Cup would be. The first round of voting delivered a crushing defeat. England received just five votes, in third place behind Germany and South Africa. In the second round, the CONCACAF bloc, never slow to get on the winning side, defected en masse. England got two votes and were eliminated.

In 2007 the FA announced its intention to bid for the 2018 World Cup. The 2006 disaster had been examined at length by a parliamentary select committee which concluded that the previous outing had been fatally undermined by the gentleman's agreement and the not-unconnected failure of FA officials to operate effectively inside UEFA and FIFA.[31] Compared to the 2006 bid, England 2018 was better staffed and better funded. It could offer noticeably improved stadiums, including the now complete New Wembley. Andy Anson, the chief executive of the bid, suggested that the Achilles heel of the last outing was arrogance. England had failed last time because the bid had played too strongly on the idea of England as football's home—a historical fact but one that deeply irritated part of the FIFA constituency. This time the message was going to be less proprietorial, inoffensive but effective. In the final stretch the glad-handing was impressive as Prince William, David Cameron, and David Beckham took up residence in the five-star quarter of Zurich. They really needn't have bothered.

The bid had already had to cope with the fallout of David Triesman's resignation and his concerns about the probity of other national football associations, as well as the universally negative international response to the Premier League's proposed 39th game– to play league fixtures outside of England. But the real problem, as Triesman was suggesting, lay elsewhere. Not only had the FA failed to improve on its pitiful record of networking and alliance-building inside FIFA but by now it was playing the wrong kind of game anyway. The new circuits of power and influence inside the organization had shifted elsewhere and the British press were instrumental in bringing this to the world's attention. First the *Sunday Times* published details of recorded conversations with current and past FIFA officials, which made it transparently clear that the votes of some members of the FIFA executive committee were for sale.[32] Normally impervious to this kind of scandal, FIFA actually suspended two members of their executive. Then, in the week preceding the vote, the BBC authorized the broadcast of a *Panorama* documentary that showed that many past and current members of the FIFA executive had received enormous secret payments from the now bankrupt company ISL in relation to the selling of World Cup TV rights.[33] While the England bid did its best to ignore these serious accusations, Zurich took notice and Sepp Blatter took the opportunity, on the eve of the final vote, to remind his executive committee of the "evils of the media."[34]

In the first round of voting England got just two votes and it was clear that the FA and the England bid had been comprehensively outmaneuvered. European support was as scarce as last time. The CONCACAF vote, shaky over the 2006 bid, never arrived at all. Andy Anson railed against the media for destabilizing the bid, but this was disingenuous. England had never been in the game. As Lord Triesman later revealed in Parliament, he had turned down flat requests for money or honors from four members of the FIFA executive, including Nicolas Leoz of Paraguay, who felt he was rich enough but thought some kind of baronetcy would be an appropriate title to put alongside the *Légion d'honneur* that the French government had bestowed upon him.[35] In one sense we should be grateful that England never had a chance and that, for all its faults, the FA and its senior officers would not engage with the flagrant corruption and abuse of power that had become the norm in international football politics. On the other hand, it defies belief that, armed with such an approach and lacking even the most basic experience of the political landscape they were operating in, the FA and the government could commit to a bid that cost £21 million and was never destined for anything but humiliation. It is worth noting that while Britain's heir to the throne and its prime minister cleared a lot of space in their diaries for the final struggle for votes, Vladimir Putin felt it necessary to put in an appearance only when Russia had won the bid for the 2018 World Cup. All the important work had been done long before.

Building the new Wembley was a more successful venture. At least the stadium got built, something inconceivable under the old order. In 1987 Ted Croker described the plan to build a new national stadium as "an eternal pipe dream" and ruefully noted that "it is an historic ground and has served the English game well, but everyone agrees it has long been overtaken by the splendour of stadia like the Santiago Bernabeu . . . and the Nou Camp."[36] That was putting it kindly. The Empire Stadium, thrown up in a few months in 1923, was showing its age and its desperate lack of basic facilities, but in the absence of the kind of capital required to truly upgrade the building the best that could be managed was some cosmetic patching and painting. The sporting–political complex beyond the FA had taken note too. All the calculations being made around Olympic and World Cup bids made it clear that Wembley would not pass muster and a new national stadium would need to be built somewhere. In 1994, flush with money from the recently launched National Lottery, Sport England announced a competition to design and locate a new national stadium.

Wembley and the FA saw off challenges from provincial alternatives, established Wembley National Stadium Limited (WNSL) to run the show and, to the sound of gasps across the nation, appointed Ken Bates, the chairman and owner of Chelsea, as the chair of the project. Graham Kelly, who had pushed for Bates' appointment, thought that his record of property development at Chelsea's Stamford Bridge would ensure the project's financial success, while his notoriously brusque demeanor was just what was required to push it through the thicket of other stakeholders involved in the new Wembley. On both counts Kelly was utterly mistaken. Bates' Chelsea Village development was being kept afloat by expensive commercial loans, while his abrasive tongue would ultimately undermine both his own position and the financial plausibility of the project for prospective funders.

Sport England released the national stadium money to WNSL with a thick book of conditions that included making the stadium usable for major athletics and rugby events. Most of the £120 million of public money was used to buy up the old stadium and the land around it. Bates' property skills were particularly in evidence here, as the value of the land rapidly dropped to a third of the overinflated price WNSL had coughed up. In 1999 the first designs of the new stadium complex were publicly unveiled—architecturally and aesthetically there was barely a dissenting voice, but on the issues of the place of athletics and finances the FA found itself embroiled in conflict. The athletics camp received a temporary boost when Tony Banks moved over to the 2006 World Cup bid and his Labour colleague Kate Hoey became Minister of Sport. She led a rancorous campaign to ensure that athletics was properly catered for at Wembley, which merely resulted in the ejection of athletics from the scheme as a whole.

The tendering process for building the stadium was conducted in a highly unorthodox manner and all the time the cost of the scheme was ratcheting upwards—now in excess of £300 million.[37] The crunch came in late 2000 when over thirty banks listened to Ken Bates make his big pitch for long-term investment and they didn't believe him. Above all they didn't believe another anodyne hotel, office and shopping complex in suburban north London was worth the investment. Bates was eventually dismissed and replaced by Rodney Walker—an altogether more sober character and, as a rugby league administrator, thankfully free of football interests—who excised Bates Village from the scheme and restored sufficient credibility to persuade the German bank West LB to underwrite the £400 million commercial loans then required to make the project happen.

Five years and £798 million later the new Wembley Stadium opened. What had the football nation bought itself?[38] Up close they had bought a large, unadorned saucer of a building, four times higher than the old Wembley. Viewed at a distance and especially on the skyline, they had acquired a building of real architectural ambition—unusual in English football—and one that has captured something of its time. The vast steel arch that rises above the stands is neither a functional structure nor an organic growth from the building's history but a deliberate calling card, an exercise in branding. Smoothly finished in glass and neutral tones, it is, like the best modern airports, designed to funnel huge numbers of people through wide concourses and up escalators to multiple destinations, and it feels like an airport too. The same high-end but ultimately bland functionality characterizes the stadium's now innumerable toilets, watering holes and commercial outlets. As with airports there is more than one way to fly. Two entire levels of the five concourses that wrap the stadium are sealed and reserved for those with access to the premium seating and entertainment boxes. Once inside they need not mingle again with anyone not in the zone.

Inside, as a venue for actually watching the football, the stadium is exceptional: 90,000 seats in undulating rings closely abut the pitch and give the space a physical and visual intensity. Although there has been some complaint about the impact of the retractable roof on the pitch, it is a brilliant stage. What it seems to lack, especially for England games, is atmosphere. This is a problem of all new stadiums and some old ones too, but the new Wembley has suffered particularly. The business model that evolved to make the astronomical costs stack up was to give over 10,000 seats to premium packages, hospitality experiences, corporate entertainment and the rest of the pampering that accompanies really expensive tickets for football. These were sold prior to Wembley's opening as debentures, guaranteeing ticket holders access to all its games for ten years and apparently subsidizing the cost of the other 80,000 seats, none of which can be had for less than £30. This part of the crowd is very clearly identifiable in the stadium. We must assume that the food is good, for their blocks of bright red seats are always empty or late to fill before kick-off and after halftime. They are a visible reminder of the club class/ economy class model of British life and a permanent dampener on the crowd's vitality. David Hill, present at England's opening game in the new stadium, wondered if this was "A tale of . . . how servile we have become before indifferent wealth, and how those left behind in the race for affluence nowadays sit and watch its winners on TV."[39] And still the bills are not all paid and the debt is not all serviced. Wembley Stadium is running at a loss and the FA has had to cut costs and programs to finance keeping Wembley open and its interest payments covered.[40]

In the new football economy the FA has trod a difficult balancing act between the imperatives of a commercial business model and the need to retain a sense of continuity with the past. This dilemma has proved hard to resolve when it comes to the FA Cup. For over a century the Cup was the jewel in the crown, the world's oldest football competition. It has been the FA's main source of income for much of its existence. Yet its true value was not measured in ticket sales but status and cultural weight. On the one hand the magic of the FA Cup was conjured from below. From the 1880s onward the Cup final had provided, for northern fans especially, a carnival trip to the capital. For many of them it was their first time in the metropolis in their lives. The uncertainties and sudden-death decisions of the knock-out format drew exceptional crowds.

On the other hand the Cup was sprinkled with establishment stardust. Edward VII accepted the role of patron of the FA in 1901 as has every monarch since. George V watched an England versus Scotland match at the FA's invitation in 1912 and then gave his reign a distinctly demotic sheen by attending his first FA Cup final in 1914. After the war, the BBC's decision to broadcast the final on the radio put it in the same category of national pageantry as the Varsity Boat Race and Armistice Day. While the Coronation of 1953 can reasonably claim to be the most significant event in Britain's first mass encounter with television, the FA Cup final of that year—the Matthews final—has a not dissimilar place in the collective memory. Bert Trautmann, Manchester City's German goalkeeper of the era, or perhaps his ghost writer, endorsed the notion of the FA Cup as a site of imagined community: united, decent and democratic. Writing about the singing of the hymn "Abide with Me," first sung at the Cup final in 1927, he observed: "Then women and children from the grimy streets of the industrial town at last are on common ground with those from the stately homes of England. What does it matter if they are off key or are not quite sure of the words . . . it is a wonderful thing, and one for which British sports lovers, regardless of politics and creed, are to be respected."[41] It was a commonplace assumption—though hardly backed up by much evidence—that the whole world turned to face Wembley on Cup final day.

This kind of cozy image of the English as a big national football family became harder to sustain as the memories of the war receded and the new cynicism and new freedoms of the postwar boom arrived. In this context, the Cup's popular status was secured for another generation by television's embrace of its quirkiness, allied to a new range of pop cultural forms. The radio broadcasts of the Cup draw on a Monday lunchtime are now fondly remembered as occasions for smuggling the new transistor radios into schools and workplaces. For over a decade there was a vogue for Cup final songs. Chelsea's "Blue Is the Colour," released in 1972, reached number five in the singles chart as did Spurs and Chas 'n' Dave's "Ossie's Dream" in 1981. Liverpool lost the final in 1988 but reached number three with "Anfield Rap." Nothing has come close since. On the eve of the 1972 final, Leeds captain Billy Bremner could still say: "I've won a Championship medal, a European medal and countless Scotland caps, but sometimes I think I'd swap the lot for an FA Cup winners' medal." But thirty years later, something has changed. In his autobiography Roy Keane referred to a FA Cup final appearance as "little more than an afterthought." Arsenal's Patrick Vieira lifted the Cup in 2005 but recalled that it "can't possibly make up for the disappointment of losing the League crown."

It is not just the players that are thinking this way. Until the mid-1980s FA Cup attendance followed the same ups and downs, mainly downs, of attendance at league football, both reaching a nadir around 1986. In the years since then league attendance has grown enormously, but average and total attendance at FA Cup games has been almost static. Bigger clubs report a significant drop from their usual attendance at games in the early rounds of the competition. In 2012, for example, attendances at third-round games were down 15 percent across the country on league averages. They were 40 percent down at Newcastle, who entertained Blackburn Rovers.[42] TV ratings have gone the same way. In the Cup's televised heyday in the 1970s the final itself could attract domestic audiences of around 14 million. Since the early 1990s, the highest ratings were recorded by the 11 million who tuned into Chelsea versus Liverpool in 2011, while as few as five million watched Arsenal defeat Southampton in 2003. In a multichannel era, TV audiences are down for everything, but then the competition as a whole and the final in particular have not made for great viewing. The last serious upset before Wigan's victory over Manchester City in 2013 was 1988 when Wimbledon beat Liverpool. The 1993 final went with form as Arsenal beat Sheffield Wednesday, but they managed it in epic style after two games and two periods of extra time. Since 1992 and the advent of the Premier League, upsets have been rare. Manchester United, Arsenal, Chelsea and Liverpool have won eighteen out of twenty-four finals and of those games only Liverpool's 2006 win against West Ham was unmissable. Many others have been mean and turgid affairs. Portsmouth's miraculous victory in 2008 came with a sting in the tail, as this victory marked the peak of the club's fortunes before a vertiginous decline into bankruptcy, administration and multiple relegations. Wigan's victory over Manchester City in 2013 was perhaps even more miraculous, but on the following Tuesday they still got relegated.

The FA's response to these shifts has been cautious, attempting to balance some semblance of the traditions, real and invented, that constitute the Cup's cultural capital, with the requirements of rich clubs, commercial broadcasters and sponsors. The FA proved—under boom conditions, but to its credit—a competent commercial negotiator. During Brian Barwick's term as chief executive in particular, the FA secured lucrative deals for coverage and sponsorship of the Cup, which allowed it to increase the prize money, maintaining the interest of leading clubs, and to divert some of the bonanza to its development work. There has however been more than a hint of the disingenuous about changes to the competition's format. When replays of the final were abandoned and the Cup was to be decided by penalties, the FA argued it was because "supporters want a decision on the day"—but it was equally likely to be connected to the scheduling needs of big clubs still in European competitions in May. The hushed tones of the Monday morning draw, broadcast live on the radio from the FA's creaky committee rooms, were cancelled and replaced by a guileless live TV evening broadcast from a neon studio. Semi-finals are now played at Wembley, on the grounds that it gives more people a big day out. Of course it also provides a crucial element in the precarious business plan to keep Wembley Stadium afloat.

There remains a quiet desperation about the FA Cup. For status, glamour, money and TV audiences it simply cannot compete with the Premier League or the Champions League. Despite the greatly expanded pool of prize money the Cup winner is unlikely to make much more than £5 million from the gig. By contrast they will more than double that with qualification for the Champions League group stages. UEFA's decision to abandon the European Cup-Winners' Cup, and with it the Cup holder's route to Europe, was a further demotion. The first sign of drift was Manchester United's withdrawal from the competition in 2000 to allow them to play in FIFA's inaugural World Club Cup in Brazil. United and the FA were vilified for this break with tradition, but United's participation had been sanctioned by the FA as part of its doomed campaign to curry favor at FIFA. Since then no club has formally abandoned the tournament but the unmistakable trend towards fielding weakened, experimental and youthful sides speaks volumes. The endless incantation of the magic of the Cup in press releases, marketing talk, newspaper columns, and TV highlight trailers suggests its terminal disenchantment.

# CHAPTER 7

# Last Man Standing?

## English Football and the Politics of Gender

A win's a win. To put it in gentlemen's terms, if you've gone out on a night and you're looking for a young lady and you pull one, some weeks they're good looking and some weeks they're not the best. Our performance today would have been not the best looking bird but at least we'd have gone home in the taxi with her . . . She wasn't the best looking lady we've ended up taking home but she was very pleasant, very nice, so thanks very much, let's have a coffee.

**IAN HOLLOWAY**

I.

Ian Holloway was explaining QPR's ugly victory over Chesterfield in 2003 in his own inimitable words,[1] yet simultaneously one could hear the voice of an older, and maybe wiser, Arthur Seaton or Alfie Elkins, the cinematic heat-seeking bachelors of the late 1950s and early 1960s. The central characters of *Saturday Night and Sunday Morning* and *Alfie*, respectively, they were affluent, single, working-class but on the up; hedonistic, hard-drinking heroes, magnetically attractive, promiscuous and resistant to every charm and bear trap on the road to the feminine worlds of domesticity and marriage. No one version of masculinity can encompass the world of English football, but it continues to have a soft spot for the hell-raisers and womanizers of the past—Stan Bowles, Rodney Marsh, and Frank Worthington remain a fondly remembered trinity of players who drank their talents into the ground—and keeps a close eye on the sexual adventures of their successors.[2] There is a similar and enduring affection, or at least tolerance, for hard men and rascals like Vinnie Jones, Neil Ruddock and Dennis Wise. Imaginatively and linguistically, English football remains in the world of Arthur Seaton and Alfie Elkins; from Holloway's extended metaphors to Tommy Smith's description of David Beckham as a "big girl's blouse," to the recent remarks of Brendan Rogers, manager of Liverpool, who told his team to "man up" and that a match against Stoke was always physical, for football is still "a man's game."[3]

Is there any other realm of public life where prominent figures proclaim the essential, enduring maleness of their world? Now, in 2014, no British politician or senior corporate executive would claim that politics or business was "a man's world" and expect to escape massive censure. Back in 1994 Ron Atkinson spoke for much of the football world when he declared, "Women should be in the kitchen, the discotheque and the boutique, but not in football." As recently as 2005, Mike Newell, then manager of Luton Town, blamed assistant referee Amy Rayner for his side's defeat saying, "This is not park football. So what are women doing here? She should not be here. I know that sounds sexist, but I am sexist."[4] Atkinson was indulged and although Newell was criticized, his dismissal soon after for because of his team's performances. Football managers and commentators still routinely proclaim that "football is a man's game," using it as an implied threat to others or as a defense of rough play.

The balance sheet of continuity and change in English football in the last quarter of a century is steadily shifting towards change. Clubs and owners still prefer winning to profits, but the economic organization of the game has been transformed out of all recognition. The English crowd retains something of the demographics of the past, but it is surely ageing and mutating. The geography of the football nation stills holds to its Victorian schema, but the map of club owners and players depicts an entirely different globalized world. In one crucial respect, however, continuity has the upper hand. English football, as a professional spectacle, as an employer, as a polymorphous popular culture, and as a recreational game, remains overwhelmingly masculine. Of course, the same could be said respectively of rugby league, the armed forces, video gaming and boxing. But none one of these other barometers can match football's social and cultural reach or the range of masculinities it encompasses. Football has its own tough northern pros, warriors, nerds and bruisers and a lot more besides. There are certainly other niche labor markets where women are as poorly represented as they are on the boards of football clubs, or the sports desks of tabloid newspapers, but few where the arrival of women has evoked such a public pantomime of a backlash. The shifting character of relationships between men and women, the new forms and norms of masculinity and femininity that are emerging, will not be resolved by English football but the nature of those changes and conflicts is discernible there in sharp relief.

This all has deep roots. Football was born of a wider elite sporting culture that consciously understood itself as an exercise in shaping masculinity and sexuality, a bromide for adolescent and potentially homosexual testosterone in all-male institutions, and a moral and physical training ground for creating Christian gentlemen. The working-class takeover of football in the early twentieth century may have swapped Corinthian for artisan heroes, but it was no less masculine. The game itself, however, showed no such bias. Despite all the medical, social, and practical prohibitions, women played and watched football in late Victorian and Edwardian England. The spread of the game among working-class women, enjoying the sporting and economic emancipation of industrial work during the First World War, looks, in retrospect, like the first stirrings of the kind of football mania that gripped boys and men in the last quarter of the nineteenth century.

In 1921 the FA, the Football League, indeed the entirety of the English football establishment, put a stop to all this. No FA affiliated club was permitted to allow women to use its facilities. The rest of the home nations followed suit. For fifty years, women's football was reduced to a tiny and stigmatized subculture subsisting in the marginal spaces of municipal recreation grounds, until it was reinvigorated by a new wave of social change in the 1970s and 1980s. For fifty years, women were almost invisible. Although there was a female presence in football crowds, somewhere between 5 and 10 percent of the audience, they are almost absent from the collective historical memory of the golden age. In football's folk chronicles, women are much more likely to feature as serving girls in the boardroom, nagging wives bemoaning their husband's monomaniacal devotion to their club or motherly landladies of homesick apprentices. In the 1960s, as the cult of celebrity first stirred and footballers' private lives acquired media currency, wives and girlfriends appeared, the former cozily domestic, the latter cast as dolly birds.

What one never saw was a woman playing. With the formation of the independent Women's FA in 1969 and two years later the lifting of the 1921 ban, this began to change, though it took until 1993 for the FA to actually incorporate women's football on notionally equal terms within its remit. Since then women's football has seen quite remarkable growth.[5] From a starting point of just 80 girls' teams in 1993 there were 8,000 by 2005. Football overtook netball in 2002 as the most widely played female recreational sport. There are now an estimated two million girls and women playing in some form or another. A women's professional league was first established in 2003 and in its current incarnation the Women's Super League (WSL) has two nationwide divisions. The women's national teams have steadily improved and in 2005, three million people watched them play Sweden on the BBC. Yet for all the remarkable grassroots work that has been done, 94 percent of the nation's football playing fields do not have women's changing rooms, and for much of the public the women's game remains in an unfair and impossible contest with the men's game, a comparison that maintains its lowly status.[6]

While the women's game has been flourishing, more and more women have made their way into the men's game, most especially as fans. From less than 10 percent at the start of the 1990s, by 2009 women were making up some 19 percent of Premiership crowds[7] and a third of recent and first-time season ticket holders. In this regard, at least, the future looks feminine. However, they have not always been welcomed. Clubs, to a great extent, continue to believe that the main value of women fans is to bring male children to the game and get them hooked. The idea that they are coming for the same reasons and in the same way that men do is beyond the reach of their imaginations. In the stands, there are plenty of first-hand reports of male uneasiness and a sense of trespass: standard heckles include, "Go home and do the ironing" and "Shouldn't you be shopping?" Many female fans report that their footballing authenticity is tested in a way that male counterparts rarely encounter, particularly with regard to technical knowledge ("Do you know what offside is?") and motivations for attending ("Just here to ogle the players?"). Masculine forms of femininity—women fans as grown up tomboys—seem to be the most easily accepted version of female fandom.[8]

In 1994 Rachel Anderson, then the only FIFA-licensed female football agent, was turned away from the PFA dinner awards, despite her invitation, the attendance of many of the players she represented and, most shamefully, the presence of female waiting staff. Her path was barred by Brendon Batson the PFA deputy secretary. Anderson recalled saying "Brendon, you're telling me, as one of the first black players, that I can't come in because I'm female?" Anderson took the PFA to court and won.[9] Karren Brady, appointed chief executive of Birmingham City in 1993, found herself excluded from club boardrooms and inner sanctums across the country.[10] This kind of formal exclusion has now ended. There are more women agents, executives, owners and directors of clubs than then, but only just. As late as 2010, there had never been a woman on the board of the FA and there was just one woman on the hundred-member-plus FA Council. Delia Smith was the chair of Norwich City, but football made the composition of the board of the average FTSE 500 company look like a paradise of sexual equality.

The media has offered more opportunities to women as television presenters, commentators and reporters, but mostly on its own terms. In the 1970s Julie Welch was the only female football correspondent on a national newspaper. In the twenty-first century she has been joined by women football writers on both national and regional papers, who make up perhaps 10 percent of the contemporary press box. Although rarely reported, a number of senior coaches have taken their presence at press conferences as an opportunity for cheap shots, and—in the case of Gordon Strachan—given deliberately monosyllabic answers to a female reporter's intelligent questions. Television has proved, at first glance, an easier environment with women presenting matches, chat shows, and rolling news on Sky, BBC and ITV, and more recently on ESPN and BT Sport. However, it is hardly been on equal terms. As Gabby Logan said, when asked if Sky Sports used women as window dressing, "the girls are basically wearing a leotard while the blokes are in suit and tie."[11] BBC Radio, although still overwhelmingly male, has acquired female voices—like Eleanor Oldroyd and Juliette Ferrington. The replacement of James Alexander Gordon, as the voice of the BBC's football scores, by the melodious Charlotte Green has been welcomed. Radio also offered the route into the commentary box. Here, the pathfinder has been Jacqui Oatley, who made her first radio commentary on BBC local radio in 2003, covering Wakefield vs Emley in the Unibond League. She broke the glass ceiling in April 2007 commentating on Fulham vs Blackburn on *Match of the Day*. Oakley's detailed command of the football and her mastery of its vernacular were unquestionable. As one press review noted, she had an identical capacity to the male commentariat for saying things like "he's in absolutely acres of space" with unwarranted emphasis. Yet columnists, insiders, and Internet forums continued to be either patronizing, willfully ignorant or simply misogynistic. Most were left only with the argument that her voice was wrong and she squawked—not a criticism levelled at her equally squawky colleague Jonathan Pearce or the maniacal high-pitched whine of Murray Walker, the Formula 1 stalwart.[12]

The toughest excursion into male territory has been made by a generation of female officials in men's professional football. Wendy Toms became the first female assistant referee in the Football League in 1995 and in the Premier League in 1998. She went on to run the line at the 2000 League Cup final and regularly refereed men's football in the Conference. It has hardly been a deluge since, but the numbers have crept up. Given that comprehension of the offside rule has served as one of the key markers of football authenticity and furnished the trope of innumerable gags that differentiate men and women, the presence of female assistant referees calling offside has been perceived as a threat to this brand of exclusionary masculinity. This was made abundantly clear by Sky Sport's perennial anchors Richard Keys and Andy Gray whose prematch banter and off mic dialogue was leaked to the press and public in 2011. Keys, remarking on Karren Brady's column in the *Sun* that day was heard to say, "The game's gone mad. See charming Karren Brady this morning complaining about sexism? Yeah. Do me a favor, love."[13] In another bit of pregame chat touchline reporter Andy Burton said, ". . . apparently a female lino today, a bit of a looker." Gray came back with, "I can see her from here . . . What do women know about the offside rule?" To this toxic brew of condescension and contempt, Keys and Gray then added some spite after assistant referee Sian Massey made a close offside call.

KEYS: Somebody better get down there and explain offside to her.
GRAY: Female linesmen . . . they probably don't know the offside rule
. . . Why is there a female linesman? Somebody fucked up big.

And so they had, but not Massey whose judgement was proved absolutely correct by the replays. When footage of these conversations was leaked to the outside world, Keys's and Gray's judgement was deemed less than correct, though they retained a small core of mainly anonymous supporters. Additional pictures of Gray inviting his colleague Charlotte Jackson to adjust a microphone stuck into the flies of his ample trousers sealed his fate and he was fired. Keys hung around for a day or two. He then crucified himself in a cringingly awful radio interview in which his grotesque sense of entitlement and his complete disengagement from reality was revealed, as he hinted at "dark forces" conspiring against him. He declared himself perplexed that it should all be such a fuss and appeared to believe himself the victim of the piece. Keys was retired too, only to resurface with Gray on their own show on Talk Sport, the saloon bar bear pit of sports radio. Massey was met at her next game by chants of "There's only one Andy Gray."[14] A similar look behind the scenes and into the email inbox of Premier League chief executive Richard Scuadamore in 2014 provided more of the same in private communications full of sexist banter.

Thus for all the changes that have occurred inside and outside football, and despite the growth of the women's game, English professional football remains a place where many men are resisting female encroachment on what they believe to be their home turf. However, as a consequence of reform from above, pressure from below and the wider transformation in attitudes to gender, they have had to concede some ground. Women who conform to the established masculine norms of authentic support, technical competence and an effortless command of football grammar are making their presence felt in every part of the game but for playing and managing. It is here alone that football is, if not a man's game, still a game of men. What remains to be seen is what will happen, if anything, to the codes of masculinity that persist among the men we choose to love and hate, deify and destroy, whom we pay to watch play and whose lives we so obsessively scrutinize.

## II.

In English football, even amongst recent coaching migrants, players are often collectively referred to by their manager as "the lads," or "the boys" and almost always they are a "good bunch of" them. Managers are the boss, the guv'nor or the gaffer. These are the echoes of a now past era of paternalism, of cast-iron hierarchies of age and deference. The lads are not quite the same anymore. The lifestyle and status of football players, their depiction in the media and their relationship with fans have all been transformed by the arrival of money. With regard to the latter, two widespread if always romantic beliefs have been fatally undermined. First, that idea that players and fans came from, and continued to live in, the same worlds has been shattered. Some players still speak of putting in a shift and doing a job but footballers are no longer working the line. English football still overwhelmingly recruits its indigenous players from the working class and from established football families, but the income gap between players and fans grew after the abolition of the maximum wage; since the early 1990s the gap has become a chasm.[15] Second, the equally tenuous idea that footballers, albeit socially mobile, remain geographically rooted in their club and city is impossible to sustain when more than half of the Premiership's players come from outside of England and the turnover of the transfer market spins ever faster. Hometown heroes, local boys made good, trusty one-club servants, all mainstays of football's sense of its own golden age, the sporting corollary of industrial Britain's lifetime employees, have become very rare characters. The almost universal affection for Manchester United's Ryan Giggs rests, in part, on his career-long fidelity to a single club. Paul Scholes and Steven Gerrard, though spikier characters, have acquired the same golden aura.

Crowds have always held grudges, disliked some players and targeted individuals for abuse, but the structure of feeling in English football has tilted from empathy to envy and from loving towards hating. Many of the most high-profile players, though often held in high regard at their own club, are widely disliked. These emotions spring from a football culture that appears to demand unwavering and narrowly cast club solidarities, and are nurtured by the anonymity of the Internet. David Beckham returned from the 1998 World Cup to a season of richly textured taunts. Made the scapegoat for England's early exit, his effigy was hung and burned at grounds and his sex life ritually abused. More recently Ashley Cole has been the object of loathing for his mercenary departure from Arsenal to Chelsea. Roy Keane, Kevin Davies, and Joey Barton were deemed to have exceeded permissible levels of violence and aggression. Cristiano Ronaldo and Didier Drogba have been singled out for their diving and theatricality, El Hadji Djouf for spitting and spitefulness, John Terry and Lee Bowyer for being thugs, Graham Le Saux for reading the *Guardian* and thus, transparently, being gay. On this evidence, at any rate, England's ideal footballer is still cast in the mould of Bobby Moore, a working-class gentleman, socially aspirant but publicly humble, vigorously physical and unambiguously heterosexual.

Disdain for individual deviants aside, there is now a more general air of collective irritation with players. As the player–fan relationship has become encased within the cash nexus that links business and customer, some fans' sense of entitlement and expectation has grown. Radio phone-ins, in particular, have given vent to the voice of disappointed consumers angrily demanding their money back or at least an exchange of goods. Player performances are described as disgraceful and shameful with alarming regularity and often only with the merest connection to what has actually happened. Yet at the same time as football players are charged with greed, indifference, cynicism, and laziness they have been elevated to the level of exalted role models. It is a notion so universally acknowledged that the last three prime ministers, Blair, Brown, and Cameron, have all very publically reiterated it.[16] Yet under no rational calculus could it be considered wise to make poorly educated and cosseted teenage millionaires, however technically gifted, personally dedicated or grittily determined they might be, the nation's moral weathervanes. This whole ridiculous apparatus of expectation and assumption goes into high gear when players' misdemeanors and bad behavior, on and off the field, are reported. It is unfair on them and helps perpetuate a dressing-room culture where widespread problems of mental illness, gambling addictions and alcoholism have been hidden.[17] As importantly, the choice of this very unrepresented group of moral paladins is indicative of the terrible paucity of our contemporary civic and ethical imaginations. The same could be said of our appetite for the footballer's biography, a literary genre almost entirely discredited in the last decade by the avalanche of the disingenuous, ghost-written, self-justifications of young adults who have barely begun to live a life, yet alone comprehend one.[18]

Only two English footballers in the last twenty years have reached a level of celebrity that has truly exceeded the sport and its own internal cultures: Paul Gascoigne and David Beckham. Both came from working-class homes. Gascoigne grew up in a tiny council house in Gateshead; his father was a laborer. Beckham was born in Leytonstone in East London; his father was a kitchen fitter. There the similarities end. Gascoigne's upbringing was chaotic and scarred by family tragedy. Beckham grew up in a very stable environment and was able to flourish at home and abroad, playing in Spain, Italy, the USA and France. Gascoigne was on a downward curve the moment he left Newcastle. He secured his place in the canon of English football at just nineteen with his performance at the 1990 World Cup where he was indisputably the best player on the team. "Daft as a brush" as Bobby Robson had called him, wayward but exquisitely gifted, Karl Miller was already registering the contradictions and frailties of this young man.

> Fierce and comic, formidable and vulnerable, urchin-like and waif-like . . . strange-eyed, pink-faced, fair-haired, tense and upright . . . "A dog of war with the face of a child," breathed Giovanni Agnelli, president of [Fiat and owner of] the Italian team Juventus. He can look like god's gift to the Union Jack soccer hooligan, and yet he can look so sweet.[19]

Gascoigne sealed his place in the nation's affections when, towards the end of England's semifinal against Germany, he was booked, effectively debarred from the final and shed a tear. For a few short years his stock rose, the money flowed and his cover of Geordie folk anthem "Fog on the Tyne," which he recorded with Chris Waddle, made it to number 2 in the charts. Utterly unequipped to cope with life in Italy and Italian football his years at Lazio were deeply disappointing. Glasgow Rangers proved a better refuge and for a few seasons he recovered something of his old form, excelling for England at Euro 96. However, over the next eight years his addictions to smoking, gambling, alcohol, junk food and energy drinks sent him into a negative spiral of personal and sporting disasters; a very public divorce driven by his violent behavior towards his wife, treatment for stomach ulcers, pneumonia, morphine dependence, bulimia, OCD and bipolarity, a terrible media circus of checking in and out of hospitals and detox clinics, climbing on and then falling off the wagon. By 2004 he was virtually unemployable, reduced to turning out for Boston United for a mere four games.

Although an exceptional footballer, Beckham never possessed the footballing talent and invention of Gascoigne. His superb dead-ball skills aside, his main football virtue was as a Stahkanovite team player. Beckham's genius was to take the raw materials of his body and football career and convert them into a level of global coverage that no player of the era, anywhere, could match. Search engines have declared him among the most sought-after name on the Internet for much of his career. His arrival in Southern California in 2007 was marked by the social event of the year, a 600-person, invite-only, A-list celebrity conclave organized by his new friends, and fellow stars on the roster of *über*-agency CAA, Tom Cruise and Will Smith. The *LA Times* gushed at the roster of Hollywood aristocracy that came to greet him: "Oprah Winfrey, George Clooney, Jim Carrey, Anjelica Huston, Steven Spielberg, David Geffen . . . Warner Bros. President Alan Horn and Universal Pictures chief Ron Meyer."[20] His marriage to Victoria Adams, aka Posh Spice, was the masterstroke, forging an alliance of pop music, fashion, and football, combined with a faultless masculine domesticity and parenthood and a brazen commercial exploitation of his sexuality that appealed to men and women, gays and straights, and most of all to corporations. In an era when as the cultural commentator Mark Simpson remarked, "unmoisturized heterosexuality had been given the pink slip by consumer capitalism. The stoic, self denying straight male didn't shop enough," Beckham was the future. His body, tailored, tattooed, and oiled, appeared everywhere, from Marks and Spencer's menswear departments to the cover of the gay magazine *Attitude*. In this respect Beckham was a true original, the first English footballer to venture into sartorial territory once deemed dangerously effeminate—Alice bands and sarongs—and to welcome his status as a gay icon. However, as Simpson, who coined the term, pointed out, Beckham was a metrosexual, whom he defined as "a young man with money to spend, living in . . . [a] metropolis—because that's where the best shops, clubs, gyms and hairdressers are. He might be gay, straight, or bisexual, but this is utterly immaterial because he has clearly taken himself as his own love object and pleasure as his sexual preference."[21]

If the playing careers of Gascoigne and Beckham took radically different courses, then their retirements are incomparable. Gascoigne has not worked in football since 2004. Over the next decade, he was made bankrupt, treated for pneumonia, fitted with an artificial hip and arrested for drunken brawling and drink driving. His alcoholic dependence was so intense that during a recent detox in America his heart stopped beating. Beckham's salad days are yet to come. Over his football career it is estimated that he has accumulated a net worth of around £150 million. Yet he will probably make more money after his playing days than he did during them. As the chief executive of M&C Saatchi Sport and Entertainment put it, "He'll have more time on his hands and more time for commercial partners and the brands he can work . . . with."[22] He has already been at work, acquiring multimillion-pound ambassadorial roles with Chinese football and Sky Sports. Thus the two most famous English footballers of the last quarter of a century occupy the emotional and financial poles of our age. The glare of the media and the game of celebrity reduced one man to a pitiful, skeletal wreck, yet made the other a ubiquitous brand and a junior member of the global super-rich. They are tangible evidence of our society's capacity for the extremes of self-destruction and self-promotion, self-hate and self-love, and the harsh epidemiology of postindustrial England; to the poor and damaged, a chaotic existence and an early death, to the rich and connected, a long life of ostentatious consumption and capital accumulation.

For the most part, real affection, real love and secular deification have been reserved for the best of the foreign players. Eric Cantona at Manchester United, Gianfranco Zola at Chelsea, Dennis Bergkamp, and Thierry Henry at Arsenal were all players of spectacular talent, who made the rest of their side play better and brought a degree of tactical sophistication, immaculate touch or spatial awareness to English football that had rarely been seen. All mastered English, albeit idiosyncratically, all had a hinterland of interests, all kept themselves in shape and their feet on the ground, displaying a degree of professional self-discipline and emotional balance that many other players, both English and foreign, have found hard to acquire. In short, rather than boys or lads, they looked and sounded like men; flawed and unfinished but human and real.

## III.

For the first half century of English professional football, the manager or coach was a peripheral figure. Club boards and secretaries picked the team, the players organized their own training in a working environment that was more like an artisanal craft workshop than a factory floor. Coaches or managers carried the net of balls, put out the cones and let them get on with it. While this kind of guild is long gone, the language of English football has retained the vocabulary of craftsmen, journeymen and apprentices. In the 1920s and 1930s Herbert Chapman, at Huddersfield and then Arsenal, revolutionized the role, carving out a distinct and powerful place in the division of labor within a football club. He assumed singular authority of team selection, tactical play, coaching regimes, and eventually transfer policy as well. It would take another couple of decades for this arrangement to become the norm in club football, a process exemplified by Matt Busby's assumption of total control at Manchester United in the 1950s and 1960s. In the 1970s executive authority was combined with a new level of media coverage of managers, which turned the most charismatic and successful coaches into national figures: above all, Bill Shankly at Liverpool and the irrepressible Brian Clough at Derby County and Nottingham Forest. Working-class autodidacts, unconventional but authentic socialists, they were unencumbered by theoretical knowledge or formal training but were exemplars of learning on the job. Both graduated from player to lower league management to underperforming clubs deep in the dying heart of late industrial England, and transformed them. Liverpool, mired in Division Two, clearly the lesser of the two Merseyside sides, was turned by Shankly and his successors into just one of a handful of football clubs with a truly global profile, a byword for its own distinct tradition of playing and supporting football. Clough never created an empire in the same way, but winning consecutive European Cup titles with Nottingham Forest—a club from perhaps England's eighth biggest city—was an unrepeatable, demography-defying achievement. Moreover, Shankly and Clough were linguistically brilliant. Shankly was more gnomic, but sardonic, sharp and funny. Clough, who helped invent the very notion of a television football pundit, was garrulous and could be cruel and arrogant, but you felt that he had earned it: "Rome wasn't built in a day, but then again I wasn't on that particular job." In the end, they were killed by the same slow horrors that took so many men of their class and generation; Shankly by the pointless empty boredom of life after work, Clough by the bottle. In retrospect it is hard not to read their achievements and their methods as the last triumph of male charisma, will and working-class wit in cities that would soon be devastated, and in a job that would soon no longer exist.

Since Shankly and Clough set the folk benchmark of what a football manager was meant to be, the coach's place in the division of labor within football clubs has shifted again. On the one hand, some of the manager's authority and tasks have been passed upwards to directors of football and chief executives, particularly with regard to transfers, wages and bonus systems. On the other hand, many responsibilities have been delegated down, to specialized position coaches, metrics, scouting and computing departments, sports psychologists and fitness experts, not to mention acupuncturists, faith healers and translators. Equally importantly, the balance of power between coaches and players has shifted. This is part of a wider decline in deference and the automatic authority once conferred by age and seniority, but it is also rooted in the very peculiar labor market conditions of elite football. Coaches may still pick the team, but players find it easier and easier to change clubs. Coaches can still fine them for leaving their gloves on the pitch or turning up late for training, but this doesn't even look like pocket money any more. Operating inside a network rather than a hierarchy, the postindustrial football coach must be a manager of complexity, consensus and coordination. Bereft of the conventional institutional weaponry of control—like the clip round the ear—they have to practice what is almost ubiquitously referred to as man-management. In an era when managerial and executive jobs are among the fastest growing segments of the labor market and their occupants make up a considerable part of the football audience, it is hardly surprising that the public often finds the manager a more interesting character than his players, and that his dilemmas and problems should evoke more empathy.

Yet despite all this the econometric evidence shows that the overwhelming determinant of a team's position in the league is the size of the wage bill. Teams might fluctuate a little from the norm, over- or underperforming, but the bands are narrow. What evidence there is on the input of managers into team performance, suggests that nearly all the benefits come in the medium-to-long term and are most likely to be achieved by managers who have garnered sufficient length of service and experience. However, the average tenure of dismissed managers has shrunk from over three years in 1992 to less than one and a half years today; most first-time managers lose their jobs between six months and twelve months after taking on the job, and half of them will never manage again.[23] The standard cliché that club owners and pundits rely upon to justify this kind of carnage in their personnel policies is that new managers will "give teams a lift." However, the econometric evidence is not good here either. By the time you have factored in the inevitable highs and lows of something as protean as a football team's performance, the honeymoon effect of a new manager in the Premier League is about two and a half points in the short term and almost nothing over the rest of the season. Things get no better further down the leagues. And all this before one has taken account of the financial, psychological and administrative costs of the transition.[24] Given this, the firing of managers is best understood as an act of ritual purification rather than a reasoned business strategy. For the apparent diminution in the scope of football managers' authority and impact has been accompanied by a huge elevation in their wages and a mode of reporting and storytelling that makes them far more culpable than any reasoned statistical analysis would support.

By the late 1990s, at the apex of the profession, Alex Ferguson, Ruud Gullit, and Arsène Wenger could command salaries in the region of £1 million a year. A decade later Ferguson, Sven-Göran Eriksson and José Mourinho could command triple this.[25] As with the structure of player's wages, these figures would rapidly decline as one descended the Premier League and then even more rapidly lower down the Football League where wages were in five rather seven figures. Media coverage of football has increasingly framed matches and seasons as psychological and emotional duels, most especially the coverage of Ferguson and Wenger's rivalry during the years between Arsenal's first Premiership title in 1998 and the arrival of José Mourinho at Chelsea in 2004. Both Ferguson and Wenger had long experience operating within this kind of framework and often fed the media fire, but the whole circus took a step up with the arrival of the Portuguese. Even in such exalted company the capacity of the "Special One" to capture, shape and manipulate the sporting spectacle, the postmatch press conference and the daily torrent of football coverage in mainstream media was unprecedented. The 2005 League Cup final is not remembered for its outcome, but for Mourinho's shushing of the Liverpool crowd after Chelsea's injury time equalizer.[26]

As these anecdotes suggest, European coaches have become much more numerous at the top of English football. The former Czech international and PhD scholar Dr Jozef Vengloš managed Aston Villa at the start of the 1990s, but the key figure in these changes was Arsène Wenger, the Frenchman who arrived at Arsenal from a coaching jaunt in Japan in 1996. Although the scale of change at Arsenal is contested by some of the older players, it is clear that Wenger's arrival marked a step change in attitudes towards players' diet, drinking habits, tactical sophistication, attention to personal psychology as well as a more measured, reflective, even rarefied voice in discussing the game. Since Wenger's arrival there have been dozens of foreign coaches in the Premier League, England has had two foreign coaches, Scotland have had a German in charge. A Frenchman and a Spaniard, Gérard Houllier and Rafa Benítez, restyled and redefined Liverpool in the first decade of the twenty-first century. Since Chelsea were bought by Roman Abramovich they have been through ten managers from six countries without a single Englishman. The foreign contingent is significantly larger if we include the Celtic presence; the Scots, Welsh and Northern Irish, generally make up as much as a third of the Premiership's managers. Notable Scots have included Kenny Dalglish and David Moyes, Northern Ireland has furnished Brendan Rogers and Martin O'Neill, Welsh managers include Mark Hughes and Chris Coleman. In 2013, half of the Premier League's managers came from overseas, a quarter from the other home countries and just a quarter from England—an even smaller domestic contingent than among players or club owners.

This English rump is a motley crew, not one of whom has won the Premier League since its inception. The archetypes of English masculinity include Harry Redknapp and Ian Holloway who did variants on the cheeky chappy cum grown-up artful dodger; Sam Allerdyce and Tony Pulis who were the no-nonsense, tough-as-old-boots northern foremen or NCOs; in a more white-collar key, we have had the grey technocracy of Alan Pardew and Gary Megson and the pyrotechnics of Kevin Keegan who was like the corporate executive who believes the motivational business books he was reading and his own messianic publicity, or did before the stress destroyed him. To this miscellany of English masculinity, the Europeans have offered something different. Wenger has been the professorial archetype, learned, considered and cool, and utterly unfazed by the kind of statement full-length puffer jacket that most English men would find suspiciously feminine and ostentatious. Mourinho combines Wenger's air of intellectual authority with a stinging tongue, a capacity to command devotion from his players, good looks and stylish dressing and a host of endorsements for high-end brands and credit cards. In contrast to the English norm, both were at home in a variety of cultures and languages and while neither could claim a distinguished playing career, they never needed to trade on those kinds of credentials.

Yet from this wide array of men and masculinities none can compare in national stature or command the widespread affection accorded to Bobby Robson or Alex Ferguson. Both made knights of the realm, and both were born into the old working classes of the great depression. Robson grew up in a small Durham mining village where his father did fifty-one years down the pit. Ferguson spent his childhood in Govan—the shipbuilding heart of Glasgow—the son of the shipyard timekeeper. Neither knew running hot water. Robson's family made do with an outside toilet, the Fergusons had to share theirs with others in their crowded tenement. Although both would have successful professional playing careers, Robson playing for England and Ferguson for Rangers, they knew the real world of work. Robson started out as an electrician's apprentice before escaping to Fulham, Ferguson was an apprentice toolmaker and an active shop steward before he got his break at St. Johnstone. Both were, of course, successful managers. Robson, the more itinerant, perhaps even cosmopolitan of the two, won titles and trophies at Ipswich, Eindhoven, Porto and Barcelona; his England team at the 1990 World Cup remains the most successful ever but for the 1966 World Cup winners. Ferguson broke the stranglehold of the Old Firm on Scottish football with his brilliant Aberdeen sides of the mid-1980s, took Scotland to the World Cup finals (now a distant memory and an even more unlikely eventuality) before going to Manchester from where he dominated English football for over a quarter of a century, and brought home United's holy grail, the European Cup, not once but twice.

They were respected and esteemed for their achievements, but we fell in love with them for the manner in which they conducted themselves. Robson remained, for the most part, long suffering, gracious and polite in the face of the relentless and unfair press scrutiny of his professional and private life. He was never loved more than when, at the end of his career, he returned home to the North East of England to repair a chaotic and broken Newcastle United. Perhaps, above all, in an era of inflated expectations and limitless appetites, he was professionally ambitious but personally stoical and content. After twenty years of cancer treatment, he was finally deemed inoperable in 2008. "I have accepted what they have told me and I am determined to make the most of what time I have left . . . everyone has to go some time, and I have enjoyed every minute." There are few of us, I suspect, who when the time comes will be able to say those words with Robson's sincerity.

Ferguson had a harder, sharper edge to him. As he put it, "When the wind's howling down the Clyde, that's what forges your character." A character so strong it seemed that, despite the economic and social transformations in football, the golden age of Shankly and Clough could return. Like them Ferguson was self-taught, and was the only manager in the country who was not required to get an official coaching qualification. Deploying a theatrical and calculated mixture of love and rage, threat and reward, the hairdryer rant in the face and the smashing of tea cups, Ferguson created a dressing room where loyalty and solidarity, self-respect and intense collective ambition appeared to trump greed and self-interest. He really was ready to part company with any player, from Jaap Stam to David Beckham, who broke the codes of conduct or whose ego threatened the project, but he also nurtured talent and personality: his squads have produced a significant part of the new generation of coaches. First as myth and then confirmed as fact, his looming presence on the touchline seemed to make the referee's watch run slower. Fergietime, when United so often acquired precious extra seconds of play and the knack of scoring devastating last minute goals. No saint, Ferguson could display contempt for authority he would never tolerate himself, conducting a one-man boycott of the BBC for almost ten years and spending plenty of time banned from his own bench after biting public criticism of referees. Yet for all this Ferguson was also a creature of our times not the past. He earned a small fortune, but worried that he was underpaid and undervalued. As at ease in the clannish inner sanctums of football as his predecessors, Ferguson moved in wider circles than they could have imagined. Brian Clough had manned a megaphone in an East Midlands by-election, but Ferguson was courted by the most senior reaches of the Labour Party and made a figure in national campaigns. He was an echo of a time when a working-class man of talent could, not by the magical alchemy of elite education, but by a lifetime of hard work and hard thinking, rise to the very top and remain true to the best of the world that he came from. Bobby Robson is dead and Alex Ferguson has ascended to the boardroom. English football lives in their shadows, and will wait for their successors, but neither England nor Scotland will forge their like again.

# Opulence and Squalor in the Football Nation

We need not only higher exports and old-age pensions, but more open-air cafes, brighter and gayer streets at night, later closing hours for public houses, more local repertory theatres, better and more hospitable hoteliers and restaurateurs, brighter and cleaner eating houses, more riverside cafes, more pleasure gardens on the Battersea model, more murals and pictures in public places, better designs for furniture and pottery and women's clothes, statues in the centre of new housing estates, better-designed new street lamps and telephone kiosks and so on ad infinitum.

**ANTHONY CROSLAND,** *THE FUTURE OF SOCIALISM,* **1956**

In a community where public services have failed to keep abreast of private consumption things are very different. Here, in an atmosphere of private opulence and public squalor, the private goods have full sway.

**JOHN KENNETH GALBRAITH,** *THE AFFLUENT SOCIETY,* **1954**

It seems inexplicable that Tony Crosland, when outlining his vision of a social democracy under conditions of affluence, should not have included in his wish list better football stadiums, and sharper movement and passing. Crosland himself was a devotee of the game and a regular viewer of Match of the Day after it began broadcasting in 1964. When Foreign Secretary in the 1970s, he took visiting American Secretary of State Henry Kissinger to watch Grimsby Town play Gillingham. Personal tastes aside, football's absence from the list is intellectually surprising. Crosland correctly anticipated that the economic and social forces at work in Britain in the 1950s would transform the lives and aspirations of much of social democracy's working-class constituency and eventually diminish the industries and occupations that defined them. The future of socialism would have to find new political constituencies, new ways of creating public spaces and tangible collective solidarities beyond the factory and the working man's club. Football surely offered this?

Moreover, English football was precisely the kind of once great, now moribund industry that the Labour Party was going to transform into a world beater. It was a cluster of institutions hidebound by unreflective adherence to tradition and a disdain for science and innovation; it was short of capital, living off a declining Victorian and Edwardian inheritance; desperately insular in an increasingly global world, it was constricted by an archaic class system that still wrapped British life in its cobwebs. But then, as now, the common culture of English football remained bound to a social democratic moral universe. The market and professionalism were acceptable within socially determined bounds; symbolic competition was combined with practical economic cooperation; individual brilliance was celebrated but collective values were prized above all. It was also conservative, paternalist, racist and sexist, but then so was everything else in the country.

Of course neither Crosland nor his colleagues embarked upon a modernizing project, or even saw it as a possibility. Mainstream Labour never had a lot of time for popular cultural projects, and football's then lowly symbolic status and limited economic size made it almost invisible to politicians. Given the fate of the industrial sectors that the Labour governments of the 1960s and 1970s did attempt to restructure, it is probably just as well. By the time the combination of social disorder and stadium disasters made it unignorable, the Conservatives were in power. Although government, mainly through the Taylor Report, set the infrastructural framework within which English football would be remade, it was inevitable the game would be reshaped by private (the Premier League, Sky, and the club owners) rather than public forces (the FA, the BBC, supporters, or indeed any other stakeholders you care to mention).

Given that English football is a social democratic game in a neo-liberal world, it is all the more remarkable that its communitarian impulses remain alive. Half a century since Crosland wrote, the institutional and ideological presence of social democracy in national life is much diminished. Trade unions are a shadow of their former selves, the Cooperative movement has been fatally undermined by its incompetence and hubris. The Labour Party, like its opponents, primarily exists in television studios and other circuits of the media. The National Health Service remains, perhaps, the only social democratic institution that is both loved and endures as a functioning presence in daily life. And then there is football, still a social democratic game, whose geography, iconography and language remain suffused with the industrial, working-class world that Crosland could see passing; that carries imagery, icons and collective memories strong enough to long outlive the passing of the world in which they were made.

The world that English football is now played in has changed again. The country is increasingly diverse; society is more individualized and more networked, and the economy has become an exemplar of a globalized and deregulated liberal model of capitalism. Given its roots, English football has come a long way in adapting to wider changes in attitudes to ethnicity and gender. The journey is hardly over, but football remains an unusually powerful popular theater in which racism and sexism are displayed and challenged. The glibness of a more commercial culture has been balanced by a rash of new fan organizations and acts of collective resistance, a wave of football NGOs tied to social, health and educational work, new forms of collective ownership and within the great gurning maw of football media—mainstream and social—more diverse and reflective voices.

Like parts of the wider economy, English football has undergone a radical globalization. The benefits, which are considerable, have been sequestered by the few: the labour market for players and coaches, the origins of many club owners, the source of the Premier League's revenues and individual clubs' commercial deals have all sharply shifted from the national to the European and the global. While the leading clubs, players and agents have negotiated this world successfully, it is notable that the English FA has proved to be at best diplomatically inept, and at worst incompetent, naïve and utterly bereft of a political strategy to cope with today's more complex global football politics. At home the rise of the Premier League and its relationship with both the FA and the government are emblematic of a much wider hollowing out of governance. The capacity of public agencies to define the common good, devise tools of intervention and create the political will to regulate powerful private actors has collapsed.

It is hard to imagine a better illustration of Galbraith's couplet than the opulence of the English Premier League and the relative squalor of the grassroots, schools and youth game in the country. In the football nation we are lucky that the fruits of such an imbalance, of the schism between the globally networked and culturally esteemed worlds of private wealth and the disconnected off-worlds of public provision and purpose, are as trifling as the performance of England at the 2014 World Cup. In the fabric of everyday life in the real nation the consequences are altogether harsher.

I continue to hope that English football might offer the moments of grace, the collective drama and invented rituals and solidarities from which a different kind of nation might be imagined: the kind of more joyous, brighter and fairer society that Crosland had in mind. But I am left wondering whether the best it can manage is to be the canary in the mine of our impending global mediocrity and domestic fragmentation.

# ACKNOWLEDGMENTS

Love and thanks for enlightenment and inspiration go to Johnny Acton, Philip Auclair, David Boyle, Mark Burman, Anthony Clavane, Robert Colls, David Conn, Gita Conn, Rafe Conn and all the boys in the blue corner, Tim Crabbe, Owen Hatherley, Alix Hughes, Simon Inglis, Simon Kuper, Dan Levy, Chris Oakley, Tim Ruck, Steve Roser, Jonathan Wilson. Special thanks to Nigel Boyle, Andre Wakefield, the President of the Faculty at Pitzer College, and especially all my fabulous students at Pitzer. Publishing love and thanks to Sally Holloway, Tony Lacey, John English, Carl Bromley, Marco Pavia, and Keith Taylor. Biggest thanks and biggest love to Sarah Bond. Here's to sanity and solvency, babe!

# NOTES

## INTRODUCTION: ENGLAND IS PARADISE

1. Quoted in Ferguson (2003).
2. R. Hattersley, "Wednesday at the weekend," in Lansdown and A. Spillius (1990).
3. D. Trelford, "A Smile on the Coventry Face'," ibid.
4. Davies (1991); Hornby (1992).
5. P. Auclair (2009), p. 351. Cantona went so far as to say, "I should have been born English. When I hear 'God save the queen' it can make me cry, much more than 'The Marseillaise.' I feel close to the rebelliousness and vigour of the youth here. Perhaps time will separate us, but nobody can deny that here, behind the windows of Manchester, there is an insane love of football, of celebration and of music."
6. See, for example, J. Dart, "100 football blogs to follow in 2011," *Guardian*, 31 December 2010: www.theguardian.com/football/blog/2010/dec/31/100-football-blogs-to-follow-2011 and www.whoateallthepies.tv/lists/14458/top-six-british-football-podcasts.html
7. Crawford (2006).
8. Gardner (2011).
9. Ian Hamilton wrote in the introduction to his superb *Faber Book of Soccer* (1992), "In my local library there are as many books about bridge, coarse fishing and badminton as there are about association football. Soccer is notoriously a sport without much of a literature: unlike cricket or rugby, it has few links with higher education. The soccer-intellectual tends to treat soccer as an off-duty indulgence . . ." (p. 1).
10. Hamilton (1998); Miller (1990); Faulks (1990); Morrison (1990).
11. M. Amis, *London Fields*, London: Jonathan Cape, 1989.
12. Taylor (1996), Peace (2007, 2013).
13. Philip Larkin, "MCMXIV," in P. Larkin, *The Whitsun Weddings*, London: Faber and Faber, 1964; Seamus Heaney, "Markings" in S. Heaney, *Seeing Things*, London: Faber and Faber, 1991; Ted Hughes, "Football at Slack," in T. Hughes, *The Hawk in the Rain*, London: Faber and Faber, 1957.
14. See "Football's first chant Laureate": http://news.bbc.co.uk/1/hi/england/london/3702313.stm
15. T. Harrison, *V*, Newcastle upon Tyne: Bloodaxe Books, 1985. On Carol Ann Duffy see "David Beckham's Achilles immortalised by poet laureate": http://news.bbc.co.uk/1/hi/8570282.stm; S. Armitage, "Why I love goalkeepers," 15 June 2010: www.theguardian.com/global/2010/jun/15/simon-armitage-goalkeepers; D. Paterson, *Nil Nil*, London: Faber and Faber, 1993.

16. "The Queen 'has supported Arsenal for over 50 years,'" *Daily Mail*, 23 April 2007: www .dailymail.co.uk/sport/football/article-450175/The-Queen-supported-Arsenal-50-years.html; "Prince of Wales supports Burnley football club," *Daily Telegraph*, 15 February 2012: www .telegraph.co.uk/sport/football/9085234/Prince-of-Wales-supports-Burnley-football-club.html

17. R. Sylvester, "Forget football. The coalition's game is different," *The Times*, 7 June 2010.

18. V. Chaudary, "Why Houllier won't vote Tory," *Guardian*, 10 January 2004.

19. V. Cable, "Arthur, Delia and another rotten bubble," *Daily Mail*, 9 May 2009: www .dailymail.co.uk/debate/article-1179868/VINCE-CABLE-Arthur-Delia-rotten-bubble.html

20. See www.channel4.com/news/sir-mervyn-king-debt-target-channel-4-news-interview

21. *Independent*, "The Booker Shortlist 1996': www.independent.co.uk/arts-entertainment /books/the-booker-shortlist-1996-1356748.html (5 October 1996).

22. R. Alleyne, "Britain faces dropping down science league," Daily Telegraph, 9 March 2010.

23. www.telegraph.co.uk/finance/8719826/Sir-Martin-Sorrells-extended-economic-metaph ors.html

24. Renton quoted in D. Batty, "Damien Hirst's split from Larry Gagosian turns heads in art world," *Guardian*, 6 January 2013. See also: "His art is seen as the result of the fat abundance of 2000s excess. Hirst stands to the public as the Chelsea football club artist – the huge ego, the wealth, the fawning customers blind to value and taste." O. Shuttleworth, "The Future of Damien Hirst': www.fineartbrokers.com/pages/news/index.asp?NewsID=53 (2012).

25. www.mirror.co.uk/lifestyle/going-out/super-rich-collectors-like-roman-abramovich-154 7218#ixzz2bquwmKDR

26. Premier League, "Prime Minister hails Premier League on India trip": www.premierleague .com/en-gb/news/news/2012-13/feb/prime-minister-david-cameron-and-richard-scudamore -take-premier-league-to-india.html (20 February 2013).

27. W. Hutton: www.theguardian.com/commentisfree/2013/jan/13/football-everything-bad -about-britain; J. Freedland: www.theguardian.com/commentisfree/2011/oct/18/premier-league -rampant-capitalism

28. C. Brown, "Oh how I hate the Beautiful Game," *Daily Telegraph*, 28 June 2008.

29. Hitchens on football can be read at http://hitchensblog.mailonsunday.co.uk/2010/06 /is-football-a-pagan-cult.html; http://hitchensblog.mailonsunday.co.uk/2006/07/boo_hoo_and _goo.html; http://hitchensblog.mailonsunday.co.uk/2013/04/miliband-shoots-at-a-footballing -fascist-and-scores-an-own-goal.html

30. Henderson on football: www.spectator.co.uk/columnists/10359/i-hate-football-so-much -these-days-that-i-can-hardly-bear-to-report-it/

## CHAPTER 1: ASPIRATION AND ILLUSION

1. *Sunday Times*, 19 May 1985.

2. Kuper and Szymanski (2009).

3. Wilson (2007).

4. Kuper and Szymanski (2009), p. 87.

5. On the coming of professionalism, see: Vamplew (1988), chapter 8; Tischler (1981).

6. Taylor (2006).

7. Conn (2013).

8. See Taylor (2000).

9. Taylor (2001).

10. On utility maximization see Sloane (1971); Vamplew (1988), chapter 8; Garnham and Jackson (2003); Dixon, Garnham Jackson (2004).

11. Chester (1983).

12. Ibid.

13. Conn (2013), p. 209.

14. Haynes (1993, 1995).

15. Cowley (2009).

16. Davies (1991). See also James Erskine's documentary *One Night in Turin* (2010).

17. Scraton (1999); Johnes (2005); Taylor (2008), pp. 338–41.

18. Between 1991 and 1995 average admission prices at Sheffield Wednesday rose by over 100 per cent, at Blackburn by 178 per cent, and by 240 per cent at Manchester United. See Football Trust (1996).

19. Football League (1990).

20. Football Association (1991). The struggle over which model would be followed is outlined in Taylor (2008), pp. 334–5; Conn (2004), pp. 49–53.

21. All the turnover data for England and other European leagues has been collated and picked over in successive editions of Deloitte Sports Business Group (1990–2012).

22. Bose (2013); Conn (2004), pp. 102–5; Bower (2003), pp. 89–92.

23. For full details on the rising cost per game of Premier League deals see BBC News, "BSkyB and BT shares fall on Premier League TV deal," www.bbc.co.uk/news/business-18438890 (2012).

24. www.independent.co.uk/sport/football/premier-league/special-report-world-will-soon-be-worth-more-to-premier-league-than-uk-8498204.html

25. Rookwood and Chan (2011).

26. See www.dailymail.co.uk/sport/football/article-2353388/Barclays-Premier-League-clubs-clock-200-000-air-miles-pre-season-tours-Asia-Australia-South-Africa-United-States.html

27. On Premier League net loss and profit see House of Commons, Culture, Media and Sport Committee (2011b), p. 28, for data on 1996–2010, and Bose (2013), pp. 370, 374 for data on 1992–2011.

28. For Leagues One and Two data see House of Commons, Culture, Media and Sport Committee (2011b), p. 28.

29. Ibid., pp. 28–31.

30. Sugar is supposed to have said this in October 1997 when speaking at the Oxford Union.

31. See House of Commons, Culture, Media and Sport Committee (2011b), p. 35 for data on 1947–2003, and Bose (2013), p. 371 for data on 1992–2011.

32. The PFA's own data can be seen here: www.sportingintelligence.com/2011/10/30/english-football-wages-since-1984-85-301001/

33. House of Commons, Culture, Media and Sport Committee (2011b), p. 51.

34. L. Taylor, "English talent gets left behind as Premier League keeps importing," *Guardian*, 20 August 2013.

35. Pini Zahavi is probably the most prominent agent in this sphere: see J. Jackson, "Pini Zahavi, football's first and only super-agent," *Observer*, 26 November 2006.

36. This data on club payments to agents is now published annually by the Premier League. See, for example, www.premierleague.com/content/dam/premierleague/site-content/News/publications/other/pl-club-agents-fees-2010-11.pdf

37. UEFA (2008).

38. PricewaterhouseCoopers (2010).

39. Kuper and Szymanski (2009), p. 98.

40. On the football creditors rule and the fate of St John Ambulance see House of Commons (2011b), p. 41.

41. Beech, Horsman and Magraw (2008); Szymanski (2012).

42. These include Barnsley, Bradford City, Charlton Athletic, Coventry City, Derby County, Hull City, Ipswich Town, Leeds United, Leicester City, Nottingham Forest, Portsmouth, QPR, Sheffield Wednesday, Southampton, Watford, Wimbledon.

43. Conn (2004), pp. 150–74.

44. Anderson and Sally (2013), pp. 81–3.

45. Michie and Oughton (2005).

## CHAPTER 2: KEEPING IT REAL?

1. Debord (1994).

2. G. Marcotti, "Actual Fans. Are they necessary?," *Wall Street Journal*, 21 September 2010: http://online.wsj.com/article/SB10001424052748703989304575503821229703834.html

3. For attendance data for 1922–99 see Dobson and Goddard (2001), pp. 57–8. Otherwise, Deloitte Sports Business Group (1990–2012).

4. Taylor (2009), pp. 193–202.

5. Sky's 1992 advert 'A Whole New Ball Game' can be seen at www.youtube.com/watch?v=MEAIyH_gDSk

6. Sky's 1997 advert with Sean Bean can be seen at www.youtube.com/watch?v=jXac8J4EoIE

7. Durkheim (1912), pp. 475–6.

8. Office for National Statistics, *Statistical Bulletin: Families and Households 2013*, ONS, 2013.

9. D. Dorling and P. Ress, "A Nation Still Dividing: the British census and social polarisation 1971–2001," *Environment and Planning* 35 (2003).

10. Crace (2012).

11. Hornby (1992).

12. Shindler (1999); Cowley (2009).

13. D. Thomas, *Daily Telegraph*, 17 July 1994, quoted in Wagg (2004).

14. G. Turner, "Fans Like Saturday 3pm," *Guardian*: www.theguardian.com/football/2005/sep/21/newsstory.sport10 (21 September 2005).

15. Premier League (2002–8).

16. Premier League (2008), p. 25; on walking, see P. Green, "Walk this Way," *When Saturday Comes* 249, November 2007.

17. D. Conn, "The Premier League has priced out fans, young and old": www.theguardian.com/sport/david-conn-inside-sport-blog/2011/aug/16/premier-league-football-ticket-prices (16 August 2011).

18. See *BBC Sport Price of Football Survey*: www.bbc.co.uk/news/uk-19842397 (2012).

19. Quoted in Conn, "The Premier League has priced out fans'.

20. Russell (2006).

21. *Guardian*, 25 February 1993.

22. H. Pearson, *The Far Corner: A Mazy Dribble through North East Football*, London: Little, Brown, 1994, p. 27.

23. "Horsemeat scandal hits Scottish football as Aberdeen remove all meat pies from menu," *Daily Record*, 26 February 2013.

24. Note, in less traditional pie country, there have also been advances with wide commendations for the quality and variety at Brighton, Norwich and Ipswich. At Bristol Rovers the distinctive smell of pasties hangs in the air, perhaps something to do with the swede and turnip they often contain; root vegetables are a rare presence otherwise on the mainstream menu. For the Scotch Football Pie awards see www.scotchpieclub.co.uk/index.php?ID=2231&CATEGORY=6-News+and+Events

25. J. Crace, "Could football supporters go veggie?," *Guardian*, 18 January 2012.

26. Full Overview of the 1882 Package: Champagne and Canapés Reception; Pre match Tour VIP Photo call with commemorative framed photo; Complimentary Bar throughout the day; Four Course Meal with Wine and Liqueurs; Match Programme and Souvenir Gift; Spurs legend seated at your table throughout the day; Match seats in your own enclosure adjacent to the Directors' Box in the Upper West Stand; Half Time refreshments; Judge the Man of the Match Award; Autographed Football Raffle; Post match Presentation to the man of the match; Company branding in the Oak Room and Matchday programme; Inscribed Silver salver; View the Parade of Spurs Legends.

27. See www.keithprowse.co.uk/football_fulham.aspx and www.fulhamfc.com/hospitality/1314-packages/george-cohen-restaurant: "When you enter the George Cohen Restaurant, you'll receive a personal welcome from George himself. A true gent, George is delighted to chat about the beautiful game and reminisce, as you enjoy Champagne and canapés, a super four-course meal and the match itself."

28. Taylor, "Will Adrian Pop the Question?'.

29. The sheer scale of the alcohol industry's involvement with football was shown by recent research: "A study of televised football matches in six of the major competitions in Britain has revealed that there were typically 111 visual references to alcohol for every hour of football that was broadcast." S. Connor, "Here for the beer? How football fans are drenched in adverts for drink," *Independent*, 11 September 2013.

30. Hornby (1992), p. 153.

31. Gambling Commission (2013).

32. P. Gallagher, "Addiction soars as online gambling hits £2bn mark," *Independent*, 27 January 2013.

33. "Arrival time," in Premier League (2002–2008).

34. "Gender," in Premier League (2002–2008).

35. "Age," in Premier League (2002–2008).

36. "Ethnicity," in Premier League (2002–2008).

37. "Foreigners," in Premier League (2002–2008).

38. "Class," in Premier League (2002–2008).

39. "Income," in Premier League (2002–2008).

40. Giulianotti (2002), pp. 25–46.

41. King (1998); Brown, Crabbe and Mellor (2006).

42. N. Andrews, "Sitting Pretty," *When Saturday Comes* 283, September 2010.

43. M. Gooding, "Fifteen Minutes of Fame," *When Saturday Comes* 280, June 2010. For the mud-spattered drum majorettes at Stamford Bridge see www.britishpathe.com/video/drum-majorettes-at-chelsea-fc

44. Editorial, "Noise Annoys," *When Saturday Comes* 116, October 1996; J. O'Driscoll, "Noise Annoys," *When Saturday Comes* 207, May 2004.

45. H. Pearson, "Last of the Line," *When Saturday Comes* 150, August 1999.

46. M. Wylie, G. Moors, N. Struthers and D. Liverman, "Mascot mania," *Manchester United: the official magazine of Manchester United Football Club* 83 (1999), pp. 28–30.

47. When, in 2003, Oldham Athletic's Chaddy the Owl wrestled Blackpool's Bloomfield Bear, the Football League was forced to introduce a code of conduct for mascots. It has not been entirely successful. Since then Chaddy has been punched in the face by one of his own fans, and Preston's Deepdale Duck was expelled from the pitch for persistently trying to distract Derby County's goalkeeper. Deepdale Duck's exit from the pitch can be seen at www.youtube.com /watch?v=WxytK0fJfLM. See also Macclesfield Town's Roary the Lion, who got a red card when it transpired that he had been making obscene gestures towards opposing players and fans while an on-pitch brawl was taking place.

48. When launching the pre-match handshake routine, Richard Scudamore said: "It's not a handshake that says everybody loves everybody else. It's a handshake that says, 'Whatever c**p's gone on before now and whatever c**p will go on after this game is over, for the next 90 minutes, let's just play a game of football'." Quoted in J. Redknapp, "It's time to end the embarrassing pre-match handshakes," *Daily Mail*: www.dailymail.co.uk/sport/football/article-2173323 /Jamie-Redknapp-No-pre-match-handshakes.html (13 July 2012).

49. A. McSmith, "A brief history of silence: when no noise is good noise," *Independent*: www. independent.co.uk/news/uk/this-britain/a-brief-history-of-silence-when-no-noise-is-good -noise-780200.html (8 February 2008).

50. For an overview of football and commemorative silences, see Foster and Woodthorpe (2012).

51. G. Cameron, "It's Cald Hearted," *Sun*, 2 January 2008; B. McLauchlin, "Calderwood apology over O'Donnell," BBC News, 11 November 2010; *The Economist*, "A Minute's Silence for the Minutes Silence": www.economist.com/blogs/blighty/2011/01/public_remembrance (27 January 2011).

52. "Hillsborough anniversary: Chelsea "embarrassed" as fans ruin minute's silence at Wembley," *Daily Telegraph*, 16 April 2012. See also the video of Chelsea fans booing at www.telegraph .co.uk/sport/football/teams/chelsea/9206300/Hillsborough-anniversary-Chelsea-embarrassed -as-fans-ruin-minutes-silence-at-Wembley.html

53. D. Waterman, "A Respectful Round of applause?," *BBC Magazine*: http://news.bbc.co .uk/1/hi/magazine/6986935.stm (2007).

54. Anderson and Sally (2013), pp. 21–7.

55. Premier League, "Wenger: Barclays Premier League has undergone tactical shift": www .premierleague.com/en-gb/news/news/2012-13/oct/wenger-barclays-premier-leagues-tactical -evolution.html (13 October 2012).

56. Ibid.

57. O. Daskal, "Injured, stressed, depressed and broke," *Soccer Issue*: www.soccerissue.com /2014/04/14/injured-stressed-depressed-and-broke/ (14 April 2014).

58. Auclair (2009), p. 278.

59. Football Supporters' Federation (2012). See also the recent green brigade at Celtic issue.

60. Home Office (annual).

61. J. Pitt-Brooke, "Poles apart: how fans of Poznan inspired City's unlikely dance craze," *Independent*: www.independent.co.uk/sport/football/news-and-comment/poles-apart-how-fans -of-poznan-inspired-citys-unlikely-dance-craze-2270018.html (20 April 2011).

62. G. Roberts, "Anfield. We're not singing anymore," *Well Red*: http://liverpoolfc.wellred mag.co.uk/Liverpool-FC-Latest-from-Well-Red/anfield-were-not-singing-any-more.html (2011).

63. I. Herbert (2012), "'Singing section' to be introduced at Old Trafford to increase decibel levels of 'dead' Manchester United fans," *Independent*: www.independent.co.uk/sport/football /premier-league/singing-section-to-be-introduced-at-old-trafford-to-increase-decibel-levels-of -dead-manchester-united-fans-7654633.html (17 April 2012).

64. For significant games there have been fan groups who have made and displayed huge flags and banners over the heads of the crowd, or club-organized paper square mosaics.

65. BBC Sport, "Power plays for laughs again": http://news.bbc.co.uk/sport1/hi/funny_old _game/2921817.stm (6 April 2003).

66. P. Bandini, "Celery banned at the Bridge," *Guardian*, 16 March 2007.

67. See www.youtube.com/watch?v=GJuGspbyQ5I

68. See report including video footage, BBC Sport (2011), "FA looks into reports of laser pen use at Chelsea match": http://news.bbc.co.uk/sport1/hi/football/teams/c/chelsea/9431990.stm (21 March 2011).

69. *Daily Telegraph*, "Football fan charged with throwing coin at Craig Bellamy": www .telegraph.co.uk/sport/football/news/7094677/Football-fan-charged-with-throwing-coin-at -Craig-Bellamy.html (29 January 2010); BBC News, "Manchester United's Rio Ferdinand hurt by thrown coin": www.bbc.co.uk/news/uk-england-manchester-20658846 (9 December 2012).

70. Morris (1981).

71. D. Conn, "Football's plutocrats resist call for living wage for staff," *Guardian*, 29 October 2008.

72. DeLillo (2001), p. 60. The chapter epigraph is from the same source, p. 11.

## CHAPTER 3: ENGLISH JOURNEY

1. The most recent updates of the *Pevsner Architectural Guides* by Yale University Press have remedied some of these deficiencies: see for example the account of St James' Park in McCombie (2009). However, Hartwell (2002), in *Manchester*, makes no mention of the City of Manchester Stadium or the renovated Old Trafford.

2. Nairn (1975).

3. Pevsner (1951–74); Hatherley (2010, 2012).

4. Pevsner (1957), p. 23.

5. Peake (2005), pp. 41–2.

6. It is worth noting that until the late 1990s, English football had an architectural chronicler of Pevsner-like proportions in Simon Inglis whose *Football Grounds of England and Wales*, later extended to all of Britain, and *Football Grounds of Europe* are, by some way, the best books ever written on the subject. It is a shame, if understandable, that he has not chosen to update these works to reflect the last two decades of frenetic rebuilding. See S. Inglis (1996, 1990, 2005). In recent years his work has focused on sports architecture more widely.

7. Priestley (1929), p. 13.

8. Priestley (1934), pp. 138–9.

9. Bryson (1999); J. Paxman (2007); R. Strong (2011).

10. Bale (2008).

11. Taylor (1993).

12. Oswalt (2006); Williams (2001, 2003), *Into the Red*; Williams, Hopkins and Long (2001); Andrews (2004).

13. Also "Who's that dying on the runaway/who's that dying in the snow/It's Matt Busby and his boys making all the fucking noise/because they can't get their aeroplane to go'.

14. One version of the chant chant goes: "In the Liverpool slums/They knock on the door when they want something to eat/They find a dead rat and they think it's a treat/In the Liverpool slums/In the Liverpool slums/Your mum's on the beat and your dad's in the nick/You can't find a job 'coz you're too fuckin' thick/ In the Liverpool slums'. In response to the chant of "Liv-er-pool, Liv-erpool," United have come back with "Murder-ers, murder-ers' and with reference to the European Cup, "We've won it three times/We've won it three times/without killing anyone/ We've won it three times'.

15. In 2012, in the wake of the Report of the Independent Panel on the Hillsborough disaster, strong statements from both clubs and activists within both sets of fans saw their derby game, at last, largely free of these chants.

16. BBC Sport, "Everton fail in King's Dock bid," 11 April 2003, http://news.bbc.co.uk /sport1/hi/football/teams/e/everton/2940481.stm

17. D. Conn, "Anfield: the victims, the anger and Liverpool's shameful truth," *Guardian*, 6 May 2013.

18. Williams and Hopkins (2011); J. Williams (2012).

19. Milward (2012).

20. D. Conn, "AFC Liverpool join the rebels with vow of football for all," *Guardian*, 8 May 2008; G. Roughley, "Liverpool's little brother prepares to enter the world," *Guardian*, 16 July 2008.

21. "Liverpool FC fans around the world tell Anfield owners Hicks and Gillett: 'You're not welcome here!'," *Liverpool Echo*, 6 July 2010; "Liverpool fans stage a rally against Hicks and Gillett," BBC News, 10 July 2010.

22. Hillsborough Independent Panel (2012).

23. Peck and Ward (2002).

24. Brown and Walsh (1999).

25. Brown (2004).

26. P. Kelso, "Football fans disrupt race to support Ferguson," *Guardian*, 7 February 2004.

27. On the tortuous history of the Glazers' and Manchester United's exotic debt, see D. Conn, "Manchester United spent £71m in 2012–13 financing debt of takeover," *Guardian*, 18 September 2013.

28. Brown (2007, 2008).

29. See Brown (2007), pp. 621–4.

30. M. Ogden, "Wayne Rooney called police after balaclava mob chanted threats outside his mansion," *Daily Telegraph*, 10 October 2010.

31. D. Conn, "How the Glazer family have milked debt-ridden United for millions," *Guardian*, 12 January 2010; D. Conn, "Manchester United title triumph shows how the Glazers have won in the end," *Guardian*, 23 April 2013.

32. S. Kuper, "Manchester United's biggest problem is not selecting next manager," *Financial Times*, 22 April 2014: www.ft.com/cms/s/2/e1e6e5d8-ca14-11e3-ac05-00144feabdc0. html#axzz32dpAEhi8

33. Ward (2003).

34. Shindler (1999).

35. See Conn (2013), pp. 261–4.

36. Ibid., pp. 271–8.

37. Ibid., pp. 321–3.

38. Kuper and Szymanski (2009).

39. Parris (2013).

40. D. Conn, "If Football League is to pass its test, Flavio Briatore must fail his," *Guardian*, 6 October 2009. See also the delightful documentary by Mal Hodgson, *The Four Year Plan* (2012).

41. BBC Sport, "I've been exploited – Fernandes": http:// bbc.co.uk/sport/football/22409888 (4 May 2013).

42. The precise cost of the Olympic Park deal for West Ham and the public purse are contested. See Press Association, "West Ham United must pay £70m bank debt before Olympic Stadium move," *Guardian*: www.theguardian.com/football/2013/jul/24/west-ham-debt-olympic -stadium (24 July 2013). In short, West Ham are getting a half a billion pounds' worth of sta-

dium and environment for a lump sum payment of £15 million and rent of just £2 million a year. They will have to sell Upton Park and clear the debts secured against it and they may end up with more debt than they would like, though this is a fragment of the debt they would have incurred had they tried to build their own stadium from scratch.

43. See, for example, *Guardian*, "Cesc Fábregas backs Samir Nasri's criticism of Emirates atmosphere": www.theguardian.com/football/2011/aug/25/fabregas-nasri-emirates-atmosphere (25 August 2011).

44. A. Levy and C. Scott Clark, "He won, Russia lost," *Guardian*: www.theguardian.com /world/2004/may/08/russia.football (8 May 2004).

45. What is so surprising then is that Abramovich has not been on the end of the crowd's anti-Semitism, indeed the fans are effectively silent on his presence and erratic decision-making. But that is the way of the bully: to know when to cower.

46. S. Collins, "Fall from Grace," *When Saturday Comes* 270, August 2009.

47. D. Conn, "Jordan makes it crystal clear: Life at the Palace has become impossible for a mere millionaire," *Guardian*, 1 October 2008.

48. BBC News, "Injured officer describes "battlefield"": http://news.bbc.co.uk/1/hi/england /1966826.stm (2 May 2002).

49. BBC News, "Mass violence mars London derby": http://news.bbc.co.uk/1/hi/england /london/8221451.stm

50. Quoted in H. Winter, "John G. Berylson proud to lead the revival of Millwall," *Daily Telegraph*, 21 May 2009.

51. See www.youtube.com/watch?v=aKZQ6xPdnlE

52. Wilson (2009), p. 109.

53. On T. Dan Smith see Hatherley (2010), pp. 172–8.

54. On Hall's rise see Conn (2004).

55. Nayak (2003).

56. D. Conn, "Former owners Shepherd and Hall got £146m from Newcastle," *Guardian*, 11 February 2009.

57. BBC News, "Newcastle directors apologise": http://news.bbc.co.uk/1/hi/sport/football /66784.stm (18 March 1998).

58. S. Field, "Middling Ways," *When Saturday Comes* 156, February 2000.

59. See "Birmingham City Council accepts findings of 'Brummie' report": www.birmingham post.co.uk/news/local-news/birmingham-city-council-accepts-findings-3908275

60. Hatherley (2012), p. 92.

61. Ibid.

62. Birmingham's ownership history has a certain local colour. The club was taken over in the 1960s by local businessman Clifford Coombs who passed the club and his home credit and car insurance empire on to his son Keith. As steady and unexciting as their businesses, the Coombs kept the show on the road, but it was never much of a show and the debts were mounting. They sold up in the 1980s to Ken Wheldon, a West Midlands scrap metal dealer. His strategy for the debt-laden club was to strip the operation bare in a frenzy of austerity. He sold the club, or rather its debt, a few years later with the side in Division Three and crowds down to 6,000. His successors, the Manchester-based Kumar Brothers, owners of a bargain clothing chain, ran the club in a similar cut-price fashion till both shops and football went bust in 1992. The administrators then sold on the club to David Gold and David Sullivan, whose connection to the city hitherto had been negligible. See Ian [King], "100 Owners: Number 76—Ken Wheldon (Walsall & Birmingham City)': http://twohundredpercent.net/?p=21429 (18 December 2012).

63. T. Davis, "Derby Daze," *When Saturday Comes* 119, January 1997.

64. D. Conn, "Derby County fraud exposes English football's 'fit and proper' test," *Guardian*, 22 July 2009.

65. D. Conn, "Coventry City's silent owners come under pressure to speak up," *Guardian*, 27 September 2011; J. Riach, "Coventry City rent stand-off threatens League One club's existence," *Guardian*, 12 December 2012.

66. D. Conn, "Coventry City move closer to a groundshare with Northampton Town," *Guardian*, 4 July 2013.

67. D. Conn, "Notts County's revolution has one outstanding debt," *Guardian*, 1 September 2009.

68. For a short period between 1959 and 1999 the League moved to the Art Deco splendour of the seaside and golf town Lytham St Annes before returning to Preston.

69. A. Hunter, "Fear and loathing on the M65 as Burnley head to Blackburn Rovers," *Guardian*, 17 October 2009.

70. See D. Conn, "Blackburn Rovers facing their nightmare scenario," *Guardian*, 8 May 2012.

71. £11 million was then paid to one of Oyston's companies, apparently as a tax planning measure for the club.

72. N. Rose, "Motorway Madness," *When Saturday Comes* 225, November 2005.

73. H. Parry, "Border Dispute," *When Saturday Comes* 217, March 2005.

74. On Oxford's schizophrenic architecture and space see "Oxford: Quadrangle and *Banlieue*," in Hatherley (2012).

75. See www.royals.org/matdoc/181299.html

76. North and Hodson (1997).

77. D. Hills, "Wife of Bournemouth's Russian co-owner 'gives half-time team talk'," *Observer*, 26 February 2012; D. Hills, "Bournemouth owner Eddie Mitchell facing sanctions for confronting fans," *Observer*, 10 September 2011.

78. For details of the rivalry see K. Mitchell, "Scummers vs Skates," *Observer*, 23 January 2005.

79. Hatherley (2012), p. 12.

80. Peace (1999, 2007).

81. J. Ferrari, "Yellow Fever," *When Saturday Comes* 108, February 1996; Ian [King], "100 Owners: Number 78 – Robert Chase (Norwich City)": http://twohundredpercent.net/?p=21377 (7 December 2012).

82. P. MacInnes, "Norwich Noveau est arrivé," *Guardian*, 2 March 2004.

83. C. Bailey, "Unjust Desserts." *When Saturday Comes* 219, May 2005.

84. "Alan Partridge commentary of Norwich City goals": www.youtube.com/watch?v=MIpc SZRM17M

85. H. Tubervill, "Football's Greatest Eccentric: Ipswich Town's John Cobbold," *Daily Telegraph*, 13 November 2009.

86. C. Abrahal and G. Barber, "Football is an Emotional Game," *When Saturday Comes* 172, June 2001; C. Abrahal, "Going for Broke—Ipswich Town," *When Saturday Comes* 194, April 2003.

87. S. Gardiner, "Who Owns Ipswich Town Football Club . . . Marcus Evans or You?" *Turnstile Blues* 1 (2012); BBC News (2012), "Arrest threat" over "provocative" Ipswich Town fanzine: www.bbc.co.uk/news/uk-england-suffolk-19883492 (9 October 2012).

88. I. Thompson, "Villain—Martin Fish »: www.ambernectar.org/blog/2007/07/villain-martin-fish/ (2007).

89. D. Conn, "The rise of a club beyond its history and dreams," *Guardian*, 19 November 2008. See also on Hull City, A. Medcalf, "Hull Pity," *When Saturday Comes* 107, January 1996;

A. Medcalf, "Fish Fingered," *When Saturday Comes* 122, April 1997; C. Ellyard, "Humber Crunch," *When Saturday Comes* 166, December 2000.

90. P. Baxter, "Allam exclusive: We WILL be called Hull City Tigers," *Hull Daily Mail*, 9 August 2013.

91. D. Conn, "'I do asset-strip' says the man who wants Mansfield," *Guardian*, 9 April 2008.

92. D. Conn, "The man who owes Mansfield over a million," *Guardian*, 7 December 2005; D. Conn, "Mansfield Town, Keith Haslam and that controversial dividend," *Guardian*, 16 November 2010; Written evidence submitted to the CMS Select Committee on Football Governance 2011, by Chris Vasper, ex-Chair Team Mansfield (Mansfield Town Supporters Trust).

93. D. Conn, "Knighton's Theatre of Dreams in Ruins," *Independent*, 28 September 2000; A. Mitten, "Juggling with an Institution," *The National*, 10 October 2009.

94. J. Wainwright, "Mark Guterman," *When Saturday Comes* 135, May 1998.

95. Ian [King], "100 Owners: Number 89 – Terry Smith (Chester City)": http://twohundredpercent.net/?p=19808) (15 July 2012).

96. Quoted in J. Sweeney, "Cocky," *Observer*, 14 May 2000.

97. A. Doyle, "Liverpool businessman Stephen Vaughan disqualified from acting as company director after alleged VAT fraud at Widnes Vikings rugby league club," *Liverpool Daily Post*: www.liverpooldailypost.co.uk/liverpool-news/regional-news/2009/11/10/liverpool-business man-stephen-vaughan-disqualified-from-acting-as-company-director-after-alleged-vat-fraud -at-widnes-vikings-rugby-league-club-92534-25138513/#ixzz2bO9TTswX (10 November 2009).

98. I. King, "Is the curse of the Vaughans striking again in Malta?": http://twohundred percent.net/?p=21878 (2013).

99. D. Conn, "Wrexham's ordeal exposes home truths," *Guardian*, 5 April 2006; I. King (2011), "Wrexham supporters prepare to man the barricades again': http://twohundredpercent .net/?p=10491; I. King, "Booth is out, but other dangers lurk at Wrexham': http://twohundred percent.net/?p=12545 (2011).

100. J. Gwinell, "West World," *When Saturday Comes* 166, December 2000; M. Walker, "Football's Lost City! But both Bristol clubs can hit the glory trail again," *Daily Mail*, 7 January 2012.

101. M. Wenham, "The Wild West," *When Saturday Comes* 120, February 1997.

102. Hatherley (2012), pp. 133–46.

103. "Rovers stadium: Councillors' fears over retail impact on Gloucester Road shops," *Bristol Post*, 10 January 2013: www.thisisbristol.co.uk/Rovers-stadium-Councillors-8217-fears-retail /story-17814128-detail/story.html#ixzz2bH2SSQZF

104. H. Pattison, "Bend it Like Uri," *When Saturday Comes* 185, July 2002.

105. BBC Sport, "Exeter eye Darth Vader": http://news.bbc.co.uk/sport1/hi/football /teams/e/exeter_city/2676443.stm (20 January 2003). Michael Jackson's extraordinary oration can be heard at BBC News, "Michael Jackson Thriller of a Devon visit": www.bbc.co.uk/devon /news_features/2002/michael_jackson.shtml (2002); BBC News, "Ex football club chairman jailed": http://news.bbc.co.uk/1/hi/england/devon/6703331.stm (30 May 2007).

106. D. Conn, "Sir Roy Gardner's return has painted Plymouth Argyle into a tricky corner," *Guardian*; D. Conn, "Five days until lights-out at Plymouth Argyle," *Guardian*, 2 March 2011; M. Scott, "Sir Roy Gardner and co-investors spent £3 million in support of doomed Pilgrims," *Guardian*, 11 May 2011.

107. J. Widdecombe, "Go West," *When Saturday Comes* 245, July 2007; Ian [King], "A Winding Up Order for Truro City," http://twohundredpercent.net/?p=15234, 22 September 2011, and "Truro City FC Takes its Final Step to the Gallows," http://twohundredpercent .net/?p=20905, 19 October 2012.

108. Martin (2007).

109. Department for Culture, Media and Sport, "AFC Wimbledon rewarded for community work": https://www.gov.uk/government/news/afc-wimbledon-rewarded-for-community-work (28 March 2012).

110. Brown (2007).

111. Brown (2008).

## CHAPTER 4: PLAYING THE RACE GAME

1 Back et al. (2001), p. 82.

2. Quoted ibid., pp. 96–7.

3. Ron Noades in Critical Eye (1991), *Great Britain United*, London: Channel 4, broadcast 12 September 1991, quoted in Back et al. (2001), p. 175.

4. Although Scottish, Irish and Welsh football have been touched by issues of ethnicity, none compares to the story of English football. This is hardly surprising given the size of England's black and minority ethnic (BME) population—perhaps five times larger per capita than any of the other home nations.

5. See BBC News, "Culture Secretary Jeremy Hunt warns on football racism": www.bbc .co.uk/news/uk-17001503 (12 February 2012).

6. Quoted in Guttmann (1994).

7. Quoted in Vasili (1998).

8. Ibid.

9. Clavane (2012).

10. Quoted in Johanneson obituary, *Independent*: www.independent.co.uk/news/people /obituary-albert-johanneson-1575592.html (2 October 1995).

11. Quoted in http://bernews.com/bermuda-profiles/clyde-best/ based on CNN interview.

12. Highfield Rangers (1993).

13. Quoted in King (2004), p. 23.

14. Ibid., p. 24.

15. Highfield Rangers Oral History Group, quoted in Burdsey (2009).

16. Holland (1997), pp. 261–77.

17. Quoted in King (2004), p. 25.

18. Quoted in Back et al. (2001), p. 49.

19. Holland (1997).

20. Quoted in King (2004), p. 28.

21. John Barnes in Critical Eye (1991), *Great Britain United*, London: Channel 4, broadcast 12 September 1991, quoted in Holland (1997), p. 273.

22. Ibid., p. 273.

23. Quoted in Back et al. (2001), pp. 146–7.

24. Quoted ibid.

25. Quoted in King (2004), p. 28.

26. Ibid.

27. Quoted in Back et al. (2001), p. 90.

28. Greenfield and Osborn (1996); Garland and Rowe (2001).

29. Back et al. (2001), p. 111.

30. Ibid., pp. 127–32.

31. Macpherson (1999), p. 30.

32. See Garland and Rowe (2001), pp. 54–9.

33. Back et al. (2001), p. 195.

34. Back et al. (2001), p. 165.

35. H. Winter, "English trio remain firm on racism," *Daily Telegraph*: www.telegraph.co.uk /sport/football/teams/england/3036133/England-trio-firm-on-racism.html (15 October 2002).

36. See the review of the night in Bradbury and Williams (2006).

37. Cited in Back et al. (2001), p. 164.

38. The first black member of the FA Council was Lord Ouseley, appointed in 2008.

39. Maguire (1991); Melnick (1988).

40. *Observer*, "Sol Campbell calls FA 'institutionally racist' after England captaincy snub": www.theguardian.com/football/2014/mar/02/sol-campbell-football-association-england -captain (2 March 2014).

41. King (2004), p. 25.

42. Ibid., p. 27.

43. J. White, "The £12 million lad done good," *Guardian*, 4 October 1997.

44. See Cashmore and Cleland (2011).

45. Quoted in Back et al. (2001), p. 182.

46. Interview in V. Chaudhary, "Players fight race bar to top job," *Guardian*, 18 September 2003.

47. Burdsey (2009), pp. 708–10.

48. Quoted in Fleming (2001).

49. Cited in Burdsey (2007), p. 58.

50. Lowles (2001).

51. Blackshaw and Crabbe (2005).

52. Milward (2008).

53. Quoted in Garland and Treadwell (2010).

54. Burdsey (2009).

55. *The Gleaner*, 1–7 April 1998, p. 30, cited in Back et al. (2001), p. 258.

56. Asians in Football Forum (2005).

57. See Burdsey (2009).

58. Quoted in Milward (2007).

59. T. Judd, "Hill defends Atkinson over racist remark" *Independent*, 13 May 2004.

60. *Guardian*, 2 April 1997, quoted in Back et al. (2001), p. 172.

61. See "What John Terry said to Anton Ferdinand": www.guardian.co.uk/football/video /2011/oct/24/john-terry-anton-ferdinand-video (24 October 2011).

62. Tottenham are not the only club to have acquired a hyper-Jewish identity despite a very small Jewish fan base; see the account of the Dutch club Ajax in Kuper (2008).

63. D. Baddiel, "So you think we've kicked racism out of football?" *Independent*, 17 October 2002.

64. C. Newkey-Burden, "The ugly truth about the beautiful game," *Time Out*, 23 May 2006.

65. D. Rosenberg, "When Spurs fans celebrate being the 'Yid Army,' are they giving racists ammunition?," *New Statesman*, 28 November 2012.

66. *Guardian*, "'I'm no racist': Nicolas Anelka defends his quenelle goal celebration": www .theguardian.com/football/2014/apr/04/nicolas-anelka-quenelle-defence-not-racist (4 April 2014).

## CHAPTER 5: FOOTBALL AT TWILIGHT

1. Quoted in D. Goodhart, "Britain rediscovered," *Prospect*, April 2005.

2. *Scotsman*, "SFA cautions players keen on Team GB Olympic spot," 11 March 2011.

3. BBC Sport, "Team GB Olympic football deal angers nations": www.bbc.co.uk/sport/0/ olympics/13854492 (21 June 2011).

4. Quoted in *Guardian*, "Put politics aside and back British football team, urges sports minister," 23 June 2011.

5. J. Macintyre, "Time for a British football team," *New Statesman*, 17 June 2010.

6. S. Kuper, "Britain's genius for childlike pop culture," *Financial Times*, 27 July 2012.

7. D. Sandbrook, "How glorious, after years of our national identity being denigrated, to see patriotism rekindled," *Daily Mail*, 10 August 2012.

8. Ibid.

9. All of which was predicted with remarkable accuracy by *When Saturday Comes*: see "Olympic Spirit," *When Saturday Comes* 260, October 2008.

10. G. Wheatcroft, "From Jessica Ennis to Joey Barton. Could a contrast be more ghastly?," *Guardian*, 16 August 2012.

11. S. Wallace, "Footballers and rowers come from different worlds, so don't compare them," *Independent*, 20 August 2012.

12. Quoted in Hassan (2002).

13. Quoted in D. Conn, "Memories of Belfast Celtic reawakened as IFA tries to soothe old wounds," *Guardian*, 23 February 2011.

14. Quoted in Hassan (2002).

15. H. McDonald, "Irish soccer's offside," *Observer*, 19 October 2002.

16. D. Millar, "Long Division," *When Saturday Comes* 144, February 1999.

17. Hassan (2006).

18. R. Meredith, "Building Block," *When Saturday Comes* 265, March 2009.

19. S. Kuper, "The Sectarian fans moved by megaphone diplomacy," *Financial Times*, 8 September 2007.

20. Hassan, McCullough and Moreland (2009).

21. *Belfast Telegraph*, "Celtic Northern Ireland player McGinn admits supporting Republic," 27 May 2011.

22. Hassan (2006), p. 79.

23. Originally eight men were charged with the murder of Kevin McDaid: see H. McDonald, "Armed police guard men in court over loyalist killing of Kevin McDaid," *Guardian*, 28 May 2009. Since then the charges have been downgraded to manslaughter but the trail has yet to commence: see *Coleraine Chronicle*, "Another Delay in McDaid Trial": http://coleraine.thechronicle.uk.com/articles/news/35662/another-delay-in-mcdaid-trial/ (5 September 2013).

24. H. McDonald, "Belfast pub wrecked as violence flares before World Cup Qualifier," *Observer*, 28 March 2009; H. McDonald, "Northern Ireland attacks on Poles blamed on Loyalists," *Guardian*, 9 April 2009.

25. S. McKinley, "Riot police deal with hooligan fans as Linfield beat Glentoran," *Belfast Telegraph*, 26 December 2008.

26. Quoted in Rogers and Rookwood (2007).

27. Johnes (2005b).

28. Johnes (2002).

29. On anti-Englishness see Rogers and Rookwood (2007), p. 61; quote from Hammam (2000), p. 14.

30. Rogers and Rookwood (2007), p. 63.

31. Ibid., p. 61.

32. Johnes (2008).

33. Quoted in Rogers and Rookwood (2007), p. 61.

34. I. Herbert, "Vincent Tan is loved by his Malaysian employees—but Cardiff fans are not so sure," *Independent*, 15 August 2013.

35. For a useful update on Tan, his son and the Kazakh student doing work experience who became chief scout at Cardiff, see www.bbc.co.uk/sport/0/football/24757037

36. D. Conn, "The 'different route' that lifted Swansea from doldrums to delirium," *Guardian*, 8 January 2013.

37. Cited in Weight (2004), pp. 556–7.

38. Bradley (2002).

39. A. Martin, "Football: Tartan Army's unbridled joy baffles Paris," *Independent*, 12 June 1998. Martin also reported: "The Scots were wild, 'well-bevied,' many topless, fearsome in their ginger wigs and tartan tummies, but they policed themselves. Old ladies with poodles were carefully guided through the mayhem."

40. Quoted in Bradley (2011).

41. Ibid.

42. A. MacGregor, "Tartan Barney," *When Saturday Comes* 138, August 1998; A. Cramb, "Tartan Army turmoil over call to back England," *Daily Telegraph*, 25 February 2002.

43. S. Cosgrove, "Tartan Army just Scots version of Morris Dancers," *Daily Record*, 5 May 2005.

44. *Scotsman*, "Tartan Army vents its fury over 'slur' by Blair," 22 June 2006.

45. S. Carrell, "Scottish knights show their colours," *Guardian*, 24 April 2007.

46. *Scotland on Sunday*, "Top academic slams sectarian 'scaremongers'," 22 April 2002.

47. Quoted in Wilson (2012), pp. 200–201, 209.

48. BBC Sport, "Fans charged after Pope jeering": http://news.bbc.co.uk/sport1/hi/football /teams/h/heart_of_midlothian/4414691.stm (11 April 2005).

49. Quoted in D. Millan, "Song Sung Blue," *When Saturday Comes* 232, June 2006.

50. J. MacMillan, "Why modern, tolerant Scotland is still disfigured by sectarian bigotry," *Daily Telegraph*, 5 December 2011: http://blogs.telegraph.co.uk/culture/jmacmillan/100058597 /why-modern-tolerant-scotland-is-still-disfigured-by-sectarian-bigotry/

51. I. Macwhirter, "This dumb, unjust law is Salmond's first own goal," *Herald*, 15 December 2011.

52. A good overview of Rangers' decline is Knight (2012).

53. On the fan campaign in particular, see Anderson (2013).

54. Taylor (1999), p. 90.

55. Weight (2004), p. 464.

56. S. Hattenstone, "There's only one George Cross," *Guardian*, 10 June 2006.

57. See Deloitte (2013), p. 36.

58. *Daily Telegraph* headline, 10 June 2006, cited in Vincent et al. (2010), p. 211.

59. On Hoddle's downfall, see A. Anthony, "Blind Faith," *Observer Sport Monthly*, 4 October 2003.

60. S. Howard, "Goodbye Tosser," *Sun*, 1 June 2006.

61. See Garland and Rowe (1999); Crolley, Hand and Jeutter (2000).

62. McKinstry (2010).

63. P. Hitchens, "Why I can't wait for it to be all over for England," *Mail on Sunday*, 2 June 2002.

64. T. R. Reid, "Hooligans? I didn't see any," *Guardian*, 22 June 2002. The NCIS report is quoted in C. Morton et al., "Rioting fans shame England," *Independent*: www.independent. co.uk/news/world/europe/rioting-fans-shame-england-712724.html (18 June 2000).

65. Editorial, "A New England?," *When Saturday Comes* 186, August 2002.

66. S. Manzoor, "A cross to bear," *Guardian*, 10 June 2004.

67. Quoted in D. Walker, "England's rising ethnic fanbase": http://news.bbc.co.uk/1/hi /uk/3833127.stm (23 June 2004).

68. D. Smith, "Archbishop of York waves flag for England," *Observer*, 4 April 2009.

69. England's defeat to Portugal in the quarter-finals of the European Championships was met with equanimity by the England fans in Lisbon, but the Portuguese population of St Helier in Jersey were pelted with coins and assaulted, while a Portuguese pub in Thetford, Norfolk, was surrounded by a hundred angry England fans baying for blood.

70. D. Crossland, "Germany's World Cup Reinvention: From Humorless to Carefree in 30 Days," Der Spiegel Online, www.spiegel.de/international/germany-s-world-cup-reinvention -from-humorless-to-carefree-in-30-days-a-426063.html (10 July 2006).

71. Vincent et al. (2010).

72. Crabbe (2008).

73. See Perryman (2010).

74. L. Ward and J. Cavell, "Growing sense of Englishness explains why less than half of country feel British," *Guardian*, 24 January 2007.

75. See Abell et al. (2007).

76. Prior to 1990 the public warmed to the pub rock sing-alongs from the squad themselves; "Back Home" (1970) made it to number one, and "This Time (We'll Get it Right)" (1982) reached number two, pipped to the top spot by Paul McCartney and Stevie Wonder. However, for the rest of the decade the English public fell out of love with the genre. The 1986 official song, "We've Got the Whole World at Our Feet," peaked at 66, only marginally worse than Stock, Aitken and Waterman's "All the Way" which shuddered along to 64 in the charts during the run-up to the 1988 European Championships. These songs were the product of a decade in which pop culture and football, still closely allied in the 1970s, had parted company. The only part of the music scene still flaunting its football colours was the Cockney Rejects, whose skinhead thrash through "I'm for Ever Blowing Bubbles" got them on *Top of the Pops* and a massive amount of publicity and fighting at their gigs as rival firms came to make trouble. A rapprochement was in the air when a new generation of artists began to advertise their football allegiances. Colourbox, an ethereal electronica outfit, released their own official World Cup theme and Half Man Half Biscuit turned down a slot on *The Tube* to attend a Tranmere Rovers game.

77. H. Pearson, "The anonymous man," *When Saturday Comes* 235, September 2006.

78. Guardian Online, Live blog, 10 June 2009.

79. It was perhaps his good fortune that John Terry, his choice of England captain, should have been charged with racial abuse after an incident with Anton Ferdinand in a Premier League game in late 2011. The FA, apparently without consulting Capello, decided that Terry would be stripped of the captaincy until after the trial. Capello went on Italian TV a few days later to complain that he had not been involved in the process and to argue that Terry was innocent till proven guilty. Either way, Capello had to go.

80. N. Rose, "Following England in South Africa," *When Saturday Comes* 282, August 2010.

81. M. Perryman, "Three Lions Ate My Shirt," *Soundings* 46, Winter 2010.

82. This amounted to a two-man squad visit to a township project near Rustenburg: see S. Wallace, www.independent.co.uk/sport/football/international/from-the-training-ground-to-the-townships-england-stars-get-a-reality-check-2001399.html (16 June 2010).

## CHAPTER 6: YOU DON'T KNOW WHAT YOU'RE DOING . . .

1. O. Gibson, "Hugh Robertson: 'Football is worst governed sport in UK'," *Guardian*: www .theguardian.com/football/2011/jan/20/hugh-robertson-football-worst-governed (20 January 2011).

2. See Tomlinson (1991).

3. Quoted in N. Fox, "Goodbye to ghosts after the Gate is bolted," *Independent*, 3 September 2000.

4. D. Davies, "Welcome to the FA's Old Curiosity Shop," *Daily Mail*: www.dailymail.co.uk /sport/football/article-1066287/David-Davies-Welcome-FA-8217-s-old-curiosity-shop .html#ixzz2SeOSdpad (2 October 2008).

5. The details of the whole sorry affair are well covered by BBC News, "The affair that rocked the FA": http://news.bbc.co.uk/1/hi/uk/4162446.stm (9 September 2005).

6. Quoted in Bower (2003), pp. 289–90.

7. On Docherty and Revie's careers see ibid., pp. 21–3.

8. Quoted ibid., p. 23.

9. Ibid., pp. 27–8.

10. Parry in *The Times*, 4 March 1997, quoted ibid., p. 28.

11. On Ashby and Venables see Bower (2003), pp. 33–7.

12. Ibid., pp. 83–8.

13. New Labour's relationship with football at a personal level is chronicled in some detail by Buckby (1997). See also Bower (2003), chapter 5.

14. Phil Shaw reported on Benn's attendance at Mansfield's sixth round tie, writing: "The unreality of it all was compounded by the sight of Tony Benn, Chesterfield's MP, beaming broadly as his constituents pledged to 'keep the blue flag flying high'." P. Shaw, "Beaumont puts Spireites in sight of twin towers," *Independent*, 10 March 1997.

15. The relationship between football and the ideological debate inside New Labour is covered in Mellor (2008).

16. The OFT decision was, of course, challenged by four of the eleven organizations accused of price fixing on football replica shirts, but the appeal was rejected. See BBC News, "Football kit 'price-fixers' fined': http://news.bbc.co.uk/1/hi/business/4565683.stm (20 May 2005). The guilty parties (and the fines) were: Manchester United (£1.5m), JJB Sports (£6.3m), Umbro (£5.3m), Allsports (£1.45m). Six other organizations were fined by the OFT but did not appeal: Football Association (£158,000); Blacks (£197,000); Sports Soccer (£123,000); JD Sports (£73,000); Sports Connection (£20,000); and online store Sportsetail (fine reduced to nil by leniency).

17. On the politics of the Task Force see Burnham (2000); Lee (2000); Brown (2000).

18. See the accounts of Crozier's downfall in Bower (2003), pp. 305–7; Conn (2004), pp. 350–66.

19. Burns' report was presented as a Letter to the Chair and Board of the FA and can be accessed at: www.thefa.com/TheFA/WhoWeAre/NewsAndFeatures/2005/~/media/Files/PDF/The FA/BurnsReview/StructuralReviewConclusions.ashx/StructuralReviewConclusions.pdf

20. D. Conn, "Burnham poses seven questions for football's authorities," *Guardian*, 17 October 2008.

21. *Guardian*, "English football is £3bn in debt, warns FA chairman": www.theguardian. com/football/2008/oct/07/footballpolitics.premierleague (7 October 2008).

22. Triesman's oral evidence to the House of Commons, Culture, Media and Sport Committee (2011b), vol. II, p. 18. He went on: "My experience is he [Richards] will put his point politely in board meetings but discussions outside are extremely aggressive. Points are made in a very colourful way. I would not use that language. This is a very macho sport and some people cultivated the language of the dressing room' (ibid., p. 17). See also P. Kelso, "Lord Triesman breaks silence on huge conflicts within the FA," *Daily Telegraph*: www.telegraph.co.uk/sport /football/teams/england/8312262/Lord-Triesman-breaks-silence-on-huge-conflicts-within-the -FA.html (9 February 2011).

23. Triesman's departure was initiated by this article in the *Daily Mail* after they published details of a conversation secretly recorded over lunch. See I. Gallagher, "FA chief Lord Triesman

accuses Spain and Russia of bid to bribe World Cup referees," *Daily Mail*: www.dailymail.co.uk /sport/worldcup2010/article-1278759/World-Cup-2010-FA-chief-Lord-Triesman-accuses -Spain-Russia-bid-bribe-referees-South-Africa.html#ixzz2fulH1ckp (15 May 2010).

24. House of Commons, Culture, Media and Sport Committee (2011b), vol. II, p. 12.

25. Quoted in P. Kelso, "Sports minister Hugh Robertson urges ruling bodies to act on promised reforms or face legislation," Daily Telegraph, 29 January 2013.

26. House of Commons, Culture, Media and Sport Committee (2011b), vol. I, p. 22.

27. Sugden and Tomlinson (1998), pp. 119–23.

28. Ibid., p. 122.

29. See Bower (2003), pp. 160–61.

30. An account of the content of this presentation is given ibid., pp. 192–3.

31. The findings of the 2000–1 select committee inquiry into the failed bid for World Cup 2006 and the lessons to be learned for the 2018 bid are set out in House of Commons, Culture Media, and Sport Committee (2011a), pp. 14–16.

32. Insight Team, "World Cup votes for sale," *Sunday Times*, 17 October 2010.

33. For extensive coverage of the ISL scandal see Jennings (2006).

34. The phrase was used by Andy Anson commenting on Blatter's role; see Press Association, "England World Cup chief: Fifa's Sepp Blatter spoke of 'evils of media'," *Guardian*, 3 December 2010.

35. See Lord Triesman's oral evidence to the House of Commons, Culture, Media and Sport Committee (2011a), Ev. 11–20.

36. Croker (1987), p. 243.

37. See critics of Bates and the tendering process in House of Commons, Culture, Media and Sport Committee (2002).

38. The figure of £798 million is in J. Glancey, "We think it's all over . . . ," *Guardian*, 9 March 2007.

39. D. Hill, "The race to affluence," *Guardian*, 4 June 2007.

40. M. Scott, "Wembley Stadium responsible for £86 million hole in FA accounts," *Guardian*, 9 September 2009.

41. Trautmann (1956), cited in Russell (2008), p. 117.

42. L. Taylor, "Magic of the FA Cup fails to cast its spell over fans and managers," *Guardian*, 9 January 2012.

## CHAPTER 7: LAST MAN STANDING?

1. Holloway can be seen at www.youtube.com/watch?v=fJB3-vEKQDc

2. On contemporary sexual mores among professional footballers, see The Secret Footballer (2012).

3. Tommy Smith is quoted in L. Rowlinson and S. Young, "Is Becks a big girl's blouse?," *Daily Mail*: www.dailymail.co.uk/tvshowbiz/article-164434/Is-Becks-big-girls-blouse.html (2003). Brendan Rodgers can be seen on this point at www.youtube.com/watch?v=fsGhEKM0Cpg

4. Newell quoted in A. Kessel, "Football's Sexism Hurt Her. But it won't stop her being a referee," *Observer*, 4 February 2007.

5. House of Commons, Culture, Media and Sport Committee (2006).

6. See, for example, R. Dixon, "Sexism and Women's Football," *Guardian*, 13 July 2011.

7. See Pope and Williams (2011). According to the Premier League's fan survey (which seems on the optimistic side), female fans attending matches has reached "almost a quarter": see www .premierleague.com/content/premierleague/en-gb/about/a-growing-fan-base/

8. On the experience of women fans in English football, see Pope and Williams (2011); Pope (2010, 2012).

9. Anderson quoted in A. Kessel, "Agent of Change Rachel Anderson gains entry to a man's world – the PFA," *Observer*, 27 April 2013.

10. See the interview with Brady in Irish (2001).

11. Logan quoted in A. Sherwin, "Sky Sports treats women presenters as 'window dressing' says Gabby Logan," *Independent*, 23 July 2013.

12. J. White, "Oatley leaves Bassett with egg on his face," *Daily Telegraph*, 23 April 2007. See also the summary of the online debate at the *Guardian*, G. Turner, "Women Can Talk Sport," *Guardian*, 4 June 2010.

13. All of the best of the Keys–Gray conversation can be heard at www.youtube.com/watch ?v=rzDtSmechXY. The Gray–Jackson encounter can be seen at www.youtube.com/watch?v= _dUrUzi_6Y8

14. The chant was reported by Associated Press.

15. See Kuper and Szymanski (2009), chapter 2.

16. P. Webster, "Gordon Brown wants footballers to be better role models," *The Times*, 1 April 2008; T. Ross, "David Cameron: Luis Suárez was 'appalling' role model for my son," *Daily Telegraph*, 26 April 2013.

17. See, for example, C. Carlisle, "Depression and suicide," BBC Sport at www.bbc.co.uk /sport/0/football/23226524 (9 July 2013).

18. Two recent and welcome exceptions to this, though both are about foreign players in foreign leagues, are Ibrahimović (2013) and Reng (2011).

19. Miller (1990).

20. C. Eller, "Hollywood aristocracy clamors to rub shoulders with Beckhams," *LA Times*, 19 July 2007.

21. M. Simpson, "Meet the metrosexual," 22 July 2002, www.salon.com/2002/07/22/metro sexual/

22. Martin quoted by Sky Sports News: www1.skysports.com/football/news/12040/8718003 /brand-beckham

23. Audas, Dobson and Goddard (2002); Dawson and Dobson (2002).

24. The best one can say of the logic of decision-making at football clubs is that the variance of team performance after mid-season managerial change is greater over the short term than usual, so around an almost negligible average impact there are a very small number of cases where performance massively improves or completely collapses. Fans and owners in desperate relegation trouble are basically buying a lottery ticket.

25. See Carter (2006), pp. 141–2.

26. Mourinho can be seen shushing at www.youtube.com/watch?v=7WMliLUCWGY

# BIBLIOGRAPHY

Abell, J., S. Condor, R. Lowe, S. Gibson and C. Stevenson (2007), "Who ate all the pride? Patriotic sentiment and English national football support," *Nations and Nationalism* 13 (1), pp. 97–116.

Alsop, W. (2005), *SuperCity*, Manchester: Urbis.

Amis, M. (1989), *London Fields*, London: Jonathan Cape.

Anderson, C. (2013), "Paying the Price," *The Blizzard* 8, March 2013.

Anderson, C. and D. Sally (2013), *The Numbers Game: Why Everything You Know About Football Is Wrong*, London: Penguin.

Andrews, D. (ed.) (2004), *Manchester United: A Thematic Study*, London: Routledge.

Araujo, M. and S. Kuper (eds), *Perfect Pitch: Dirt*, London: Headline.

Archbishop's Council (2012), *Church Statistics 2010/11*: http://www.churchofengland.org/media/1477827/2010_11churchstatistics.pdf

Asians in Football Forum (2005), *Asians Can Play Football: Another Wasted Decade*, Asians in Football Forum.

Auclair, P. (2009), *Cantona: The Rebel Who Would be King*, London: Macmillan.

Audas, R., S. Dobson and J. Goddard (2002), "The Impact of Managerial Change on Team Performance in Professional Sports," *Journal of Economics and Business* 54 (6).

Back, L., T. Crabbe and J. Solomos (2001), *The Changing Face of Football: Racism, Identity and Multiculturalism in the English Game*, Oxford: Berg.

Bale, J. (2008), *Anti-sport Sentiments in Literature: Batting for the Opposition*, London: Routledge.

Beech, J., S. Horsman and J. Magraw (2008), "The circumstances in which British football clubs go into administration," *CIBS Working Paper Series*, No. 4, Coventry: Coventry University.

Blackshaw, T. and T. Crabbe (2005), "Leeds on Trial: Soap opera, performativity and the racialization of sports related violence," *Patterns of Prejudice* 39 (3), pp. 327–42.

Bose, M. (2013), *Game Changer: How the English Premier League Came to Dominate the World*, Singapore: Marshall Cavendish.

Bower, T. (2003), *Broken Dreams: Vanity, Greed and the Souring of British Football*, London: Simon and Schuster.

Bradbury, S. and J. Williams (2006), "New Labour, Racism and 'New' Football in England," *Patterns of Prejudice* 40 (1), pp. 61–82.

Bradley, J. (2002), "The Patriot Game: Football's famous Tartan Army," *International Review for The Sociology of Sport* 37 (2), pp. 177–97.

———— (2011), "Scottishness in the Tartan Army," *The Bottle Imp* 10 (Association of Scottish Literary Studies e-zine): http://www.arts.gla.ac.uk/ScotLit/ASLS/SWE/TBI/TBIIssue10/Bradley.html

Brown, A. (2000), "The Football Task Force and the 'regulator debate'," in S. Hamil et al. (eds), *Football in the Digital Age.*

———— (2004), "Manchester is Red? Manchester United, Fan Identity and the Sport City," in D. Andrews (ed.), *Manchester United: A Thematic Study.*

———— (2007), "Not for Sale? The Destruction and Reformation of Football Communities in the Glazer Takeover of Manchester United," *Soccer and Society* 8 (4), pp. 614–35.

———— (2008), "Our Club Our Rules: Fan Communities at FC United of Manchester," *Soccer and Society* 9 (3), pp. 346–58.

Brown, A. and A. Walsh (1999), *Not For Sale: Manchester United, Murdoch and the Defeat of BSkyB*, London: Mainstream.

Brown, A., T. Crabbe and G. Mellor (2006), *Football and its Communities: Final Report and Findings*, London: Football Foundation.

Bryson, B. (1999), *Notes from a Small Island*, London: Transworld.

Buckby, S. (1997), "The People's Party Game," in S. Kuper and M. Mora y Araujo (eds), *Perfect Pitch 4: Dirt.*

Burdsey, D. (2007), *British Asians and Football: Culture, Identity and Exclusion*, London: Routledge.

———— (2009), "Forgotten Fields? Centralizing the experiences of minority ethnic men's football clubs in England," *Soccer and Society* 10 (6), pp. 704–21.

Burnham, A. (2000), "The Task Force and the future Regulation of Football," in S. Hamil et al. (eds), *Football in the Digital Age*, in ibid.; A. Brown (2000), "The Football Task Force and the Regulator debate," in ibid.

Butler, B. (1986) *The Official History of the FA Cup*, London: Headline.

Carlisle, C. (2013), "Depression and suicide: Football's secret uncovered," BBC Sport at http://www.bbc.co.uk/sport/0/football/23226524

Carrington, B. and I. McDonald (eds) (2001), *Race, Sport and British Society*, London: Routledge.

Carter, N. (2006), *The Football Manager: A History*, London: Routledge.

Cashmore, E. and J. Cleland (2011), "Why aren't there more black football managers?," *Ethnic and Racial Studies* 34 (9), pp. 1594–1607.

Chester, Sir Norman (1983), *Report of the Committee of Enquiry into Structure and Finance*, The Football League.

Clavane, A. (2012), *Does Your Rabbi Know You're Here? The Story of English Football's Forgotten Tribe*, London: Quercus.

Conn, D. (2004), *The Beautiful Game? Searching for the Soul of Football*, London: Yellow Jersey.

———— (2013), *Richer Than God: Manchester City, Modern Football and Growing Up*, London: Quercus.

Cowley, J. (2009), *The Last Game: Love, Death and Football*, London: Simon and Schuster.

Crabbe, T. (2008), "Fishing for community: England fans at the 2006 FIFA World Cup," *Soccer and Society* 9 (3), pp. 428–38.

Crace, J. (2012), *Vertigo: One Football Fan's Fear of Success*, London: Constable.

Crawford, G. (2006), "The cult of Champ Man: the culture and pleasures of Championship Manager/Football Manager gamers," *Information, Communication & Society* 9 (4), pp. 496–514.

Croker, T. (1987), *The First Voice You Will Hear Is . . .*, London: Collins Willow.

Crolley, L., D. Hand and R. Jeutter (2000), "Playing the identity card: Stereotypes in European football," *Soccer and Society* 1 (2), pp. 107–28.

Darby, P., M. Johnes and G. Mellor (eds) (2005), *Soccer and Disaster: International Perspectives*, London: Routledge. Independent Commission.

Davies, P. (1991), *All Played Out: The Full Story of Italia 90*, London: Mandarin.

Dawson, P. and S. Dobson (2002), "Managerial Efficiency and Human Capital: An application to English association football," *Managerial and Decision Economics* 23 (8).

Debord, G. (1994), *Society of the Spectacle*, London: Zone Books.

Deloitte (2013), *The Full Picture (2nd edn): Measuring the Contribution of the British Betting Industry*, report for Association of British Bookmakers: http://www.deloitte.com/assets/Dcom-UnitedKingdom/Local%20Assets/Documents/Industries/THL/uk-thl-measuring-economic-contribution-march-2013.pdf

Deloitte Sports Business Group (1990–2012), *Deloitte Annual Review of Football Finance*, London: Deloitte.

DeLillo, D. (2001), *Underworld*, London: Picador.

Dixon, P., N. Garnham and A. Jackson (2004), "Shareholders and Shareholding: The case of the football company in late Victorian England," *Business History* 46 (4), pp. 503–24.

Dobson, S. and J. Goddard (2001), *The Economics of Football*, Cambridge: Cambridge University Press.

Durkheim, E. (1912), *The Elementary Forms of the Religious Life* (1954 edn), trans. J. W. Swain, New York: The Free Press.

Faulks, S. (1990), "Upton and other Parks," in H. Landsdown and A. Spillius (eds), *Saturday's Boy*.

Ferguson, N. (2003), *Empire: How the Modern World Was Made*, London: Allen Lane.

Fleming, S. (2001), "Racial Science and South Asian and Black Physicality," in B. Carrington and I. McDonald (eds), *Race, Sport and British Society*.

Football Association (1991), *Blueprint for the Future of Football*, London: Football Association.

Football League (1990), *One Game, One Team, One Voice: Managing Football's Future*, London: Football League.

Football Supporters' Federation (2012), *Analysis of the 2012 Football Supporters' Federation survey on the policing of football fans in England and Wales*: http://old.fsf.org.uk/media/uploaded/file/Police-FSF-Survey-7-Nov-final.pdf

Football Trust (1996), *Digest of Football Statistics, 1994–95*, London: Football Trust.

Foster, L. and K. Woodthorpe (2012), "A Golden Silence? Acts of remembrance and commemoration at UK football games," *Journal of Sport & Social Issues* 36 (1), pp. 50–67.

Gambling Commission (2013), *Industry Statistics 2009–2012*.

Gardner, L. (2011) "Where are our great plays about football?," *Guardian*: http://www.theguardian.com/stage/theatreblog/2011/sep/26/great-plays-football-theatre (26 September 2011).

Garland, J. and M. Rowe (2001), *Racism and Anti-Racism in Football*, London: Palgrave.

Garland, J. and J. Treadwell (2010), "'No surrender to the Taliban': Football hooliganism, Islamophobia and the rise of the English Defence League," *Papers from the British Criminology Conference*, vol. 10, pp. 19–35.

Garland, M. and J. Rowe (1999), "War Minus the Shooting? Jingoism, the English Press, and Euro 96," *Journal of Sport & Social Issues* 23 (1), pp. 80–95.

Garnham, N. and A. Jackson (2003), "Who Invested in Victorian Football Clubs? The case of Newcastle Upon Tyne," *Soccer and Society* 4 (1), pp. 57–70.

Giulianotti, R. (2002). "Supporters, Followers, Fans, and Flaneurs: A taxonomy of spectator identities in football," *Journal of Sport & Social Issues* 26 (1), pp. 25–46.

Goodhart, D. (2005), "Britain rediscovered," *Prospect*, 17 April 2005.

Greenfield, S. and G. Osborn (1996), "When the Whites Go Marching In? Racism and resistances in English football," *Marequette Sports Law Review* 6 (2), pp. 315–37.

Guttmann, A. (1994), *Games and Empires: Modern Sports and Cultural Imperialism*, New York: Columbia University Press.

Hamil, S., J. Michie, C. Oughton and S. Warby (eds), *Football in the Digital Age: Whose Game is It Anyway*, London: Mainstream.

Hamilton, I. (1998), *Gazza Agonistes*, London: Bloomsbury.

Hamilton, I. (ed.) (1992), *The Faber Book of Soccer*, London: Faber and Faber.

Hammam, S. (2000), *Follow The Dream: An Overview 2000*, Cardiff: Cardiff City FC.

Hartwell, C. (2002), see *Pevsner Architectural Guides*.

Hassan, D. (2002), "A People Apart: Soccer, identity and Irish nationalists in Northern Ireland," *Soccer and Society* 3 (3), pp. 65–83.

———— (2006), "An opportunity for a new beginning: Soccer, Irish Nationalists and the construction of a new multi-sports stadium for Northern Ireland," *Soccer and Society* 7 (2–3), pp. 339–52.

Hassan, D., S. McCullough and E. Moreland (2009), "North or South? Darron Gibson and the issue of player eligibility within Irish soccer," *Soccer and Society* 10 (6), pp. 740–53.

Hatherley, O. (2010), *A Guide to the New Ruins of Great Britain*, London: Verso.

———— (2012), *A New Kind of Bleak: Journeys through Urban Britain*, London: Verso.

Haynes, R. (1993), "Vanguard or Vagabond? A history of *When Saturday Comes*," in S. Redhead (ed.) *The Passion and the Fashion: Football Fandom in the New Europe*.

———— (1995), *The Football Imagination: the Rise of the Football Fanzine Culture*, Aldershot: Arena.

Highfield Rangers (1993), *Highfield Rangers: An Oral History*, Leicester: Leicester City Council Living History Unit.

Hillsborough Independent Panel (2012), *The Report of the Hillsborough Independent Panel*: http://hillsborough.independent.gov.uk

Holland, B. (1997), "Surviving Leisure Time Racism: The burden of racial harassment on Britain"s black footballers," *Leisure Studies* 16 (4), pp. 261–77.

Home Office (annual), *Statistics on Football Related Arrests and Banning Orders*, London: Home Office.

Hornby, N. (1992), *Fever Pitch*, London: Gollancz.

House of Commons, Culture Media and Sport Committee (2002), *Wembley National Stadium Project: Into Injury Time*, London: The Stationery Office.

———— (2006), *Women"s Football, Fourth Report of Session 2005–06*, London: The Stationery Office.

———— (2011a), *2018 World Cup Bid: Sixth Report of Session 2010–12*, London: The Stationery Office.

———— (2011b), *Football Governance: Seventh Report of Session 2010–12*, 2 vols, London: The Stationery Office.

Ibrahimovich, Z. (2013), *I am Zlatan*, London: Penguin

Inglis, S. (1990), *The Football Grounds of Europe*, London: Collins Willow.

—— (1996), *The Football Grounds of Britain* (3rd edn), London: Collins Willow.

—— (2005), *Engineering Archie: Archibald Leitch—Football Ground Design*er, London: English Heritage.

Irish, O. (2001) "Women in a men"s game," *Observer Sport Monthly*, 4 November 2001.

Jarvie, G. (ed.) (1991), *Sport, Racism and Ethnicity*, London: The Falmer Press.

Jennings, A. (2006), *Foul! The Secret World of FIFA: Bribes, Vote Rigging and Ticket Scandals*, London: HarperCollins.

Johnes, M. (2002), *Soccer and Society in South Wales, 1900–1939, That other game*. Cardiff: University of Wales Press.

—— (2005a), "Heads in the Sand: Football, politics and crowd disasters in twentieth-century Britain," in P. Darby, M. Johnes and G. Mellor (eds), *Soccer and Disaster: International Perspectives*.

—— (2005b), *Sport, Wales and the Welsh*, Cardiff: University of Wales Press.

—— (2008), "We Hate England? National identity and anti-Englishness in Welsh soccer fan culture," *Cycnos* 25 (2), pp. 143–57.

King, A. (1998), *The End of the Terraces: The Transformation of English Football*, Leicester: Leicester University Press.

King, C. (2004), "Race and Cultural Identity: Playing the race game inside football," *Leisure Studies* 23 (1), pp. 19–30.

Knight, S. (2012), "Terminal Blues," *Prospect*, 18 July 2012.

Kuper, S. (2008), *Ajax, The Jews and the War*, London: Orion.

Kuper, S. and S. Syzmanski (2009), *Why England Lose*, London: Orion.

Landsdown, H. and A. Spillius (eds) (1990), *Saturday's Boys: The Football Experience*, London: Collins Willow.

Lee, M. (2000), "The Football Task Force: A Premier League View," in S. Hamil et al. (eds), *Football in the Digital Age*.

Lowles, N. (2001), *White Riot: The Violent Story of Combat 18*, Preston: Milo Books.

Macpherson, Sir W. (1999), *The Stephen Lawrence Inquiry: Report by Sir William Macpherson of Cluny*, London: HMSO.

Maguire, J. (1991), "Sport, Racism and British Society: A sociological study of England's élite male Afro/Caribbean soccer and rugby union players," in G. Jarvie (ed.), *Sport, Racism and Ethnicity*, pp. 71–94.

Martin, P. (2007), "Football, Community and Cooperation: A critical analysis of supporter trusts in England," *Soccer and Society* 8 (4), pp. 636–53.

McCombie, G. (2009), see *Pevsner Architectural Guides*.

McKinstry, L. (2010), *Sir Alf*, London: HarperCollins.

Mellor, G. (2008), "'The Janus-faced sport': English football, community and the legacy of the 'third way'," *Soccer and Society* 9 (3), pp. 313–24.

Melnick, M. (1988), "Race segregation by playing position in the English Football League: some preliminary observations," *Journal of Sport and Social Issues* 12 (2), pp. 122–30.

Michie, J. and C. Oughton (2005), *Competitive Balance in Football: An Update*, Football Governance Research Centre, Birkbeck University of London.

Miller, K. (1990), "World Cup 1990: A Diary," *London Review of Books*, 26 July 1990, in I. Hamilton (ed.) (1992), *The Faber Book of Soccer*.

Milward, P. (2007), "True Cosmopolitanism or Notional Acceptances of Non National Players in English Football: Or, why 'bloody foreigners' get blamed when 'things go wrong'," *Sport in Society* 10 (4), pp. 601–22.

———— (2008), "Rivalries and Racisms: 'closed' and 'open' Islamophobic dispositions among football supporters," *Sociological Research Online* 13 (6) 5.

———— (2012), "Reclaiming the Kop? Analysing Liverpool supporters" 21st century mobilizations," *Sociology* 46 (4), pp. 633–48.

Mora y Araujo, M. and S. Kuper (eds) (1999), *Perfect Pitch 4: Dirt*, London: Headline.

Morris, D. (1981), *The Soccer Tribe*, London: Jonathan Cape.

Morrison, B. (1990), "Turf Moor, and other fields of dreams," in H. Landsdown and A. Spillius (eds), *Saturday's Boys*.

Nairn, I. (1975), "The Towns Behind the Teams," *Listener*, 21 & 28 August 1975.

Nayak, A. (2003), "Last of the "Real Geordies"? White masculinities and the subcultural response to deindustrialisation," *Environment and Planning D: Society and Space* 21 (1), pp. 7–25.

North, S. and P. Hodson (1997), *Build a Bonfire: How Football Fans United to Save Brighton and Hove Albion*, London: Mainstream.

Oswalt, P. (2006), *Shrinking Cities, Volume 1: International Research*, Ostfildern Ruit: Hatje Cantz.

Parris, C. (2013), "The Homes of the Super-rich: Multiple residences, hyper-mobility and decoupling of prime residential housing in global cities," in I. Hay (ed.), *Geographies of the Super-rich*, Cheltenham: Edward Elgar.

Paxman, J. (2007), *The English: A Portrait of a People*, Harmondsworth: Penguin.

Peace, D. (1999), *Nineteen Seventy Four*, London: Profile Books.

———— (2007), *The Damned Utd*, London: Faber and Faber.

———— (2013), *Red or Dead*, London: Faber and Faber.

Peake, L. (2005), "Smashing Icons," in W. Alsop, *SuperCity*, pp. 39–49.

Pearson, H. (1994), *The Far Corner: A Mazy Dribble through North East Football*, London: Little Brown.

Peck, J. and K. Ward (eds) (2002), *City of Revolution: Restructuring Manchester*, Manchester: Manchester University Press.

Perryman, M. (2010), *Ingerland: Travels with a football nation*, London: Simon and Schuster.

Pevsner, N. (1951–74), *The Buildings of England*, 46 vols, Harmondsworth: Penguin.

———— (1957), *An Outline of European Architecture*, Harmondsworth: Penguin.

*Pevsner Architectural Guides*: C. Hartwell (2002), *Manchester*, London: Yale University Press; G. McCombie (2009), *Newcastle and Gateshead*, London: Yale University Press.

Pope, S. (2010), "'Like pulling down Durham Cathedral and building a brothel': Women as 'new consumer' fans?," *International Review for the Sociology of Sport* 46 (4).

———— (2012), "'The love of my life': The meaning and importance of sport for female fans," *Journal of Sport and Social Issues* 37 (2).

Pope, S. and J. Williams (2011), "'White shoes to a football match!': Female experiences of football's golden age in England," *Transformative Works and Culture* 6.

Premier League (2002–2008), *National Fan Survey*, London: Premier League.

PricewaterhouseCoopers (2010), *Annual Financial Review of Scottish Premier League Football Season 2009–2010*.

Priestley, J. B. (1929), *The Good Companions*, 1976 edn, Harmondsworth: Penguin.

———— (1934), *English Journey*, 1977 edn, Harmondsworth: Penguin.

Redhead, S. (ed.), *The Passion and the Fashion: Football Fandom in the New Europe*, Aldershot: Avebury.

Reng, R. (2011), *A Life Too Short: The Tragedy of Robert Enke*, London: Yellow Jersey.

Rogers, G. and J. Rookwood (2007), "Cardiff City Football Club as a Vehicle to Promote Welsh National Identity," *Journal of Qualitative Research in Sports Studies* 1 (1), pp. 57–68.

Rookwood, J. and N. Chan (2011), "The 39th game: fan responses to the Premier League's proposal to globalize the English game," *Soccer and Society* 12 (6), pp. 897–913.

Russell, D. (2006), "'We All Agree, Name the Stand after Shankly': Cultures of Commemoration in Late Twentieth Century English Football," *Sports in History* 26 (1), pp. 1–25.

——— (2008), "Abiding Memories: The community singing movement and English social life in the 1920s," *Popular Music* 27(1) (2008): 117–33.

Scraton, P. (1999), *Hillsborough: The Truth*, Edinburgh: Mainstream.

Secret Footballer, The (2012), *I am the Secret Footballer*, London: Guardian Books.

Shindler, C. (1999), *Manchester United Ruined My Life*, London: Headline.

Simpson, M. (2002), "Meet the metrosexual," 22 July 2002, http://www.salon.com/2002/07/22/metrosexual/

Sloane, P. J. (1971), "The Economics of Professional Football: The football club as a utility maximiser," *Scottish Journal of Political Economy* 18 (2), pp. 121–46.

Strong, R. (2011), *Visions of England*, London: Bodley Head.

Sugden, J. and A. Tomlinson (1998), *FIFA and the Contest for World Football: Who Rules the People's Game?*, Cambridge: Polity.

Szymanski, S. (2012), "Insolvency in English professional football: Irrational exuberance or negative shocks?," *NAASE Working Paper Series*, Paper No. 12-02.

Taylor, D. J. (1993), "Just Accept it Hansen: Norwich City, 1992–93," in N. Hornby (ed.), *My Favourite Year*, London: Witherby.

——— (1996), *English Settlement*, London: Vintage.

——— (1999), "Will Adrian Pop the Question? The sociology of the soccer programme," in M. Mora y Araujo and S. Kuper (eds), *Perfect Pitch 4: Dirt*.

——— (2006), *On the Corinthian Spirit*, London: Yellow Jersey.

Taylor, M. (2000), "Labour Relations and Managerial Control in English Professional Football, 1890–1939," *Sport History Review* 31 (2), pp. 80–99.

——— (2001), "Beyond the Maximum Wage: The earnings of professional footballers in England, 1900–39," *Soccer and Society* 2 (3), pp. 101–18.

——— (2008), *The Association Game: A History of British Football*, London: Longman.

——— (2009), *The Association Game: A History of British Football*, Harlow: Pearson Longman.

Tischler, S. (1981), *Footballers and Businessmen: The Origins of Professional Soccer in England*, New York: Homes and Meier.

Tomlinson, A. (1991), "North and South: the rivalry of the Football League and the Football Association," in J. Williams and S. Wagg (eds), *British Football and Social Change: Getting Into Europe*.

Trautmann, B. (1956), *Steppes to Wembley*, London: Robert Hale.

UEFA (2008), *Football Club Licensing Report 2004–2008*, Nyon: UEFA.

Vamplew, W. (1988), *Pay Up and Play the Game: Professional Sport in Britain, 1875–1914*, Cambridge: Cambridge University Press.

Vasili, P. (1998), *The First Black Footballer: Arthur Wharton 1865–1930*, London: Frank Cass.

Vincent, J., E. Kian, P. Pedersen, A. Kuntz and J. Hill (2010), "England Expects: English newspapers" narratives about the English football team in the 2006 World Cup," *International Review for the Sociology of Sport* 45 (2), pp. 199–223.

Wagg, S. (ed.) (2004), *British Football and Social Exclusion*, London: Routledge.

Ward, K. (2003), "Entrepreneurial urbanism, state restructuring and civilizing 'New' East Manchester," *Area* 35 (2), pp. 116–27.

Weight, R. (2004), *Patriots: National Identity in Britain, 1940–2000*, London: Macmillan.

Williams, J. (2001), *Into the Red: Liverpool FC and the Changing Face of English Football*, Edinburgh: Mainstream.

——— (2003), *The Liverpool Way: Houllier, Anfield and the New Global Game*, Edinburgh: Mainstream.

——— (2012), "Walking alone together the Liverpool Way: fan culture and 'clueless' Yanks," *Soccer and Society* 13 (2), pp. 426–42.

Williams, J., S. Hopkins and C. Long (2001), *Passing Rhythms: Liverpool FC and the Transformation of Football*, Oxford: Berg.

Williams, J. and S. Hopkins (2011), "'Over here': 'Americanization' and the new politics of football club ownership—the case of Liverpool FC," *Sport in Society* 14 (2), pp. 160–74.

Williams, J. and S. Wagg (eds) (1991), *British Football and Social Change: Getting Into Europe*, Leicester: Leicester University Press.

Wilson, J. (2007), *Inverting the Pyramid: The History of Football Tactics*, London: Orion.

——— (2009), *Sunderland: A Club Transformed*, London: Orion.

*Wilson, R. (2012), Inside the Divide: One City, Two Teams . . . The Old Firm, Edinburgh*: Canongate.

# INDEX

**David Goldblatt** was born in London in 1965 and lives in Bristol. He shares his affections between Tottenham Hotspur and Bristol Rovers. In 2006 he published *The Ball Is Round: A Global History of Football.* Since then he has made sport documentaries for BBC Radio, reviewed sports books for the *TLS* and the *Guardian*, and taught the sociology of sport at Bristol University, the International Centre for Sports History and Culture, De Montfort University, Leicester and Pitzer College, Los Angeles.

# The Nation Institute

## NATION BOOKS
New York

Founded in 2000, **Nation Books** has become a leading voice in American independent publishing. The inspiration for the imprint came from the *Nation* magazine, the oldest independent and continuously published weekly magazine of politics and culture in the United States.

The imprint's mission is to produce authoritative books that break new ground and shed light on current social and political issues. We publish established authors who are leaders in their area of expertise, and endeavor to cultivate a new generation of emerging and talented writers. With each of our books we aim to positively affect cultural and political discourse.

Nation Books is a project of The Nation Institute, a nonprofit media center dedicated to strengthening the independent press and advancing social justice and civil rights. The Nation Institute is home to a dynamic range of programs: the award-winning Investigative Fund, which supports ground-breaking investigative journalism; the widely read and syndicated website TomDispatch; the Victor S. Navasky Internship Program in conjunction with the *Nation* magazine; and Journalism Fellowships that support up to 25 high-profile reporters every year.

For more information on Nation Books, The Nation Institute, and the *Nation* magazine, please visit:

www.nationbooks.org

www.nationinstitute.org

www.thenation.com

www.facebook.com/nationbooks.ny

Twitter: @nationbooks